INTRODUCTION
TO THE STUDY OF
RELIGION

INTRODUCTION
TO THE STUDY OF
RELIGION

SECOND EDITION—
REVISED AND EXPANDED

Nancy C. Ring, Kathleen S. Nash,
Mary N. MacDonald, and Fred Glennon

ORBIS BOOKS

Maryknoll, New York 10545

Second Printing 2014

Founded in 1970, Orbis Books endeavors to publish works that enlighten the mind, nourish the spirit, and challenge the conscience. The publishing arm of the Maryknoll Fathers and Brothers, Orbis seeks to explore the global dimensions of the Christian faith and mission, to invite dialogue with diverse cultures and religious traditions, and to serve the cause of reconciliation and peace. The books published reflect the views of their authors and do not represent the official position of the Maryknoll Society. To learn more about Maryknoll and Orbis Books, please visit our website at www.maryknollsociety.org.

Published by Orbis Books, Maryknoll, New York 10545–0302.

Manufactured in the United States of America.

Manuscript editing and typesetting by Joan Weber Laflamme.

Unless otherwise noted, scripture quotations are from the NRSV, copyright © 1989 by the Division of Christian Education of the National Council of the Churches of Christ.

Acknowledgments: Excerpt from *Collected Poems* by Wallace Stevens. Copyright © 1936 by Wallace Stevens and renewed 1964 by Holly Stevens; reprinted by permission of Alfred A. Knopf, Inc. Excerpt from *Yimikirli: Warlpiri Deamings and Histories*, translated by Peggy Rockman Napaljarri and Lee Cataldi. Copyright © 1994 by Peggy Napaljarri et al. Reprinted by permission of HarperCollins Publishers, Inc. Purusa Sukta excerpt from *The Rig Veda: An Anthology of One Hundred and Eight Hymns*, selected, translated and annotated by Wendy Doniger O'Flaherty (Penguin Classics, 1981). Copyright © Wendy Doniger O'Flaherty, 1981. Excerpt from "The Buddha's Enlightenment," from Stephen Beyer, *The Buddhist Experience: Sources and Interpretation* (Encino: Dickinson, 1974), 191–97. Thanks to Flickr/Creative Commons and the Maryknoll Photo Library/Archives for many of the photos used throughout.

Library of Congress Cataloging-in-Publication Data

Introduction to the study of religion / Nancy C. Ring . . . [et al.].—2nd ed.
   p. cm.
  Includes bibliographical references and index.
   ISBN 978-1-57075-997-0 (pbk.); ISBN 978-1-60833-231-1 (ebook)
   1. Religion. I. Ring, Nancy C.
BL.48.R455 2012
200—dc23

2012015183

Contents

PART II: RELIGIOUS ACTION

PART III: RELIGIOUS LANGUAGE

Introduction to the Second Edition

This book is an introductory college textbook on the study of religion, and the authors are long-time colleagues in a department of religious studies. Over the years we have held countless conversations about religion with our students and almost as many conversations with one another about teaching religion. Writing the book back in the late 1990s gave us the opportunity to continue our conversations and take them to a wider audience. Revising it in 2012 enables us to observe contemporary expressions of religion and to think about the role that religion is playing in the early twenty-first century. Following the events of September 11, 2001, we found ourselves thinking about how religion is employed not only in constructive but also in destructive ways. At the same time we observed religious practitioners addressing issues of environmental sustainability and eco-justice and making common cause with those of other faiths and those of no faith at all. In an increasingly globalized and pluralistic world we all need to know about a variety of cultures and religions and to better understand the role of religion in global politics.

Our goal is to help students think through basic questions that arise in the study of religion. What, for example, is the nature of religious experience? In what ways is religion intertwined with our everyday lives, and in what ways is religion an experience set apart? How does religion shape the actions of individuals and communities? In what ways does language mediate our experience of the sacred, the ultimate? By what processes does religious change occur? And, finally, does religion promote or inhibit human flourishing? We rely on examples from both world religions and indigenous religions to explore these questions. We teach at a Jesuit college, and our students tend to come from Christian backgrounds. Because it is often easiest to begin with what is familiar, we draw most frequently on examples from Christian traditions. We hope that we are also successful in leading students to think about traditions other than their own and that the book will be accessible to students from a wide range of backgrounds.

Students arrive at our classrooms with a variety of life experiences. Perhaps most of them fit the mold of traditional late-adolescent, full-time college students, but we also teach part-time students, parents, workers who have been laid off, retired people, former military personnel, and others who have never had a chance to complete a college education. As we wrote we tried to keep all these people, as well as others, in mind. We trust that this book will be useful to college students and to others who would like to think more systematically about religion, for example, parish groups that want to expand their understanding of the role that religion plays in people's lives.

We have made every effort to make this volume easy to read and easy to use. At the end of each chapter we list suggestions for further reading, films, and Internet resources. We expect that professors who use this book will select supplementary readings for students from these lists or from other texts that they find helpful. In addition, each chapter includes suggested activities that students may pursue on their own or that professors may assign as class activities. Many of these activities are research based, and many of them culminate in a public presentation of some sort. We want you to continue the conversation that we have begun.

Each chapter includes several activity text boxes, titled "Thinking about . . . " or "Thinking with. . . . " We hope that as people read the book they will take some time to reflect on the questions we have posed in these sidebars; perhaps some professors will assign these sidebars as quick homework assignments or use them to stimulate class discussions. The purpose of the sidebars is to help students connect what are sometimes abstract concepts with their own life experience and ideas. All terms that appear in bold type are included in the glossary at the end of the book.

As we have worked on this volume, we have spoken not only to one another about its concepts but also to our friends and our families, many of whom have taken the time to read and comment on the manuscript. We owe special thanks first of all to our students, who inspired us to collaborate on this text in the first place and who have provided invaluable insight over the years as we pondered revising the text. We also want to thank our many friends and colleagues who gave us suggestions, advice, and encouragement and who read the text for us in its formative stages. For their contributions to the first edition we particularly want to thank David Andrews, Amy Glancy, Charles Goldsmith, Jo Ann Nelson, Barbara Olmstead, and Paul Petersen; and we are grateful to Kathy Gervase for technical assistance and to Penny Sandoval of Maryknoll for her help in choosing illustrations. For their contributions to the revised edition we extend our deep appreciation to Tom Peterson, Matthew Plafcan, Martha Reineke, and Deanna Thompson. For her contributions to the first edition and support for the revision, we are deeply indebted to our colleague Jennifer Glancy. Finally, as any writer knows, editors play an enormous role in seeing a book through from inception to completion. We could have wished for no better an editor than Susan Perry, whose care, astuteness, and insistence that we keep students central to our work governed our writing. Susan, we thank you.

During our many editorial sessions for the first edition we would often ask one another, "How do you think this will work for the reader?" As we worked on the second edition, we also asked, "How will this book work for students who have grown up with the Internet?" We hope that working with this volume and the resources to which it points will enable students to think through for *themselves* the importance of religion in human lives. We share many of our own ideas and refer students to classic works in the study of religion. We trust that students will also search the web with discrimination. We do not aim to deliver the final word about religion. After all, our goal is to begin a conversation. We want to know what you think. Won't you join us?

PART I

HUMAN EXPERIENCE AND RELIGION

This book invites you to the study of religion, asking you to frame questions and think about evidence that we take from the religious behavior and beliefs of several cultures. It suggests that we can develop disciplined and imaginative ways of approaching the phenomena that we describe under the rubric of religion. Since we live today in a pluralistic world, our study is an invitation to open-mindedness, to a serious and enjoyable excursion into a variety of religious ways and the approaches that scholars have taken in studying them.

Why in the twenty-first century do we study religion? Many students and many citizens regard religion as a personal matter and are reluctant to have their faith placed under scrutiny. Others, interested in obtaining academic and professional training that will result in a secure job, would rather study something "practical," leaving religion to those who seek a career in ministry and to those who are embarked on some religious quest. There are, in fact, good practical reasons, as well as vocational and avocational reasons, for studying religion. Today, religion plays a significant role in world politics, including conflicts among nations and ethnic groups. It is also a significant factor in the personal choices that people make. If you become a doctor, you are likely to find that your patients' religious beliefs influence their attitudes toward illness and its treatment. If you become a small business owner, you will have employees who may require certain days off to fulfill religious obligations. If you become a caterer, you will need to take into account the dietary restrictions that are part of religious practice. The study of religion is an excellent way to enter the worlds of other people and thus to see your own world from a new perspective.

There are many ways to practice religion and many ways to study religion. We each bring our own experiences, our own convictions, and our own questions to the practice and to the study of religion. Since the first edition of this book appeared in 1998, the events of 9/11 have led religious people to reflect on the role that religion plays in global politics and to think about the potential that religion has to produce bad as well as good. Over the past decade, too, religious communities have given increasing emphasis to what they might do for the environment as well as for all the peoples of the world. Religion, we can see, interacts with what is happening in the world. It is constantly changing as people's understanding of their place in the universe evolves. The first of the five sections in this book comprises three chapters concerned with human experience and religion. It asks us to think about our own experiences and also to consider experiences that are different from our own. In the first three chapters of our conversations about religion we consider the human quest for order and meaning, examine religious understandings of life, and assess ways in which scholars go about the study of religion.

Chapter 1, "Creating Order and Meaning," reflects on our experiences of organizing the undifferentiated landscape of our lives. We think about how we arrange the spaces where we live and work, how we organize the times of our day and week, and how we manage our relationships. The chapter calls on us to observe how the human imagination draws on experiences within particular ecological and cultural contexts. From these experiences we forge symbolic representations of life, as we experience it in the world and of life as we want it to be. In order to see the religious imagination at work we explore two religious texts, one a hymn from the Hindu scriptures and the other a **sacred** story from the Haudenosaunee (Iroquois). Each text gives a vision of how the world should be and how we should live in it. Chapter 1 proposes that we can think about religions as processes for creating order and meaning in an ultimate sense, and also that we can think about them as processes for learning to be human.

Chapter 2, "Religious Understandings of Life," considers responses to the power and mystery of life. The chapter begins by exploring experiences of power and mystery in two communities: among the Warlpiri people of Central Australia, an indigenous community still living in its traditional land despite a disruptive colonial history; and among Jews, a community claiming a common religious heritage but that today is dispersed throughout the world. Each community sustains a relationship with a particular land. The chapter ponders the role of religion in the construction of personhood and the ways in which religions understand the human condition. Building on the previous discussion of order, we examine the distinction made between sacred and profane and consider the notions of the sacred, sacred space, and sacred time.

Chapter 3, "The Study of Religion," demarcates religion as an area of **culture**. The chapter begins with discussion of the ideas of nature, culture, and religion. These ideas are pursued in reflecting on a Zuni ritual in which a newborn child is presented to the sun. In order to discuss the ritual, a prayer of which is given in the text, we find that it is necessary to provide considerable information about Zuni culture. Using the Zuni ritual as a point of reference, we examine some of the ways in which scholars go about the study of religion. Since some scholars are sympathetic to religion and some are not, we explore what is necessary for scholars in both situations to produce accurate and responsible descriptions of the religious expressions they study.

We use the word *religion* in both an abstract sense and a more concrete sense. As an abstract noun, *religion* signifies a human propensity to seek order and meaning within the mystery of life. By a *religion* or *religions* we mean particular traditions (for example, Judaism, Buddhism, Christianity, Hopi religion), which in their constellations of ideas and practices provide order and meaning for their followers, connecting them to what are considered the ultimate powers of life.

Chapter 1

Creating Order and Meaning

SHAPING HUMAN EXPERIENCE

We human beings are always trying to get our lives in order. We make lists and hatch plans. In small ways and large we strive to bring harmony and significance to our individual and communal pursuits. We sort our class notes, we count our money, and we arrange our bills in an order of priority for payment. Periodically we tidy our closets and check our cars. We take stock of our friendships and work on repairing those that we value that have gone awry. We organize the space in which we live and the time we have for living. We designate certain spaces and times as private and others as public. We make places to play, places to work, places to pray. We establish times to relax, times to concentrate, times to be with those we hold most dear, times to engage with what we hold sacred.

Religion, some would say, is the human recognition that there is an ultimate order and meaning within the mystery of our lives. Others would say that religion is the human impulse to create order and meaning. The American poet Wallace Stevens (1879–1955) captures something of the latter understanding in a poem called "The Idea of Order at Key West."[1] The poem is part of a collection, published in 1935, titled *Ideas of Order*.

Stevens suggests that we construct our own worlds of meaning through the use of imagination. In that sense we are all poets, composing our lives. The Greek verb *poiein*, the origin of the word "poet," means "to make, to create, to compose." Stevens describes a woman walking and singing beside the sea. She cannot exactly replicate the noise of the ocean, but she can create something that suggests or approximates it. Her voice interprets and gives meaning to her experience

5

of the sea. She, as it were, sings a world into being. She is a maker, an artificer. The poet writes:

> She was the single artificer of the world
> In which she sang. And when she sang, the sea,
> Whatever self it had, became the self
> That was her song, for she was the maker. Then we,
> As we beheld her standing there alone,
> Knew that there never was a world for her
> Except the one she sang and, singing, made.

The poem concludes:

> Oh! Blessed rage for order, pale Ramon,
> The maker's rage to order words of the sea,
> Words of the fragrant portals, dimly-starred,
> And of ourselves and of our origins,
> In ghostlier demarcations, keener sounds.[2]

Stevens recognizes that we create or assert order; from the chaos and mystery of our lives we shape worlds of meaning. Others say that an ultimate order is given to us, that it is part of the structure of human reality. On the one hand, many people regard God as the first maker and the source of order, while, on the other, some people say we human beings in our search for order and meaning have created God and other religious conceptualizations. Regardless of whether we see order as given or created we can probably agree with Stevens that a "rage to order" or a passion to overcome chaos is central to the human condition.

The monotheistic religious traditions of Judaism, Christianity, and **Islam** have a notion of a maker—called God or **Allah**—who gives order to the universe and sustains all that exists in it. In contrast to monotheism, the main philosophical tradition within Hinduism (**Vedanta**) postulates that there is only one reality and that the individual self is identified with the absolute and with every other individual self. The indigenous religious traditions—in other words, the traditions of native communities closely connected to a particular environment—present the search for order and meaning in terms of sustaining a network of relationships. The indigenous traditions recognize many manifestations of life-giving power—gods, spirits, ancestors—each of which contributes to the order of the world.

In comparing various religious understandings of the ordering of life scholars refer to experiences or manifestations of the **sacred**. Such experiences or manifestations are understood by those reporting them to empower the life of an individual or community. The historian of religions, Mircea Eliade (1907–86), regards the sacred as a structure of reality that is manifested in particular historical circumstances.[3] Others would say it is not a structure of reality, a given to which human beings respond, but a human conceptualization of ultimate value and meaning, and that at a further distance religion is an area defined for the purposes of study. Eliade's former colleague at the University of Chicago, J. Z. Smith, says, for example, that religion is "a creation of the scholar's study."[4] Although scholars may differ in their interpretations of the sacred, the notion that particular objects, times, places, and experiences provide an opening to that which bestows order and meaning is almost universal. The interrelated themes of order and meaning are never far from conversations about the sacred and

Mircea Eliade (1907–86)

Mircea Eliade was born in Romania. As a university student he lived and studied in India. Later he resided in the United Kingdom, in Portugal, and in France, and in 1956 he moved to the United States, where he taught at the University of Chicago. In the United States he is best known as a historian of religions who, through his teaching and books, influenced the teaching of religious studies in colleges and universities. In Romania, though, he is better known as a writer of fiction. Eliade held that hierophanies (appearances of the sacred) are foundational for religion, and he divided the experience of reality into the realms of the sacred and profane. In his book *The Myth of the Eternal Return* (1971). Eliade proposes that myth and ritual are vehicles that enable people not only to remember hierophanies but actually to take part in them. As a student and young professor in Romania, Eliade was influenced by the far-Right philosopher and journalist Nae Ionescu and during the late 1930s Eliade publicly expressed his support for the Iron Guard, a fascist political organization. Today, scholars debate the significance of these associations. Noted for his encyclopedic knowledge of the world's religions, Eliade was fluent in five languages (Romanian, French, German, Italian, and English) and had a reading knowledge of at least three others (Hebrew, Persian, and Sanskrit).

religion. At issue is whether order and meaning are given or are created by human beings. People seek to connect with and participate in the fundamental power of life. Thus, they either recognize or create the order of the universe. Indeed, seeing (gaining insight, recognizing the true situation) and making (structuring the world through intellectual and physical work) are complementary ways of undertaking the religious quest.

In periodic rituals religious communities may create the order of the world anew. The annual **Sun Dances** of the Plains peoples of the United States and Canada, for example, are based on the understanding that human beings have a responsibility for sustaining the natural and social world. The performance of rituals at certain points in the year and at certain points in the life cycle facilitates carrying out of that responsibility. Rituals such as the Sun Dance permit people to connect with sacred power and to make it active in the world. For Muslims, the order of the world is revealed by God, and the tradition encourages recitation of the words of the **Qur'an,** the holy book of Islam, in which the revelation is recorded. For Muslims, submission to God and proper relationship to neighbors are fundamental. It is, according to the Islamic insight, acceptance of Allah and his law that brings order and meaning to the world. Despite differences in religious conceptualization and expression, the conviction of most people is that order—a system of life-giving connections—is possible, that our lives are potentially meaningful, and that they connect to a larger pattern of life beyond our immediate knowing.

In creating order in our lives we produce networks of relationships that connect us to the world, to our fellow human beings, and to whatever we consider to have greatest value. Some of us are more successful than others, of course, in creating order. At one extreme are people who are obsessive about order. They seem to want order for order's sake. We all know someone who has every piece of paper in its proper drawer, every pencil in its designated compartment, and the paper clips in their appointed box. We may liken the tidy-desk fanatic to the religiously obsessive person who follows every prescription of his or her religion to the letter. At the opposite extreme is the disorganized-desk person whose room is in such disarray that it may take some time to find paper and pencils. This person searches among clothes and books for pen and paper when something needs to be written. We might compare the person with a disorganized desk to those who pray when the spirit moves them, recall a prayer learned in childhood when they are in need of help, report an awareness of the Holy or the mystery of life when a child is born, and go to church at Christmas. In the work of ordering our lives, and in our religious observances, most of us are somewhere between the extremes. We try to establish an order that is flexible and facilitates our living to the fullest rather than an order that is controlling and burdensome.

Tidy rooms, messy rooms, or rooms that are somewhat ordered but still comfortable? Tidy lives, messy lives, or something in between? We want enough order to give predictability and coherence to our lives. We do not want so much order that it stifles our spontaneity and restricts our possibilities. Our "rage for order" is a desire to establish conditions in which we can live fully and authentically. However, even when we get things "just right," in our rooms and our lives, something will happen to challenge the order we have established—the gift of a beautiful carving challenges us to redecorate, the departure of a dear friend obliges us to rearrange our social network, the death of a loved one negates the very notion of order.

The opposite of order is chaos. Chaos is a state of being in which chance is supreme. It is, however, a state of potentiality. In many **myths** of origin storytellers contrast chaos (from Greek *chaos,* "an empty space"), a confused unorganized state of primordial matter, and cosmos (from Greek *kosmos,* "order"), an orderly and harmonious world system. The stories of our individual lives as well as the stories of communities are made up of an ongoing reciprocity of chaos and cosmos. At certain stages in our journey everything lies in chaos around us, a confusing and mysterious mess. Yet, chaos offers possibilities. We can make something of it; we can bring order to it. At other stages on the way everything is under control, well organized into a tidy world, perhaps too well organized. We may feel crushed by it; we may want to destroy the order, revert to chaos, and forge a new order.

Our order is constantly shifting and sometimes even falling apart, and we are constantly realigning and reconstituting it. Sometimes we accept an order established by others. A school or college has curricula and rules established prior to the arrival of a particular class. Each new class grumbles about the order, and some even boycott classes or protest outside the dean's office in order to get it changed. Religions, like other institutions, are constituted of practices and ideas that, in most cases, were put in place before the present generation was born. In its own way each generation remakes the tradition, challenging the old order and prescribing a new order.

In 2001 the order of our world was shaken by the 9/11 terrorist attacks in which four commercial airliners were hijacked. Two were intentionally crashed into the Twin Towers of the World Trade Center in New York City, killing all those on board as well as thousands of people working in the towers. A third airliner was crashed into the Pentagon in Arlington, Virginia, just outside Washington. The fourth plane, which the hijackers had directed toward Washington, DC, crashed into a field near Shanksville, Pennsylvania, after some passengers and crew members attempted to retake control of it. None survived the flights. Nearly three thousand people of various religions and nationalities died in the attack. Suspicion quickly fell on al-Qaeda, a global militant Sunni Islamist group founded by Osama bin Laden in the late 1980s; al Qaeda means "foundation" or "basis." Bin Laden was raised in the Wahhabi branch of Sunni Islam that is dominant in Saudi Arabia. It is named for the Muslim theologian Muhammad ibn Abd al-Wahhab (1703–92), who strove to return Islam to the "pure" message and practice of the Prophet Muhammad. The United States responded to the 9/11 attacks by launching a "war on terrorism," invading Afghanistan to depose the Taliban, a militant Islamist group that had ruled much of Afghanistan from 1996 to 2001 and had harbored al-Qaeda members, by enacting the USA Patriot Act, and by pursuing Osama bin Laden, who was finally found and killed in May 2011. Supporters of al-Qaeda maintain that a Christian-Jewish alliance is intent on destroying Islam and that true Muslims should resist with force. They want to banish foreign influences from Muslim countries and to institute a new caliphate. Since 9/11 the countries of the world and their religious communities have been working to create order anew. In the area of religion we find some religious people advocating for interreligious dialogue and cooperation and for trying to understand the perspectives of religiously conservative Muslims who fear the corruption of traditional values by Western culture. Unfortunately, the events of 9/11, perpetrated by fanatical fundamentalists, have led some Americans and Europeans who are also of a fanatical bent to engage in hate crimes against Muslims.

Before we venture further into considerations of what religion is and how religion functions in our lives, we shall reflect on how college students "order" their lives. The exercise below will give us some ideas about the sense of order and meaning that we try to establish in our lives. If you are not a college student, adapt the exercise to your own circumstances. For example, reflect on how your family "orders" its life. If you wish, discuss your responses with a classmate or friend.

ORDER AND MEANING

Through the exercise below we move from reflection on making order and meaning in daily life toward a consideration of religion as a

Thinking about a Day in the Life of . . .

A. Imagine that you are sharing a dorm room or apartment with another person. First, think about some of the things you might do over a twenty-four hour period to bring order to:

1. Your Space: Where do you put things? Where do you carry out various activities? Is lack of space a problem? If so how do you resolve the problem? Are some spaces in your room special? How are they special?

2. Your Time: What do you fit into the day? How do you establish priorities? What do you do when there are too many things to fit into the available time? Are some times in the day special? Which times? How are they special? Are some times in the day difficult for you? If so, how do you cope with them?

3. Your Relationships: With whom do you talk, work, play? Who is important to you? How do you sustain relationships? When there are conflicts, how do you choose between giving attention to people and giving attention to work and study? Are some relationships special? How are they special?

B. Think about how sharing a room or apartment with someone else influences your decisions and behavior. To what extent are your plans contingent upon the cooperation of your roommate? Is having a roommate calming or disruptive? How?

C. What principles or understandings guide you in making decisions about ordering your space, your time, and your relationships? How did you acquire or develop these principles or understandings?

process of making order and meaning in the largest possible sense. We shall be thinking about religions as systems that create networks of significant relationships. As you know from your consideration of order in daily life, a good order is not just a matter of everything in its place. A life-giving, satisfying order is a harmonious network of connections to environment and people and, perhaps, to God and/or spirits. An important dimension of such order is that it be purposeful or meaningful and open to growth. Most people regard order for the sake of order as empty and stultifying.

There are many ways to think about religion. Some scholars attempt to define religion. That is, they try to say what religion is in its essence. Others see too many difficulties in defining religion. If we say religion is "belief in God" and/or "practices for relating to God," they would ask how we classify a tradition that does not believe in God but carries out rituals to facilitate a relationship with ancestors. If such a tradition is not a religion, what is it? Perhaps we could expand our definition to say religion is "belief in superhuman beings." We would then be including those who believe in a variety of supernatural beings but excluding from the domain of religion those who recognize a powerful mystery in the universe but do not conceptualize it in terms of gods, spirits, or other superhuman beings.

Scholars who place a greater emphasis on describing than on defining will recount activities and institutions that could possibly be construed as religion. They will, for example, describe the Mid-Winter **Shalako** Festival of the **Zuni,** in which energy is danced back into the dormant earth, and they will report on the Easter liturgy, in which Christians celebrate the resurrection of Jesus and the hope in life despite the evidence of death. We could elaborate on each of these rituals as a process of creating order in the lives of individuals and communities and, indeed, in the life of the cosmos. These are key rituals that encapsulate the Zuni and Christian understandings of the world. Scholars who define and scholars who describe also interpret. That is, they say something about what religion does in the lives of its practitioners; they elaborate on its role in creating meaning and order.

We began by thinking about order in our daily lives. We continue by reflecting on the role that religion plays in ordering human experience: we consider how religion establishes fundamental understandings and structures for individuals and communities and how religion facilitates and inhibits people's participation in the fundamental power of life. A Christian may understand that the world is basically a good place created by God but that it is also flawed by the sinfulness of human beings. Furthermore, that person may believe that God has sent Jesus Christ to show us how to live in the world and how to overcome sin. Hence, Christianity provides an understanding of how the world is, and it provides certain structures, including the **church, sacraments,** and **prayer,** to help a person live in the world. Thus, Christianity is a set of ideas and practices that orders the Christian's life. Yet, we must remember that order can be freeing or inhibiting. A good order can facilitate participation in life; it can lead us to live authentically. A bad order can unduly restrict participation in life; it can lead to a sense of alienation. For example, some religions place control in the hands of a few and stifle the participation of the many.

In authentically proclaiming their messages, religions may create disorder. There is a prophetic side to religion that calls the established order into question and highlights values and principles by which individuals and communities should reorder their lives. We find this challenge in the prophets of the Jewish scriptures, the **Tanakh.** The prophets protest the hypocrisy of people who claim to be followers of the Israelite God but act unjustly toward their fellow human beings. We find it in the **Gospels** of Matthew and Luke. Looking toward the end of an age and the way that followers of Jesus should live, they portray Jesus as saying, "Do not think that I have come to bring peace on earth; I have not come to bring peace, but a sword" (Mt 10:34; Lk 12:51). In Chapter 8 and Chapter 9 we look at changes that occur in the lives of individuals and communities as a result of challenging the religious and social status quo.

Hindu religious texts and practices emphasize the realization of the identity between the individual self and a cosmic principle of unity called **Brahman**. According to Hindu traditions there is a religious and moral law, called **dharma**, governing all of life. Dharma is a principle of ultimate order, and those who attune themselves to it will, Hinduism suggests, realize their relationship to Brahman and their mode of participation in the life of the cosmos. Sometimes translated as "duty," dharma includes the carrying out of duties related to one's class and status. The Hindu worldview imagines cycles of rebirth that are dependent upon one's actions (karma) in previous lives. Liberation from rebirth, it is held, may be obtained by following three overlapping paths. These paths, which are given different emphases in the various Hindu traditions, are **karma** marga, the path of work (with work usually interpreted as ritual or disinterested action); **jñana** marga, the path of light (with light interpreted as true knowledge); and **bhakti** marga, the path of love (with love interpreted as devotion to the divine). Thus, Hinduism suggests that there is an ultimate order to the world and provides its devotees with paths by which to order their individual lives so that they may also participate in the larger order.

If we look on religions—such as Judaism, Christianity, Native American religions, and Buddhism—as systems that enable people to order their lives in the world in an ultimate as well as immediate sense, we have made a beginning in the study of religion and religions. We have found an element that is common to religious traditions and enables us, for purposes of study and comparison, to group diverse traditions together. As we progress in our study we will think about how the "order" proposed by religious traditions becomes institutionalized in rituals, ethical **codes**, myths, and doctrines. We will think about how and why the order changes over time, and we shall consider how the order can be helpful and harmful.

In keeping our houses tidy, our work in good shape, our friendships intact, we try to bring order to the everyday world of home, work, and social interactions. In engaging in religious actions we try to order our lives in relation to a larger world of which we have a sense or that our religious tradition tells us is the eventual reality. The sociologist Emile Durkheim referred to the first area of our lives as the profane and to the second as the sacred. In both areas we are makers or, to use Wallace Stevens's old-fashioned word, *artificers*, creating, through our actions and words, the world in which we want to live.

Some people say there is no need to distinguish two worlds and two kinds of ordering activities. Why not, they ask, just see the world as a whole, a material whole? Why identify some acts of ordering as religious rather than as social? In place of sacred powers they posit material causes and reject the non-rational and the supernatural. Such questions lead at times to the drawing of a distinct line between the proponents of science and the proponents of religion. However, the defenders of science and the defenders of religion are not necessarily opposed. For objective scientists it can be difficult to find suitable methods for studying human subjectivity and social processes. There is no laboratory experiment to prove or disprove claims concerning the sacred. However, there is a wealth of rituals and myths and doctrines as well as abundant accounts of ancient and contemporary religious experience that enable us to explore the "rage for order" that is part of human history.

As we interrogate the constellations of human experiences and practices that we call religions we accept that knowledge, whether it is "religious" knowledge or "scientific" knowledge, is socially con-structed. That is, knowledge results from the ways that individuals and communities choose to study and interpret evidence that is before them. For religious people experience of manifestations of sacred power is taken as part of the evidence. Both practitioners of religion and practitioners of the scientific method attempt to bring cosmos out of the confusing and often overwhelming, but nevertheless fascinating and exciting, chaos of human experience.

When we are ordering that which is near to us (room, friendships, manner of working), we are dealing with matters that we understand relatively well; when we try to order our place in the ultimate scheme of things, we are dealing with matters of which we understand rela-tively little, matters that stretch our imagination. Who knows what happens after death? Who knows what power or energy gives life to the world? There is, then, a qualitative difference in the two kinds of ordering activity. Religions grapple with difficult-to-answer questions. Like science, they use reason and imagination to create models of the world. Like poetry, they employ **symbols** to describe ultimate realties. Like dance and drama, they act out, in ritual, their visions of the world as it is and as it may yet be. Along the way religions pick up folk wisdom and songs and stories, some of which contradict each other, but all of which are concerned with how people should live their lives here and now. Although the complexes of ideas and practices that we call religions differ in their particular depictions of the world and of ultimate reality, they all sustain a concern that an empowering order should prevail in our lives.

For their adherents, religious traditions provide some commentary on the mystery of the universe and on how to live with it. Islam, for example, proclaims that there is no god but God (no *allah* but *Allah*) and that Muhammad is the messenger of God. Then, the revelations recorded in the Qur'an lay out a system of ethical monotheism—in other words, a system that holds that there is one god and that this God requires a certain kind of behavior from human beings. Islam insists that all human beings are children of the one God and maintains that they should, therefore, act toward others as they would toward their brothers and sisters. The teachings of Islam are summarized in **Five Pillars**, five devotional-ritual duties with social implications: (1) *Shahada*, the proclamation of faith in God as the only god and acknowledgment of Muhammad as his messenger; (2) *Salat*, five daily prayer services acknowledging one's relationship to God and the human community; (3) *Zakat*, almsgiving, the support of those in the community who are in need; (4) *Sawm*, fasting during daylight during the holy month of Ramadan; and (5) *Hajj*, pilgrimage to Mecca for those financially and physically able to make the journey. Islamic spirituality elaborates on the beauty that God has inscribed in the universe and thus provides a framework to connect everyday experience with the divine. **Muslims** do not have to work it all out for themselves in each generation. The Qur'an, the Pillars, the community, and the weight of tradition are there to guide them. Islam provides an order for life, and Muslims form their children within that order.

If a person born into a religious tradition is to grow into an authentic member of the tradition, he or she needs to internalize what the tradition prescribes and practices. Of course, there are various understandings of what is "authentic." One Roman Catholic may say that the church's commandment to attend **mass** on Sundays and Holy Days is to be observed with exceptions only for grave causes. Another may say it is a good guideline but that attendance at mass is only one component in one's religious observance. Such differences in interpretation lead at times to divisions in religious traditions. Moreover, some members of a religious tradition may take an image or a precept literally while others may understand it symbolically. One Christian reading the first chapter of the Gospel of Luke may take the author's description of Mary, the mother of Jesus, as a virgin in a literal, physical sense. Another may understand it as a representation of Mary's total availability to the plans of God and a depiction of an attitude of openness that should characterize all Christians in their relationship to God's Spirit, a metaphorical rather than a literal reading.

In sacred stories and songs and in religious doctrines our faith communities provide us with understandings of the world, and, in rituals and ethical guidelines, they provide us with ways to engage the world. At certain points in our lives we may want to ask whether what we have received in our tradition accords with our particular experience. We may investigate, question, and even challenge the tradition in which we were raised. For example, in recent times many Jews and Christians, both women and men, have come to ask whether their scriptures and ritual practices discriminate against women. Some say, "I don't want to belong to a religion that makes women subservient to men." Since religion is concerned with relationships, the way that a religion looks at the relationship between men and women is significant. The person who starts out saying, "I don't want to belong to a religion that makes women subservient to men," has several options in dealing with the dilemma. One option is to submit to the discipline of the tradition and compromise his or her original position. A second is to leave the **synagogue** or church. A third is to accept that religions change over time and to recognize that in our time Jews and Christians are rethinking and reformulating their understandings of sex and gender. Some people will choose to stay with a religion and become advocates of change within the tradition. Our personalities and our early socialization have some role in determining which option we choose.

THE SYMBOLIC PROCESS

Human beings think with symbols. We encode our experiences in words, in gestures, in images. We craft **similes** and **metaphors**—the former signaled by "as" or "like"—making an explicit comparison, the latter implying an identity based on a few or on a myriad of sensory and mental associations. We see a bird floating in the air and it evokes a sense of freedom; we look forward to being "as free as a bird" when chores or end-of-semester exams are done. We observe the mountains, and they evoke permanence and stability; for many religions they suggest the abode of gods. We experience the rage and chaos of the storm; it provides an image with which to capture the turmoil of life. We carve statues and compose music. We tell stories and sing songs. We use sounds and marks and images to denote and connote experiences and intuitions. In symbols we articulate experiences that defy everyday language. We mentioned above the symbolic, rather than literal, interpretation of a gospel image, suggesting that the image of a virgin evokes an understanding of openness and commitment to God. The meaning and power of symbols depend on their contexts. In the context of the Gospel of Luke, for example, the virginity of Mary can serve as a figure of speech, a metaphor, denoting the freshness and openness the Christian should bring to service of the Lord.

In the Jewish scriptures the image of marriage is used to speak of God's faithful relationship to Israel. We also use the image in expressions like "He's married to his work" to suggest the restrictions our commitments impose on us. Whether marriage as metaphor denotes faithful companionship or a restrictive contract or something else depends on the context in which it is presented.

Religions, we could say, are systems of symbols in which the ideals, the aspirations, and the experiences of a community are represented. The symbolic process is part of the way we think. Usually it operates at a largely unconscious level, but we can become more aware of how we think with symbols by reflecting on particular symbols (such as a flag, the cross, a mosque, the hammer and sickle) and symbol systems (such as Christian baptism, the Jewish **Sabbath** service, American Thanksgiving observances, national anthems). Symbols are powerful tools that groups employ in socializing their members. Religious leaders use symbols to encourage insight and to inspire, to foster spiritual growth. They also use symbols to induce conformity and to brainwash their followers. We are so conditioned to accepting the validity of the tradition in which we are raised that it may be difficult to recognize its manipulative tendencies. While religious symbols—such as gods and spirits, creeds and hymns, shrines and icons—are shared by groups, they are also powerful repositories of meaning for individuals. From the repertoire of symbols a religion offers its members, each person will have favorites—hymns, saints, icons, passages of scripture—that help him or her in the human work of creating order and meaning.

Symbols carry meanings. If we drink water, it sustains our physical life. If we use water to wash we experience it as cleansing and refreshing. If it rains for a long period of time and the rivers flood, washing away our crops and our houses, we experience water as destructive. Before birth we all had the experience of the watery abode of our mother's womb. Think of your own best and worst experiences of

J. M. SUAREZ

Pilgrims at the Ganges River at Varanasi in India, 2008. The Ganges is preeminent among the sacred rivers of India and is worshiped as the goddess Ganga, yet today it is one of the most polluted rivers in the world.

water. What adjectives would you use to describe the impact of water on you at those times? When we extract the word *water* from particular contexts, it exists as a natural symbol overflowing with meanings. It has the potential to evoke a range of emotions and thoughts that are related to the qualities of water and our experiences of water. Water is a symbol that suggests life itself, fertility, cleanliness, refreshment, and destruction.

Devout Hindus make pilgrimages to mountain shrines and sacred rivers. At the Ganges River in India we see pilgrims washing away impurity and throwing the ashes of the dead into the stream. They pray that through their ritual cleansing they will deepen their union with the Divine. The Ganges, which is said to flow from the toe of the life-giving god, **Vishnu**, is sacred to all Hindus. Hindus approach the Ganges, dirty and smelly though those waters may be today, with solemnity. Their gravity is in contrast to the cheerful, undignified splashing of water in the **Holi** festival. Holi is a popular Hindu spring festival that celebrates the death of winter and the birth of spring. Its theme of new life and regeneration is presented in joyful erotic images.

In northern India the Holi festival celebrates the affection between the god **Krishna** and his beloved, Radha, the wife of a cowherd who, in the epic **Mahabharata**, leaves her husband to be with Krishna.

Legend says that as an infant Krishna killed a demon that was in the service of the king of winter. In some parts of India, however, the festival is dedicated to Kama, the god of sexual love. Holi includes boisterous games in which the symbolism of water is employed in welcoming the new life of spring and, for the space of the festival, dissolving the usual class distinctions. The festival plays on water's fluidity and its fertilizing qualities, as spring rain and as seminal fluid, in the continuation of life. The eroticism in the stories about Radha and in the water games of Holi is criticized by some Hindus, while others see the love between Krishna and Radha as a type of the love between the divine and the human.

The meaning that we take from the symbol of water at a particular time depends on its context. For example, in ritual washings, which in the technical language of religion are called ablutions, water suggests cleansing and renewal. The word *baptism*, which comes from the Greek verb *baptizein*, "to dip, to bathe," and translates into everyday English as "washing," has these connotations. In his Letter to the Romans Saint Paul goes beyond the symbolism of cleansing and suggests that the one baptized has been drowned. In Romans 6:1–4 Paul says that the Christian has died to the old life of sin and has a new life in Jesus Christ. Paul's symbolic way of speaking of baptism as drowning is reflected in the early Christian practice of baptism by immersion, a practice continued in some Christian communities today. The religious imagination works with water and fire and trees and other natural symbols. It also constructs pictures and stories and rituals to convey its understanding of the world.

The symbolic process is part of the way we think. It is essential to the creation of art and literature, to scientific breakthroughs, and to religion. The sacred narratives, the good stories that have borne the test of time and that religious traditions pass on from generation to generation, are symbolic. They speak indirectly and evocatively, presenting us with images and metaphors with which to explore the human condition. Each offers its own characteristic understanding of the person in the world and gives guidance for individual and communal life. The ritual actions that religious traditions prescribe are also symbolic. They provide ways for their members to align themselves with what the traditions suggest is the real or ultimate nature of the world. These rituals, some of which focus on events in the individual life cycle, and others that celebrate the seasons and commemorate historical events, provide experiences of participating in the fundamental power of life. In some religious traditions icons—such as statues, paintings, and masks—are part of the symbolic system and evoke the power of God, saints, and spirits. From our capacity to connect and focus our experiences of life in symbols we construct the systems of symbols that in the European intellectual tradition are known as religions.

CULTURES AND COSMOLOGIES

Human beings organize their relationships with their environment and with one another. They create communal designs for living that social scientists call cultures. *Culture,* a word derived from the Latin *colere,* "to till," has at least two usages. The first refers to personal refinement, the result of much "tilling," which is reflected in such things as a preference for classical music over popular, an interest in fine arts and philosophy, a taste for gourmet cuisine. The second usage, which concerns us here, is that of anthropology, the discipline that is most concerned with culture as shared and learned behaviors. Whereas we are born with certain biological capacities, we learn our particular culture from our families and our social groups. One of the first American anthropologists, Ruth Benedict (1887–1948), described cultures as "patterns for living."[5] Another American anthropologist, James F. Downs, defines culture as "a mental map which guides us in our relations to our surroundings and to other people."[6] In anthropological usage, rap music or reggae is just as much a part of culture as opera. And, in the anthropological sense of culture, the indigenous peoples of the South Pacific have culture, as do North Americans, Africans, and all the people of the earth.

	DIACHRONIC →		
	2000	**2005**	**2010**
S Y N C H R O N I C ↓	Religion	Religion	Religion
	Science	Science	Science
	Technology	Technology	Technology
	Economics	Economics	Economics
	Music	Music	Music

Diachronic and synchronic axes of culture. A diachronic view shows changes occurring over time. A synchronic view shows how the different areas of culture connect with one another at a given time.

For purposes of exploring a culture we may, as it were, freeze it in time. We may stop the clock at a particular time so that when we look at the culture at that moment we can see how our economic transactions relate to our social patterns and how our religious observances have an impact on our production of fine arts. That is, we can see how the various components of culture are affecting one another at that moment. At the same time, however, cultures are constantly changing. Even as we stop to look at the current situation some of the actors are moving and changing the pattern. The terms *synchronic* and *diachronic* refer to these two perspectives. A synchronic perspective is like a snapshot. It looks at the various parts of a system at a particular moment in time to see how the parts work together.

Social scientists often take a synchronic perspective toward culture. They study how the various components of a culture fit together—how economy influences religion and vice versa, how social structure interacts with ideology, and so on. In contrast, a diachronic perspective is more like a movie than a photograph. It shows how something changes through time. In the study of Christianity a synchronic perspective on baptism looks on baptism in relation to a larger network of Christian beliefs and rituals, while a diachronic perspective looks at the changes over time in the ways that baptism has been practiced and understood. We can see that the two perspectives are complementary and that both are needed in the study of religion. However, in the division of labor within studies in religion some scholars focus on one and some on the other.

Each culture develops within a particular ecological context and makes use of the resources of that context. Yet, cultures differ one from the other not only because of the availability, or lack of availability, of certain material resources, but also because of the different ways in which human beings make choices and exercise their imaginations. Many peoples have fish available to them. For example, the Solomon Islands peoples of the South Pacific have access to abundant marine resources. Therefore, it is not surprising that seafood is an important element in their diet. Nor is it surprising that Solomon Islanders have rituals for attracting fish to their hooks and nets, and that those who can attract fish are said to possess a quality called *mana*. What might be surprising to those of us raised in other cultures is that traditional Solomon Islands societies conceive of fish spirits and have rituals that celebrate their relationship to fish.[7] Within each Solomon Islands community some marine species are of greater significance than others. For example, the people of Auki look upon sharks as guardians who take a particular interest in their welfare.

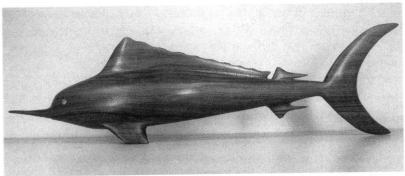

MARY N. MACDONALD

Fish carving from the Solomon Islands (c. 1980). Traditional Solomon Islands art includes ritual items such as carved masks and decorated items ranging from small combs and hooks to large canoes.

Many indigenous cultures have ceremonies that are similar in orientation to the fish rituals of the Solomon Islanders. In these rituals people celebrate their relationship to particular animals and particular plants. Communities may use the animal or plant as food and thus give thanks to it for making itself available to them. Native communities of the American Pacific Northwest give thanks to the salmon and Plains People to the buffalo. Pueblo women give thanks to the clay—neither animal nor plant but, even so, a gift of the earth—that they gather in order to make pots. On the other hand, communities may avoid eating an animal or plant because they regard it as an ancestor or a close relative. The people of Auki in the Solomon Islands refrain from eating shark. In both cases communities are affirming that animals and plants are part of their essential network of life.

Like Solomon Islands communities, contemporary New England societies have a good supply of fish. However, New Englanders do not think about fish as their relatives. They do not celebrate their kinship with fish. New Englanders and Solomon Islanders exercise their imaginations about fish in different ways. Nevertheless, Christian groups in New England do, like traditional Solomon Islanders, employ ritual to acknowledge the fact that their well-being depends on fish. They recognize that they have a relationship to fish, even though they experience that relationship in different ways, emotionally and intellectually, from the Solomon Islanders. They think about fish not in terms of kinship but in terms of God's care of them through the gift of fish. New England coastal communities have ceremonies, such as the annual blessing of the fishing fleet, in which they give thanks to

God for the fish. In the fishing town of Gloucester, Massachusetts, the Portuguese American community celebrates Saint Peter's Fiesta in the last week of June. A statue of Saint Peter, who was a fisherman when he was called to follow Jesus, is carried in procession. Along with an outdoor Mass and the blessing of the fleet, the festival also includes entertainments and sporting events.

Solomon Islanders and New Englanders have fish in common. They share an attitude of thankfulness for the fish. Yet, just as they have different recipes for cooking the fish, they have different rituals for celebrating their relationship to the fish. Indeed, they have different views of the way the world is constructed and the way the world works. When we speak of a people's "worldview," a term which is a translation of the German *Weltanschauung* (*Welt,* "world"; *anschauung,* "way of viewing, perception, intuition"), we are referring to their characteristic philosophy of life or ideology, their way of imaginatively ordering the world, their conceptual framework.

The Solomon Islanders have a notion of a world in which people and animals are interdependent and in which a number of ancestral spirits and land spirits influence human lives. Given their worldview, it is appropriate that they give thanks to the fish for making themselves available to human communities. Most New Englanders have a notion of a world in which God is the ultimate source of all good. Thus, for them, it is God who gives fish to people. Therefore, their rituals focus on God as the giver of the fish rather than on the relationship between people and fish. They thank God for providing the fish and ask God to help them catch the fish. Given their worldview, it is appropriate that their thanks be directed to God. The ultimate world of the New Englanders is more hierarchically structured—fish are below people, and people are below God. The ultimate world of the Solomon Islanders is more communally structured—fish are relatives playing their part in the ocean of life. Culturally and religiously the two groups have created different imaginative orders. They think about their lives in the world, or "imagine" them, in different ways. In the academic study of religion we do not say that one ordering/imagining is right and the other ordering/imagining is wrong. Both are ways of understanding the world and living in the world. Both constructions are viable possibilities for human beings; both, like all symbolic constructions, have limitations.

Not all cultures have a term that corresponds exactly to the Latin-derived *religion*. The Latin word *religio* had political and moral overtones. In Ancient Rome *religio* expressed proper behavior and attitudes for a Roman citizen. The Roman statesman and scholar

Marcus Tullius Cicero (106–43 BCE), and the Latin church father Caecilius Lactantius (240–320 CE),[8] who is dubbed the Christian Cicero, give different accounts of the word's origin. Cicero said it came from the verb *relegere*, "to reread" or "to pass on." Thus, he understood religion as "tradition." Lactantius said that the word "religion" came from the verb *religare*, "to bind fast." Thus, he understood religion as that which binds people to one another and to the gods or God. Both understandings are reflected in the way we use the word *religion* today. We think of religion as a way of ordering the world that is passed on from generation to generation and also as a process for connecting people to gods or powers and to one another.

While not all cultures have a concept of religion, all cultures have at least an implicit **cosmology,** or an understanding of how the universe is ordered or structured. The word *cosmology* means "an account of the world," and the term has particular usages in philosophy and astronomy in referring to the structuring of the universe. In conversations about religion *cosmology* refers to the understanding of the world's structure that is found in a culture's significant rituals and stories. For scholars of religion, cosmologies are starting points for the study of human experience.

We may enter a people's cosmology through listening to their stories and observing their actions. Hopi myths and rituals, for example, tell of nine potential worlds, of which four have already been inhabited by human beings. Hopi origin stories narrate the emergence of ancestor beings from three former worlds into the fourth world in which, by following an inner voice or song, they were able to journey to the center where they now live. The Hopi place an emphasis on right thinking, conceived of as following the inner voice, the song in one's heart. Following the song is the way to negotiate one's life in the present world, and, in times of transition, to negotiate the route from one world to another. The members of a culture have a plan of the cosmos in their heads, and, the Hopi might say, a song of the cosmos in their hearts. It reverberates in their rituals and their stories. They transmit it, with adjustments at times, from generation to generation. In fact, a culture may have a number of variant cosmologies, and groups within the culture may understand the generally accepted cosmology in different ways.

Cosmologies are encoded in traditional narratives and rituals. They are also present, implicitly or explicitly, in scientific texts, philosophical treatises, and theological documents. They have their echoes in folk wisdom, in cultural mores, in etiquette. All cultures have their oral texts, and some their written texts, in which accounts of the physical and moral structure of the world are inscribed. All cultures employ rituals, scripted symbolic behaviors that echo and recreate the structure of the world and point to what the culture considers to be life giving and ultimately significant.

EXPERIENCE AND IMAGINATION

People talk a lot about beginnings. We recall our first days in school, our first jobs, our first meetings with those who became our dear friends. We ask, "How did this custom begin?" "Who built this city?" "From where did these people come?" Sometimes our questions become more profound and we wonder, "Who or what started it all?" "How did human beings come to be such bundles of creativity and fragility?" However, we do not all frame our questions in the same way and even those who do arrive at different answers. The various peoples of the world have their own stories about why human beings and the world are the way they are. Like Spider Grandmother, a creator and storyteller in Hopi mythology, they have spun stories that they project back to "the beginning." By placing the human situation in some ultimate perspective these stories of beginnings assist people in thinking about their lives now. Perhaps you are familiar with the biblical accounts in Genesis 1—2 in which God creates the world. There are, in fact, two distinct creation accounts in Genesis that differ in their presentations. What they share is the outlook that there is an ultimate being and source, existing before everything else, from which all creation receives the gift of life. These accounts will be discussed in detail in Chapter 7.

We look now at two contrasting accounts that describe the shaping and ordering of the world in the beginning. Such accounts, even as they tell of beginnings, are powerful in the here and now. At the same time, as they encode traditional cosmologies they prescribe how people should live now. They can be a source of meaning and guidance; they can also be a source of frustration and alienation. In one account, a later hymn of the Hindu **Rig Veda**, a primeval being, Purusa Sukta (first person), is sacrificed and dismembered. From the many parts of his body come the various parts of the cosmos and of social life. The image of the one cut into the many gives us a monistic view of the world. Monism is the doctrine that all is one; monism denies the duality of matter and mind.

The other account comes from the Haudenosaunee or Iroquois. *Haudenosaunee,*[9] an Iroquois term meaning "People of the Long-house," is the name the Six Confederate Nations of Mohawk, Oneida, Onondaga, Cayuga, Seneca, and Tuscarora give themselves. They think of their confederacy as a large house in which each nation occupies its allocated place. *Iroquois* is the term used by the French for the members of the confederacy. In the Haudenosaunee story of the beginnings of life on earth, the curiosity of a woman sets in motion a train of events that leads to her grandchildren, Left-Handed-Twin and Right-Handed-Twin shaping a physical and social world that contains both harmony and competition. Some say that the worldview of the Haudenosaunee account is dualistic since it tells us that in the world, and in ourselves, we find two competing principles—straight minded and crooked minded—and suggests the importance of the straight mind overcoming the crooked. However, lest we oversimplify, the story also suggests that the world was shaped and continues in existence through the interaction of straight and crooked.

Before reading the two accounts we shall venture briefly into the culture and history of the peoples to whom they belong. As you read the accounts ask yourself what insight each gives into the human condition. Although one is a Hindu story and one is a Haudeno-saunee story, both have something to say to all of us because both are stories about our human condition. Both answer the question "How did we come to be like this?" and both give guidance as to how we are to live here and now. In entering into the worlds of the stories we find differences of time and culture, yet we also find perspectives on the human situation that apply to our own lives.

THE ARYANS AND VEDIC RELIGION

The Rig Veda[10] is a collection of 1,028 hymns that was made between approximately 1200 and 900 BCE. The hymns are written in an archaic dialect of Sanskrit and are ascribed to various seers. The Sanskrit word *veda* means "sacred knowledge" or "wisdom." It is derived from the same Indo-European root as the English words "wit" and "wisdom." *Rig* is a transliteration of the Sanskrit word for "praise." Hence, this is a collection of hymns of praise and wisdom. The Rig Veda is the oldest of four Vedas that belong to the Vedic religion that preceded Hinduism. They have become part of the scriptures of Hinduism. The

Vedas were the sacred hymns of invaders who entered the northwest of India from the region of Iran around the middle of the second millennium BCE. The invaders called themselves Aryans (lords). The Indo-European languages of South Asia descend from their language, which is also called Aryan.[11]

Literary and archeological evidence suggest that the religion of the Aryans included rituals in which a drink prepared from the *soma* plant was offered to the gods and consumed by worshipers, sacrifices in which food and animal offerings were made to the gods, and the recitation of hymns. The chief **priest** would draw material from the Rig Veda for his recitations. In time the Vedic religion of the newcomers merged with indigenous Indian traditions to produce a variety of practices and ideas that we speak of collectively as Hinduism. For Hinduism, the Vedas constitute that which was heard, and thus revealed, in the beginning. The Vedas are the basis of Hindu religious authority, although the commentaries written upon them offer a wide variety of interpretations. The Vedas were transmitted by oral recitation, passed from teacher to student, for more than two thousand years. Then, over a period of several hundred years, they were written down, so that by the fifteenth or sixteenth century CE, the Sanskrit text as we know it today had been established.

The Rig Veda has several hymns that describe the shaping of the world. Some of the older hymns present the creation of the world as the result of a cosmic battle, while other hymns, including the one given below, Purusa Sukta (Hymn 90 from Book 10), show the world and the people in it being brought into being through a process of sacrifice.[12] A hymn from the Chandogya Upanishad, a philosophical part of the Vedas that we shall explore in Chapter 6, employs the metaphor of an egg hatching. In Purusa Sukta—which is sometimes referred to as The Hymn of Man—the gods cut up the primal person and from the parts of his body shape the physical and social world. This is one of the later hymns of the Rig Veda and the only one in which the four social classes or castes are mentioned (v. 12). Creation by dismemberment is a common theme in Indo-European mythology. The cutting up of Purusa Sukta produces four groups of people, each with its own role in the community. The mouth becomes the priests (the Brahman caste), with the duty of speaking to the gods; the arms become the warrior caste; the thighs become the farmers and tradespeople; and the feet on which all else rest become the laborers.

PURUSA SUKTA, *OR* THE HYMN OF MAN

1 The Man has a thousand heads, a thousand eyes, a thousand feet. He pervaded the earth on all sides and extended beyond it as far as ten fingers.

2 It is the Man who is all this, whatever has been and whatever is to be. He is the ruler of immortality, when he grows beyond everything through food.[1]

3 Such is his greatness, and the Man is yet more than this. All creatures are a quarter of him; three quarters are what is immortal in heaven.

4 With three quarters the Man rose upwards, and one quarter of him still remains here. From this[2] he spread out in all directions, into that which eats and that which does not eat.

5 From him Viraj[3] was born, and from Viraj came the Man. When he was born, he ranged beyond the earth behind and before.

6 When the gods spread[4] the sacrifice with the Man as the offering, spring was the clarified butter, summer the fuel, autumn the oblation.

7 They anointed[5] the Man, the sacrifice[6] born at the beginning, upon the sacred grass.[7] With him the gods, Sadhyas,[8] and sages sacrificed.

8 From that sacrifice in which everything was offered, the melted fat[9] was collected, and he[10] made it into those beasts who live in the air, in the forest, and in villages.

9 From that sacrifice in which everything was offered, the verses and chants were born, the meters were born from it, and from it the formulas were born.[11]

10 Horses were born from it, and those other animals that have two rows of teeth;[12] cows were born from it, and from it goats and sheep were born.

11 When they divided the Man, into how many parts did they apportion him? What do they call his mouth, his two arms and thighs and feet?

12 His mouth became the Brahman; his arms were made into the Warrior, his thighs the People, and from his feet the Servants were born.[13]

13 The moon was born from his mind; from his eye the sun was born. Indra and Agni came from his mouth, and from his vital breath the Wind was born.

14 From his navel the middle realm of space arose; from his head the sky evolved. From his two feet came the earth, and the quarters of the sky from his ear. Thus they[14] set the worlds in order.

15 There were seven enclosing-sticks[15] for him, and thrice seven fuel-sticks, when the gods, spreading the sacrifice, bound the Man as the sacrificial beast.

16 With the sacrifice the gods sacrificed to the sacrifice.[16] These were the first ritual laws.[17] These very powers reached the dome of the sky where dwell the Sadhyas, the ancient gods.

Notes

[1] This rather obscure phrase seems to imply that through food (perhaps the sacrificial offering) Purusa grows beyond the world of the immortals, even as he grows beyond the earth (v. 1 and v. 5). He himself also transcends both what grows by food and what does not (v. 4), i.e. the world of animate and inanimate creatures, or Agni (eater) and Soma (eaten).

[2] That is, from the quarter still remaining on earth, or perhaps from the condition in which he had already spread out from earth with three quarters of his form.

[3] The active female creative principle, Viraj is later replaced by Prakrti or material nature, the mate of Purusa in Sankhya philosophy.

[4] This is the word used to indicate the performance of a Vedic sacrifice, spread or stretched out (like the earth spread upon the cosmic waters) or woven (like a fabric upon a loom). Cf. 10.130.1–2.

[5] The word actually means "to sprinkle" with consecrated water, but indicates the consecration of an initiate or a king.

[6] Here "the sacrifice" indicates the sacrificial victim; they are explicitly identified with one another (and with the divinity to whom the sacrifice is dedicated) in verse 16.

[7] A mixture of special grasses that was strewn on the ground for the gods to sit upon.

[8] A class of demi-gods or saints, whose name literally means "those who are yet to be fulfilled."

[9] Literally, a mixture of butter and sour milk used in the sacrifice; figuratively, the fat that drained from the sacrificial victim.

[10] Probably the Creator, though possibly Purusa himself.

[11] The verses are the elements of the *Rig Veda*, the chants of the *Sama Veda*, and the formulas of the *Yajur Veda*. The metres often appear as elements in primeval creation; cf. 10.130.3–5 and, 1.164.23–5.

[12] That is, incisors above and below, such as dogs and cats have.

[13] The four classes or *varnas* of classical Indian society.

[14] The gods.

[15] The enclosing-sticks are green twigs that keep the fire from spreading; the fuel sticks are seasoned wood used for kindling.

[16] The meaning is that Purusa was both the victim that the gods sacrificed and the divinity to whom the sacrifice was dedicated; that is, he was both the subject and the object of the sacrifice. Through a typical Vedic paradox, the sacrifice itself creates the sacrifice.

[17] Literally, the *dharmas*, a protean word that here designates the archetypal patterns of behavior established during this first sacrifice to serve as the model for all future sacrifices.

THE HAUDENOSAUNEE
AND LONGHOUSE RELIGION

The second account, a Haudenosaunee narrative, is still passed on in oral form from generation to generation. For hundreds of years the five original nations of the Haudenosaunee—the Mohawk, Oneida, Onondaga, Cayuga, and Seneca—have occupied separate territories in New York State and Canada. Today, the Oneida also have territory in Wisconsin. At some stage prior to European settlement the five nations formed a confederacy. The Tuscarora joined later to make what we now refer to as the Six Nations. A confederacy narrative tells that warfare was a way of life among the five nations. According to this story it took the efforts of a peace maker, Deganawidah, who came from the Huron people to the north, and an Onondaga chief, Hayenwatha (Hiawatha), to establish peace among them. Degana-widah is so revered that many today will not pronounce his name. The confederacy strengthened the nations against outside enemies and encouraged peace among them.

Traditionally, the Haudenosaunee were agricultural and hunting people. Therefore, their ritual cycle is related to the seasonal cycle of crops and game. For example, in the summer, after the corn, beans, and squash are ripe, they hold the Green Corn Festival to rejoice and give thanks. In winter, after hunting is over for the year, they hold their New Year or Mid-Winter Festival, a celebration that emphasizes cleansing and new life. The Haudenosaunee Creation Account, Confederacy Narrative, and Thanksgiving Address complement one another, each echoing themes of right-mindedness, thankfulness, competition, and balance.

In the time since European contact, more than forty versions of the Haudenosaunee creation story have been written down in English. The following account is based on them. When a story is transmitted orally, the storyteller is able to accommodate the basic story to the circumstances of the community for which it is told. Knowing the situation of the audience the storyteller may, for example, highlight points that are pertinent at the time the story is told. It is not surprising that so many written versions of the Haudenosaunee story may be found because those who wrote them heard the story told for different communities by different storytellers. Thousands upon thousands of tellings of the story have resided not on written pages, but in the lives of those who heard them and used them as a framework for thinking about our situation as human beings in the world.

SHAPING THE WORLD:
A HAUDENOSAUNEE STORY

In the beginning, in the Sky World, lived a husband and wife. The wife was expecting a child and craved various delicacies as pregnant women are wont to do. Her husband was kept busy fetching them for her. In the middle of the Sky World grew a Great Tree with huge roots and many branches. Those who lived in the Sky World were not permitted to take leaves or wood from the tree or to injure it in any way. The woman wanted some of the bark from one of the roots of the Great Tree, but her husband was reluctant to take it. Eventually, he gave in to his wife's desire and scraped away some soil to bare the root. In fact, the floor of the Sky World was not very deep, and he made a hole that revealed an empty space beneath. He was afraid and would not take any of the root.

The woman was curious. She looked down through the hole and saw the ocean. Then, she fell. Perhaps she slipped. Perhaps her husband pushed her. As she fell she grasped at the edges of the hole and pulled away bits of the small roots of the tree and parts of the things growing in the soil under the tree. When the birds saw the woman falling some of them came to her aid and, flying wingtip to wingtip, made a raft to support her. Other birds flew down to the ocean and called to the ocean creatures for help. The great sea turtle agreed to receive her on his back, and so the birds placed her there.

The woman wanted to plant the bits of root and plant material that she had brought from the Sky World. The diving birds and animals took it in turns to dive down into the ocean to see if they could find some soil that could be placed on the turtle's back to enable the woman to plant the things from the Sky World. Finally, the muskrat was successful, but he was completely out of breath and almost dead when he emerged from the ocean. They hoisted him up onto the turtle's back, sang and prayed over him, and breathed air into his mouth until he recovered. The woman took the soil and placed it in the middle of the turtle's back. Then she walked around in a circle, moving in the direction that the sun goes. This is still the direction for dance rituals. The soil spread out, and the earth grew until it was big enough for her to plant the roots she had brought from the Sky World. These grew, and thus we have plants in the Earth World.

The woman who had fallen from the sky was after some time delivered of a daughter. The child knew nothing of the Sky World, but she knew the animals and birds and ocean creatures who had helped her mother. One day, after the girl had grown up, a man appeared. Some say he was the West Wind and had been sent from the Sky World. The girl was so surprised to see him that she fainted. The man lay two arrows across her body, one sharp and one blunt. When the girl awoke she continued, as before, to walk with her mother around the earth that had been formed on the turtle's back. Soon it became clear that she was pregnant. In fact, she was pregnant with twins.

While still in their mother's womb the twins began to quarrel. They even argued about the way they should be born. The right-handed twin wanted to be born in the usual way that babies are born, emerging through his mother's birth canal. The left-handed twin said he could see light in the opposite direction and wanted to go that way. He could not be born through his mother's mouth or nose, but he forced himself out through her left armpit and killed her in the process. When Right-Handed Twin, who had been born in the normal way, saw what had happened, he accused Left-Handed Twin of murdering their mother. However, Grandmother, who tended to favor Left-Handed Twin, told them to stop arguing. They buried the woman, who now is referred to as Our Mother, and Corn Mother. From her grave grew the staple foods of the Haudenosaunee. From her head grew corn, beans, and squash, which are referred to as Our Supporters, the Three Sisters. From her heart grew sacred tobacco, which is used in ceremonies to send messages and thanks to the Sky World.

The two brothers represented two different ways of living in the world, and they were always competing with each other. Right-Handed Twin always told the truth and always did things in a reasonable way. Left-Handed Twin lied and did things in unusual ways. Right-Handed Twin, people say, had the straight mind, and Left-handed Twin had the crooked mind. The brothers shaped the world as we know it now. They took clay and molded it into animals. Right-Handed Twin made the deer and Left-Handed Twin made the mountain lion, which kills the deer. Then Right-Handed Twin made the ground squirrel, which was able to dig a hole and get away from the mountain lion. Left-Handed Twin responded by making the weasel, which is able to pursue the ground squirrel into its hole. Right-Handed Twin then made the porcupine and, of course, the weasel could not kill it. However, Left-Handed Twin made the bear, and the bear was not afraid to flip the porcupine over on it back and tear out its stomach.

Just as Right-Handed Twin and Left-Handed Twin competed with each other in making animals, so they competed with each other in making plants. Right-Handed Twin made fruits and berries that the animals could eat. Left-Handed Twin made plants with thorns and poisons, and he made medicines, some for healing and some for harming. Right-Handed Twin made human beings and, therefore, he is called our Creator and The Master of Life. However, it is said that Left-Handed Twin also had some part in this creation, and it is he who is responsible for the rituals of sorcery and healing. Together the twins built a world that embraced both competition and cooperation. Even when they were adults, they still argued. Eventually their arguments led to a series of contests and to the departure of both of them from the world they had shaped.

First, they gambled. They took wild plum pits that they had burned on one side, so that they were white on one side and black on the other, and tossed them in a bowl to see how they would fall. In this way they gambled all day, but neither was the winner. Then they played lacrosse all day, but neither was the winner. Then they fought with clubs, but neither won. Each knew deep in his mind that he had a weak point. They talked about this as they dueled, and the deep mind of each entered into the deep mind of the other. However, the deep mind of Right-Handed Twin lied to his brother while the deep mind of Left-Handed Twin told the truth. Finally, they both knew that Right-handed Twin would vanquish Left-Handed Twin, and so it was. Left-Handed Twin took a stick for the final contest. Right-Handed Twin took a deer antler. With one touch of the deer antler he destroyed his brother and threw his body off the edge of the earth. Left-Handed Twin now lives somewhere off the edge of the world. People say that the day is the domain of Right-Handed Twin and night the domain of Left-Handed Twin.

After killing his brother, Right-Handed Twin went home to Grandmother. She was angry over what he had done and said he was a murderer. He told her she had always favored Left-Handed Twin, and in his fury he cut off her head. He threw her body into the ocean and her head into the sky, where still she keeps watch. People call her Our Grandmother, the Moon. Today Right-Handed Twin lives in the Sky World. People burn sacred tobacco in order to honor him and to send thanks to him. Left-Handed Twin lives in the world below. At Mid-Winter and other festivals the day is dedicated to rituals honoring Right-Handed

Thinking with Stories

Storytelling and ritual performance provide opportunities to think about our situation in the world. We might even say that storytelling and ritual performance are ways of thinking because they tell or enact possible ways of understanding ourselves and our world. They provide models with which, or against which, we can test our experience. In telling of beginnings the Vedic hymn and the Haudenosaunee story call on us to think about our life in the world here and now.

1. Summarize the cosmologies (accounts of the world's structure) to be found in the Vedic hymn and the Haudenosaunee story.
2. What does each account suggest about social order?
3. What does each account suggest about the power of life?
4. Religious rituals and texts contribute some insight into the human situation and raise issues for further reflection. What insights do the Vedic and Haudenosaunee accounts provide for you? What issues do they raise?

Each of us makes our world within—and sometimes against—the cultural pattern that our forebears have transmitted to us. We inherit religious images, such as those in the Vedic Purusa hymn and the Haudenosaunee creation account. These images help us in shaping our human experiences and reassuring ourselves that they have meaning. These images are so influential that most of the time we take them for granted. However, in studying religion our task is to move beyond the attitude of "taken for grantedness" and to ask what understandings of life are embodied in religious conceptualizations and practices.

Twin, and the night is given to social activities, to feasting and singing and dancing under the auspices of Left-Handed Twin. Thus, the balance the twins built into the world is reflected in the structure of rituals even today.

RESOURCES

ACTIVITIES

1. Divide the members of your class into several groups and ask each group to watch one of the episodes in the PBS series *Worlds of Faith with Huston Smith*. Have each group report on the worldview, symbols, and values of the tradition(s) being discussed. How does Huston Smith approach traditions other than his own? (You could modify this exercise for use with other documentaries, or you could make use of library resources to prepare reports on the worldview, symbols, and values of selected traditions.)

2. Divide into several groups and have each group prepare a thumbnail sketch of the search for order and meaning as it is exemplified in the following traditions (or traditions of your choice): Hopi religion, Dogon religion, Hinduism, Buddhism, Judaism, Islam, Christianity, **Sikhism**, Shinto, Confucianism.

3. Join an Internet list or blog in which people discuss religious issues. What is the focus of the list or blog that you joined? What ideas about religion and human experience are expressed by those posting messages? Do the participants have a positive or negative attitude toward religion? How is this manifested?

4. Visit websites that provide material on a religious issue in which you are interested. What resources do the sites provide? In making use of the Internet, as in making use of a library, one cannot take information at face value. It is necessary to establish the qualifications of the person providing information and to check the information against other sources.

5. Make use of your library and the Internet to
   a. Find out more about Vedic religion and its relationship to modern Hinduism.
   b. Find out more about present-day Haudenosaunee religion.

6. Choose a poem that you consider to have a religious theme. Discuss the symbols in the poem and the messages that it conveys.

7. Choose a film that you consider to have a religious theme. Discuss the symbols in the film and the messages that it conveys.
8. Choose a natural symbol (water, fire, tree, mountain, animal, fish). Find out how the symbol has been used in secular and religious contexts (in literature, art, ritual, and so on). Then, with other students, prepare a multimedia presentation on the symbol.

READINGS

The Bible. Since biblical texts are referred to throughout this book, it is useful to have a Bible on hand while reading. For example, when reflecting on the creation stories you could turn to the Book of Genesis. The New Oxford Annotated Bible, New Revised Standard Version with the Apocrypha (New York: Oxford University Press, 2011) is a good choice. It gives an introduction to each of the books of the Bible and provides notes to the text. Another suitable edition is The New American Bible, rev. ed. (Charlotte, NC: Saint Benedict Press, 2011).

Cooey, Paula, William R. Eakin, and Jay B. McDaniel, eds. *After Patriarchy: Feminist Transformations of the World Religions*. Maryknoll, NY: Orbis Books, 1991. The contributors grapple with the possibilities and problems of developing religious communities that transcend sexism.

Jones, Lindsay, ed. *The Encyclopedia of Religion*. 2nd ed. Detroit: Macmillan Reference USA, 2005. This encyclopedia, the most complete and up-to-date encyclopedia on religion available in English, is a good starting point for research on particular topics in religious studies.

Esposito, John. *The Future of Islam*. New York: Oxford University Press, 2011. A discussion of Islam in the twenty-first century and in several countries.

Eliade, Mircea. *The Sacred and the Profane: The Nature of Religion*. New York: Harcourt, Brace and World, 1959. A classic introduction to the history of religion that delineates the idea of the sacred in several cultures.

Geaves, Ron. *Islam Today*. New York: Continuum, 2010. Geaves discusses Muslim diversity, ethics and morality, challenges of textual interpretation, gender issues, fundamentalism, Islam and the West, and the future of Islam.

George-Kanentiio, Doug. *Iroquois Culture and Commentary*. Santa Fe: NM: Clear Light Publishers, 2000. An introduction to the history and culture of the Haudenosaunee with attention to the challenges the community faces today.

Jacobs, Stephen. *Hinduism Today*. London/New York, Continuum, 2010. Jacobs introduces the basic teachings and practices of Hinduism and discusses Hinduism in India and in the Diaspora, while also addressing social and political aspects of the religion.

Smith, Huston. *The World's Religions*. San Francisco: Harper, 1991. This is a revised and updated edition of Smith's 1958 classic *The Religions of Man*. He presents Hinduism, Buddhism, Confucianism, Taoism, Islam, Judaism, Christianity, and Primal Religions. An illustrated version is available.

Smith, Jonathan Z. *Imagining Religion: From Babylon to Jonestown*. Chicago: University of Chicago Press, 1982. In a series of essays on various expressions of religion, Smith makes a case that religion be seen not as the result of divine intervention in human affairs but as a product of the geographically and historically located human imagination.

Tooker, Elisabeth, ed. *Native North American Spirituality of the Eastern Woodlands*. New York: Paulist Press, 1979. This volume makes available texts of myths, dreams, visions, speeches, healing formulas, rituals, and ceremonials of native peoples of the Eastern Woodlands of North America. It includes a chapter on Iroquois ceremonials.

AUDIO-VISUALS

Many of the audio-visuals mentioned throughout the book can be found in school or public libraries as well as through the publishers.

Journey of the Universe (2011). Northcut Productions. This documentary film developed from the work of the historian of religions Thomas Berry, who believed that we needed a "new story" of the universe. Following Berry's death it was brought to fruition by Mary Evelyn Tucker with co-writer and narrator Brian Swimme. Tucker and John Grim were also the producers. Swimme, an evolutionary philosopher, leads us through a day on a Greek island and in the process brings together the fields of astronomy, geology, biology, and ecology with humanistic insights into the nature of the universe.

Trail of Tears: Cherokee Legacy (2006). Rich-Heap Films. With narrator James Earl Jones this documentary explores the dark era of Andrew Jackson's Indian Removal Act of 1830 and the forced removal of the Cherokee Nation to Oklahoma in 1838. Almost a quarter of the Cherokee Nation died on the journey to Indian Territory.

The Wisdom of Faith with Huston Smith: A Bill Moyers Special (1996). PBS. Available from Films for the Humanities and Sciences. Order online or from 132 West 31st Street, 17th Floor, New York, NY 10001. Huston Smith, the son of American missionary parents, was born and grew up in China. He has devoted his life to the study and practice of religion. In five one-hour programs, each presented with art, architecture, music, and poetry from the traditions being presented, Smith discusses the wisdom that humankind embodies in its religions. The programs are I. Hinduism and Buddhism; II. Confucianism and

Yoga; III. Christianity and Judaism; IV. Islam and Sufi Mysticism; and V. A Personal Faith: Religions as Windows on Truth.

YouTube. A wealth of audio-visual materials concerning religion is found on YouTube and other media sites. Among them are lectures and presentations on many of the topics included in this book. Search for relevant programs and learn from them, but be careful to assess where they are coming from and whether they are reliable.

NOTES

1. Wallace Stevens, *Collected Poems* (New York: Alfred A. Knopf, 1936).

2. Ibid., 129–30.

3. Mircea Eliade, *The Sacred and the Profane: The Nature of Religion* (New York: Harcourt, Brace and World, 1959).

4. Jonathan Z. Smith, *Map Is Not Territory* (Leiden: Brill, 1978).

5. Ruth Benedict, *Patterns of Culture* (Boston: Houghton Mifflin, 1934).

6. James F. Downs, *Cultures in Crisis* (Beverly Hills, CA: Glenco Press, 1971), 35.

7. On Solomon Islands societies, see Raymond Firth, *We, the Tikopia* (London: Allen and Unwin, 1936); Ian Hogbin, *A Guadalcanal Society: The Kaoka Speakers* (New York: Holt, Rinehart and Winston, 1965); Roger Keesing, *Kwaio Religion: The Living and the Dead in a Solomon Islands Society* (New York: Columbia University Press, 1982). Hogbin's chapter on religion includes a discussion of shark spirits and fishing rituals. Works that reflect the Solomon Islanders' adoption of Christianity include Michael W. Scott, *The Severed Snake: Matrilineages, Making Place, and a Melanesian Christianity in Southeast Solomon Islands* (Durham, NC: Carolina Academic Press, 2007); and Ben Burt, *Tradition and Christianity: The Colonial Transformation of Solomon Islands Society* (Philadelphia: Harwood Academic Publishers, 1994).

8. It is usual in religious studies today to use CE (common era) to designate years that in the past were given as AD (anno Domini, in the year of Our Lord), and BCE (before the common era) to designate years that in the previous nomenclature were given as BC (before Christ). The use of CE and BCE recognizes that the Gregorian calendar is in general use but does not privilege it on religious grounds over other calendar systems such as the Muslim calendar that is used by most Arab countries and the Hindu and Jewish calendars that are used for religious purposes.

9. For further information on the Haudenosaunee, see Hazel W. Hertzberg, *The Great Tree and the Longhouse: The Culture of the Iroquois* (New York: Macmillan, 1966); Doug George-Kanentiio, *Iroquois Culture and Commentary* (Santa Fe, NM: Clear Light Publishers, 2000); Dean R. Snow, *Iroquois* (Cambridge, MA: Blackwell, 1994); Elisabeth Tooker, *The Iroquois Ceremonial of Midwinter* (Syracuse, NY: Syracuse University Press, 1970); Elisabeth Tooker, ed., *An Iroquois Source Book*, 3 vols. (New York: Garland

Publishers, 1985–86); and Anthony F. C. Wallace, *The Death and Rebirth of the Seneca* (New York: Knopf, 1970).

10. For background and commentary on the Rig Veda, see Wendy Doniger, *The Rig Veda: An Anthology* (Harmondsworth, UK: Penguin, 1981); Ralph T. H. Griffith, trans., *The Rig Veda*, in *Sacred Writings*, ed. Jaroslav Pelikan (New York: Book-of-the-Month Club, 1992).

11. In the nineteenth century the term *Aryan* came to be used synonymously with *Indo-European*. The French diplomat and ethnologist Comte Joseph Arthur de Gobineau (1816–82) spread the idea that those who spoke Indo-European languages were superior to "Semites," "yellows," and "blacks." De Gobineau's followers saw the Germanic peoples as the purest Aryans. Although the idea of an Aryan race was discredited by anthropologists, it was taken up by Adolf Hitler and the Nazis as the basis of their policies for disposing of non-Aryans.

12. This translation of the Purusa Sukta is reprinted from *The Rig Veda: An Anthology: One Hundred and Eight Hymns*. Selected, translated, and annotated by Wendy Doniger (Middlesex England: Harmondsworth; New York: Penguin Books, 1981).

Chapter 2

Religious Understandings of Life

THE POWER OF LIFE

Human beings desire life, and yet they suffer diminishments of life and they experience death. Religious communities grapple in their teachings and practices with the paradox of life and death. Religions express the human desire to understand and to engage the powers of life. They speak of the power of life in terms of the sacred, the holy, the transcendent, the absolute, the good, the beautiful, the true, the energy to effect change. The religious imagination gives the powers of life location and character. The Aztecs looked to the heavens whence the sun and the rain sent their warmth and moisture to the earth. Confucianists, Shintoists, and many indigenous communities turn to the ancestors, to whom we are in debt for both biological and cultural life, to give them wisdom and strength. The Plains peoples of North America imagine the powers of life to be dispersed throughout nature. Theists see them centered in a God or gods. Zen Buddhism teaches that we can experience the real power of life by living intensely in the present.

Conceptualizations of life-giving power and of power that is inimical to life differ, but there is an understanding common to religious communities that we are part of a powerful mystery of life. Religious texts speak of that mystery and what they deem to be appropriate responses to it; they also struggle with the reality of illness and suffering. Religious rituals provide opportunities to connect with the mystery and commit to living in accord with it; they grant absolution to sinners and afford solace for those who suffer a weakening of their own life or the loss of loved ones.

The symbolic formulations with which communities capture a sense of the power and mystery of life suggest that there is something "more" than the world that we know through our five senses. Religious words and actions and images bear a surplus of meaning and feeling that points to the "more." Just as individuals and communities conceive of life and the ultimate power of life in various ways, so they devise various ritual ways to tap into the power of life. For example, the tribes of the Central Desert of Australia understand that their world was shaped by ancestors in the beginning of time. They have daily, seasonal, and life-cycle rituals to link them to the originating time/space and to continue its empowering process in the here and now. In contrast to the Australian Aboriginal representation of life-giving power, the Jewish community conceives of a God who dwells in a realm apart but graciously intervenes in the history of his people. In their annual **Passover** ritual, Jews stand with their ancestors and celebrate God's power and love in freeing them from Egypt long ago and continuing to free them from whatever inhibits their life today. They, too, have daily, seasonal, and life-cycle rituals that above all, connect them to God and the orienting events in their history.

In this chapter we explore understandings encoded in an Aboriginal **initiation** story and in the Jewish Passover Seder ritual. Both the Warlpiri story and the texts and actions that compose the Passover Seder suggest that life is good and blessed and that human beings participate in the fundamental power of life. A dialogue of the two accounts uncovers areas of both commonality and difference. Such a dialogue reveals that the Central Desert peoples of Australia and the Jewish community, with its origins in the Middle East but spread today throughout the world, have ideas about their relationship to land that shape their religious experience. In the search for an ultimate order and meaning the communities think both with similar and with different images. Both focus on land, although they conceive of it in different ways. The Jewish community tells of a God who chose them and established them in a particular land. The Warlpiri community of Central Australia tells of kangaroo ancestors who traced out the boundaries of the land in whose life they participate. Both communities seek to develop appropriate relationships with what they understand to be the fundamental power of life.

Even as human beings seek life, they experience suffering, evil, and death. On the surface of it we say that sickness, hunger, aging, loneliness, and grief diminish life. We say that children should not be tortured and murdered. We say that all people should have food and shelter. Yet things are not the way we want them to be. Since religions purport to provide frames of reference within which human experience has purpose and meaning, suffering and death put them to the test. Buddhism addresses the test by asserting that suffering is an intrinsic structure of transitory existence. The point with which the **Buddha** begins his discourse on life is the universality of suffering. From the fact of suffering the Buddha moves to an analysis of its causes (desire and ignorance) and to the prescription of a path that will lead to non-attachment and wisdom. For the theistic religions suffering raises the problem of theodicy, of reconciling the existence of evil with a God who is held to be all powerful, all knowing, and all good.

Religions suggest that this world of the senses, with all its unsatisfactory aspects, is not all that there is. They propose that we are in some way presently alienated from ultimate reality. Some religions teach that death is a path to true life. As individuals we may refuse to recognize the inevitability of death in our own case (most of us recognize it in general), we may resign ourselves to it, or we may accept it willingly. Our attitude is often governed by our religious formation. The images that a religious community employs in setting life and death within a larger design may seem unusual, or strange and confusing, to outsiders. However, we can uncover something of their import if we take the time to reflect on these images in their historical and cultural contexts.

LAND IN WARLPIRI EXPERIENCE

The Warlpiri (Walbiri) of Central Australia understand that they belong to the land, and for them, the land is imbued with sacred power. The Warlpiri tell of ancestors who in the original space/time traveled from place to place shaping the land and establishing the laws by which people would live. Some of the ancestors of whom they tell have animal forms and some have plant forms. The power of the founding ancestors is still available to people through the telling of their stories and the performance of rituals that replicate their actions of long ago. The Warlpiri do not talk about "religion," but they talk about the original shaping work of the ancestors and of their ongoing work in molding the land and community. The term *hierophany*, as we saw in Chapter 1, is used in religious studies to refer to appearances of the sacred. In the Warlpiri case songs, journeys, dances, dreams, paintings, rituals, storytelling, and places where the ancestors stopped on their mythic journeys are opportunities for hierophany. They are occasions for people to participate more intensely in their myth history and to experience the power of a sacred geography.

Jukurrpa, the term the Warlpiri use in speaking of the journeys of their ancestors and also in claiming their connection to the path taken by the ancestors, is usually translated as "dreaming." Each person has his or her own dreamings, inherited from both mother's and father's sides of the family. Notice that the story is about two kangaroos, not one, and that the storyteller speaks of them affectionately as "my two kangaroos." Dreamings are mental and emotional maps that situate the person in relationship to the ancestors, to other people, and to the land. They provide an orientation in life. The story of the Two Kangaroos is a male **initiation** myth that is told in a simple form to children and in a more detailed form to candidates for initiation. Notice the humor in the transformation of the small rat-like animal into a noble kangaroo. What happens in the story is comparable to what happens in all our lives. We start out as puny rat-like creatures focused on our own needs, but through the care and instruction of our elders we grow physically into adults and socially into citizens. Notice also that the tale has been transcribed and translated from an oral account. Hence, we need to imagine the storyteller, with his gestures and pauses and emotional overtones, and the audience for whom the territory through which the characters journey is home.

The Warlpiri story tells of kangaroo ancestors who marked out the territory of the storyteller's dreamings, brought water places (soaks or soakages) into being, planted fruit-bearing shrubs, and gave people the songs to use for initiations. The power of the ancestral figures is, in Warlpiri conceptualizations, embedded in the landscape. Providing water, the condition of physical life, in the desert country of Central Australia is regarded as the work of powerful and benevolent beings. The two kangaroos, however, give not only physical life but also the ritual means to produce social life. Traces of their journey are to be found in the landscape and rituals are carried out at places where they stopped along the way. Those who follow their tracks invoke their power for the here and now.

The account that follows was narrated in 1990 by Henry Cook Jakamarra.[1] Read the story as though you were the storyteller telling of your heroes, punctuating the story with gestures, and outlining the kangaroos' journey with marks in the desert sand. Since the context of the story is most likely unfamiliar, you will need to read it a few times. Remember that the story is about land and initiation—about the Warlpiri association with a particular area of land in Central Australia and about the possibility of transformation into a real kangaroo-person.

THE TWO KANGAROOS: A WARLPIRI INITIATION STORY

These are my two kangaroos. There they went, along the east side. The two kangaroos travelled along the east side. They went, where, where, am I trying to remember? They went to Parntarla. They stayed at Parntarla. Then they departed. They stopped again. They went to Lawarri next. They stayed at Lawarri. There they stayed, the two kangaroos belonging to that place. These two places belong to them, Lawarri and Parntarla. These places belong to them both. They are the two who belong to these places. They brought many places into being, many soakages in the surrounding area.

They stayed. Then they left. A little later on they set off, then they stopped. You know, in the old days they walked about during the Dreaming. There they were travelling, the two of them. They travelled south, along the west side to the Granites, then back along the east to Yurlpuwarnu, along the east side again. From the Granites they went along the west side again, near the Granites. Then they left the Granites. Then one of the two kangaroos was taken away. He was carried away in a big flooded stretch of water. Thus he was taken away. The other looked for him all around.

"Now I will have to travel alone. What has happened? Maybe he was carried off by all that water? The water has been running everywhere, it has spread out everywhere. That lake, that lake has swallowed him up."

He was taken from there, one of the two was taken away. Then, from that place the one who was left, went away. He went off, and put the other one out of his mind.

He looked around. "What is this sitting here?"

It was a type of little mouse, a little rat, somewhat related to a mouse but slightly different, called a wulyu-wulyu. He approached it and picked it up. He looked at it closely.

"Ah, it had two ears, two ears and it has a tail, it has two feet, and it has a tail." He looked at it carefully. In particular he looked at its tail.

"What will I do with this creature? I'll take it with me, I'll take it along." He carried it to Mulyu, he carried it to Mulyu. There he remade it, completely. He made it into a kangaroo. Now that he was a kangaroo, he started to hop about. Where did he go? He went away. Now that he was a kangaroo, now that he had been completely remade into a kangaroo, he went away.

Now there were two kangaroos. One had come from the little animal we call wulyu-wulyu. The two kangaroos stayed in that place for a considerable time, in that place which belongs to them. The two kangaroos stayed there for a long time.

"Let's go on a journey."

"Yes."

The one that had spoken was probably the older brother, I am not sure, probably the older brother. The other was now also a real kangaroo, the one that had been made from a little rat. At first it hopped around on all fours, on all four legs. It went. It stopped. It went on.

"I am going on a journey. I am going on a journey."

"Yes, yes, on a journey, then, yes."

"All right, you go in front, like that."

He made the little one, the one made from the little rat, travel in front of him. The other one followed him. In this way, he went along. Then they found another place, called Nyurrijardu, which is a very important place. They created that place, the two of them, and there they stayed for a while. They were the two belonging to that place. In that southern part of the country there are all those places that belong to them, all those soaks, there in the south.

Then they travelled east to Jalyirrparnta. They slept there, they stayed out there. Then they went on into the south for a long time. They also visited a soak on the way. Now what is that name I am looking for? Somewhere behind Jalyirrlparnta. Warrarna, Jupurrurla's father, knows that place. I have never visited that particular country.

From there they went to another soak, further away, to Kuyujarra, Kuyujarra. I do not know of another soak there, either to the south or the north. To Kuyujarra. From Kuyujarra to Yintawalyarri. From Yintawalyarri they went along the west side to Warnirriparnta. They went a long distance away, along the west side. There they encountered another dreaming. At that place, the Pirlarla dreaming follows the same path.

Then they arrived at Lirrawarnupatu. At Lirrawarnupatu, they mistakenly made contact with that other dreaming. From Lirrawarnupatu they went to Japiya-jarra. In that area, many, many soakages, some very big, lie across the basin there. I learned about those places when I was growing up, a little at a time. I can follow this dreaming as it goes along the west side, as it has been told to me, as it has been shown me.

The two kangaroos continued their journey. They went into Japiyajarra. From there, now, into another country, into Yintaramurru, which is in the west. White people call that place Mount Singleton. That country, in the west. They went away over there. There they put down bush tomato plants, the fruit that we call ngayaki, which is like jarlparrpa as well. In that country they deposited the bush tomato plants.

They came back this way. At Yarrpawangu, there is a stone knife, a stone knife at Yarrpawangu. From there they went back to eat the bush tomatoes. They went back to Yintaramurru. From there they went on to Butcher Creek to Yanijiwarra. At Yanjiwarra those two sang the kurdiji (initiation) songs for others. Then they left there, just the two of them. They went away towards that place, they climbed up towards Pikilyi, from Yanjiwarra. They climbed up towards Pikilyi. That is as far as I will take the story, as far as Pikilyi.

That is all.

FREEDOM
IN JEWISH EXPERIENCE

For the Jewish community, as for the Warlpiri, relationship to a particular land is an important element of identity. Archeological evidence indicates that there have been people living in Australia for more than fifty thousand years. Prehistorians say that there have been people in Israel for an even longer period, for some one hundred thousand years, and that the ancestors of the Jews were established there by the thirteenth century BCE. In the Book of Genesis, the first book of the **Bible,** we read the story that the Jewish people came to relate of their establishment in the land they call their own. Genesis tells that God led the patriarch Abraham, his wife Sarah, and their family, from Ur of the Chaldeans to a land that he promised them, the land of Canaan (Gen 12). The biblical account narrates that, after some years in Canaan, a famine occurred, and Abraham's grandson, Jacob, brought his family into Egypt, where they remained for four hundred years and became enslaved to Pharaoh, the king of Egypt (Gen 42—50). In the Book of Exodus, the second book of the Bible, we are told that the Lord had compassion on his people and delivered them out of this slavery and brought them back to the Promised Land. That land, referred to today as Eretz Israel, has become a symbol of freedom for Jews. The story of God's intervention to release the Hebrews from slavery in Egypt has become central to the Jewish self-understanding. God is the hero of Exodus and acts on behalf of God's people.

If we study the history of the land of Israel, we find that during most of the time that Jews lived in Israel other nations governed them. From 1550 to 1200 BCE Egypt had jurisdiction over Palestine but lost control with the coming of the Sea Peoples, of whom the Philistines were a significant power, until subdued by the Israelites under King David and King Solomon. Solomon's reign in the tenth century BCE is remembered as a golden age for Israel and during it the First Temple of Jerusalem was built. His death brought division of the kingdom into two—Israel in the north and Judah in the south. The ancient Canaanites had developed a linear alphabet, which was adopted by the Israelites around 1000 BCE. Hence, the stories of the Israelite ancestors and their legal and religious codes began to take written form and, as will be discussed in Chapter 7, underwent revision until the present canon of the Tanakh was established. Jewish teachers and, later on, writers reflected on the saga of their relationship to the land—on the graciousness of God in giving it to them, on his interventions to restore it to them, and on their own transgressions that merited such punishment as loss of the land.

The northern state of Israel fell to the Assyrians in 722 BCE while the southern state of Judah survived as an Assyrian vassal until 625 BCE, when Assyria lost power to Babylon. The Babylonians destroyed Judah in 587 BCE and took many of the priests and scholars into exile in Babylon. Under the Persian ruler Cyrus II (c. 550–529 BCE) the exiles returned to Jerusalem and built the Second Temple. After the invasion of Alexander the Great (356–323 BCE), Palestine came under Greek suzerains. It enjoyed a period of independence from 141 BCE, following a revolt led by Judas Maccabeus, until 65 BCE, when dissension in the ruling family led to civil war and Roman intervention. The Romans crushed subsequent attempts at revolt. After a final revolt in 135 CE the Jewish population of Palestine was drastically reduced and Israel ceased to exist as a separate state, even though Jews continued to live there.

Members of Diaspora communities in North Africa and Europe still remembered the land of their ancestors, a land they understood to have been given to them by God. Connection to the land of Israel remained a part of Jewish identity. In the centuries that followed the establishment of Roman hegemony, Palestine became part of the Byzantine Empire and then fell to the Ottoman Turks. After World War I it became a League of Nations–mandated territory governed by Britain. European Jews, fleeing anti-Semitism, began moving there in the 1880s, and the Zionist Movement, under the leadership of the Viennese journalist Theodor Herzl (1860–1904), advocated the establishment of a Jewish homeland. In the 1930s, Jews fleeing Hitler's persecutions joined them. Finally, following the partition of Palestine into Arab and Jewish areas, the United Nations created the modern state of Israel in 1948.

Today, Jews live in all parts of the world, so it is not surprising that they have a variety of ideas about the land of Israel. Some maintain that every true Jew should live in the present-day geographical equivalent of the Promised Land. Others do not see the modern state of Israel as equivalent to the biblical Promised Land. Rather, they see Zion as the ideal land of freedom in which people live in faithfulness to God and loyalty to one another, and they take it upon themselves to build Zion wherever they might be. However, since the **Holocaust**, in which almost six million Jews were murdered by the Nazi leadership during the Second World War, the land of Israel has also come to be seen as a safe haven, a place in which Jews might govern themselves and live free of the anti-Semitism that marked their life in the European Diaspora. Today, the United States, with some six million Jews, has the largest and most diverse Jewish community in the world. Many American Jews see it as a duty of solidarity to give material support to Israel.

The Israeli-Palestinian conflict is seldom absent from our news media and causes us to reflect on the complex mixing of politics and religion. Jewish settlements inspired by the Zionist movement were established in Palestine from the end of the nineteenth century until today. They have resulted in tensions and hostilities between Arab peoples, both Muslim and Christian who have been resident for centuries in Palestine, and the Jewish community returning, as it were, from exile to their historical homeland. While militants in the Pan-Arab movement consider the territory occupied today by the state of Israel to belong to the Palestinian Arabs, those seeking peace in the Middle East acknowledge that both communities have claims in the region and that compromises are necessary to bring about a settlement of the conflict.

Despite different understandings of the relationship between symbolic Israel and the modern state of Israel, the image of God as savior and liberator who intervenes to free his oppressed people is central to Judaism. Each year Jews echo the theme of God's saving love as they gather to celebrate Pesach or **Passover**, a springtime festival of new lambs, which Judaism has transformed into a historical commemoration. Passover brings into present consciousness the liberation from bondage in Egypt. At Passover, Jews pray for freedom for themselves and for all the peoples of the earth. Their own experiences of persecution and loss of freedom make them sensitive to oppression. In their sacred narratives, telling of a God who intervenes to save Israel, they point, however, to the possibility of universal liberation. Although the symbolic structure of Judaism has been shaken by the events of the Holocaust, nevertheless, millions of Jews gather each year to celebrate Passover and thus to assert the value and possibility of freedom.

Passover is celebrated in the home on the first new moon after the Spring equinox with a Seder, a meal that follows a particular order. The word *seder* in fact means "order." The Seder arranges readings from the Bible, prayers, songs, and the consumption of symbolic foods into an orchestrated order. Passover is the most widely observed Jewish holiday. The Passover home service enables all Jews to remember their heritage and to become part of the ongoing movement from slavery to freedom. The sequence of the Seder meal, along with all the prayers and readings and songs used in the service, is published in a text called the **Haggada**. Some parts of the Haggada are passages from the **Torah**, the first section of the Hebrew Bible; some parts were composed by rabbis around two thousand years ago; other parts date from the Middle Ages.

A plate containing six symbolic foods is placed on the Seder table. The foods are *karpas*, a mild green vegetable such as parsley, which symbolizes the new growth of spring and is dipped in salt water or vinegar to recall the tears of the enslaved Hebrews; *maror*, a bitter herb such as horseradish to suggest the bitterness endured by the slaves; *hazeret*, another bitter herb such as romaine lettuce, pointing to a double portion of bitterness; *haroset*, a sweet mixture of fruit, nuts, and wine said to resemble the mud and mortar that the slaves molded into bricks, and which suggests that even harsh slavery is tempered with sweetness and optimism; *zeroah*, a roasted lamb shank bone to recall the Exodus account of the last meal eaten by the slaves as they prepared to leave Egypt and also to recall the days of the Temple when a lamb was sacrificed and then roasted for the family Passover meal; *baytzah*, a roasted egg, symbolic of new life and of the second festival offering brought to the Temple, and also seen as symbol of mourning for the Second Temple. Three pieces of unleavened bread *(matzot)* are set on the table and are consumed throughout the course of the meal. The bread is unleavened because in the Exodus account it is said that the Hebrews left Egypt in such haste that there was not time to wait for bread to rise. The ritual meal begins with a blessing that recalls God's creation of the world, God's choice of Israel, the distinction God makes between sacred and profane, and the distinction God has

Seder plate: The names of the six symbolic foods are written in Hebrew on the plate.

established between the days of work and the Sabbath and festival days. A ritual washing of hands follows and then the leader—traditionally the head of the household—distributes the *karpas* that he has dipped in salt water or vinegar. Then the middle one of three sheets of unleavened bread, the second *matzot*, is broken.

To prompt the telling of the Exodus story the youngest child present asks four questions to which the company makes an initial response. Then the readings, prayers, and songs spread throughout the evening constitute a longer response to the questions. We shall read a section from near the beginning of the Passover service. It includes the four questions with the company's response, an anecdote concerning why the Exodus story is narrated at night, and a passage that concerns the instruction of four sons: one wise, one wicked, one simple, and one too young to even ask questions. At the same time as the Haggada narrates the story of God's intervention to save the Hebrews and to make of them a nation, it speaks of the need to pass on the tradition and to accommodate the teaching of it to the disposition of the student. The Jewish liturgical renewal of recent years has produced several new scripts for the Seder that accommodate themselves to the situations of people today. Some of the new scripts give attention to humanist and feminist issues and to the relationship of Judaism and other religions.

FROM THE PASSOVER SEDER

Child: How is this night different from any other night? On any other night we eat leavened and unleavened bread. Why on this night only unleavened bread? On any other night we eat all kinds of herbs. Why on this night only bitter herbs? On any other night we do not dip our herbs into anything even once. Why on this night do we do it twice? On any other night we eat either sitting upright or reclining. Why on this night do we all recline?

The leader uncovers the dish of *matzot* and places it on the table.

Company: We were slaves to Pharaoh in Egypt and the Lord our God brought us out from there with a mighty hand and an outstretched arm. If the Holy One, Blessed be He, had not brought our fathers out of Egypt, then we and our children and our children's children would still be enslaved to Pharaoh in Egypt. Therefore, if all of us were wise, all mature, all versed in the Torah, it would still be our duty to tell the story of the Liberation from Egypt. The more one dwells upon the details of the Exodus, the more he is praised.

It once happened that Rabbi Eliezer, Rabbi Joshua, Rabbi Eleazer ben Azariah, Rabbi Akiba, and Rabbi Tarphon gathered together in Bene Berak and they discussed the Exodus throughout the night until their disciples came and said to them: "Our teachers, it is time to recite the morning Shema."

Rabbi Eleazer ben Azariah said, "I am like a man of seventy and yet I did not understand why the story of the departure from Egypt would be related at night until Ben Zoma explained the reason: It is said, seven days shall you eat unleavened bread 'so that you may remember the day when you came out of the land of Egypt all the days of your life' (Dt 16:3). Had the text stated 'the days of your life' it would have meant the days only, but 'all the days of your life' includes the nights also. The sages further maintain that 'the days of your life' refers to this world while 'all the days of your life' is taken to include the days of the Messiah.

Blessed be the Omnipresent, Blessed be He. Blessed be the One who gave the Torah to His people Israel. Blessed be He. The Torah speaks of four kinds of children: the wise, the wicked, the simple and the one who is too young to ask.

What does the wise son ask? "What mean the testimonies, the statutes, and the ordinances, which the Lord your God commanded you?" (Dt 6:20). It is then your duty to tell him all the laws of the Passover down to the last detail of the Afikoman.

What does the wicked son say? "What does this service mean to you?" (Ex 2:26). Since he says "To you" and not "to himself" he excludes himself and thus denies God. Refute his arguments and tell him: "This is done because of that which the Lord did for me when I came out of Egypt." "For me" and not for him, implying that if he had been there he would not have been redeemed.

What does the simple son ask, "What is this?" (Ex 13:14). You shall say to him: "By strength of his hand, the Lord brought us out of Egypt, from the house of bondage."

To the son who is too young to ask, you shall tell him, for it is said (Ex 13:8), "On that day you shall tell your son, 'This commemorates what the Lord did for me when I came out of Egypt.'"

Construed in a large sense, as a quest for significance or as a structuring of a world of meaning, religion is, according to some scholars, a defining characteristic of human life. Historian of religions Mircea Eliade, as we have already observed, talks about the sacred as a structure or modality of human consciousness. That is, he sees the sacred as

Thinking about Our Place in the World

Both the Warlpiri story and the section of the Passover Seder picture what we might call sacred geographies. That is, they describe places in which powerful life-giving events occurred.

1. Draw maps to summarize the sacred geographies pictured in the two accounts.
2. How do members of the Warlpiri community and the Jewish community today connect themselves to the sacred power that is evoked in their mythic geographies?
3. Draw a map or picture showing your place in the world. Are there sources of power and energy that you need to include? What do the Warlpiri story, an initiation myth, and the Passover Seder, a liturgy structured around scripted questions posed by children, suggest about the education of children?

Mosque, Egypt. Most mosques have an outer courtyard for ablutions and a large unfurnished inside area for worship. Muslims are called to prayer from a tower, called a minaret, attached to the mosque.

one mode of human awareness, a mode that apprehends a transformative power of life. Eliade contrasts this modality with another, which he calls the profane.[2] By *profane* (prior to the temple) he means that which is not yet sacred, not yet aware of the transformative power of life. For Eliade, religion is the process in which the sacred irrupts into the profane and transforms it, making it holy or powerful, filling it with true life. Another way of thinking about religion, which we explore in Chapter 3, is to consider religion as an awareness expressed in symbols of participation in the fundamental power of life.

SACRED SPACE AND SACRED TIME

Human beings are aware of space and time. We notice our closeness to, and distance from, other things and other people. We notice the succession of events and the cycles of the seasons. We are people of particular places and particular times—contemporary Warlpiri of the Central Desert, ancient Hebrews in Egypt, Americans of the twenty-first century, Solomon Islanders of the late nineteenth century. Our experience of ourselves is conditioned by the time and place in which our larger community lives and by the particular times and places in which each of our lives is lived. To some extent our time and place are given, and to some extent we create them. We work with time and place to structure our lives, to bring order to our existence.

We have offices and factories for work, classrooms for study, kitchens for cooking, bedrooms for sleeping, chapels for praying. We have times in our daily schedule to sleep, to eat, to study, to play, to worship. Each of these places and times has its own quality. The locker room and dance hall feel different from the synagogue and church. The time of a lecture feels different from a time of eating or a time of praying. There are times that we call relaxing, times we name boring, times we call powerful, times we call painful. There are beautiful places and ugly places, inviting places and repulsive places, places we find stressful, places we find peaceful, places we feel disturbing, places we feel are exciting. In special spaces and times we sense the potential to change ourselves and our communities for the better. For some people a library is such a space. It is a quiet space, conducive to reflection, that contains materials that carry us beyond the more restricted space of our daily lives, beyond our local communities, beyond the boundaries of our nations, to the larger world. It is a space of possibilities.

We characterize some places and times as religious, or sacred, because they are places and times, distinct from the other places and times of our lives, in which we are more aware of our relationship to the powers of life. On the Sabbath, Jews take a day in the weekly cycle to refresh themselves and to rejoice in their relationship to God and community. It is a time taken out of ordinary time and separated from it by Sabbath conventions. Jews also take a place, the synagogue—a place within, but separated from, profane space—and set it aside for worship, study, and community activities. Characterized primarily as a gathering place, the synagogue affords opportunity to dwell on, and in, relationship to God and community. Sacred space may be a natural space that becomes sacred to a religious community because God or ancestral spirits have manifested themselves in it, or because it has been the place in which a paradigmatic figure such as the Buddha achieved insight. Sacred space may also be architecturally created space such as a Shinto shrine, a Mayan temple, or a mosque.

Some Christians give time each day to prayers and Bible reading; these are sacred times within the daily cycle. Similarly, spaces set aside for the Bible and for religious objects are sacred places within the home. They have a different feeling from the places where we put our pots and pans and clothes. Jews and Christians pray that the power of God, the grace, that is encountered in sacred times and places will come to transform all of life. Buddhism looks on such times and places as opportunities to gain insight into reality. Buddhism, its followers say, is not a religion of God but a religion of wisdom, enlightenment, and compassion. For **Taoism**, sacred times and places are windows into the natural way of all things. For indigenous traditions such as that of the Warlpiri, they are opportunities for empowering the whole of life.

The biblical Book of Qoheleth, often referred to in English as Ecclesiastes, outlines a succession of the times of our lives. *Qoheleth,* a proper noun meaning "speaker in the assembly," suggests one who conducts a school or assembly. The word *Qoheleth* has been translated into Greek as "Ecclesiastes." The writer was probably a Jewish wisdom teacher writing in the third century BCE who had been influenced by Greek thought. He writes of the shallowness or vanity of life and echoes a distaste for conventional wisdom. Qoheleth describes the seasons of our lives without finding a completely satisfying order or meaning. He even makes us wonder whether the search for order and meaning is futile. His observations could come as easily from a Gentile as from a Jew, from an atheist as from a theist. However, Qoheleth situates the perennial human problem of the shortness of life and the difficulty of knowing how to act within a Jewish religious context. Qoheleth's God may be more remote and inflexible than the God we encounter in other parts of the Hebrew Bible, but he is God nevertheless, and it is he who has given life to human beings. Qoheleth gives people the commonsense advice that "it is God's gift to man that everyone should eat and drink and take pleasure in all his toil" (3:13), yet he concludes that human wisdom is not sufficient to comprehend the work of God.

TIMES (Ecclesiastes 3:1–11)

> For everything there is a season, and a time for every matter under heaven:
>> a time to be born, and a time to die;
>> a time to plant, and a time to pluck up what is planted;
>> a time to kill and a time to heal;
>> a time to break down, and a time to build up;
>> a time to weep, and a time to laugh;

Fushimi Inari-taisha shrine, Kyoto. The torii *(gateway) leads to the shrines for the* kami *(spirits).*

> a time to mourn, and a time to dance;
> a time to throw away stones, and a time to gather
> stones together;
> a time to embrace, and a time to refrain from em-
> bracing;
> a time to seek, and a time to lose;
> a time to keep, and a time to throw away;
> a time to tear, and a time to sew;
> a time to keep silence, and a time to speak;
> a time to love, and a time to hate;
> a time for war, and a time for peace.

What gain have the workers from their toil? I have seen the business that God has given to everyone to be busy with. He has made everything suitable for its time; moreover he has put a sense of past and future into their minds, yet they cannot find out what God has done from the beginning to the end.

People live through the stages of their lives in particular ecological and social contexts. There is no "human life" in the abstract but only human lives lived out in various circumstances. There are people with their various drives and desires connected in social networks, connected to their land with its plants and its animals. There are people in relationships that may be cooperative or competitive, encouraging or exploitative. Religions posit an ultimate context, a large scheme of things, a cosmos or world. When they help us locate ourselves within that world and to make life-giving connections to all else within it, they are inspiring and freeing. Tragically, though, religions have a negative side. Religious leaders may use their authority to dominate and control their followers. Adherents may take hope in an afterlife as reason to suffer unjust working and social conditions in the present. Patriarchal traditions may interpret their dogmas to the detriment of women.

In Chapter 1, following Mircea Eliade, we used the word *hierophany*, which means "manifestation of the sacred," to denote appearances of the sacred. Sacred times, sacred places, sacred objects, and sacred persons facilitate hierophany. A hierophany is a point of contact between life that stands in need of meaning and empowerment and that (the sacred, the holy, the true, the good, the beautiful) which is able to transform it. Hierophanies occasion reverence and also fear on the part of believers. That which is potentially life giving is also potentially life destroying and needs, therefore, to be approached with caution and reverence. Hence, rituals that cultivate the manifestation of the sacred may be surrounded with taboos in order to avoid an unregulated release of power.

Some religions emphasize a separation between the sacred and the profane; others stress their mutuality and, hence, the accessibility of the sacred to human experience. However, even for traditions that stress the separation of sacred and profane, notions of transcendence and immanence are not mutually exclusive. Those who stress transcendence say that we may "climb across" (transcend) from our everyday experience to the experience of another realm. In this view ultimate power, the transcendent, is located primarily beyond our ordinary experience. Traditions emphasizing transcendence say that the Creator, or the company of the gods, or the spirit of creativity, or the power of life, lies beyond the limits of ordinary experience but may, on occasion, enter directly into our existence. We might, through a spiritual journey or mystic experience, cross to the realm of the transcendent, or the transcendent may graciously come to us.

In contrast to understandings ordered by an emphasis on transcendence, in the so-called *nature religions* the power of life is conceived of as immanent, as "remaining in place." *Immanent*, like the words *remain* and *mansion*, comes from the Greek *menein*, "to remain." In religious discourse immanence suggests that the sacred, or the power of life, is to be found in the world of ordinary existence. For example, Purusa Sukta, the primal person or divine being conceptualized in the Vedic hymn we considered in Chapter 1, is diffused throughout the universe. Or, in the Solomon Islands, to recall our discussion of relationships to fish, **mana**, a quality that empowers technical processes and relationships, is accessible and manifests itself within the realm of community life. Mana has, in fact, become a technical term in religious studies denoting supernatural power of various kinds.

PERSON, SELF, AND EXPERIENCE

We experience ourselves in space and time, in relationship to the earth, and in relationship with others. Just what is the self or the person realizing such experiences? A body, mental states, a spiritual substance? Our understandings of self and personhood are conditioned by our cultures. Ethno-psychologists, those who study the relation of psychology and culture on a comparative basis, consider self-awareness to be a human universal and the "self" to be the individual, but never fully individuated, human being. They define the person as the culturally constructed point of intersection between the subjective and the social. Some cultures permit the person to be more individually than communally defined; others see the person as part of a network of relationships. Even cultures that define the person in more social terms may permit considerable idiosyncrasy.

The English empiricist and moral and political philosopher John Locke (1632–1704) defined a person as "a thinking intelligent being that has reason and reflection, and can consider itself as itself, the same thinking thing, in different times and places; which it does only by that consciousness which is inseparable from thinking and essential to it."[3] Someone who in his early life shared Locke's understanding of the person as basically "a thinking intelligent being" was the French Protestant missionary Maurice Leenhardt (1878–1954), who early in the twentieth century worked in New Caledonia, a French colony in the South Pacific, adjacent to the Solomon Islands. Leenhardt was to find his notion of "person" challenged by the ideas of the indigenous people of New Caledonia. In *Do Kamo*,[4] a book whose title means "the true person," he presents the idea of the New Caledonians that the person has identity only in relationship to a land and to a community. Returning to France, Leenhardt taught at the Sorbonne. He influenced scholars such as Lucien Lévy-Bruhl and, as studies in

Thinking about Personhood

1. What are the advantages of thinking, as Leenhardt did in childhood and young adulthood, of the true or authentic person as someone conscious of his or her individuality and capable of making individual decisions?
2. What are the advantages of thinking, as the New Caledonians described by Leenhardt did, of the true person as a locus in a network of relationships connecting land, traditions, ancestors, and others?
3. How would you describe the true or authentic person in your community? What accommodations for a variation in values and behaviors does a multicultural situation require you to make in describing the true or authentic person?
4. How has your self-understanding been shaped by your experiences of place and community?

cross-cultural psychology advanced, *Do Kamo* became a classic in the cross-cultural discussion of personhood.

In Maurice Leenhardt's European Protestant upbringing, the person was seen as an autonomous being whose dignity lay in the ability to make free individual decisions. In New Caledonia he encountered a notion of person in which authentic identity partook also of the social and the mythic worlds. That is, the true person experienced himself or herself as connected to kin, to ancestors, to land, and to tradition. The notion of the person embedded in the landscape and the community, a notion similar to that we encountered in the Warlpiri story about the two kangaroos, so entranced Leenhardt that he spent the rest of his life thinking about it and writing about it. Leenhardt's life is truly a record of learning to appreciate ways of thinking, and ways of being religious, that were radically different from those he learned in his own upbringing.

As Leenhardt listened to the stories and analyzed the complex social structures of the Melanesians among whom he lived, he sensed that people dwelt in a mythic landscape that extended beyond his French-conditioned imagination. He perceived that they understood the self not so much as an individual entity but more as one locus of a larger pattern of life. It seemed that they allowed the mythic to exert a living influence on the present time and place. In trying to capture this understanding Leenhardt coined the term "living myth." He observed that not only did the New Caledonians have rules about marriage, and stories that set out patterns for relations between the sexes, but that the complementarity of male and female was even echoed in the spatial arrangements of New Caledonian gardens and villages. "The couple," he wrote in his analysis of the New Caledonian landscape, "is inscribed in the earth."[5]

In the New Caledonian context of the late nineteenth century, in which French mines and missionaries were still newcomers, the true person, *Do Kamo*, was intrinsically a part of a cosmos that included land, people, ancestors, animals, plants, and spirit beings. The authentic person was powerfully connected to the world of his or her culture's making. As a missionary and a French citizen, Leenhardt had qualms about what was happening to this "person" as a result of French annexation of the land and the introduction of Christianity. He saw that the dialectical relationship between the person and the person's Melanesian world was in danger of being lost to consciousness. The true person was in jeopardy of becoming an alienated person.

Religions suggest that, in one way or another, we can overcome all that inhibits our existence and attain to a fullness of life. Or, looking at it from another perspective, Buddhists might say that religion is a path by which we can attain to an emptiness of life, that is, to a state of not clinging to life. And if this fullness or emptiness is not achieved in this world, then it may be achieved in another. Religions provide their followers with central symbols with which to focus their vision of life and with ritual means and moral guidance for achieving that vision. At their best, religious understandings of life are open minded and life enhancing, encouraging and inspiriting; at their worst they are narrow minded and life destroying, discouraging and dispiriting. At both ends of the spectrum religions afford their members ways of putting individual and communal lives, and life itself, into an ultimate perspective, and of participating in whatever the tradition imagines to be the fundamental power of life.

RESOURCES

ACTIVITIES

1. Assign groups within the class to visit houses of worship of various religious traditions. Groups should give attention to arrangement of the sacred space and to ritual and instruction taking place there. Each group will report on what it learned about the worldview and values of the religious community.
2. Read the story of "Two Kangaroos" again. Describe the characters and outline the plot of the story. What does the story say about life and death? What does it say about relationship to land? What can we learn from the Warlpiri understanding of life?
3. Obtain a copy of the Haggada, the liturgical text used for the Passover service from which the extract in this chapter is taken. After reading the service, answer these questions: What is the structure of the Seder? What understanding of the human condition does the Seder narrate and enact? What can we all learn from the Jewish understanding of life?
4. Choose a story that helps you to understand your life. Is it a story that is generally recognized as religious? Do you regard it as religious? Why, or why not? How does it portray authentic life?
5. Describe an example of religious architecture. How has the space been arranged and embellished? What messages does it convey? What mood does it create? What does it suggest about the power of life?

Consult books and articles on religious architecture to obtain the vocabulary and framework for describing the building you have chosen.

6. Work with a group to prepare a multimedia presentation on religious
architecture in your community.

READINGS

Birch, Charles, William Eakin, and Jay B. McDaniel, eds. *Liberating Life:
Contemporary Approaches to Ecological Theology*. Maryknoll, NY:
Orbis Books, 1990. The contributors to this volume draw on their
religious traditions in seeking an ethic of life that will respect life
in its many forms and will encourage justice and peace in human
communities.

Cohn-Sherbok, Dan. *Judaism Today*. New York: Continuum, 2010. An introduction to Judaism that addresses sources of authority, effects of the
Jewish enlightenment, modern biblical scholarship and the rise of
science, the religious impact of the Holocaust, the status of women,
Jewish ethics, and the future of Judaism.

Frishnan, Martin, and Hasan-Uddin Khan, eds. *The Mosque: History, Architectural Development and Regional Diversity*. New York: Thames
and Hudson, 1994. A discussion of the spiritual and aesthetic
principles of Islamic architecture, along with an exploration of the
development and diversity of mosque architecture.

Lane, Belden C. *Landscapes of the Sacred: Geography and Narrative in
American Spirituality*, 2nd ed. Baltimore: Johns Hopkins University
Press, 2011. This book explores how Native American and settler
traditions have developed their spiritualities in relation to the places
they inhabit. Lane addresses the symbol-making process of religious
experience and discusses the tension between place and placelessness
in Christianity.

Maslow, Abraham. *Religions, Values, and Peak-Experiences*. Columbus: Ohio
State University Press, 1964. Maslow, the founder of humanistic
psychology, discusses the role of religion in helping the person to
become a "self-actualizing individual."

Muecke, Stephen. *Textual Spaces: Aboriginality and Culture Studies*. Sydney:
University of New South Wales Press, 1992. A study of misunder-
standings and miscommunication in relationships between Aborigi-
nes and European Australians since colonization.

Napaljarri, Peggy Rockman, and Lee Cataldi, collectors and translators.
Warlpiri Dreamings and Histories. San Francisco: HarperCollins,
1994. A collection of Warlpiri stories. The collectors explain, "The
narrative is simultaneously an account of the creation of the places
in the story, an account of the mythical but human behavior of
the ancestral figures, and a mnemonic map of the country with

its important, life-giving features for the purpose of instructing a younger listener. These elements make up Warlpiri Jukurrpa, commonly translated as the Dreaming."

Potok, Chaim. *The Chosen.* New York: Fawcett Crest, 1967. This story of two Jewish boys and their fathers in the Williamsburg section of Brooklyn during the Second World War introduces the diversity of Jewish tradition and its profound influence from generation to generation.

Telushkin, Joseph. *Jewish Literacy: The Most Important Things to Know about the Jewish Religion, Its People, and Its History.* New York: William Morrow and Company, 1991. An accessible introduction to Judaism arranged in fifteen areas.

Yezierska, Anzia. *Bread Givers.* New York: Persea Books, 1975 (original edition 1925). An autobiographical novel that brings a woman's viewpoint to the Jewish immigrant experience in New York City in the early twentieth century and raises enduring questions about the position of women in religious traditions.

AUDIO-VISUALS

Sabbath of Peace (1979). Commentator, Eli Wallach. New York: Jewish Chataqua Society. A presentation of the course of a Sabbath and a discussion of its significance in Jewish life.

Walbiri Fire Ceremony (1977). Australian Institute of Aboriginal Studies; distributed in the United States by University of California Extension Services, Berkeley. Documents the fire ceremony by which the Walbiri (Warlpiri) negotiate relationships among moieties.

Women of the Sun (1982). Hyllus Maris and Sonia Borg, produced by Bob Weis. Generation Films, distributed in the United States by University of California Extension Services, Berkeley. Four television dramas, each concerning a period in the experience of Australia's Aboriginal people after the arrival of white settlers. The chief protagonist in each drama is a woman.

YouTube has many presentations on sacred geography.

NOTES

1. Henry Cook Jakamarra, "Marlujarrakurlu: The Two Kangaroos," in *Yimikirli: Warlpiri Dreamings and Histories,* collected and translated by Peggy Rockman Napaljarri and Lee Cataldi (San Francisco: Harper Collins, 1995), 46–53.

2. Mircea Eliade, *The Sacred and the Profane,* trans. Willard R. Trask (New York: Harcourt, Brace, and World, 1959).

3. John Locke, *An Essay concerning Human Understanding*, ed. and intro. John W. Yolton (London: Dent, 1965; originally published in 1690).

4. Maurice Leenhardt, *Do Kamo: Person and Myth in the Melanesian World* (Chicago: University of Chicago Press, 1979; originally published in French in 1947).

5. Maurice Leenhardt, *Gens de la Grande Terre* (Paris: Gallimard, 1937).

Chapter 3

_____

The Study of Religion

NATURE, CULTURE, AND RELIGION

We turn now from reflection on the ways that human beings order their lives and the ways that religions assist them in doing so, to the ways that scholars study the ordering process they call religion. In talking about the ways in which we structure our lives we have used the terms *culture* and *religion*. Implied in our discussion has been a third term, *nature*. Nature and culture are complementary frames, reciprocal mental constructs, that many scholars use in their study of religion. They are concepts that help us talk about our life in the world and, therefore, they are useful to us in the study of religion.

Nature, in our usual way of speaking, is what is given. Nature includes land, water, sun, sky, trees, animals, and people in their biological being. *Culture,* on the other hand, is what human beings create. Culture includes technical processes for obtaining food and shelter, conventions for interacting with other people, and ideas about the structure of the world. Religion is part of culture. The constructs of nature and culture can be used to frame discussions about the lives of human communities and about the creative activity of human beings. However, the terms have their limitations. Much of what we call nature (rolling meadows, herds of cattle) is not given but is the result of human decision-making and activity. Moreover, human life is both natural and cultural. Nature requires that we eat; culture dictates how we prepare food and the conventions to be observed in eating it.

As we have seen in our discussion of communities in the Southwest Pacific, people can think about their life in the world without resorting to the mental constructs of nature and culture. That is, we can draw boundaries and forge linkages with other constructs, such as that of kinship. The indigenous people of New Caledonia of whom Leenhardt wrote, the Solomon Islands whose relationship to fish we considered, and the Warlpiri on whose initiation story we reflected, all construct the interrelationship of land and animals and people in terms more like kinship than like nature and culture. Then, some people construct

MARY N. MACDONALD

The Three Sisters painted on bark by Native American artist Marla Skye (c. 2011).

their world as a vast organism. Each way of thinking about the human and cosmic condition yields its particular insight but falls short of being the last word.

Even cultures with similar material resources available to them and cultures in similar ecological niches differ considerably from one another. They differ because of the varied ways that human beings use their imaginations in symbolically structuring their worlds. In fashioning human communities we live with the possibilities and constraints of our ecological contexts. We are not going to be farmers if we have no land. We may well become hunters of game if we live in a forest where there are animals. Yet, just living in a forest where there are animals does not determine that we shall be hunters. We may choose not to eat certain animals, or we may choose to be vegetarians and not to eat animals at all. Regardless of our ecological contexts we are, as Wallace Stevens reminds us, the makers of the worlds in which we live. Our exercise of imagination results in diversity in our understandings of the world and in the symbol systems we use to express our relationship to the world. We create different economic systems, different social structures, and different understandings of the human condition and the fundamental powers of life.

Culture, as anthropologist Ruth Benedict says, is a pattern for living. Anthropologists tell us that cultures provide us with ways to live and reasons for living. The social sciences understand culture to be a pattern that embraces the domains of:

1. economy (the use of the resources available to us to sustain our physical existence—from Greek *oikos*, "house," and *nomos*, "manager"),
2. social life (our conventions for relating to others, including marriage and kinship rules, processes of warfare and alliance making, strategies of cooperation), and
3. ideology (ideas about how the world is constituted and the use of symbols to reinforce those ideas and to facilitate engagement with the world).

Within this threefold schema, religion and philosophy and literature all belong in the domain of ideology. They have to do with understanding the human situation and the context in which human beings find themselves. Of course, the three domains overlap. Yet, seeing them as separate provides a tool to help us think about the ways that people create order and meaning. If a community supports its physical existence by growing corn, the chances are corn will be part of the exchange network by which social relationships are sustained and part of its symbolic system in which understandings of human life are

CULTURE—A SHARED PATTERN FOR LIVING

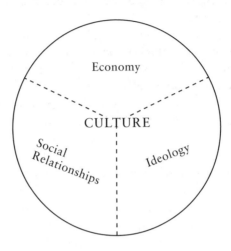

imaged and articulated. This, as we shall see, is the case for the Pueblo Peoples of the American Southwest such as the Hopi, Tewa, and Zuni.

In the understanding that is couched in terms of "nature and culture," nature is a context, a resource, and a locus of power. Human beings, as they create their cultures, including the domain of religion, develop characteristic attitudes toward nature. They may seek to subdue nature, to harness its powers to satisfy their desires—cutting forests for farmland, using swift-flowing streams to generate electric power. They may seek to work with nature, to use its products without destroying their sources—fishing and hunting in ways that do not destroy habitats or herds. People may strive with or against nature; they may respect nature, fear nature, or both respect and fear it. Whatever their attitude, they are obliged, on occasion, to accommodate themselves to nature, to live with the fact that nature will demolish the order they have created. Despite their careful efforts there will be floods and blizzards. We are not obliged to frame our understandings of the world and of ourselves with the "nature and culture" dichotomy. We may choose to see our human communities as part of nature. Or, we may choose to see our human cultures as parallel to, and in interaction with, other communities or cultures, such as those of plants and insects and animals. Today, many people like to use the image of a web of life, which is common in a number of indigenous traditions, when they work at bringing order to their experience of the world.

Each culture is a pattern for living created within a context of constraints and possibilities. It is transmitted from generation to generation, and the pattern changes over time. Changes may result from external or internal causes. The Solomon Islanders and New Caledonians, to whom we referred in Chapter 1 and Chapter 2, have changed their ways of life over the past century as the result of colonial incursions and Christian missions, both external causes. Many of their communities have forsaken subsistence agriculture, hunting, and fishing for wage labor or have come to supplement their subsistence economy with wage labor in colonial and neocolonial enterprises such as plantations and mines. Around the time that colonial officials and traders reached the Solomon Islands and New Caledonia, missionaries, the majority of whom were Pacific Islanders, also arrived. Hence, for better or worse, new religious options were added to the repertoire of indigenous myths and rituals. Today, most people in these neighboring areas of Melanesia have appropriated biblical stories and Christian practices and consider themselves Christians.[1]

While cultures develop their own characteristic ways of understanding the human condition, modern circumstances bring people from different cultural backgrounds together within the same nation and even within the same city. Hence, people may be, at one time, exposed to several worldviews, each employing its own metaphors, each proposing a model for understanding the human condition. Sometimes a person of one culture marries a person of another culture. Such multicultural situations call for respect, and they afford opportunities to stretch our imaginations as, along with our fellow human beings of various cultural backgrounds, we try to comprehend and negotiate our time and place in the world. In order to reflect on religion in multicultural contexts, openness and willingness to dialogue are essential.

Cultures propose different understandings of what it means to be human, and they educate the potential human being so that it may approach the cultural ideal of personhood. That area of culture that we refer to as religion is employed in inculcating such understandings. Religion provides guiding narratives and paradigmatic rituals to encourage the development of the person and community. Through word and ritual, religion transmits its vision of true humanity from generation to generation. The vision is, of course, challenged and modified. It is experienced by some as true and harmonious and by others as false and alienating.

When in the last decades of the twentieth century scholars began to speak of **globalization** and global culture, they were observing that, in many respects, the peoples of the world were coming to live as a single social unit. In particular, the various peoples of the world were participating in an interconnected economy, a global economy. Religions have contributed to, and been affected by, *globalization,* even before a word was coined to describe the process. In the Age of Discovery, for example, Christian missionaries and explorers together left Europe for Africa and the New World, collaborators in bringing Christianity to those who had not heard of it. At the same time, they were collaborators in acquiring the rich resources of foreign lands for the coffers of Europe. The separation of church and state, which many of us take for granted today, was not part of the worldview of Europe in the fifteenth through seventeenth centuries when explorers such as Christopher Columbus set out on their voyages in the name of God and monarch. Some religions aspire to become global or universal, to carry their message to all the peoples of the earth. These are missionary religions, and among them are Christianity, Islam, and Buddhism.

Indigenous religions tend not to be missionary in outlook, though their members may be willing to share their understanding of the world with outsiders. Very often the religion of outsiders has been thrust upon them. For instance, the Zuni of the Southwest United States have been affected by missionary incursions of the Catholic Church, the Presbyterian Church, the Christian Reformed Church, and other groups. Nevertheless, they have preserved much of their traditional vision of the world. The Zuni encapsulate their understanding of the world in rituals and storytelling and prayers. The matrilineal Zuni live in a multi-storied adobe pueblo, into which they incorporated six or seven earlier pueblo communities after conflicts with the Spanish in west central New Mexico. They tell that their ancestors emerged from underground and then journeyed to their present location. Their relationship with rain beings called "dwellers in the clouds" (*uwanammi*) and their messengers (*kachinas*) was established at that time, and priesthoods, including twelve rain priesthoods charged with responsibility for moisture of four different kinds, were instituted. Unlike traditions in which religious expertise is attributed to individual shamans, the Zuni, a long-settled agricultural people whose traditional way of life remains largely intact, have developed groups of ritual practitioners. In English we would call them societies or priesthoods. Each priesthood has responsibility for an area of ritual performance.

A **shaman** is a religious practitioner who is able to induce a trance experience in which to contact spirits; this ability depends on innate and individual qualities. A priest, one authorized by the community to carry out ritual, depends more on training in traditional practices. Religious officiants fall somewhere along a spectrum between the shamanic and the priestly. In traditional Native America, priestly religious practitioners tend to be found in communities with a primarily agricultural economy. Shamanic religious practitioners are more likely to be found in communities with a primarily hunting economy. Modern industrial societies, in which book education is highly valued, tend to have religious practitioners who, like Zuni priests, have undergone a long period of training followed by a form of investiture. However, these societies, which prize individualism, also have a number of charismatic religious practitioners who claim a personal religious empowerment like that of a shaman.

Despite the incursion of modern life, Zuni ceremonialism continues today with *kachinas* and clowns dancing in the plazas each summer as part of the process of maintaining a right relationship between the people and the *uwanammis*. Zuni ritual regulates the annual cycle of the corn; it also regulates the cycle of human life. The prayer that the Zuni say for an infant on the eighth day of its life, as it is taken outdoors for the first time and presented to the sun, suggests that corn is the stuff of life. Like many Native American peoples, the Zuni refer to corn, beans, and squash as "our three sisters." On the morning of the infant's presentation its head is washed by its father's female relatives. Corn meal, which is used in Zuni prayers and healing rituals, is placed in its hands. Then, at the moment of sunrise, the child is taken out and symbolically placed on the road of life, linked to its ancestors, and introduced to the sun who does his part to ripen the corn and other crops on which human life depends.

In the Zuni prayer for the presentation of a newborn child to the sun, good wishes are addressed to the child, and corn meal (prayer meal) is given to the sun. The prayer expresses the community's desires for the child and, moreover, like the Warlpiri initiation songs, its powerful and evocative words have a role to play in the shaping of the person. The infant has been born; it has biological life. However, the infant is not yet a cultural and religious person. For the child to become an authentic Zuni person, it must be introduced to the sun and set on the road of life. Then, as the child proceeds on life's way, there will be more prayers and rituals and stories to instruct it and shape it until the child becomes a real person. Notice that in the Zuni idiom the sun and stars are spoken of in kin terms—"our sun father," "our night fathers."

ZUNI PRAYER
FOR PRESENTATION OF AN INFANT

Now this is the day
Our child,
Into the daylight
You will go out standing.
Preparing for your day,
We have passed our days.
When all your days were at an end,
When eight days were past,
Our sun father
Went in to sit down at his sacred place.
And our night fathers
Having come out standing to their sacred place,
Passing a blessed night
We came to day.
Now this day
Our fathers,
Dawn priests,
Have come out standing to their sacred place.
Our sun father
Having come out standing to his sacred place,
Our child,
It is your day.
This day,
The flesh of the white corn,
Prayer meal,
To our sun father
This prayer meal we offer.
May your road be fulfilled
Reaching to the road of your sun father,
When your road is fulfilled
In your thoughts (may we live)
May we be the ones whom your thoughts will em-
      brace,
For this, on this day
To our sun father.
We offer prayer meal.
To this end
May you help us all to finish our roads.[2]

Thinking with Corn

Maize, known in some English-speaking countries as corn, is a starchy grain that was domesticated by the indigenous peoples of Mesoamerica to become a staple food. Between 1700 and 1250 BCE several varieties of corn spread throughout the Americas. Following European entry into the region, corn was carried to Europe, Africa, and Asia. Toward the end of the twentieth century corn was genetically modified to resist insect pests and to favor desirable traits. In 2009, 85 percent of corn produced in the United States was genetically modified.

1. What experiences have you had with corn and corn products? Have you eaten it, cooked with it, used it for decoration? Is it a regular part of your diet?
2. What sayings and images do you have that depend on the qualities of corn? What times and places does corn evoke for you?
3. What experiences do the Zuni have with corn in sustaining their natural, cultural and religious life? How do these experiences differ from your experiences with corn? What foods and/or drinks sustain your natural, cultural, and religious life?
4. What qualities of corn are evoked in the Zuni prayer given above?
5. In the United States in the early twenty-first century, corn, particularly as high-fructose corn syrup, has been accused of being detrimental to health. How would you put the good and the bad possibilities of corn in context? How do you assess the advantages and disadvantages of genetically modified corn?

STUDYING RELIGION

Religion is a term that ordinary people use when they talk about gaining access to whatever it is they consider ultimately life giving. In addition *religion* is a term that scholars use when they study people's ideas and practices concerning whatever they consider ultimately life giving. We have been discussing religion as the area of culture that orders life in an ultimate sense. Human beings link themselves to other people in social networks. They recognize a relationship to other sentient beings and to the world in which they live. These relationships may be life giving or, at times, life inhibiting. Human beings also link themselves to whatever they regard as most empowering. Christians, Jews, and Muslims appeal to God. Melanesians nurture relationships with their ancestors and their land spirits. Buddhists seek **nirvana**, release from all the attributes of sensory existence. Taoists attune themselves to nature. When scholars study all these quests for life in its fullness, they do so under the rubric of religion. They may be assisted in their study by insights from history, anthropology, and other disciplines but religious studies is also seen as a discipline in its own right.

The modern study of religion grew out of the **Enlightenment**, a philosophic movement that questioned traditional authority and emphasized the use of reason. In eighteenth-century Europe the Enlightenment motivated people to think for themselves. A consequence was that many abandoned the teachings of their churches and synagogues, saying that they wanted to reason things out for themselves and not to accept blindly what was passed on from generation to generation by priests and rabbis. For Enlightenment thinkers the scientific method, not tradition, was the way to true knowledge. Even those who remained within their faith traditions were affected by the spirit of the Enlightenment, some trying to understand religious teachings in humanistic ways, others becoming defensive about religious teachings that seemed to be opposed to reason.

The Enlightenment encouraged scholars to be more critical in their study of religion, to make use of tools from the study of languages and literature, and to employ scientific and historical methods. For example, biblical scholars came to rely more on archeology and philology in establishing contexts for the religious texts they sought to explicate. The Enlightenment began a movement that has taken the study of religion beyond the confines of religious institutions to the larger academy. Today people study religion not only because they might themselves be religious and therefore want to know more about something that is important to them, but also because religion is a part of the experience of humankind and, as such, is worth studying. The modern critical study of religion looks not only to the positive contributions that religion has made, but also to the suffering it has caused and the destruction it has wrought.

Contemporary religious scholarship makes a distinction between natural religion and revealed religion. This distinction appears in the work of Immanuel Kant (1724–1804), one of the pioneers in the modern study of religion. Kant understood natural religion as a sensibility or faculty common to all people, an aspect of the human spirit, whereas he understood revealed religion as a set of beliefs and practices passed on within a community that claims to have received them from God. Obviously, claims that a religion is revealed, meaning divinely given, are made by people inside a tradition. They accept the content of the revelation in a commitment of faith; then they devote themselves to explicating it. For example, Christians who accept that Jesus is Lord and Savior will say that they do so on faith. However, in explicating what it means to say that Jesus is Lord and Savior, they might use psychological analysis to tell us why human beings are in need of salvation, and historical and literary analysis to situate Jesus and his message in a particular time and place. They might present archaeological evidence indentifying sites connected with Jesus' ministry. Scholars not belonging to the religious tradition they are studying may be more concerned with looking at how the religion functions than in explicating its basic tenets. They ask: Does a particular religious belief or practice, or a religious tradition as a whole, help people to lead happy and generous lives? Does it stifle their creativity and result in guilt complexes? Whether insiders or outsiders, scholars are concerned both to obtain accurate descriptions of the insiders' experiences of religion and to assess the ways that religion functions in the lives of individuals and communities.

Tu Wei-ming, a professor of Chinese history and philosophy at Harvard University, teaches and writes about Confucianism and contributes to discussions of the role that religion plays, and might play, in the modern world. Tu was born in mainland China, studied in Taiwan, and has taught for many years in the United States. He says that when he first studied Confucianism, an ethical system based on the teachings of **Confucius** (551–479 BCE), he approached it as a historian. Next he adopted a philosophic stance, analyzing the ideas and the concepts in the teachings of Confucius and his followers. More recently, he says, he has examined it as religionist, seeing it as a religious system that holds out the possibility of perfecting human nature through self-effort. Tu told interviewer Bill Moyers that he had come to look on Confucianism as "a process of learning to be human," and that what Confucianists call the mandate of heaven he took to be "one's ability to go beyond anthropocentrism."[3] That is, he understands the Confucian "mandate of heaven" as the ability to go beyond human self-interest. Taking this Confucian concept as a starting point, he can then bring Confucianism into dialogue with other religious traditions and see what they say about going beyond human self-interest. Tu Wei-ming's work is important as a bridge

MARY N. MACDONALD

Maya Temple, Pacbitun, Belize. This major ceremonial site was first occupied around 1000 BCE. Archeology is expanding our knowledge of many ancient religions, including that of the Maya.

between Eastern and Western approaches to the study of religion, and also as a bridge between practitioners of religion and scholars of religion. He is a prominent representative of the New Confucian movement, which seeks to extend Confucian insights beyond their original Asian contexts.

Since the Enlightenment the study of religion has taken three major directions. The first, an outcome of the Enlightenment's stress on reason, suggests that religion is part of the world of ideas, a matter of thinking, concerned with truth and wisdom. The second, which is a development from the first, proposes that religion is part of the moral order, a matter of discrimination and behavior, concerned with goodness. The third, which places the other two in a wider context, says that religion is part of aesthetics, a matter of a feeling for relationships and patterns, concerned with order and beauty. The three perspectives, corresponding to the classical triad of the good, the true, and the beautiful, are interconnected. It might seem that by framing our discussion in this book in terms of the human propensity to order our individual and communal lives, we have adopted a primarily aesthetic perspective. However, in the following chapters we shall also be examining the efforts of religious people to find truth and live good lives.

DEFINING RELIGION

In thinking in a systematic way about an area of experience, such as religion, we can be helped by definitions. Definitions set boundaries on what it is we are studying, and the attempt to define obliges us to clarify our ideas. Definitions tell us a lot about the interests and orientations of the people who make them. Definitions, however, are not value free. For example, the French writer, philosopher, and social activist Jean Paul Sartre (1905–80), characterizes religion as an attempt to escape responsibility. His definition is part of a pattern of ideas about human freedom and responsibility that leads him to a negative evaluation of religion. On the other hand, the Christian theologian and philosopher Rudolf Otto (1869–1937) defines religion as "the experience of the Holy." As a young student of **theology** Otto had studied the life of the Protestant reformer Martin Luther (1483–1546) and become intrigued with the human response to what he called the *mysterium tremendum et fascinans*, the "awe-inspiring and attracting (appealing/enchanting) mystery." Luther, of course, saw himself standing before an awe-inspiring and fascinating mystery that he called God. Otto speculated that in other than Christian traditions there were comparable objects. In his writings he referred to them as "the numinous," the "wholly other," the "transcendent," or, his preferred term, "the Holy."

In studying religion as a general field, and in studying the religions of Oceania in particular, we have used the following working definitions:

1. Religion is awareness expressed through symbols of relationship to, or participation in, the fundamental power of life.
2. Religions are symbol systems that facilitate relationship to, or participation in, what the members understand to be the fundamental power of life.

The first definition presents religion as a disposition, a way of apprehending the powerful and life-giving mystery of the world and engaging with it. The second definition recognizes that religions, as human constructions, are usually developed by communities and so become systems that communities share but that may admit of variation in individual or group usage. These definitions allow that practitioners of religion may believe in God or spirits or the influence of ancestors but does not require that they do so. Using these definitions one could study Taoism and Confucianism as religions because both are systems of symbols that encourage and facilitate participation in the fundamental power of life, even though they do not posit the existence of a god. If one's interests were more theological, or more psychological, or more philosophical, a different definition could be crafted.

Defining is an analytic Enlightenment way of going about the study of religion. A definition circumscribes an area of experience and thus sets it out for further investigation. The *HarperCollins Dictionary of Religion* proposes that religion be understood as "a system of beliefs and practices relative to superhuman beings."[4] The believer has faith in the superhuman beings of the definition. The nonbeliever may not ascribe objective reality to the superhuman beings but recognizes their significance to the members of a religious community. The focus on superhuman beings excludes Nazism, Marxism, and secularism as religions, whereas someone could conceivably make a case for including them under our working definition. Taken at face value, this dictionary definition also excludes the religion of Taoists and Confucianists and many Buddhists, who look on their faiths more as ways of wisdom than as ways of devotion to a superhuman being.

Definitions of religion tend to take one of two directions. Some, including ours and that of the dictionary quoted above, focus on religion as a system of symbols, or a system of beliefs and practices, embedded in human experience. Others focus on religion as experience of the transcendent. For theologians such as Karl Rahner and Paul Tillich working within a religious tradition, and for scholars such as Mircea Eliade, experience of the transcendent is recognized as part of the human condition. It is accepted as a structure of reality. There are, however, scholars of religion who would neither affirm nor deny the reality of the transcendent. While they regard formulations such as God, sacred, holy, mana, and transcendence as important encapsulations of human experience, these scholars say they cannot think of any way in which claims of transcendence can be proved or disproved. Hence, they may "bracket" their own belief or disbelief and proceed to study how religion functions in human communities. Or, like Tu Wei-ming, they may seek to discover in ancient formulations some wisdom for going beyond anthropomorphism to a larger view of life in the world. Both the scholars who doubt that transcendence is anything more than a human way of speaking of the mystery of life and scholars who wholeheartedly profess faith in a transcendent reality recognize the importance of the transcendent to faith. All of them report on the ways it is conceptualized and made part of religious practice.

Thinking by Defining

Analyze the definitions that follow and if possible discuss them with another person. After reading each definition, consider: Does the definition accord with the way you have been accustomed to think about religion? Why, or why not? Would you be able to use it as a framework for describing the religious experience of people you know? Why, or why not?

1. Religion is a "feeling of absolute dependence." Religion is "the consciousness that the whole of our spontaneous activity comes from a source outside of us." (Friedrich Schleiermacher, 1768–1834, theologian)
2. Religion is "an institution of culturally patterned interaction with culturally postulated superhuman beings." (Melford Spiro, 1920– , anthropologist)
3. "Religion is the aspect of depth in the totality of the human spirit" and "Religion is an expression of ultimate concern." (Paul Tillich, 1886–1965, theologian and philosopher)
4. Religion is "the recognition of all duties as divine commands." (Immanuel Kant, 1724–1804, philosopher)
5. Religion is "a set of symbolic forms and acts that relate man to the ultimate conditions of his existence." (Robert Bellah, 1927– , sociologist)

We saw that the European philosophical movement known as the Enlightenment stressed reason. On the one hand, it prompted those who valued religion to show the reasonableness of their faith and to use scholarly tools in studying their religion. On the other hand, the Enlightenment prompted scholars to study religions as social phenomena without respect for the reasonableness of their particular truth claims. In the wake of the Enlightenment the modern social sciences, such as anthropology, sociology, and psychology, developed. Social scientists, such as sociologist Emile Durkheim, psychologist William James, and anthropologist E. E. Evans-Pritchard, have given attention to the ways that religion operates both functionally and dysfunctionally in individual lives and in communities. The social sciences have, for example, considered the role of religion in politics, in economics, and in class and gender construction. Archeology has made a large contribution to our study of prehistoric cultures and led most scholars to the conclusion that all known societies have had some forms of religious expression.

SCIENCE AND RELIGION

In the latter part of the twentieth century an interdisciplinary field of study arose that is referred to as science and religion. This field grapples with the relationship between modern science, which is concerned with empirically derived truth, and religious traditions, which have passed on their understanding of the world and human life over numerous generations in symbolic forms such as myth and rituals. Of course, the religion and science debate is not entirely new. The Christian theologians Tertullian (160–220 CE) and Augustine of Hippo (354–430 CE) asked themselves what believers in God and in the redemptive work of Jesus Christ were to make of the natural philosophy of the Greeks. Tertullian asked, rhetorically, "What has Athens to do with Jerusalem?" suggesting that Christian theology had precedence over Greek thought, while Augustine saw Greek science and philosophy as welcome "handmaids to theology." Some scholars see science and religion as quite separate fields that, at best, can be in dialogue with each other, while others contend that religion and science are integrally connected.

Let us consider the perspectives of two paleontologists (scientists who study early life forms), Pierre Teilhard de Chardin (1881–1955) and Stephen Jay Gould (1941–2002), to see two of the many positions that may be taken on the relationship of science and religion. Both scholars, one a Catholic and the other an agnostic whose heritage was Jewish, were committed to the theory of evolution. Teilhard de Chardin, who came from the Auvergne region of France, was both a Jesuit priest and a distinguished scientist; he never saw a contradiction between his two callings. He refused to separate matter and spirit, seeing them as interrelated aspects of the emergent reality of the universe. On the one hand, he rejected mechanistic Cartesian forms of science that separated matter and spirit, and on the other hand, he rejected religious worldviews that, similarly, separated the realms of the transcendent and the material. He saw the cosmos, which he experienced as a "divine milieu," as being in a continual state of evolution. For him, God was to be found in the ongoing process of the world. Science and religion were necessary parts of an integrated whole. Several of his biographers have described him as a mystic, meaning one who has had a personal experience of the divine.

Gould, an American raised in New York City, spent most of his career at Harvard University. In addition to significant contributions to evolutionary studies, he was a great popularizer of science. Gould maintained that science and religion deal with fundamentally separate aspects of human experience and that when each stays within its own domain, they can co-exist peacefully. He articulated a position that he called "non-overlapping magisteria" (NOMA). He believed that science and religion were separate discourses about the world and could learn from each other but could not be merged. In Chapter 9, as we think about communal religious change, we shall have more to say about the challenges that advances in science pose for religious worldviews. Gould was an opponent of attempts to have creation science taught in American schools and testified in court against it. Creation scientists attempt to use science to show that the creation narratives in the book of Genesis are literally accurate, something Gould regarded as impossible.

SYMBOLIC FORMS

Some scholars, including Ernst Cassirer (1874–1945) of the University of Marburg, have thought that the Enlightenment project carried out by people like Kant was incomplete because it stressed reason but neglected the consciousness of symbolic forms. Cassirer, whose three-volume work *The Philosophy of Symbolic Forms* has influenced contemporary religious studies, believed that there was more to thinking than the exercise of formal logic. He saw his reflections on symbolic awareness as extending the work of Kant. Cassirer gives place to both mythical consciousness, which emphasizes participation in life, and scientific consciousness, which analyzes parts of life. An awareness of and openness to symbolic language is, in his view, basic to any philosophy. Most people working in religious studies would say that it is basic to the study of religion.

Human beings communicate with symbols, that is, with words, gestures, and objects that evoke feelings or stand for other things. Symbols carry meanings and emotions. They help human beings to interpret their experience. We saw that in Zuni experience corn has come to represent the very stuff of life, to the extent that special corn meal, known as prayer meal, is used in most rituals. Similarly, in the experience of Christians bread and wine have come to symbolize the fullness of life and self-giving. French philosopher Paul Ricoeur (1913–2005) contends that symbols are multivalent; that is, they carry multiple meanings that will be revealed according to the way we approach them and according to our own life experience. It is not only, Ricoeur would say, that we interpret symbols but that the symbols provided by our religious and cultural traditions help us to interpret ourselves.[5]

The twenty-third psalm from the biblical Book of Psalms presents us with reciprocal images of shepherd and lamb in order to have us reflect on the relationship of God and his people. Many Jews and Christians have learned this psalm by heart as children. Even those who have grown up in surroundings where sheep are rare and those who have grown up in places, like Australia and New Zealand, where flocks of sheep are so huge that the relationship of sheep and shepherd is very different from that of the psalmist's Israel, have been schooled in the significance of the hymn's central image. In reading the psalm, note its evocative quality and the concreteness of its language.

PSALM 23

> The Lord is my shepherd, I shall not want;
> He makes me lie down in green pastures;
> he leads me beside still waters;
> he restores my soul.
> He leads me in paths of righteousness for his name's
>   sake.
> Even though I walk through the darkest valley,
> I fear no evil;
> for you are with me;
> your rod and your staff—
> they comfort me.
>
> You prepare a table before me
> in the presence of my enemies;
> you anoint my head with oil;
> my cup overflows.
> Surely goodness and mercy shall follow me
> all the days of my life,
> and I shall dwell in the house of the Lord
> my whole life long.

Would we be able to express the sentiments of the psalm in more straightforward, less symbolic language? "God cares for me" does not say as much as "The Lord is my shepherd." Children can uncover some facets of the psalm's imagery; adults are able to plumb further depths. As children, the psalm may help us to trust and to see the world as basically a benevolent place in the hands of God. As teenagers who have suffered losses, we may uncover other aspects of the shepherd's care for the sheep and may become attentive to our need

Teenager Bette Tuso, an Aymara Indian of Peru, cares for a new lamb in her Andean village.

for healing. As adults, the image of the valley of death may move us to reflect on our own mortality and our experiences of alienation. As we accept responsibility for caring for others—as parents, teachers, community leaders—we may come to identify with the shepherd. In other words, the meaning of religious symbols is not limited to one-to-one correspondences. Symbols are evocative, drawing on our life experiences and the shared history of the communities that employ them.

A distinction may be made between representational symbols and presentational symbols. Some would call this a distinction between signs and true symbols. Representational symbols or signs point to or stand for something else but do not necessarily participate in the realities for which they stand. Presentational symbols are necessarily connected to that which they symbolize. A green light is a representational symbol. It means "go" because we have arbitrarily agreed that it means "go." We could just as easily have agreed that a red light means "go." Religious symbols are more likely to be presentational. For example, in Christian iconography the church is presented as a ship, a barque. A ship is a temporary home, transporting its passengers over calm and stormy seas to their destination. In the context of early Christianity the church, a community set upon by a dangerous world yet secure in its faith, could seem like a ship tossed by the seas. Thus, the early Christians came to see the ship as a symbol of the church because it had qualities analogous to those of the church.

A presentational symbol is something that suggests something else by virtue of analogous qualities. It "presents" the other through its own qualities. The analogous qualities may be colors or shapes or patterns of behavior. In the association of the shepherd with God in Psalm 23 a comparison is made between the way a shepherd cares for and protects the flock and the way God cares for and protects his people. Think of symbols with which you represent your relationships with friends and family. What does each of the symbols suggest? Is there anyone you would call a shepherd—or a bus driver or doctor or coach—not because that is the person's actual occupation but because of qualities or attributes that suggest such an occupation?

The meaning of symbols is determined by the contexts in which they are located. In Chapter 1 we considered, for example, the way that water was employed in Christian baptism and in the Hindu Holi celebration. Rituals and religious narratives are replete with symbols. The ritual sharing of food in the Eucharist and the poetic image of the shepherd and the sheep point to the fundamental power of life, to the sacred. They draw us beyond our everyday lives into the power and mystery of life. To put it another way, symbols suggest an ultimate order and meaning that we are encouraged to create in the world. Moreover, since symbols are usually shared by groups, they serve as rallying points, vehicles to articulate and reinforce group loyalties.

Thinking with Symbols

Symbols may awaken our consciousness to new ways of thinking about ourselves and our world. Take any religious symbol with which you are familiar, or on which you would like to do some research, as a basis for reflection. It may be a statue of the seated Buddha, which suggests peace and enlightenment. It may be a wampum belt, used by the Haudenosaunee to send messages and to seal commitments. It may be an image from a prayer or poem, a character from a hero myth, or a ritual action.

1. What do you know about the symbol's religious context?
2. What does the symbol suggest to you? How does it appeal to your senses (sight, touch, taste, smell, hearing)?
3. How does your interpretation of the symbol coincide with, and differ from, that of the tradition to which it belongs?
4. How does the symbol interpret you? How does it help you think about your own life, your relationships to other people, the world about you, the mystery of life?

In this section of our conversations about religion we have explored religion as an area of human experience. We have suggested that religion is a symbolic process that enables us to make connections to the world beyond ourselves, to think about, and get in touch with the fundamental power of life, to bring order and meaning to the time and space in which we live. We have seen that people who study religion may or may not be religiously inclined themselves. Those who are religious and who study religion want to understand the nature and practice of religion. Those who are not religious are, nevertheless, often fascinated with the role that religion has played, and continues to play in the world. In succeeding sections we shall explore the ways that people act religiously and the ways that people talk about their religious experience. We shall see how religions assist and also inhibit the quest for authenticity. And, we shall see the resilience of religious traditions in recreating themselves from age to age. The study of religion on which we have embarked is very much a study, as Wallace Stevens might say, of the "idea of order" in the experience of human communities.

RESOURCES

ACTIVITIES

1. Arrange a debate within the class to defend and oppose the following statement: We live in a multicultural and multi-religious world. It is, therefore, impossible to hold particular religious commitments without slighting the commitments of others.

2. Construct a working definition of religion. Write a page commenting on each significant phrase in your definition. Modify your definition as you reach the end of each chapter in this book. As you modify a part of the definition, write a note indicating why you made the change. Think about the definition as a practical tool that will help you by circumscribing the area of human life that you are exploring.

3. In the Public Television series *Cosmos* (1980) the eminent popularizer of science Carl Sagan (1934–96), makes a case for the scientific method as the way to plumb the mysteries of the universe. In his last book, *The Demon-Haunted World*, Sagan reiterates that good science is our only hope in understanding the world.[6] Sagan does not deny that religions may have some insight into the human condition, but he clearly regards science and religion as opposed worlds. Consult works by Sagan in order to understand his point of view and then write a page summarizing his perspective titled "Sagan's Point of View." Think about how a religious person, such as Pierre Teilhard de Chardin, who also takes science seriously, might respond to Sagan's point of view and then write a paragraph entitled "Response to Sagan."

4. Rewrite Psalm 23, or another psalm, in everyday language. (If you choose a long psalm, rewrite only part of it.) Which version do you prefer? Why? Post your rewriting of the psalm to your class computerized bulletin if you have one. If not, make copies to distribute in class.

5. Identify the specializations of the members of your religious studies department or its equivalent. How does each of these scholars go about the study of religion? You may work in groups and interview the scholars to find out how each understands his or her contribution to the study of religion.

6. Imagine that you are a non-Christian scholar who has been sent to report on a celebration of the Lord's Supper at a local church. Write a report saying (a) what you observed, and (b) how you interpreted it. You will need to attend a celebration of the Lord's Supper in order to carry out this activity. If it happens that you are a Christian, you will need to set your own presuppositions aside in recording your observations.

READINGS

Braude, Ann. *Sisters and Saints: Women and American Religion*. New York: Oxford University Press, 2007. An examination of the role of women in American religious history and their struggles for equality. Attention is given to, among others, Margaret Winthrop, Jarena Lee, Mary Baker Eddy, Henrietta Szold, and Aimee Semple McPherson.

Deloria, Vine, Jr. *For This Land: Writings on Religion in America*. Edited and with an introduction by James Treat. New York: Routledge, 1999. Reflections on indigenous religion and its encounters with Christianity by a renowned Native American leader.

Elder, John, and Steve C. Rockefeller. *Spirit and Nature: Why the Environment Is a Religious Issue*. Boston: Beacon Press, 1992. A discussion of ecological issues and religious responses to them.

Ginsburg, Carlo. *Clues, Myths, and the Historical Method*. Baltimore: The Johns Hopkins University Press, 1989. Historian Ginsburg reflects on how we construct knowledge and what we might do to retrieve a "history" that is fuller and richer than that our current methodologies make available to us.

Hick, John. *An Interpretation of Religion*. New Haven, CT: Yale University Press, 1992. A philosophical approach to the study of religion that suggests that religions may be looked upon as culturally conditioned responses to the mystery of Being.

Olupona, Jacob, ed. *African Traditional Religions in Contemporary Societies*. New York: Paragon House, 1991. A collection of papers by African scholars discussing indigenous sacred ways in modern contexts.

Orsi, Robert A. *The Madonna of 115th Street: Faith and Community in Italian Harlem 1880–1950*. New Haven, CT: Yale University Press, 1985. A narration of the religious experience of an Italian immigrant community in New York City.

Pope-Levison, Priscilla, and John R. Levison. *Jesus in Global Contexts*. Louisville, KY: Westminster/John Knox Press, 1992. An exploration of the symbol of Jesus in a variety of cultures, with particular attention to materially disadvantaged peoples and the perspectives of women.

Rosenberg, Charles E. *No Other Gods: On Science and American Social Thought*. Revised edition. Baltimore and London: Johns Hopkins University Press, 1997. Rosenberg, a social historian of medicine, examines the ways in which our conception of knowledge and our search for knowledge are conditioned by the culture of which they are part.

Tu Wei-ming, ed. *Confucian Traditions in East Asian Modernity: Moral Education and Economic Culture in Japan and the Four Mini-*

Dragons. Cambridge, MA: Harvard University Press, 1996. Seventeen scholars reflect on the Confucian influence in East Asia, addressing such matters as self-cultivation, family relations, social civility, moral education, the well-being of the people, governance of the state, and universal peace.

AUDIO-VISUALS

Did Darwin Kill God? (2009). BBC. Philosopher and theologian Conor Cunningham and a range of experts trace the history of the evolution/religion debate. Cunningham argues that evolution and religion are not mutually exclusive.

Hopi: Songs of the Fourth World (1985). Produced and directed by Pat Ferrero. Wayne, NJ: New Day Films. This documentary presents the traditional worldview and way of life of the Hopi. It shows how their religion and art are integrated with experiences of a particular landscape and community. Their relationship to corn, their staple crop and a central religious symbol, is highlighted. Through interviews with a number of Hopi people the documentary describes Hopi experiences with the Anglo world and the changes that these have brought to the community.

Religion and Ethics News Weekly. A weekly PBS program available on the pbs.org website. It may be searched by date, by faith, and by topic.

Searching for God in America (1996). Hosted by Hugh Hewitt. PBS. Consists of eight thirty-minute programs in which Hewitt interviews religious leaders about their commitments and about the spiritual quests of contemporary Americans. Those interviewed are Rev. Charles Colson (Evangelical), Rabbi Harold Kushner (Jewish), Rev. Cecil Murray (African Methodist Episcopal), Father Thomas Keating (Catholic), Rev. Roberta Hestenes (Presbyterian), Dr. Seyyed Hossein Nasr (Muslim), Elder Neal A. Maxwell (Mormon), and His Holiness the XIV Dalai Lama (Buddhist).

Sir Edward Evans-Pritchard: Strange Beliefs (1985). Available from Films for the Humanities and Sciences, 132 West 31st Street, 17th Floor, New York, NY 10001. This fifty-two-minute film examines the career of the first trained anthropologist to work in Africa. Evans-Pritchard's reports on the religious beliefs and practice of the Azande and the Nuer challenged religious-studies scholars to take seriously the religious worlds and sentiments of "primitive" peoples.

Tu Wei-ming: A Confucian Life in America (1990). Available from Films for the Humanities and Sciences, 132 West 31st Street, 17th Floor, New York, NY 10001. This thirty-minute film introduces modern Confucian scholar Tu Wei-ming, a professor at Harvard University, who explores Confucian teaching from the points of view of both secular humanism and religion.

NOTES

1. For a history of Christianity in Oceania, see Charles Forman, *The Island Churches of the South Pacific* (Maryknoll, NY: Orbis Books, 1982); John Garrett, *To Live among the Stars: Christian Origins in Oceania* (Suva: University of the South Pacific Press, 1982).

2. Ruth Bunzel, *Zuñi Ritual Poetry*, Smithsonian Institution, Forty-seventh Annual Report of the Bureau of American Ethnology, 1929–1930 (Washington, DC: US Government Printing Office, 1932), 635.

3. Bill Moyers, *A World of Ideas II* (New York: Doubleday, 1990), 110.

4. Jonathan Z. Smith, ed., *HarperCollins Dictionary of Religion* (San Francisco: HarperCollins, 1995).

5. See, for example, Paul Ricoeur, *Interpretation Theory* (Fort Worth: Texas University Press, 1974).

6. Carl Sagan, *The Demon-Haunted World: Science as a Candle in the Dark* (New York: Random House, 1996).

PART II

RELIGIOUS ACTION

Leaving the familiar surroundings of our hometowns, families, and friends to face the unknown worlds of college or work can intimidate, confuse, and even scare us. To help calm our fears we fill our rooms and apartments with treasures from home: pictures of friends and family, an iPod loaded with our favorite music, a comfortable blanket and pillow. Through sight, sound, and touch these treasures symbolize what we find meaningful in our lives and help us to order our new environments. Yet we cannot stop there. To make the transition to college or work life we seek to make new friends, to familiarize ourselves with the campus or workplace, and to discern the expectations of our new institutions. Fortunately, returning students or co-workers are there to orient and to guide us. Eventually we develop a routine that helps us to order our new worlds: we fix our rooms and apartments to make them comfortable and to express our personalities, we set our schedules to accommodate our work patterns, and we develop relationships (personal and virtual) and engage in activities that reflect our values and interests.

As the previous chapters make clear, the search for order and meaning is not a passive enterprise. Finding meaning and purpose in a world often filled with ambiguity, suffering, and confusion requires some action on the part of us all, as individuals and as members of communities. The next two chapters discuss two types of action: ritual and ethical. Ritual and ethics are symbolic and practical actions that help us make sense of our lives, to give life order and direction, to relate us to one another, in harmony with the worldviews we affirm.

Chapter 4 explores the nature of religious ritual as a form of symbolic action that provides meaning and order for religious people. The chapter begins with a review of the nature of ritual action, the distinctiveness of religious ritual, its symbolic/expressive dimensions, and its personal and social functions. We follow this with a discussion of three types of religious rituals: life-cycle rituals, life-crises rituals, and periodic rituals. Life-cycle rituals refer to those rituals that are chronological, occurring over the lifetime of an individual. These rituals celebrate and commemorate key transitions in the life of an individual and reflect a certain structure that we analyze in the context of various religious rituals associated with birth, adulthood, marriage, religious vocation, and death. Life-crises rituals enable individuals and communities to cope with natural and human calamities, including illness, accident, and death. Periodic rituals are rituals that celebrate seasons in the year or commemorate specific historical events. These rituals provide an opportunity for reflection, to take stock, and to re-direct individual and communal life. We discuss the rituals associated with **Kwanzaa** to illustrate these functions.

The focus of Chapter 5 is on the nature of ethical action—a form of practical action that religious traditions prescribe as in keeping with their perception of the ultimate orderings of life. The chapter begins with a general discussion of ethics followed by consideration of the relationship between religion and morality. We contend that religion and morality are intricately connected; one cannot be religious without being moral. The focus then turns to the ways in which religion pro-vides ethical action with its source, sanction, and goal. In particular, we look at how religion provides norms for both moral conduct and moral character. Under the rubric of norms for moral conduct, we explore two types of moral obligations religions provide: laws and ends. The section on norms for moral character includes discussions of the development of moral **conscience**/consciousness, moral affec-tions and virtues, and illustrations of how these are embodied in moral exemplars. This is followed by a discussion of how religions not only provide norms for individuals but also for societies. We conclude the chapter, and the section, with a detailed discussion of the interrelation-ship between ritual and ethical action.

Chapter 4

Ritual Action

Rituals are symbolic, routine, and repetitive activities and actions through which we make connections with what we consider to be the most valuable dimensions of life. They are often associated with significant events or places in our individual and communal lives. Rituals set aside specific times and places and provide us opportunity to ponder their meaning and to connect emotionally. The birthday candles, the cake, the giving of gifts—all celebrate the value of a person's life and make room for reflection upon what that life has meant over the past year and the year ahead. The bedtime rituals between parents and children—sharing a favorite story, giving a kiss and a hug, saying a prayer—solidify the parent-child bond and affirm the importance of family.

Ritual actions enable us to maintain continuity with significant persons and events from the past. The ceremonial first pitch in baseball's fall classic, the World Series, is often thrown by a member of the baseball Hall of Fame, a person remembered for his contributions to the sport. The Baseball Hall of Fame itself, in Cooperstown, New York, is the place that enshrines the great ones of baseball, such as Babe Ruth and Hank Aaron, and enables fans to celebrate and to pay homage to their accomplishments. Traditional African families build shrines on the burial sites of those considered to be ancestors, deceased prominent members of the family or community, to honor their spirits and to seek their favor in the ongoing life of the community.

Rituals also commemorate significant events in the life of our communities and provide a means for renewing the meaning of those events among us. For example, the Fourth of July holiday and rituals celebrate the beginnings of the United States of America. Community picnics and fireworks pay tribute to the sacrifices made by the revolutionaries; the prolific display of flags celebrates the emergence and the unity of the nation; and the playing and singing of patriotic songs declare anew the values of freedom and equality. In the Passover ritual Jews celebrate the freedom of their Hebrew ancestors from Egyptian oppression and their development as a people. During the Passover Seder, participants sing songs and the leader asks specific questions about the ritual foods and the Exodus event that prompt reflection on the meaning of being chosen as God's covenant partners.

Rituals can be exciting and dramatic, engaging all of our senses. Many people travel to New Orleans or to Rio de Janeiro to participate in the *Mardi Gras* (Fat Tuesday) and *Carnival* (farewell to the flesh) celebrations that mark the days before the beginning of the Lenten season on Ash Wednesday for Christians. The sights of the decorated parade floats and ornate costumes, the smells of gumbo and smoky grilled meats, the sounds of jazz bands and samba music, serve to heighten the experience of revelers prior to the sacrifice expected during Lent. In the Yoruba festival of Odun Egungun, the sounds of the rhythmic drums, the sights of the colorful masks, the smells of the sacrificial food, and the whirling motions of the dancers, remind the community of the presence and power of the ancestors.

Rituals help us individually and communally to make sense of life's transitions; they provide some structure to move from the familiar to the unknown. Becoming an adult is a significant event in our lives. We move from the familiarity of dependence and protection of childhood to assume the mantle of responsibility in the adult world. To aid in that transition, among the Yupik, an indigenous people of Alaska, fathers instruct their sons on the skills needed to kill their first seal. The ability to hunt seals is an essential attribute of a man and an important component of the community's survival. At the ceremony following the kill, the boy shares his kill with the entire community. This symbolizes that the boy has also developed the generosity to provide for others.

Moreover, although rituals have formalized patterns, they are still subject to change. Ritual actions often adjust to changes in values or worldviews. For example, wedding vows once included the promise to obey for women. This reflected a patriarchal structure of the family, in which the husband was the head of the household and the wife played a subordinate role. Because of changing gender roles and the affirmation of equality between the partners in the marriage covenant, most wedding ceremonies today have dropped this vow. Some have gone a step further to emphasize the equality of the partners by having the parents accompany both the bride and the groom.

Like all symbolic action, our rituals can have different meanings depending upon the context or our experiences. The rituals associated with Christmas bring many Christian families together, providing opportunities for gathering with relatives and friends and for reaffirming the faith tradition they share. For Jews, however, Christmas rituals can be a source of frustration and alienation, partly because of the religious prejudice some Christians still harbor against Jews, and partly because of the pressure to embellish what were once quite simple Hanukkah rituals. Moreover, to some extent Jews have to participate in Christmas rituals even against their inclinations because they have become so much a part of our culture. Similarly, Italian Americans celebrate Columbus Day, stressing the significance of the Italian-born explorer's discovery of the New World. The celebration of Columbus's birthday, on the other hand, reminds some Native Americans of their oppression and exploitation by Europeans, whose lust for resources and power resulted in the near destruction of indigenous traditions and civilizations, a catastrophe to be mourned rather than celebrated.

RELIGIOUS RITUAL

Religious rituals share many of the features of ritual described above; some of the examples used are drawn from religious contexts. Some people who study religious ritual, however, want to distinguish it from other rituals. They see ritual as a critical component of religion and thus note the distinctiveness of religious ritual. Various definitions of religious ritual are available. Consider the following examples:

> Rites are the rules of conduct which prescribe how a man should comport himself in the presence of . . . sacred objects.
> —EMILE DURKHEIM

> A religious ritual can be defined as an agreed-on and formalized pattern of ceremonial movements and verbal expressions carried out in a sacred context.
> —JAMES C. LIVINGSTON

Although different, each definition suggests that there is a regularity or pattern to religious rituals (rules, formalized patterns) and that rituals are social in origin (prescribe, agreed upon). Of course, all ritual activity can be described in this manner. What makes religious ritual distinct is its intention. Religious rituals connect our individual and communal efforts to order life and create a relationship with what we perceive as ultimate or sacred orderings (sacred objects, sacred context).

When many of us define religion, we generally include beliefs and rules for living that provide some sense of meaning and direction for our lives. Missing in our definitions is any mention of practices. When pushed, we often speak of how the traditional rituals with which we grew up no longer provide meaning, order, or connect us with a sense of the Ultimate. For many of us, just the thought of having to attend another religious service raises concern. We look around and see people who participate in these rituals who have no sense of the meaning dimension attached to them. In fact, we sometimes describe the rituals and practices we grew up with as a part of "organized" religion. A growing number of us feel that we can still be "spiritual" without observing religious rituals.

Upon further exploration, we admit that what alienates us are particular rituals, not ritual itself. We engage in other practices that provide meaning for us. We may pray freely instead of using the formal prayers we learned. We may hike through the woods to get in touch with our perception of the sacred. In other words, although we may not define our practices as religious rituals, they share similar ends. Our practices enable us to express our spirituality and provide a way to order our lives in concert with our sense of perceived ultimacy.

Thinking about Ritual

What do you think about the rituals of your youth? Which ones still provide meaning for you? Which ones have lost their meaning? Have you substituted other practices in their place to help you understand or get in touch with what you perceive to be ultimate in the universe? What are those other practices? How do they provide meaning for you?

SYMBOLIC/EXPRESSIVE DIMENSIONS OF RITUAL

The previous chapters speak of the significance of symbols and signs. In that vein, religious ritual is significant action. Religious ritual expresses the connection with our perception of ultimacy or the sacred in the universe. Religious ritual expresses our deepest understandings of the world. Here the connection between ritual and **myth** emerges. Many religious rituals act out the great myths and stories of our religious traditions. They help to express a community's worldview and understanding of the ultimate ordering in the universe. As a result, many rituals are dramatic and performative. Christmas pageants have become ritualized for many churches. The children of the church practice for weeks as they assume the various roles surrounding the Christmas myths. The adult volunteers provide costumes and props: robes for the shepherds, wings for the angels, and gifts for the magi. Young people are given the important roles of Mary and Joseph. The magi come bearing their gifts. The drama sets the stage for the retelling of the myth. Often the congregation joins in by singing key Christmas carols. "Angels We Have Heard on High" accompanies the angels' announcement to the shepherds of the birth of Jesus. "We Three Kings" follows the entrance of the magi bearing their gifts. And "Silent Night" often concludes the dramatization.

Religious rituals are often expressive of our imaginative capacities. Religious ritual opens the door for imagining another realm and new possibilities. The meditation rituals associated with Zen Buddhism are a good example. The person who meditates may recite a **koan** received from a master, a phrase or saying that defies the logic or worldview dominant in society. An example would be: "What did your face look like before your parents were born?" The purpose of reciting or reflecting on this word or phrase is to imagine a different world, to break free from the cognitive constraints of one's culture and so to achieve some sense of enlightenment. Similarly, the singing of spirituals by slaves in the United States helped them to get through the day by providing some hope. "Sometimes I hangs my head an' cries, But Jesus going to wipe my weep'n eyes." The spirituals spoke about a world different from the pain and suffering they knew and enabled them to envision a life beyond slavery.

Many talents and abilities are expressed in religious ritual actions. Music, dance, art, and architecture often play critical roles. Many great works of music were composed to set the mood and tone for religious celebrations. The music of Johann Sebastian Bach (1685-1750) is a good example. Although he may be best known for his Brandenburg concertos, written for the private enjoyment of a prince, the vast majority of Bach's works express his deep religious faith. Bach spent most of his life as an organist and music director for churches in Germany. During his twenty-seven years as director of music at Saint Thomas Church in Leipzig, Bach wrote hundreds of masses, oratorios, motets, and cantatas in which he displays a wide range of religious sentiments, from joyful celebrations of life to reflective meditations on death. Through his musical talents he explored the deep mysteries of his Christian faith and enabled his listeners to do the same. As a Lutheran, Bach realized that, regardless of one's chosen occupation or vocation, one could express one's love for God. That is why he signed each piece *Sola Deo Gloria*, which means "to the glory of God alone."

Some of the world's great architectural achievements are dedicated to religious purposes and for religious space. Cathedrals are good examples. The beautiful **stupas** associated with the Golden Temple in Bangkok, Thailand, are others. Initially, stupas were mounds of earth built over the remains of great persons as places of remembrance and worship. Mounds were built at places where the Buddha visited, preached, or some relic was found. With the development of the notion of merit, and the belief that the power of the great person is still present with the relic or place, people began to make pilgrimages to the stupas. With the rise of the cult associated with Buddhism, larger, more ornate stupas were built. In Bangkok, the golden stupas house various sculptures of the Buddha (golden Buddha, emerald Buddha, reclining Buddha) that are the objects of religious veneration and devotion. These bell-like structures (they are dome-shaped in India) have elaborate carvings of mythic beings from popular local beliefs. The reverence paid by visiting pilgrims is not like the worship of a god. Instead, the pilgrims pay respect to the Buddha's attainment of enlightenment, the experience of full insight into the nature of reality as suffering, and they commit themselves to follow the Buddha's example.

Religious rituals also express our embodiedness in the world. They often transform routine bodily experiences, such as eating, drinking, bathing, and experiencing pain, into symbolic experiences of spiritual potency and ultimacy. Christians of all denominations imbue the routine acts of gathering to break bread and drink wine (or grape juice) with cosmic significance when they connect it with God's saving grace in the life, death, and resurrection of Jesus. Similarly, many religious traditions associate the act of bathing with purification and cleansing before coming into the presence of the sacred. Native Americans of the Plains bathe before pursuing a vision quest to prepare themselves for the connection with the sacred they are about to undertake. In preparation for the Sun Dance, Oglala Sioux pierce their bodies with leather thongs as they dance and gaze into the sun. The pain they experience reflects the pain associated with the birth and rebirth of creation.

FRED GLENNON

Burial stupa outside a Tibetan monastery in Southwest China.

Suggesting that religious rituals are expressive and symbolic or provide a sense of meaning does not mean that they always do so. Sometimes we lose sight of the meaning of our religious rituals. For example, Ash Wednesday marks the beginning of Lent for Christians, a time of reflection, prayer, and fasting in honor of Christ's sacrifice. Having ashes placed upon one's head symbolizes one's commitment to reflect, pray, and fast. Many people walk around on this Wednesday with ashes on their forehead. When asked why they have ashes placed on their head each year, most simply respond that they do it because of their tradition. Others say, "Ashes to ashes, dust to dust." In doing so, they are attempting to suggest the symbolic meaning of the ritual activity. When asked what that statement means, however, many are unable to tell.

If we cannot express the purpose or aim of the ritual action, then why do we do it? Is it a waste of time? Some theorists of religious ritual conclude from this that ritual activity is action and that the ritual has intrinsic value even if we cannot connect it with any explicit meaning. One does the ritual even when one does not find conscious meaning. Its significance comes from orthopraxy, right action, not orthodoxy, right thought. The ritual may have secondary effects, such as creating bonds between participants and reinforcing solidarity. But these are not their intention.[1]

PERSONAL AND SOCIAL FUNCTIONS OF RITUAL

Others who study religious rituals speak of their personal and social functions. The function of ritual for individual and social harmony is beautifully summarized by the Confucian scholar, Hsun Tzu:

> It is through rites that Heaven and earth are harmonious and sun and moon are bright, that the four seasons are ordered and the stars are on their courses, that rivers flow and that things prosper, that love and hatred are tempered and joy and anger are in keeping. They cause the lowly to be obedient and those on high to be illustrious. He who holds to the rites is never confused in the midst of multifarious change; he who deviates therefrom is lost. Rites—are they not the culmination of culture?[2]

This view illustrates the potential of ritual to help individuals find a sense of meaning and direction for their lives. They are able to make connections with the broader communities out of which they emerge.

Finding meaning and purpose in our lives is an important element of human experience. Religious communities have developed rituals to enable members to make this discovery and to celebrate its occurrence. For example, the Oglala Sioux developed the vision-quest ritual mentioned above. Through the vision quest a young person receives guidance and direction for his or her life. After undergoing some purification rituals, a guide takes the person seeking the vision to a distant sacred hill. The only provisions the person may take are a blanket and a sacred pipe. While on this hill the seeker prays for a vision from the spirits. The spirits may speak to the seeker through animate or inanimate objects, such as a bird, a tree, or a rock. The experience lasts from two to four days. When the time is over, the guide retrieves the seeker, and the community celebrates the seeker's adulthood status.

Religious rituals enable us to make connections with our heritage and history. They provide an understanding of the historical significance of our faith and a sense of belonging to a broader, even cosmic, community. One of the five pillars of Islam, the foundations of Islamic life, is the pilgrimage to Mecca (**hajj**). Those who take this journey travel to a sacred place, where Muslims believe Adam and Eve lived, where Abraham and his son Ishmael built the **Ka'ba** as the first house of worship for Allah, and where Muhammad and his followers prayed. They reenact the rituals of significant persons in their tradition: they run in search of water like Hagar, Abraham's maidservant, did for her son Ishmael; they circumambulate the Ka'ba seven times on three occasions like the monotheistic worshipers of old; and they make a blood sacrifice of a consecrated animal as Abraham did at God's direction, the flesh of which is then distributed to the poor. Pilgrims get to see and meet fellow believers of all races and languages. They experience the unity and equality of the **Umma**, the worldwide Muslim community, in all of its rich diversity.

Religious rituals often provide benefits for us as individuals and for our communities. This dual function can be seen in the Buddhist ordination ritual. At the individual level, the ordinand receives a sense of mission, vocation, and purpose; he becomes a member of the **Sangha,** the community of monks who live together and participate in the practices and rituals that line the path that leads to enlightenment. At the communal level, the ordinand's spiritual energies are released for the benefit of the community, especially for his relatives and those ancestors who may be suffering in hell. By renouncing all worldly

ALI IMRAN

Plains of Arafat on the day of the Hajj, Mecca, Saudi Arabia (2003).

pleasures, he becomes a storehouse of spiritual power that others can draw upon. Some communities believe that the sexual renunciation of the monks enhances the fertility of the entire community. For this reason the ordination rituals are often done prior to the rainy season.

TYPES OF RELIGIOUS RITUAL

There are many types of religious rituals. Some occur at significant moments in the life of the individual or community. They tend to be chronological in that the key actors in the ritual engage in such rituals only once in their lifetime. Some religious rituals, such as annual festivals, however, are cyclical; they occur periodically in the course of a year. If one looks at the research on religious ritual, one quickly discovers that researchers do not agree on any one typology. Instead, they use a variety of typologies and classifications. As with any typology, there is the danger of oversimplifying.

LIFE-CYCLE RITUALS

Life-cycle rituals occur throughout our lives, celebrating key transitions, especially birth, initiation into adulthood, marriage, vocation, and death. Many of these events are marked by **rites of passage**. Rites of passage involve a variety of significant actions and rituals to mark the process of moving from one status in our lives or communities to another.

French anthropologist and ethnologist Arnold van Gennep (1873-1957), in his classic work *Rites of Passage*, speaks of three phases associated with a rite of passage: *separation, transition (liminality),* and *incorporation.* The *separation* phase is marked by symbolic behaviors or actions that stress the separation or detachment of the individual or group undergoing the rite from a previous status. For example, the vision quest often begins with purification rituals, such as bathing or time spent in the sweathouse. The person then leaves the tribe and goes alone to a place to await the vision. These activities separate the person from his or her former status within the community.

The *transition* or *liminal* phase prepares one for the next status one will assume. This phase is ambiguous; the person no longer possesses the old status but the new status has not been conferred. In the words of symbolic anthropologist Victor Turner (1920-83), the person is "betwixt and between." The behavior and actions done in this phase prepare one for one's new status. The liminal phase is crucial because during this phase the person is outside of the structures of ordinary life and potentially exposed more to the sacred. The stage is set for new experiences of the sacred. In the vision quest the vision seeker has no status within the community. The person is left to his or her own devices with just a blanket and a pipe. At this stage the person has no real direction for his or her life but is seeking it from the spirits who will come to visit. The spirits often come in the form of animals or birds, melting away the distinctions that are normal within the community.

The final phase of *incorporation* involves a variety of rituals and actions that confer the new status upon the person and welcome him or her back into the community. The guide retrieves the person seeking the vision and brings him or her back to the community. The person receives a new name, often associated with the animal form the spirit takes. There is a celebration and feast commemorating the new status of the person as an adult in the community. If the person is also a medicine man, then that person becomes the apprentice of an experienced medicine man. Finally, the person receiving the vision shares the wisdom of that vision with the entire community.

The three phases are not developed to the same extent in every ceremony or rite of passage. Some ceremonies stress one phase over the other. For example, with birth rites the phases of separation and incorporation are more significant than the transition or marginal phase. Rites of initiation into adulthood, however, often have longer transitional phases. Thus, while all rites may express some aspects of these three phases, the phases are not always equally important or developed by all religious peoples or cultures.

The birth of a child is a significant event in our lives, our families, and our communities, and numerous rituals accompany it. Friends and family give baby showers for the expectant couple, filled with gifts for caring for the child (including books on how to parent). The parents select a name that has some significance for the couple or connects the child with the broader family. The family sends out a birth announcement, including a picture of a rather wrinkly newborn. In all of these rituals the family commemorates the importance of this event for their lives and their families.

Similarly, religious communities have developed rituals to celebrate the birth of a child and to connect it with its communal and cosmic significance. Often there are separation and purification rituals attached to the celebration of the birth. One aspect of the traditional baptism ritual in Catholic churches is that it represents the washing away of original sin—the propensity of disobedience toward God inherent in the human condition that was transmitted to humanity

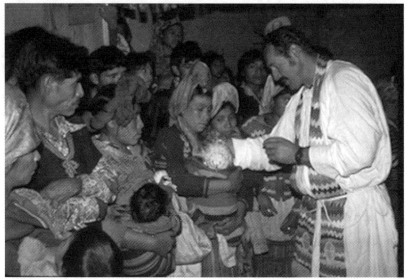

CREDIT: MARYKNOLL MISSION ARCHIVES/P. GAUDVIS

Infants being baptized in Guatemala.

through the disobedience of Adam. Baptism, by imparting the life of Christ's grace, purifies the child from that condition and initiates the child into a community that pledges to provide nurture in the Christian faith. Some churches have the baptismal font in a separate building. Infant baptisms in some Protestant churches follow a similar pattern. The baptismal liturgies speak of the baptismal font as the place where the old person of Adam is washed away and the child becomes a new person in Christ. Then they challenge the parents, the godparents, and the congregation to provide appropriate Christian care and nurture.

In some traditional African religions the heads of newborns are shaved to symbolize the cutting off of anything bad—shaved off with the old hairs—and the separation of the baby from its mother's womb for membership in the community. The communal significance of the birth can also be seen in the separation and naming rituals attached to it. Because the family's continuation is dependent upon the survival of the child, families separate their children from contact with others for a period of time and say prayers to ensure the survival of the child. The naming of the child in some instances reflects the belief that the ancestors, important persons in the life of the family, are often reborn into new children. This is significant because ancestors are spiritually potent and can provide help to the community. A family presents the names of ancestors to the child until the child stops crying. When this occurs, the family chooses a name that reflects the belief that this ancestor has been reborn in that child.

Thinking about Birth

Think about the birth of your child (real or imagined). How do you feel about the experience? How have you prepared for it? What will you name the child? How will you involve family and friends in the experience?

Now think about your religious community. How do the members welcome children into the community? Are there specific rituals, like baptism, attached to this event? Are these rituals private? public? both? What words are spoken by the leaders of the ritual? What role does the child play? What role do the parents play? What role does the congregation play?

Initiation rituals associated with moving into a new status are common occurrences. Graduation events celebrate the move from adolescence to the adult world of work and family. College campuses with fraternities and sororities are familiar with initiation ceremonies during Greek Week through which pledges become full members in the community. Ceremonies mark inductions into academic and athletic honor societies, such as Phi Beta Kappa and the Baseball Hall of Fame. What all these rituals have in common is that they reflect significant achievement and membership in a new status.

Religious rituals associated with initiation into adult status in the community reflect this same significance. There is usually some separation or gathering together, instruction in the ways of the religion or group, and a public ceremony welcoming the new members. From their youth, Jewish boys, and in some communities girls, receive instruction in the Hebrew language and Jewish tradition in preparation for their formal membership in the Jewish community. At about the age of thirteen, the age at which Jews believe their intelligence and self-consciousness has matured sufficiently, the boy and girls become a **bar/bat mitzvah,** literally a "son/daughter of the commandment." At this time the community expects them to perform all the commandments and to take responsibility for their religious behavior. During the ceremony the young people publicly read from the Torah in the synagogue, symbolizing their new status as members of the religious majority, and the parents and the community say **blessings** in their honor. The service is followed by a celebration welcoming the young people as members of the religious majority.

In cultures where the lines between religion and society are less clearly drawn, the rituals attached to the transition to adulthood are significant because of their connections with the whole meaning of adulthood; not only do those initiated assume adult religious responsibilities and privileges, but they also assume the responsibilities of marriage and family. In some traditional African cultures male and female **circumcision** is reserved for this time. The Dogon believe that males and females are born with both sexual components. The cutting away of the foreskin of the penis (the female part) or excision of the clitoral hood (the male part) allows the individuals to become fully male and female and ready to assume their respective adult gender roles. The young people are gathered together, circumcised by an adult skilled in the procedure, and then separated from the community for a period of instruction on the responsibilities and expectations of religious and sexual adulthood. During this time they are often dressed alike, representing their commonality and liminal status. At the end of the training period the whole community welcomes them back with a public ceremony celebrating their new status.

Marriage is another significant stage in the life cycle that has various rituals attached to it. Historically, marriage brought families, rather than two individuals in love, together. Societies regulated and arranged marriages to reinforce kinship ties or enhance the social and economic status of the families involved. Traditional societies also stressed procreation in marriage as a central means for the survival of the community. In some modern societies romantic love and personal happiness have become the primary motivations for marriage. In spite of this, however, the economic, social, and communal significance of marriage continue to play a role, as evidenced in the arguments put forward by both proponents and opponents of same-sex marriage. This significance is then reflected in various marriage rituals.

In the United States friends and families often hold wedding showers for the couple, where the couple receives gifts of dishes, cookware, and other items they will need to set up their own household. The activities surrounding the marriage ceremony often take months of preparation and planning. The couple must decide when and where to have the ceremony and reception; whom to invite as participants and guests; what costumes, flowers, and music to adorn the event, and how to orchestrate each activity. The presence of flowers and children historically represented the promise of fertility. Leaving the home of

CREDIT: MARYKNOLL PHOTO ARCHIVES

Newlyweds at San Miguel Acatan, Guatemala.

the parents, entering the door of the church, and being carried over the threshold of the new home all signify the change in the status of newlyweds from adolescents, sons and daughters of their parents, to adults, when they will establish a household and family of their own. Arnold Van Gennep writes, "The door is the boundary between the foreign and the domestic worlds in the case of an ordinary dwelling, between the profane and sacred worlds in the case of a temple. Therefore to cross the threshold is to unite oneself with a new world."[3]

For many religious traditions the significance of marriage is not simply about the personal connection made between two people. There is also the importance of children for the life and well-being of the community. In Jewish tradition marriage receives spiritual significance because the creation myths suggest it is ordained by God as the ideal human relationship and because it is the appropriate context for fulfillment of the commandment, "Be fruitful and multiply." Traditional Jewish marriage rites begin with the engagement, which at one time was a formal commitment to marry but is now a social occasion when the two people announce their intention to marry. The engagement period marks the separation from their formal single status and preparation for what is about to take place. The liminal status of their situation is reflected in the marriage contract, the **kettuba**. The contract provides a sense of equality between the partners; they covenant together and it protects them. The seven blessings reflected in the nuptial prayer connect the couple being married to the mythic couple, **Adam** and **Eve**. This moment reflects an immediacy with the sacred. The conclusion of the ceremony is marked by the groom's stomping on a drinking glass and the communal welcoming of the couple into the life of the community. In past times the couple was taken to a room to consummate their marriage. Today, the period of privacy is brief and symbolic. The couple is then welcomed into the community and expected to fulfill the commandment to "be fruitful and multiply." They fulfill the obligations associated with house and home.

Religious communities often associate certain activities and rituals with entrance into a religious vocation. The structure or order of those rituals can be similar across different religions. Future religious leaders may experience some sense of call or vocation, or the mantle of leadership may be passed on from one generation to another. (It is quite common to discover that ministers have parents and grandparents who are also ministers.) Sometimes this occurs because the person or the community attaches religious significance to a specific event, experience, or vision/dream. The community often validates the experience and provides a period of training for the person in the ways of religious leadership and the performance of religious rituals. Upon completion of the training, the community has a public ritual to celebrate the transition into religious leadership and to affirm the person's calling. Finally, the newly appointed religious leader undergoes some time in apprenticeship with an experienced religious leader to learn the practices and nuances associated with religious leadership.

Buddhism ordains monks in two ways. First, there is lower ordination. In many ways this is similar to a rite of passage from youth to adult responsibility, similar to a Jewish *bar/bat mitzvah* or Catholic confirmation. In **Theravada Buddhism** the monastic path is expected of everyone who reaches nirvana, including women. The first ordination is an attempt to provide early training and instruction in the way and teachings of Buddhism. The young men who become ordained generally do not remain monks; most stay monks for about four months. They engage in monastic rituals, such as walking the streets begging for food, and perform some priestly functions, such as the blessing of houses. But generally they assume the role of an apprentice and learn Buddhist doctrine. Ordination associated with religious vocation is known as the higher ordination. This time commitment to the monastic community is for life; one has dedicated oneself to become an **arhant** (worthy one).

Both forms of ordination follow the pattern typical of rites of passage: separation, transition, and incorporation. The ordinands ritually die and are reborn. The ordinand leaves behind family and friends to live at the monastery. He leaves his clothes, shaves his head, undergoes a ritual bath, and receives a new name. All of these elements reflect the separation phase, the separation from a past life. The transition phase includes instruction in the ways of the monastic order. The ordinands vow to keep the **Ten Precepts** of Buddhism, which include the **Five Precepts** (listed below on page 131) plus the precepts not to take food from noon to the next morning; not to adorn their bodies with anything other than the three robes; not to participate in or be spectator to public entertainments; not to use high or comfortable beds; and not to use money. Those of higher ordination also commit themselves to

AKUPPA

Ordination ceremony. Friends and relatives celebrate with the young ordinands who will live in the monastery where they will receive instruction in the Buddhist doctrines and way of life.

keep the 227 rules of the monastic code. Any infractions of the rules are confessed publicly in the presence of other monks. They study together and learn the practice of meditation. They are taught how to perform the various rituals and blessings for the lay community.

Incorporation occurs in two stages. First, friends and relatives in the lay community provide cloth for the robes the ordinands will receive from the monks. Eventually, those undergoing lower ordination return to their communities. A public ceremony and celebration accompanies this event. Those of higher ordination in Theravada Buddhism commit themselves to celibacy and remain in the community for life. Their interactions with the lay community are still important. The laity provides food and the other basic material needs of the monks. These gifts enable the monks to practice the monastic path, to become models of spiritual and moral ideals, and to generate spiritual power. The exercise of this spiritual power through blessings and rituals brings prosperity to the lay people. In **Mahayana Buddhism**, after their training at the monastery most monks marry and serve as priests to local congregations, performing rituals for families who belong to the temple.

The final life-cycle rituals we will discuss center on dying and death. When someone we love dies, the loss generates a variety of emotions: shock, denial, anger, grief. Not only do we experience loss, but we also confront our own mortality. To deal with our loss and anxiety, cultures develop funeral rites. These rites not only honor the dead, but they also provide aid and comfort to the living. Wakes and funerals provide opportunities for people to come together and remember the significance of the dead in their lives, their families, and their communities. These rites also provide opportunity and social space to weep together; to express anger, grief, and anxiety; and to prepare one another for life without the deceased.

Similarly, religions have generated a vast array of funeral rites to honor the dead, prepare the person for passage into the next life, and provide aid and comfort to the bereaved. A common practice in Jewish and Islamic funeral rites is the bathing, preparation, and dressing of the body. As in other life-cycle rituals, the bathing and cleansing mark the separation phase—the dead become separated from the living. The preparation and dressing signify the transition or liminal phase of the ritual. Often the person is dressed in a simple white cloth. This notes the common status of the dead. There is no division of wealth before the creator of the world. At this point all are equal. For Jewish men the prayer shawl (**tallit**) they received at their bar mitzvah and used as their wedding canopy becomes their burial gown. Similarly, many

Islamic men are buried in the white linen robe that they wore when on the pilgrimage (*hajj*) to Mecca. Both traditions stress burial as the norm, reflecting the biblical notion of "ashes to ashes, dust to dust," an allusion to the reincorporation with the source and substance of their creation. Both traditions also stress the importance of burial taking place as soon as possible, preferably on the day of death. The mourning period is marked by the suspension of normal social activities. In Judaism the mourning period is marked by seven days; in Islam the period is three days. The mourning period allows the living to face the separation that death brings.

Some religious traditions believe that not all of the deceased pass immediately into the next life. They become the "walking dead" of Buddhist tradition or *wanagi yuhapi* (ghost) of the Oglala Sioux. This reflects a liminal phase where the dead are "betwixt and between" the realm of the living and the realm of the dead. If left there, they can generate problems for the living through various mischievous and malevolent acts. To keep this from happening and to aid the living dead to move into the heavenly realm, the family performs a variety of rituals.

Thinking about Life-Cycle Rituals

Think about a life-cycle ritual that you have observed or in which you have participated. Describe the ritual. Look at your description and ask yourself the following questions: Was there a time when the participants were separated from the rest of the community? What were they doing? What was that experience like? Was there a feeling of community among the participants? Did they wear special clothing? How did the ritual conclude? What symbols were used? What words were spoken? How did the rest of the community respond to the ritual participants? How were they welcomed?

LIFE-CRISIS RITUALS

Disorder and chaos threaten the meaning and order we have created in our lives through the inevitable life crises we encounter. To counter their effects we develop various rituals to help us cope and to get us through them. People erect temporary shrines on the streets or roadsides where loved ones were killed through violent acts or tragic accidents. They adorn them with pictures, memorabilia, prayers, and other artifacts to mark the spot, to honor the dead, and to proclaim

FRED GLENNON

A makeshift shrine outside St. Paul's Chapel in New York City that commemorates the 9/11 tragedy at Ground Zero.

to the larger community that the senselessness of their deaths and the value of their lives will not be forgotten.

Religious communities also develop rituals aimed at helping individuals and communities deal with human and natural calamities, such as an accident, a sudden illness, a drought, a death, or war. For example, a key component of some indigenous religious worldviews is that there is a balance or harmony in human life and in the universe. Crises, whether natural or human in origin, reflect a break in that balance. A fundamental way to restore the balance is through ritual activity. Whether through sweat, music, or dance, the rituals seek to restore the harmony in the world and in so doing bring an end to the affliction suffered by the community or the individual.

The practice of divination, using certain signs to understand the cause or cure of an affliction, is a common practice. When a catastrophe or problem emerges unexpectedly, we often ask, "Why is this happening to me?" We want to know what we did. We may even decide to call an expensive psychic hotline or to have our palm read to get answers. Many indigenous cultures have developed elaborate systems of divination and value the role of diviner. The Ndembu of

Africa believe that most individual and communal misfortunes are a result of moral problems within the community. A diviner's task is not to tell the future but to scrutinize the past and to disclose the spiritual and moral causes for the crisis. By asking a series of questions of the people involved, the diviner seeks to construct a picture of the events and the relationships involved that led to the misfortune. Because each relationship in Ndembu life carries certain moral responsibilities, the diviner is able to identify potential moral conflicts that might be the source of the crisis. In addition, the diviner uses a winnowing basket filled with approximately twenty objects that symbolize relationships, problems, and motives common to Ndembu society. By shaking the basket, certain objects rise to the top, providing clues that the diviner uses to discern the cause of the crisis.

Healing rituals may seem puzzling in this day of modern medicine. But the rituals continue. Lighting a candle, mentioning the names of the sick during the worship service, and saying brief prayers are all rituals practiced by Christians today in hopes of aiding the healing process for themselves and for their loved ones. In some traditional Jewish communities people change the name of a person who is deathly ill or dying in hopes that the new name will trick the Angel of Death into believing that the person is already dead and provide the person with a new lease on life. In the rituals people are *doing*; they are being agents in the process and the hope is that their action will have some effect.

In some evangelical traditions in the United States healing services are fairly common. Those who participate in these services take seriously the promise of Jesus that, if they are faithful followers, they too will be agents of God's healing power to others. The power of touch is especially important to them. Either through the special connection the person leading the service has with God's Spirit, or through the power of the faithful community, laying on of hands is a common healing practice in which the healing power of the Holy Spirit passes through the individual or community to the sick.

As society recognizes the complex nature of suffering, pain, and disorder, religious communities develop new healing rituals. In her book *Women-Church* Rosemary Ruether discusses various rituals that Christian women have developed to provide healing from the sexual and physical violence to which they have been subjected, including rape, incest, and wife battering. The Women-Church movement (which today is known as the Women-Church Convergence) seeks to liberate women and men from the chains of the patriarchal subordination of women to a community where men and women are equal partners.

Such liberation requires the development of new liturgies that reject the violence that is so much a part of that subordination and bring healing for the victims and the community. The rituals reaffirm the importance of healing traditions that recognize the emotional and spiritual aspects of an illness or injury. This is especially true in the suffering caused by sexual violence, which creates emotional scars for the victims and often isolates and alienates them from community. The "rite of healing from rape" Ruether describes incorporates many elements of traditional healing rituals, including ritual bathing, anointing with oils, and laying on of hands. It also includes rituals for purifying and rededicating the woman's home if the rape took place there. What is significant about these rituals is that they recognize that the violence has created disorder for the woman with her world. The rituals bring communal recognition of the violence and seek to reincorporate the woman back into community and empower her to create new order by integrating the event into her life without shame or blame.

The importance of rituals in life crises came home to me as a young chaplain in a hospital in Louisville, Kentucky. I was working in the Emergency Room when I received a call requesting that a chaplain come to the Delivery Room to comfort a woman who had delivered a premature, stillborn infant. When I arrived, I discovered that the mother of the child wanted me to baptize the child, the thought of which terrified me. Not only had I never performed a baptism, but my Baptist tradition taught me that baptism is a rite reserved for persons professing their faith in Christ, something infants could not do. I explained this to the nursing staff who, although listening sympathetically, proceeded to dress me in a surgical gown and to provide me with a basin of water. Apparently, they had done this before. As I entered the room, I saw an eighteen-year-old African American woman lying in a bed and holding a beautifully formed but lifeless child. As I spoke with her, we talked about her sorrow and about the hopes she once had for her child. I finally asked if there was anything I could do for her. After giving the child a name, she looked into my eyes and requested that I baptize her child so that her spirit and her daughter's spirit could be at peace with God. Confused and uncertain, I took her child in my arms, placed my fingers in the water basin, and baptized her daughter in the name of the Creator, the Christ, and the Comforter. Baptists say that there is nothing sacramental about the ritual of baptism; no saving grace comes from it. Perhaps. In that ritual act in that Delivery Room, however, I experienced the presence of the Sacred in a way I have not since, an experience I can only describe as grace. As I looked at the woman, I could see that she had experienced it as well. The peace the woman requested had come to her, to her daughter, and, unexpectedly, to me.

PERIODIC (CYCLICAL) RITUALS

Periodic rituals are rituals that celebrate seasons in the year or commemorate specific historical events. As with all rituals, there are often several layers of meaning attached to them. The rituals associated with Easter have various religious and secular meanings. The specifically religious dimensions include the rituals associated with Holy Week, Good Friday, and Easter morning. In them, the new life and salvation God brought about through the life, death, and resurrection of Jesus the Christ are celebrated. Easter also includes rituals associated with spring and the birth of new life. Some Christians believe that the dogwoods bloom only during Easter, even though the dates for Easter change. The Easter bunny, the decorated eggs, the colorful flowers, and the bright clothes all reflect and celebrate the new life that appears after the winter season has ended.

New Year rituals also have multiple levels of meaning. They are rituals of thanksgiving and gratitude for all that the Sacred has provided. But they are also periods of penitence and renewal, full of recognition of past wrongs and promises to change in the year ahead. The festivals and celebrations provide an opportunity to reflect, to take stock, and to redirect one's life.

An intriguing recent ritual development within the African American community is the **Kwanzaa** celebration that begins on December 26 and ends on January 1. Kwanzaa was developed as a cultural holiday by African American historian Dr. Maulana Karenga in 1966. He did so in the aftermath of the August 1965 riots that took place in Watts, a predominantly African American community in Los Angeles; the riots lasted for four days in response to an alleged incident of police brutality. Thirty-four people were killed, hundreds more were injured, and over two hundred million dollars in property damage was incurred. As a result, the African American community joined together to rebuild Watts and to make it a stronger community. Karenga's goal in developing the holiday was to bring about a sense of pride and unity among African Americans by setting aside a special time for this purpose. Although not connected to a specific religious tradition, the ritual embodies many features of the harvest festivals in the traditional African cultures Karenga researched. It is a time for African Americans to join together to honor the traditions of their ancestors. More important, it is a time for participants to take stock of the past year and to prepare themselves for the year ahead with the hope of improving their lives and their communities. Thus, Kwanzaa reflects the elements of many religious festivals associated with the New Year.

The reflective dimension of the holiday centers on the **seven principles** (in Swahili, *nguzo Saba*). The principles include unity (working together as a people), self-determination (accomplishing goals set), collective work and responsibility (working together to solve problems), cooperative economics (maintaining individual businesses to profit the community), purpose (a plan for life), creativity (making the community and world better), and faith (trust in the rightness of our efforts). The principles provide the basis for reflection and discussion during the festival. Such reflection, it is hoped, will lead to actions throughout the year that will enhance the lives of the individuals and communities who take part.

Various rituals are attached to the festival, involving all of the senses. Many adults fast from sunrise to sunset in order to purify and prepare themselves. Participants wear colorful traditional African clothing to commemorate their African heritage. Seven candles, one black, three red, and three green, representing the seven principles are lit, one each day. The black candle is placed at the center, and it represents unity. It is lit on the first day of the celebration. The red candles, placed on the left side of the black candle, represent purpose, creativity, and faith. The green candles, placed on the right side of the black candle, represent self-determination, collective work and responsibility, and cooperative economics. Fruit and vegetables are also displayed, representing the connection with the African harvest festivals. Ears of corn represent the children and are displayed even by childless couples to reflect the African belief that it takes a village to raise a child.

Each day one candle is lit. Discussion of the principle it represents takes place in the glow of the candle. On the sixth day families and friends have a feast and exchange gifts. The gifts are meant to improve the life of the recipient, such as books about African culture. The gifts are opened the following day. Before the feast all of the candles are lit and the principles they represent are discussed. Then there is time for stories, songs, and dances. Many of the stories center on the lives of significant African Americans. After the festivities there is a time for all to commit themselves again to the seven principles. A unity cup filled with water, the essence of life, is passed, and everyone sips from it. Then drums are played, signaling the beginning of the feast. The final day of Kwanzaa is New Year's Day. The gifts are opened and the day is spent reflecting and planning how to put into place the seven principles in the year ahead.

SUMMARY

From this discussion on religious ritual we can see the tremendous use of ritual activity to help participants find meaning, order, and relationships in their lives. Religious rituals encompass every facet of life, from daily practice and annual celebrations to significant transitions and crises in the lives of individuals and communities. These symbolic actions reenact and make conscious religions' understanding of reality and enable participants to make their lives meaningful by connecting to their perceptions of the ultimate orderings of life. Symbolic action, however, is but one form of significant, ordering action. Religions also prescribe practical or ethical actions that are in keeping with the worldview.

RESOURCES

ACTIVITIES

1. Research specific celebrations on your college campus, such as Founder's Day, that commemorate the beginnings of the institution. What rituals are associated with them? What members of the community, past and present, participate in those rituals?

2. Research and observe (individually or in groups) a religious ritual in which you have never participated. The research will enable you to understand the meaning of the symbols and activities you observe. Write a reflection/reaction paper in which you describe the rituals and what they mean for the participants. In addition, compare/contrast the ritual with a similar ritual from your own tradition.

3. Divide the class into small groups (assigned or self-chosen) and create your own religions using a collaborative wiki page or YouTube channel. Be sure to include a religious worldview and a religious ethos that corresponds to that worldview, including ritual performances and symbols.

4. Engage in a religious ritual activity in the classroom, such as a meditation or rhythmic dance. Upon completion of the ritual reflect upon your experience, highlighting your reactions/responses and what you took from the experience. Then read about and discuss the ritual experience in the context of one or more religious traditions.

5. Recall a crisis you once experienced. Write a reflection paper or journal entry that answers these questions: What did you do? What actions helped you to make sense of the experience? What actions provided comfort? What were the actions of those around you? Were they helpful? If you feel comfortable, you may want to share this with the class by posting it in a blog or an online discussion folder.

READINGS

Bell, Catherine. *Ritual Theory, Ritual Practice*. New York: Oxford University Press, 1992. This book looks at theories of ritual and how they function in academic discourse. Bell questions whether ritual should be associated with action rather than thought. Instead, she sees ritualization as always strategic and, hence, political.

Driver, Tom F. *The Magic of Ritual*. San Francisco: HarperCollins, 1991. Driver argues for a theological reclamation of ritual's transformative capabilities. He argues that ritual has the ability to evoke moral and social transformation because of the way ritual both changes things and is subject to change.

Durkheim, Emile. *The Elementary Forms of Religious Life*. New York: The Free Press, 1965. Durkheim maintains that ritual and belief are what constitute religion. He contrasts the religious realm, the sacred, with the secular realm, the profane. Because of this dichotomy, he defines ritual in a way that makes it fundamentally religious, a step with which other ritual theorists disagree.

Grimes, Ronald L. *Readings in Ritual Studies*. Upper Saddle River, NJ: Prentice-Hall, 1996. This collection of essays seeks to illustrate and to foster the interdisciplinary discussion of ritual studies that has developed by including writers from a variety of disciplines, including religious studies, anthropology, theology, history, psychology, and the arts. In addition, the volume includes selections from theorists who shaped the field, such as Durkheim, Eliade, and Freud.

Karenga, Maulana. *Kwanzaa: A Celebration of Family, Community, and Culture*. Los Angeles: Kawaida Publications, 2007. This book, written by the creator of the holiday, provides a concise overview of the celebration, discusses the seven principles and their related symbols, and includes suggested activities for those seeking to participate.

Ruether, Rosemary Radford. *Women-Church: Theology and Practice of Feminist Liturgical Communities*. San Francisco: Harper, 1985. The book reflects the perspective of religious feminists who seek to reclaim aspects of their religious tradition but see the need to reform its patriarchal roots. It discusses special liturgies for moments of crisis and healing, especially from sexual violence and abuse, with the hope of providing resources for the liturgical work of religious communities.

Turner, Victor. *The Ritual Process*. Ithaca, NY: Cornell University Press, 1977. This book provides a detailed discussion of the concepts of *liminality* and *communitas* Turner developed to expand Van Gennep's understanding of the phases of rites of passage.

Van Gennep, Arnold. *Rites of Passage*. Chicago: University of Chicago Press, 1960. In this book Van Gennep develops his understanding of the three phases of rites of passage: separation, transition, and incorporation. He contends that transition from one social status to the next requires some means of negotiating them, namely, rites of passage.

AUDIO-VISUAL RESOURCES

Beliefs and Traditions. Available from National Geographic on the video .nationalgeographic.com website. These short video clips introduce students to various ritual traditions, including the *hajj*, the Hindu festival of Diwali, male circumcision, and exorcism.

The Five Pillars of Islam (1983). Available from Films for the Humanities and Sciences, 132 West 31st Street, 17th Floor, New York, NY 10001. The five pillars of Islam are discussed, described, and put into historical context. The film places them in an international context and also introduces the conflict between traditional teaching and the effects of industrialization.

Hindu Spiritual Pathways (2006). Available from Films for the Humanities and Sciences, 132 West 31st Street, 17th Floor, New York, NY 10001. This short video program introduces the viewer to a group of young Hindus who examine the practices and philosophies of the paths to Hindu devotion, explaining that Hinduism accommodates many ways to worship. The teens also touch on the concepts of Brahman and *atman*, and their families' use of devotional music, meditation, and ritual to connect with the Divine.

Holy Places and Pilgrimages (1991). Available from Films for the Humanities and Sciences, 132 West 31st Street, 17th Floor, New York, NY 10001. This film, part of the *Religions of the Book* series, explores the meaning of holiness and its implications for ritual practice and holy places in the religions of Judaism, Christianity, and Islam.

Ritual: Three Portraits of Judaism (1990). Produced by Brenda J. Goodman and Oren Rudavsky. Interfaith Broadcasting Network. Judaism has rituals for blessing each day, rituals for blessing each life, and rituals for blessing the annual cycle. This documentary presents daily rituals in the life of a woman seminarian, a periodic or holiday ritual (Sukkoth) celebrated by a family, and a life-cycle ritual (circumcision) that involves a community of family and friends. Each ritual links the individual to God and to the Jewish community. The documentary illustrates the engagement of the senses, as well as the mind, in ritual.

Wheel of Time (2005). Available from Wellspring Media, 419 Park Ave. S, 20th Floor, New York, NY 10016-8410. This film looks at the largest Buddhist ritual in Bodh Gaya, India. It is said that Buddha found enlightenment under a tree in Bodh Gaya, and today Buddhist monks are ordained in this holy place. The film captures the lengthy pilgrimages (for some, over three thousand miles) and the monk's creation of the beautiful and intricate sand mandala (the wheel of time), along with many secret **rituals** that have never been seen before on film.

NOTES

1. Frits Staal, "The Meaninglessness of Ritual," in *Readings in Ritual Studies*, ed. Ronald L. Grimes (Upper Saddle River, NJ: Prentice-Hall, 1996), 483-94.

2. Hsun Tzu, "On Rites," quoted in *Essential Sacred Writings from around the World*, ed. Mircea Eliade (San Francisco: Harper Row, 1977), 234-35.

3. Arnold Van Gennep, *The Rites of Passage* (1960; reprint London: Routledge, 2004), 20. Available online.

Chapter 5

Ethical Action

Ethical or moral action is another way we order our lives and engage our world. Ethics helps us to answer the significant human questions: What should I do? What kind of person should I become? How should I act in relationship to others? How do I connect to the world? The moral feelings, habits, values, and codes that we develop individually and communally help us to discern directions for our behavior and relationships.

Where do our ethics come from? Recent research suggests that morality, like language, is in part genetic and in part social and cultural. The feelings, habits, values, and codes of ethical action have evolved from the interplay of developments in the brain and the social and institutional circumstances in which we live. They, of course, reflect the worldview, the picture of how things are and ought to be, of our particular culture or tradition. For example, European philosophical ideas that continue to influence our political and economic institutions posit the freedom of the individual as the ultimate value of society. The rights of the individual to life, liberty, and property are inalienable. This view answers the question, What should I do? negatively: do no harm. Individuals are free to do as they please so long as their actions do not harm or interfere with the ability of others to do the same.

Anthropologists note the connection between our worldviews and our ethical actions. Worldviews not only serve the ordering process by helping us make sense of how things are, but they also suggest how life ought to be lived. The power of myth, a key element in a community's worldview, demonstrates this connection. Myths are both models of the world and models for the world; they are both descriptive and prescriptive. For example, the Horatio Alger stories in the late nineteenth century of poor individuals who moved from rags to riches championed the worldview in American culture that

America is a land of opportunity and that there are no restrictions to social mobility. These stories also served to encourage a certain way of life; that is, hard work and persistence are virtues that all Americans should emulate if they want material success. This myth is so strong that it continues to be held even in the face of evidence to the contrary.

In many cultures, ethical action is action that conforms to the moral code generated by the community and reflected in its worldview. Members understand ethical action in this way. What should I do? is answered with, What is the relevant rule or principle? Children's initial experience with ethical action is usually abiding by the rules or facing the consequences of failure to do so. Families, schools, and religious organizations all socialize children to these codes. As children grow and develop cognitive skills, parents introduce them to the rules of the house that are designed to respect persons, pets, and property: no hitting or biting, no playing with matches, and no writing on the walls. When they get to school, teachers and principals introduce children to a similar set of rules that reflect the need for order in the broader social context. This reflects most of our initial experience of ethical action.

Moral codes, and the values embodied in them, begin external to us. They are "out there," and we confront them. They exist before us, we abide by them, and they go on existing after us. The hope of most communities, however, is that we will internalize the moral codes and values, make them our own, that they will become a part of our moral **conscience**. Parents hope their children will someday do the right thing without the need for punishment or reward. When that happens, they encourage their children to let their conscience be their guide. The Old Testament prophet Jeremiah reflects this hope of internalizing the moral code when he proclaims, "But this is the covenant that I will make with the house of Israel after those days, says the Lord: I will put my law within them, and I will write it on their hearts; and I will be their God, and they shall be my people" (Jer 31:33).

If we could imagine a society where a single worldview and ethos dominated all cultural and institutional life, ethical action might be simple and certain types of moral problems might never emerge. We live in a culturally pluralistic society, however, where communities have different worldviews and institutions embody different values. Moral ambiguity and conflict are everywhere. In the American context this conflict is no more evident than in the debate over abortion. Believing in the humanity and sanctity of the life of the fetus, a belief drawn from their religious communities, many conservative Christians form picket lines outside abortion clinics to protest with words and gestures the killing of unborn children. Across the street, stressing the values of freedom and the sovereignty of the individual over her own body—values that are embedded in American culture, religion, and politics—an equally vocal group of Christians seeks to protect the right of women to choose. Each group claims that the weight of morality is on its side.

CREDIT: FIBONACCI BLUE

Protest against Planned Parenthood.

Sometimes the moral conflict and ambiguity occurs within us. This is often referred to as **moral perplexity**. When faced with an ethical choice or dilemma, we are often unsure of which course of action to take. We cannot make one choice over another without experiencing some moral blame. For example, a Congressional representative may vote in favor of closing a military base in her district because she feels it is in the best interests of the community or country as a whole. The closing, however, may result in some dislocation or joblessness within her district. When she returns home, she may question the moral worth of her decision when visited by her unemployed constituents and their families.

The moral perplexity we experience often arises from the competing values or obligations that social and institutional locations place upon us. They demand commitment and loyalty. For example, imagine that you work as a resident assistant (RA) for a small Catholic college. One of the requirements of being an RA is to provide educational programs for the students living in the residence hall. Several of the other RAs want to have a program on contraception because most of the students have become sexually active and want to know the best ways to prevent unwanted pregnancies and sexually transmitted diseases (STDs). As a Catholic you accept the church's teaching on the inappropriateness of artificial forms of birth control and sex before marriage because they violate the procreative purpose of sexuality. Although you agree that an unwanted pregnancy or STD would be a terrible burden for a college student to bear, you feel that providing a program on contraception would suggest to students that having sex without intending procreation is morally acceptable.

All the RAs except you vote to have the program and, because you are an RA, you are expected to participate in the planning and implementation of the program. What should you do? Regardless of the choice you make, you are likely to feel conflicted or to experience guilt. These feelings illustrate the difficulty of resolving the moral conflicts created by competing values and loyalties.

RELIGIOUS ETHICS

Religions provide not only a worldview but also an ethos, a way of being in and relating to the world. They present their followers with a way of life that is considered to be in keeping with the ultimate ordering of life. Religious ritual is one aspect of this ethos; religious ethics is another. The connection with the ultimate or sacred ordering is a central dimension of religious ethics. Historian of religion Joachim Wach (1898–1955) suggests:

> To recognize an order in the universe (as profound religious experience would prompt man to do) means that in his every act man would strive to sustain that order. Where this order is interpreted as an expression of a divine will, the divine commands will have to be obeyed. They may be obeyed because they are commands, because they promise rewards, because they are believed to be conducive to well-being, success, or happiness, and finally because they are deemed to be expressive of the nature of the Supreme Reality.[1]

If, as a result of religious experience, we see an order in the universe, we would in all our actions strive to sustain, enhance, or restore that order. Thus, religion can become a fundamental source for our ethics.

In today's secular society we may not see the intricate connection between religion and ethics clearly. We may agree with Sam Harris,

Christopher Hitchens, and other so-called new atheists who contend that religion and ethics are really separate and distinct human endeavors that do not necessarily go together. It may be possible (or from the perspective of new atheists preferable) for us to have ethics without religion. In support of our view we can point to numerous ethical decisions we have made that had nothing to do with our religious beliefs. We tell the truth because we feel that lying undermines the possibility for genuine relationships. We tutor disadvantaged children in reading and math because we think that all children deserve a good education regardless of economic status. What do these actions have to do with religion? The answer may be nothing or everything, depending upon the source of these underlying values.

While it may be possible to have ethics without religion, we would contend that the reverse is not true. Religions help people focus on or provide answers to human questions of ultimacy, including questions about morality: What should I do? What kind of person should I be? How should I relate to others and to the nonhuman world? Religions suggest possible answers to these questions based upon their perceptions of the ultimate ordering of life. Thus, what distinguishes secular morality—ethical ideals or norms without conscious religious support—from religious ethics is that the latter are grounded in some perception of ultimacy or sacred ordering.

Thinking about Religious Ethics

As a way of seeing whether or not you have done religious ethics, do the following exercise. First, think about an ethical situation you faced recently. Write the situation out in a paragraph or two. Then write what decision you made or what course of action you took in this situation. When you are finished, look at your decision or action and ask yourself the following questions: Why did you take this course of action? What beliefs and/or values motivated your action? List those beliefs and values as completely as you are able. Now, looking at your list of values and beliefs, put a mark next to those that came in full or in part from the religious tradition or community in which you grew up. The religious dimension can be from parents or directly from the religious organization. How much did your religious background influence the moral action you took? To the extent that your religious background influenced you, you have done religious ethics.

RELIGION AS A SOURCE OF ETHICS

In discussing the relationship between religion and morality in the Jewish and Christian traditions, religious ethicist John Reeder contends that religions attempt to synthesize the worldview and ethos of the religious community, providing the moral order with its source, its sanction, and its goal or salvation.[2] Religions provide the norms for both conduct and character for their practitioners. By advocating particular moral principles, laws, and virtues, religions prescribe what religious people and communities should do and the kind of people they should become. Thus, they encompass both moral doing and being.

Moreover, religions sanction particular ways of doing and being as most in keeping with the perceived ultimate ordering in the universe. Religions help their practitioners to believe that their way of living in relationship to one another and to the world is not simply what ought to be but also what is "really real." How many children have been told that the reason they should respect their parents is because this is what the Bible says? By invoking the name of the sacred text, parents declare that this is not simply what they think is good behavior, but also what God wants. The reverse is also true: acting contrary to what the Bible says can bring about divine judgment. Such examples are a part of what sociologists of religion define as religion's legitimating role, an explanation and justification of society's moral order. The moral authority that religions assert may be oppressive or liberating or both. Regardless, religions enable people to answer the question of why a particular moral order is in place.

Often, this legitimation comes in the form of a religious community's founding myths. Recall the Indian and Iroquois creation myths discussed in Chapter 1, the Purusa Sukta and the Haudenosaunee creation story. Both accounts provide not only understanding of how the world came to be but also some indication of the moral world their respective communities inhabit. The first account, Purusa Sukta, has been used historically by Hindus to justify a particular social order, the caste system of India. There are four castes identified in the myth: the Brahman (priests), the Rajanya (warriors/rulers), the Vaisya (merchants/artisans), and the Sudra (unskilled workers). These castes are hereditary; one remains in the particular caste into which one is born. These castes also have specific religious and moral duties and responsibilities associated with them, known as dharma. This is important because these duties connect to the religious understanding of **reincarnation** and karma. Reincarnation refers to the cycle of birth and rebirth in which all creatures are enmeshed. Karma refers to the cause-and-effect nature of the universe. By fulfilling the duties associated with one's caste faithfully, a person generates good karma, and will be rewarded by a better life upon rebirth. Failure to fulfill one's duties has the opposite effect. This connection, in effect, justifies or legitimates the caste system. Those born into higher castes deserve their status because they have earned it by their good deeds; those born into lower castes deserve their position as well.

This example not only illustrates how religion sanctions morality, but it also points to the third tie that Reeder suggests exists between religion and morality: salvation. The religious goal—salvation, liberation, enlightenment—is often achieved as a result of moral actions. By fulfilling the responsibilities of dharma, the religious and moral duties associated with each caste, Hindus believe they will attain higher positions and social status in future lives. Ultimately, they are able to break free of the cycle of birth and rebirth through the three paths noted in Chapter 1. It is the path of karma marga, the path of works, that most people follow. Works include religious as well as moral duties, but fulfilling one's moral responsibilities is required as well in order to achieve the goal of Hinduism.

To suggest that religious traditions are the source, sanction, and goal of religious ethical action does not necessarily answer the moral questions that concern us. We want to know what we should do and what kind of persons we should be. How does religion help us here? From the examples given above, it is clear that religion provides particular norms for human conduct and human character. The next two sections focus on the norms religions provide.

NORMS FOR MORAL CONDUCT

For many of us, thinking about morality and ethics occurs most when deciding what we ought to do in specific contexts or situations. Religious ethicists call this the ground level of reflection, trying to discern the appropriate action in the heat of the moment. It is this question of "oughtness" that leads many to suggest that our primary experience of ethics is as an ethics of obligation. When we seek to act morally we are looking for particular norms or principles to guide our action. As the source and sanction of ethical action, religions have provided such norms for the ethical and moral action of their followers. These norms are generally of two types: laws and ends. They may appear singly or in some combination in different religious traditions. In all cases, however, followers experience these norms as obligations; they are expectations that followers must abide by in their lives.

LAW

For many of us, our early moral experiences are with laws or rules. In response to the basic moral question, What should I do? we ask, What is the relevant rule, principle, or law? Using our reason, we discern which rule applies, and we follow the appropriate rule. What makes the action right is that our behavior conforms to the rule. The virtue that is praised here is the virtue of obedience; the actor is obeying the moral law in this situation.

Clearly, this approach to ethics is nonconsequential; that is, one abides by the rule, law, or principle regardless of the consequences. For example, those who oppose abortion for religious reasons point to the sanctity of human life as a fundamental, God-given, principle. From this they derive a basic rule or law: it is morally impermissible to do any action that undermines the sanctity of human life. Abortion violates this principle and is, therefore, an immoral practice. Abortion opponents may agree that having a child may be financially ruinous for the person or the family involved. They may feel sympathy for the woman who does not want the child and offer counseling on adoption. The bottom line, however, is that the consequences for the woman or the family or even society are ultimately immaterial. What matters, abortion opponents argue, is that the child has a fundamental right to life, and we ought to respect that right.

In modern moral philosophy, law as the norm for moral action is connected with the experience of duty. Most people, at one time or another, experience ethical action in the form of duty. In our relationships with others we develop certain obligations and responsibilities that people expect us to fulfill. Sometimes we may not want to meet those expectations. Fulfilling our obligations may not be enjoyable, or we might prefer to do something else. Yet we keep our obligations because we know it is the right thing to do. For example, we make a promise to a friend that we will help her move into her new apartment on Saturday afternoon. Saturday morning, another friend calls to say she has free passes to an afternoon movie matinee and asks us to join her. Our preference that morning is to go to the movie; the weather is rainy, and we really want to see that movie. Because of our promise to our other friend, however, we decline the invitation and spend the day moving furniture and getting wet. By keeping our promise, we have done our duty. Duty is often understood in contrast to inclinations to do differently. In fact, it is the presence of these other inclinations and desires that make duty so forceful.

Many researchers in religious ethics refer to this dimension of religion as code. As we see in the examples of the Ten Commandments, the Five Precepts, and the Golden Rule, many religions codify the ethical actions they prescribe. Why? Part of the reason is that codes are easy to remember and are helpful in the moral socialization process. Children growing up morally can learn a set of rules or codes that they can cherish. Many children in the Jewish and Christian traditions can recite the Ten Commandments; many more can recite the Golden Rule. Codes also embody the collective wisdom of the group or the deity. If the worldview and the ethos of a community are mutually reinforcing, then we can expect that a rule expresses the community's wisdom regarding how life ought to be lived.

THE FIVE PRECEPTS
(Buddhism)

I undertake to observe the rule to abstain from taking life; to abstain from taking what is not given; to abstain from sensuous misconduct; to abstain from false speech; to abstain from intoxicants as tending to cloud the mind. (*Buddhist scriptures*)

THE GOLDEN RULE
(Christianity)

Do to others what you want them to do to you. (Mt 7:12)

THE TEN COMMANDMENTS
(Judaism and Christianity)

You shall have no other gods before me.
You shall not make for yourself an idol.
You shall not make wrongful use of the name of the Lord your God.
Remember the Sabbath day, and keep it holy.
Honor your father and your mother.
You shall not murder.
You shall not commit adultery.
You shall not steal.
You shall not bear false witness against your neighbor.
You shall not covet your neighbor's possessions. (Ex 20:2–17)

Theistic religions (those that believe in a transcendent being or beings) see the moral order in the universe as coming from that being(s). Two important ways the transcendent being makes the moral order known are by issuing divine commands and by revealing divine character. Most theistic religions have elements of a divine command moral system; the moral rules or principles are directly related to the commands of the deity. This idea is captured in the Hebrew scriptures in various places, including the prophet Micah: "He has told you, O mortal, what is good; and what does the Lord require of you but to do justice, and to love kindness, and to walk humbly with your God?" (Mi 6:8). Obedience to the divine command is considered the fundamental expression of one's religious piety and devotion.

Of course, people have questioned the validity of a divine command as a basis for morality. In his dialogue *Euthyphro*, Plato suggests two possible ways of construing the connection with the deity: either God commands a certain act because it is right, or an act is right because God commands it. If the former is true, then the basic standard of morality is logically independent of God's commands. In the context of the biblical passage quoted above, God requires followers to do justice and to love kindness because justice and kindness are good in and of themselves. Divine revelation or authority ("He has told you . . . what is good") may provide the basis for understanding these moral duties or the motivation for accepting and doing them. Yet, they would still be good even if God did not require them. If an act is right because God commands it, on the other hand, then there is no independent reason to do what God commands except that God commands it, which, for some, makes morality seem arbitrary. For example, if God required injustice and cruelty of followers, then justice and kindness would lose their moral value. Certainly we can point to numerous religious texts and stories that make the deity seem capricious. Whatever we may think about divine-command theory, however, should not keep us from exploring those religious groups that affirm divine command as a foundation for ethics.

Related to divine command is divine character. One of the ways in which theistic religions connect their moral laws with the ultimate moral ordering in the universe is by suggesting that the deity reflects these laws in its own being. In the Deuteronomic code—which includes the Ten Commandments—found in the Hebrew Bible, the people of Israel are commanded to care for the sojourner, the widow, the orphan, the poor, and all of the marginalized members of the community. Part of the rationale for this is because it reflects the same care and concern that God expressed for the Hebrew people when they were enslaved in Egypt. Similarly, in the prophetic literature, the call for the people to embody justice, righteousness, and steadfast love is a call to imitate their God. In the words of the psalmist, "Gracious is the Lord, and righteous; our God is merciful" (Ps 116:5).

In the case of divine command, the moral question, What should I do? is answered by the question, What does the deity command? Then the person performs the action that follows the appropriate command. Here again, obedience is the primary virtue. We may know some religious people who have this approach to ethics. When confronted with a moral situation, they pause to pray, asking what God would want them to do. One of the appeals of this ethical stance is that it provides a measure of certainty about their moral action, connecting it with the ultimate moral ordering. If they can discern what God commands, through Bible study or prayer, then the moral decision-making seems relatively simple. They can do what God commands without regard for the consequences of their actions.

Some would contend that Islamic ethics are an example of a divine-command moral system. This makes sense when you understand that the word *Islam* means "submission." Muslims are those who submit their life totally to the will of God. An action is not inherently right or wrong, but rather is either commanded or forbidden by God. The key is that Muslims submit all of their life to God, and the emphasis is on conformity to God's law. How do you know what God wants? The connection with the revealed dimension of religion becomes apparent. The divine will is revealed in the Qur'an, the sacred text of Islam, which has the status of the word of God. It is the ultimate judge between what is good and what is evil. Because the divine laws entailed in the Qur'an tend to be stated in general principles rather than detailed commands for specific situations, the need arose for specific interpretations. It was in this context that Islamic law, shari'ah, developed.

The *shari'ah* is a collection of interpretations and extrapolations from learned members of the Islamic community. It has its source in both the Qur'an and the *hadith*—the record of customs derived from the words and deeds of Muhammad—both of which are considered to be divinely inspired. Because the *shari'ah* is human interpretation, and humans cannot fully know and comprehend God's transcendent law, the *shari'ah* does not carry the same status as the Qur'an and is subject to debate among legal scholars. However, in Islamic societies it does carry the status of law, and people are expected to obey. The duties included are both individual and collective. The actions are further divided into five categories: obligatory, recommended but not obligatory, permitted, disapproved, and forbidden.

Even though much of ethical thinking is duty oriented, and thus rules and principles are critical, people continue to be frustrated with moral rules. The source of their frustration is often that rules seem to be restrictive and oppressive. People contend that many rules lose sight of the bigger picture or do not always apply in a given situation. However, many religious traditions affirm rules and laws because they are grateful for the guidance. This is expressed in the Jewish notion, "The reward for keeping one mitzvah is another!"

Not all religious affirmation of moral laws is in the form of divine-command theory. Many accept the difficulties of knowing exactly what the divine will is, even in sacred texts, and suggest that there is a significant set of rules or principles that people can know through the use of reason. These rules and principles represent the collective wisdom of the community, or are part of the structure of reality itself, and ought not to be violated easily. Moral action, then, is the action that conforms to the moral law that is discernible through the use of reason. This moral law has its foundation in divine law and thus has a connection with the transcendent moral order in the universe. This is certainly behind those systems of ethics that affirm **cosmic law** or **natural law**.

The concepts of cosmic and natural law enable us to comprehend the notion of a moral order in the universe. Certain ways of acting are more in keeping with that order than others. They contribute to balance and harmony. Acting contrary to that order causes chaos and disruption. Nontheistic religions (those that see the sacred as impersonal) suggest that the source of morality comes from some sense of order inherent in the cosmos. As the previous chapter noted, some Eastern religions, such as Hinduism, see a religious and moral law that governs all of life. Hinduism and Buddhism refer to this law as the dharma, although they have some different ideas about it. Chinese religions, including Confucianism and Taoism, refer to this cosmic law as **Tao,** which refers to the "way" or order that underlies all reality. Although there are spiritual and metaphysical aspects of the Tao, both religions stress the ethical dimensions of it. By discerning and following the Tao, individuals and society find the ethical guidance they need to live in harmony with nature and to achieve the ends they seek, including order, prosperity, and peace.

A well-known proponent of natural law was Saint Thomas Aquinas (1225–74). In the nineteenth century the Roman Catholic hierarchy found in Aquinas the basis for its moral and social norms. For Aquinas, law always has some good, generally the good of the individual or the community, in mind. Underlying all of the created order is the eternal law, through which God is guiding all things in the universe toward their intended end. This guidance has the significance of law. The natural moral law is that law embedded in all rational creatures—namely, humanity—that directs us toward our own right ends or good. We discover those ends by reflecting on human nature through the use of our reason. On the one hand, human beings share certain ends with other creatures, such as self-preservation, the union of males with females, and the education of offspring. On the other hand, as uniquely rational creatures, human beings also have a natural inclination to know the truth about God and to live in society. Once we have discovered those ends, then we can discern the means for achieving them. This understanding of God's intent for us, built into our nature by God's creative activity, Aquinas refers to as natural law. Thus, those rules or principles of reason that guide us to promote human good and avoid evil carry the weight of natural law. For example, most human societies have laws or principles against the unjustified killing of human beings. Many societies call such actions murder. For Aquinas, such laws are natural laws, because they preserve human life and do not harm it.

ENDS

The notion that somehow laws are in keeping with the order in the universe and reflect what is good for human life and flourishing leads to a second norm for ethical action: ends. As John Reeder notes, people often follow religions because of some goal: salvation, liberation, or the like. Many times, achieving those ends is dependent upon moral behavior. Human beings are valuing beings. This means that we have certain ideas about goods that we think make human life meaningful and worthwhile, and so we pursue those values. Codes, laws, and principles embody certain values deemed worthy on the part of the community. For example, the rule not to kill other persons embodies the notion that life is intrinsically valuable and not simply there for someone else's use.

The idea of acting morally to gain a desired goal or value is a common experience for us. As children, many of us acted a particular way deemed moral by our parents or other adults to gain some reward or to keep from being punished. The same is true for children when their moral action is tied to their religion. Children have done the right thing from a desire to gain God's blessing or out of fear that God would punish them if they did not. Of course, parents hope that eventually their children will act morally because of some other moral end, such as world peace, loving community, or justice. In other words, the ends are moral or a moral state of affairs.

The term most often used for this approach to ethical obligation is **teleology.** The word comes from the Greek word *telos*, which means "end." The response an ethics of ends provides to the moral question, What should I do? is, What ends am I seeking to achieve? What are the best means for achieving them? People then use the most efficient means for achieving their ends. Unlike law, the moral action has more to do with the actions themselves and their consequences than with the intention of the actions. That is why this approach has been labeled consequential. No matter how good the intention of the actor is, if the action does not result in the goal or end sought, the morality of the action is called into question. For example, a person stops to help an accident victim and in the process of helping ends up causing more serious injury. We understand and appreciate the intention of the helper, but we judge such actions by their consequences as well.

With regard to the goal of religious morality, John Reeder says that religions provide both moral ends and also ends that transcend morality. For example, the biblical record advocates the norms of justice and mercy because they will generate a specific kind of moral community, enabling all members of the community to experience meaningful, fulfilling, and moral lives. So visions of community are moral ends that require certain moral actions to achieve them. This understanding was evident in the Civil Rights movement in the United States. Martin Luther King, Jr., and others advocated nonviolent resistance as the means to achieve their end, the "beloved community." The beloved community entailed the norms of equality, justice, and peace for all. To achieve that end using means that were destructive was inappropriate. Violence was destructive of the very community they were hoping to achieve. Violence could not be accepted as a means to that end, and thus participants in the struggle were trained in the principles of nonviolent resistance.

In religious ethical action, the goal can also be the promise of a trans-moral state. When we Christians describe heaven, the goal of our religion, we often depict a state of being that is beyond morality. We envision a society where there are no wants or needs, where there is no sexuality, no economic relations, no political structures. We are tired of having to make moral decisions, of having to do the right thing, of having to be a particular type of person. For us, heaven means salvation and liberation from the trials and tribulations that the moral condition brings. We want a world where we no longer face moral decisions or questions. We want a return to the pre-moral bliss of childhood. Those who accept a particular reading of the second creation account in the Book of Genesis want a return to the Garden

Martin Luther King, Jr., addresses a large rally in front of the United Nations protesting the Vietnam War.

of Eden, before the man and the woman ate fruit from the tree of the knowledge of good and evil.

The goal of Buddhism is liberation from the suffering that is endemic to the cycle of birth and rebirth in the universe. People refer to this liberation as nirvana, a concept difficult to describe. In fact, most do so only negatively by describing what nirvana is not. It is the experience of nonbeing, the loss of self, the loss of desire and craving. Clearly, critical to achieving the experience of nirvana is to follow the **Eightfold Path,** which will be discussed shortly. Some of the actions required to achieve liberation are moral, such as not killing living creatures. In Mahayana Buddhism, the ideal person for entry into nirvana is the **bodhisattva,** a person who chooses to delay entry into this state in order to help all living creatures reach this end, a person full of compassion for others. Yet the goal of Buddhism clearly transcends morality. Breaking free from the cycle of birth and rebirth means breaking free from the human condition itself and all that it involves, including the moral condition.

One final way of looking at the teleological approach to religious ethics is to explore the metaphors of path, way, and road that are used by many religious traditions to speak of moral obligation. We often hear of moral action as action that is on the right path or going the right way. The image of path carries with it the notion of destination. Those who follow the path are seeking some end or goal; they are going somewhere for a purpose. One of the **Four Noble Truths** of Buddhism is that the end to suffering comes by following the Eightfold Path. This path consists of various religious and moral practices aimed at achieving this end. The end or goal determines the kind of actions deemed moral. The requirements of *sila* (morality) include right speech, right conduct, and right livelihood. Right speech refers to not speaking falsely about others. The notion of right conduct embodies the remainder of the Five Precepts: not killing, not stealing, not engaging in sexual immorality, and not using intoxicants. Right livelihood means not earning one's keep by work that violates these precepts, such as prostitution, pornography, or the sale of alcohol. The problem with each of these activities is that they lead to desiring and craving, the source of suffering in human life and the stumbling block to the goal of liberation from this suffering. Engaging in the activities leads to a perpetuation of the cycle of birth and rebirth. Thus, the path one follows is intricately connected to the destination at which one arrives.

Thinking about Moral Obligations

To help you grasp the notion of ends as moral obligation, write four or five of the most important goals in your life. Next to each of the goals, write what values are implicit in those goals. Do they reflect what you think is most important in life? Reviewing those goals and values, think of the ways that they determine the actions you do today. Do you choose some activities over others because they are more in keeping with your goals and values, even though you might want to do those other activities? Do you ever experience your decision to do certain activities as an obligation in that you feel you have to do those activities or you will not accomplish your goals? Do you ever feel remorse or regret when you fail to do those actions you know are in keeping with your goals or values?

NORMS FOR MORAL CHARACTER

Discussion of moral norms limits our focus to the actions themselves, the *doing* of ethics. We also make moral judgments about people, however, as when we say someone is a moral or ethical person. When we make these judgments, we are making judgments about character, the *being* of an ethical person or community. Being and doing are obviously related. It is because a person is a certain type of character that we know that he or she will do a certain type of action. The difference is that the moral judgment of character focuses more on the inner motivations—the traits, habits, or dispositions a person has to act a certain way—than on the actions themselves. For example, when we say that someone is a good person or has a moral character, we are declaring that when moral situations arise, that person tends to do the right thing, the moral thing. Good people are predisposed to act in moral ways because they have a certain way of being in the world. Often our description of those persons includes various virtues or emotional traits, such as compassion, caring, wisdom, or courage. In part, we determine our moral character is determined by us, by the choices and decisions we have made over the years that shape our moral orientations and perspectives. In part our moral character is determined by our environment, the social, cultural, and institutional contexts in which we grow up.

For many of us, one of the environmental influences on our moral character is religion. Religious morality generally speaks as much about character as it does about conduct. For example, in Yoruba religion, ethics is best described by the term *character (iwa)*. The focus of Yoruba ethical teachings is on the essential nature or being of the person. People are either good characters or bad characters. To help us understand this aspect of religious ethics, we discuss three elements connected to the formation of moral character: moral development, moral conscience and consciousness, and moral affections and virtues. We conclude with a discussion of moral exemplars, those who embody the moral character deemed significant by their respective religious communities.

MORAL DEVELOPMENT

When we ponder the moral character of a person, we are making a judgment about the person at that particular moment. Moral character, however, has a history as well. The notion of moral development suggests that human beings are not born morally mature; rather, their capacity for moral and ethical action grows and develops gradually with their other capacities as they get older. For many, a key component of moral development is cognitive development, the reasoning process one uses to make judgments. For example, if we find a five-year-old boy and girl together exploring one another's genitalia, we generally do not judge them by the same standards of sexual ethics we might judge a sixteen-year-old boy and girl doing the same thing. The reason is that we feel that the five-year-olds do not know any better. Their cognitive capacity to understand their actions has not developed sufficiently to warrant such a judgment. We might use the opportunity to instruct them on appropriate versus inappropriate behavior with each other, but until they are older, we don't think they can fully understand the nature of their actions.

The concept of cognitive moral development is often mythically portrayed in religious traditions. Many creation myths regarding humanity reflect the movement from some pre-moral condition to the condition of morality. The second creation myth in Genesis can be seen in this light. Often, the second creation myth (Gen 2:4–23) is seen as a fall from some state of moral perfection to a state of moral imperfection. The Genesis story can also been seen as a story depicting the movement from a pre-moral state into a moral state. The prohibition against eating of the tree of knowledge of good and evil reflects that initially they related to one another without concepts of good and evil. They were in a state of childlike innocence. After eating the fruit, however—after desiring moral knowledge—they entered the moral condition. This is symbolized in their recognition of their nakedness. Their sexuality becomes conscious to them, and the need for moral structure (the fig leaf) enters into their cultural understandings. They begin the moral history of humanity. From that point forward, the direction of Genesis and Exodus can be seen as a movement to establish some moral dimensions to life, culminating in the giving of the Law at Sinai. The movement reflects the struggle of living within a moral universe.

MORAL CONSCIENCE OR CONSCIOUSNESS

Related to cognition is the notion of moral conscience or consciousness in moral development. Most people claim to have a conscience, some inner sense of what is right and wrong that leads them to do the right thing most of the time. This is implicit in such questions as, Didn't your conscience bother you?, which parents often ask children who have done something wrong. In fact, people who don't have a conscience are referred to as psychopaths or sociopaths. Some philosophical and religious traditions suggest that human beings are born with an innate moral sense. We have the capacity from birth to know the difference between right and wrong. Many identify this innate faculty as the conscience. It is a faculty that we believe is universal among people. When we suggest, "Let your conscience be your guide," we are assuming that people have the capacity for conscience and that it will lead them to do the right thing. In so doing, we imply some type of unity between moral knowing and moral doing.

There is some debate about whether or not this innate capacity for moral discrimination or conscience needs development. The Confucian philosopher Mencius suggests that people are basically good. If left to our natural inclinations, or allowed to follow the dictates of our conscience, we will do the right thing. Others are not so sure. They suggest that the conscience is shaped by our social and cultural location. Sigmund Freud suggested that the conscience, which he called the superego, is primarily the internalization of parental and societal restrictions that act to keep our sexual and aggressive tendencies in check. Theologian Walter Conn suggests that conscience is not simply some innate human faculty or the internalization of a moral code; rather, conscience refers to moral consciousness, a consciousness that can be informed, self-critical, and can move toward self-transcendence. Conscience enables moral consistency in that there is coherence between our moral knowing and moral doing. A person does not *have* a conscience, a person *is* a conscience.

An example from literature that illustrates the self-transcendent dimension of conscience can be found in Mark Twain's *Huckleberry Finn*. Huck helps Jim, Miss Watson's slave, escape into free territory. Throughout the experience Huck battles his conscience, a conscience formed by a community that accepted slavery as a way of life and labeled helping runaway slaves a crime. In a memorable scene after Jim's capture, when he was thought to be someone else's slave, Huck wrestles with his conscience over whether to write a letter to Miss Watson informing her of Jim's whereabouts. Huck ponders, "The more I studied about this the more my conscience went to grinding me, and the more wicked and low-down and ornery I got to feeling." He was afraid he might go to hell. He decides to pray but realizes that he cannot until he writes the letter. After doing so, he feels "clean of sin" for the first time in his life. Before praying, however, Huck reflects on the relationship he had developed with Jim in the course of their journey. He realizes Jim was more than a slave; Jim was his friend. Then he picks up the letter and reflects: "I was a-trembling, because I'd got to decide, forever, betwixt two things, and I knowed it. I studies a minute, sort of holding my breath, and then says to myself: 'All right, then, I'll go to hell'—and tore it up." For many who read this text, this marks a step in Huck's moral development, from unquestioned acceptance of society's norms to critical moral consciousness in the face of new experiences and insight (even if Huck's insight was fleeting and did not last).

Of course, it is important to realize that when we say our consciences ought to be self-critical—that we ought to include moral consciousness and awareness in our understanding of conscience—we need to be sure what this includes. What are the sources that inform and shape our consciences? Conn writes:

> While it may be true that a person must follow his own conscience, and I for one think it is, it will not be enough on that symbolic Day of Judgment for him to say, simply, "I followed my conscience." For . . . he will surely be asked not only how faithfully he *followed* his conscience, but also how authentically he *formed* it.[3]

Conn's point is that, when we judge people who claim to have followed their conscience, we have a normative view of conscience. It is not simply some faculty that everyone has. Rather, it is a moral consciousness that grows and develops and is always self-critical. This means that the mature conscience is always expanding and deepening its understanding by critical engagement with and openness toward various sources of moral wisdom and insight.

For example, some of the Nazi doctors who participated in Hitler's euthanasia program claimed they did so in good conscience. Karl Brandt, the chief medical administrator in Germany at the time, was charged with responsibility for carrying out various human experiments, including exploding a man's brains out of his ears in a high compression chamber. He spoke these words before the Nuremberg Tribunal:

> Somewhere we must all take a stand. I am fully conscious that when I said "Yes" to Euthanasia I did so with the deepest conviction, just as it is my conviction today, that it was right. . . . I bear a burden, but it is not the burden of crime. I bear this burden of mine, though with a heavy heart, as my responsibility. I stand before it, and *before my conscience* as a man and as a doctor (emphasis added).[4]

Even though they claimed good conscience, Brandt and other doctors were hanged for crimes against humanity. These doctors provided moral justification for their actions, citing both compassion for those unworthy of life and a commitment to the betterment of humanity. Before their conscience, they felt free of guilt. The decision to hang them for crimes against humanity reflects the judgment that they had not allowed their consciences to be fully or appropriately developed.

From the perspective of religious ethics, an informed conscience is always one that is shaped and open toward the wisdom that comes through the religious tradition, wisdom that has its source in some divine or transcendent order. When the prophet Jeremiah suggests that God will write his law upon the hearts of his people, the point is that the moral consciousness of the person will be directed by God. Similarly, the Jewish tradition contends that the study of written and oral Torah is the path to a fully formed conscience and a moral life. Both the impulse to do good and the impulse to do evil exist in the human heart. God has given the study of Torah as the antidote to the evil impulse.

For Buddhism, the moral conscience can find wisdom in the Five Precepts and the Eightfold Path. The Eightfold Path is a guide to action to achieve the goal of Buddhism: enlightenment. The first two precepts, right views and right aspiration, reflect the consciousness expected of persons seeking to live rightly. Right views means that one accepts the Four Noble Truths about the cause and cessation of suffering. One is not deceived by one's immediate desires and cravings but knows that desiring is the source of suffering in the world. Right views also means understanding that change and becoming—including the impermanence of the self—are at the heart of reality. Right aspiration, purpose, or thought means, negatively, freeing oneself from all sensual and material cravings and desires; positively, it means embracing thoughts of nonviolence, detachment, and compassion. These cognitive aspects of the Eightfold Path are a means to generating right living among people.

The notion of a conscience that is informed by religious tradition, a transcendent ordering in the universe, is reflected in the defense Martin Luther King, Jr., provides for breaking segregation laws in his "Letter from a Birmingham Jail." People wanted to know how King could advocate obeying some laws and not others. The answer he provided was that some laws were just and others were unjust. "Any law that uplifts human personality is just. Any law that degrades human personality is unjust." By recognizing a transcendent basis for law, King was suggesting that moral consciousness must be shaped by more than human convention. For King, the source of that transcendence was his religion. "A just law is a . . . code that squares with the moral law or the law of God." But in the practice of civil disobedience, to accept the penalty is not just to act on the individual's own conscience, it also has the goal of raising the moral consciousness of the community as well. "I submit that an individual who breaks a law that conscience tells him is unjust, who willingly accepts the penalty of imprisonment in order to arouse the conscience of the community over its injustice, is in reality expressing the highest respect for the law."[5]

EMOTIONS AND VIRTUES

At this point the reader may feel that the discussion about religious ethics and moral character has been too cognitive. Too much focus has been placed on the development of moral consciousness. Not all moral or ethical action, however, is the conscious action of applying moral codes to specific contexts. Some psychologists, such as Jonathan Haidt, even suggest that moral intuition, which comes from the unconscious mind, precedes moral reasoning.[6] When a moral situation arises that calls for action, we simply respond without conscious reflection. It is a part of who we are. Very often, our ethical action flows from the moral dispositions, feelings, and virtues that constitute our character. For example, when we come across a child who is hurt and there are no other adults around, our immediate response is to attend to the needs of the child. We do not ask ourselves whether we should help or not, or what moral principle applies in this situation. Instead, we respond from our hearts with compassion because we have become caring people.

The power of emotions or affections that religions instill within us is that they can move us from indifference to action. They can be the motivations or triggers that lead us to put our beliefs or dispositions into action. Many ethicists have seen this power in the moral affection known as empathy or sympathy, which some evolutionary biologists believe is one of the building blocks of human morality. Sympathy is fellow feeling, an affective identification with the situation of others, especially situations that involve sorrow or suffering. Our ability to feel someone else's pain or suffering is often a precondition for us to do something to relieve it. Without sympathy, we may never get interested enough to act even if, as some contend, such empathy does not always lead us to moral action (in other words, it may be a necessary but not sufficient condition). For example, in 1985, a group of musicians, aware of the plight of the people in several African nations, spawned the USA for Africa campaign, which continues to this day. They were "moved," "affected" to the point of action on behalf of those in need. One might argue that they became aware of their obligation to all of humanity because we live in an interdependent world. Some of the words in the song they dedicated to this work, "We Are the World," may affirm this interpretation. Or one could say that a sense of guilt or shame for the situation in Africa was responsible. For some this is surely true. But to hear the originators of the program tell it, what moved them was their concern for hungry people, their identification with the pain and suffering these Africans were experiencing, an affective response that we would identify as sympathy. The source of the response of millions of people to provide aid and assistance when a natural catastrophe strikes a community, such as the earthquake in Haiti, the Christmas Day tsunami in Asia, or the floods caused by hurricane Katrina, can also be identified as sympathy.

Within the Jewish and Christian traditions, the human capacity for sympathy has been a mediator or symbol for construing the experience of the sacred. Many key myths and symbols portray God as a sympathetic power. The Bible contains numerous stories about God's intervention on behalf of the lowly and the poor who have cried out to God. The biblical account of the Exodus suggests that God heard the cries of the Hebrew slaves and was moved to act to liberate them from their bondage in Egypt. "The Israelites groaned under their slavery, and . . . their cry for help rose up to God. God heard their groaning . . . and God took notice of them" (Ex 2:23–25). The covenant law called upon the Israelites to care for the stranger and the sojourner, for they can identify and sympathize with what it is like to be strangers and sojourners. "You shall not oppress a resident alien; you know the heart of an alien, for you were aliens in the land of Egypt" (Ex 23:9). The Christian tradition's understanding of the person and work of Jesus the Christ is that God identifies with our sufferings and sin and acts decisively to redeem us. "For God so loved the world that he gave his only Son, so that everyone who believes in him may not perish but may have eternal life" (Jn 3:16). Even today, many Jews and Christians conceive of God as being concerned for their well-being.

Emotions can also lead us to restrict our actions. We often experience emotions when we do the right thing *or* when we go against the dictates of our conscience. In the former instance, we may feel pride, joy, or contentment; in the latter case, we may feel guilt or shame. Our emotions lead us to do some self-assessment or assessment of others. We take stock of ourselves, see what things need to change, and act to make those changes. (Of course, we may deny the wrongdoing and repress the feelings, which, psychologists tell us, can lead to a variety of unhealthy behaviors.) The point is that the emotions we experience are the triggers. When someone else does something wrong, we may feel anger or outrage at the person or events. For example, whenever we feel unfairly treated, we experience a sense of anger at the person who, we feel, has mistreated us. We are suggesting that this person has violated an important value in the life of the community. Here, again, the emotions trigger a response on our part or on the part of the community.

Within indigenous religious traditions this connection between emotions and moral judgment is seen in the concept of taboo. Ethicist John Ansah tells us that in some African cultures, taboos form an extremely important part of their ethical code. "They are charged with a high degree of religious fervor, being associated with divine power."[7] By claiming something is taboo, the community generates such an emotionally charged aura around the action that the breaking of the taboo can trigger emotions of shame or guilt on the part of the individual and outrage or abhorrence on the part of the community. For example, taboos associated with sexual conduct are so highly respected that deviations from them are deeply detested. This level of emotion is understandable when we realize that, in the African worldview, such offenses can have disastrous consequences for the society as a whole, such as epidemics, drought, or famine.

In addition to moral feelings, religious traditions emphasize virtues as norms for moral character. Many of us have a narrow concept of virtue. We see virtue primarily as a type of self-restraint, especially with regard to human wants and desires. We are virtuous when we do not give in to our seemingly insatiable desires for fame, fortune, and sex. The dictionary reflects this view when it includes "chastity, especially in a woman," as one of the definitions of virtue. But the basic moral meaning of virtue signifies strength, power, and excellence. Moral virtues are certain excellences, skills, habits, and traits that develop over time and that dispose us, intellectually and emotionally, to act in ways that are in keeping with our understanding of the moral ordering in the world. Not only do virtues make us ready to act in morally good ways, they make it easy for us to do so; it becomes part of our nature. Virtues also generate emotions of joy and intrinsic satisfaction when we act morally, thereby reinforcing these moral habits. If we have developed the virtue of generosity, we readily and easily act generously when the opportunity arises, and we feel happy when we do.

As conceptions of the good life or moral order differ among religious communities, so do their accounts of the virtues. The Greeks affirmed four virtues: wisdom, courage, temperance, and justice. When acquired, these virtues enabled persons to find happiness. Christianity stressed these same moral virtues but added the theological virtues of faith, hope, and love, which all people need to find their true happiness in God. These virtues are infused into believers by the Spirit of God working within them. In Buddhism the virtues include self-restraint and compassion, which lead to enlightenment for the self and others. The Yoruba religious tradition of Africa upholds the virtues of honesty and loyalty because of their significance for maintaining relationship and community.

One way religious communities contribute to the cultivation of virtue is through their stories of what the good life or moral ordering is all about and the virtues or "habits of the heart" needed to achieve salvation. For example, the Gospel of Luke includes the story about the good Samaritan. In this story a man asks Jesus what he needs to achieve salvation. Jesus tells him that salvation is achieved through living out the twofold command to love God and to love one's neighbor. The man responds with a question, seeking to limit his ethical obligations: "Who is my neighbor?" Instead of answering this question, Jesus responds with the story of the good Samaritan, a story that stresses the moral character of the hero over the fulfillment of the commandment. Briefly, three individuals encounter someone who has been robbed and beaten and is lying by the roadside. The good Samaritan is the one who stops and goes out of his way to ensure that the victim receives the care and assistance needed to restore him to health. After telling the story, Jesus asks which of the three persons who passed by embodied the norms of love and care essential to being a neighbor. It is the Samaritan who is the neighbor; it flows from his being because he has the covenant written on his heart.

It is not always easy to differentiate between moral affections and virtues. For example, compassion is an emotion that a person may feel for others, but it is also a habitual response on the part of a person. It is cultivated over time and held up as a virtue by various religious traditions, especially Buddhism. In Buddhist scriptures the **Buddha** exemplified his deep sympathy and compassion for the sufferings that all living things experience: in the face of temptation by the Evil One (Mara) to disappear into nirvana at the time of his enlightenment, the Buddha delayed so that he could teach the path of enlightenment to others. In doing so the Buddha modeled the depth of compassion that all Buddhists should emulate.

In Mahayana Buddhism compassion becomes a central moral trait. Mahayana Buddhists are critical of Theravada Buddhists, who hold up what appears to be a selfish ideal, the arhant (worthy one) who achieves enlightenment in monastic isolation. By contrast, Mahayana Buddhists point to the pattern of life exemplified in bodhisattvas (Buddhas-to-be), who sacrifice their own welfare through countless lives out of compassion for the suffering of other living creatures. Moreover, they postpone their own liberation until all are liberated. In many ways bodhisattvas are like ship captains who will not leave a sinking ship until they are sure that all of the passengers and crew are safely on lifeboats.

Guanyin, pictured in this statue in Dali, China, is a key heavenly bodhisattva to whom many Chinese Buddhists pray for compassion and mercy.

FRED GLENNON

One final element that must be stressed here is that all communities charge certain institutions or groups with the task of assisting others in their character formation. In the United States the family is given the primary role for the moral development and character formation of children. This is one reason why so many people contend that the rise in immoral behavior is directly related to the dysfunction of many families, which for various reasons no longer provide the moral training needed to develop moral children. Others argue that, while families play an important and even central role, moral development is the responsibility of the whole community. The African proverb that it takes a village to raise a child reflects this perspective. Thus, many communities charge their schools with the task of values education as well as academic preparation, including a community-service requirement for graduation to stress the importance of service to others.

Religions have played and continue to play a significant role in moral development in many cultures. They are communities of character. Alexis de Tocqueville noticed how religion cultivated "habits of the heart"—habits that included benevolence and concern for others—that limited the effects of growing self-interest and excessive consumption taking place in the nineteenth-century United States.[8] Today, the various religious traditions struggle to continue that tradition. Religious instruction by lay and clergy leaders at churches, synagogues, mosques, and temples also includes instruction in the ethical obligations and virtues cherished by those traditions. Similarly, in African Traditional Religion communities, while the locus of moral development and character formation is with the family, the religious leaders are also given responsibility for the moral development of children. Rituals associated with initiation into adulthood include instruction in the proper use of sexuality and other adult responsibilities.

MORAL EXEMPLARS

Moral exemplars are those persons or communities that live a life deemed preeminently moral. They most fully embody the norms of conduct and character advocated by the community. Many religious communities hold up their founders as moral exemplars in their scriptures. The Qur'an describes Muhammad as "a fine example" (33:22), full of "high moral excellence" (68:4). We noted the model provided by the Buddha above. Some would contend that this general attitude of compassion holds the same status as *agape* (love) for Christians. Jesus describes the nature of this love in the Gospel of John: "No one has greater love than this, to lay down one's life for one's friends" (Jn 15:13). Here again, Christians recognize that the best exemplar of this love is Jesus. The notion of moral exemplar or ethical model may be reflected either in a specific individual or group, or in a way of life that is highly esteemed by the tradition. In both instances what is key is that people live out the life they believe is right and good. They model that way of life in their own actions, and that way of life is deemed to be ultimately connected to sacred orderings.

Wangari Maathai (1940–2011), 2004 Nobel Laureate from Kenya, is a good example of a contemporary moral exemplar. Her life's work was influenced by the religious and spiritual traditions of her youth.[9] Although born to peasant parents during the time of British rule in Kenya, she was nurtured in a cultural worldview that spoke about the beauty, splendor, and sacredness of the land and the interdependence of all life within it; and she grew up in a family where women were respected with the same rights and responsibilities as men. Her family made sure that she was educated; taught by Catholic missionary nuns at a girls' high school, she went on to earn a bachelor's degree in biological sciences at what is now known as Benedictine College (Kansas), a master's degree from the University of Pittsburgh, and a Ph.D. (the first woman in east and central Africa to do so) from the University of Nairobi in 1971, where she taught and became chair of a department.

In the 1970s Professor Maathai became active in a variety of environmental and humanitarian organizations. Through this work she came into contact with poor rural women in Kenya, where she learned about the horrible environmental and social conditions they faced—where wood for cooking and heating, clean water, and food were becoming scarce. It was then that a confluence of her spiritual and educational formation came to fruition in the Green Belt movement that was formerly established in 1977. Although Maathai had encountered and practiced various forms of Christianity over the years, she was deeply saddened by the ways in which colonialism and narrow Christian views became inextricably linked—views that saw nature merely as a resource for humanity to be dominated, used, and abused and where the rights of women became subordinated to the power of men. Her own reading of the creation accounts of Genesis led her to reject the domination-of-nature motif and instead affirmed the goodness of the created order and the responsibility of humanity to replenish the earth for the sake of all creatures. Moreover, her education at the hands of Catholic sisters and monks provided numerous examples of the significance of service to others and taught her about the importance of justice for all people, especially the poor and the marginalized.

The mission of the Green Belt movement, a grassroots tree-planting program, is to restore respect for the land and the development and rights of women by addressing the challenges of deforestation, soil erosion, and the lack of water while also empowering women throughout Africa to become stewards of their natural environment. Participants in the movement embody the virtues of honesty, accountability, and hard work. Underlying these virtues are four core values: love for the environment, respect and gratitude for earth's resources, self-empowerment and self-betterment, and cultivating the spirit of service and volunteerism. Maathai likened her work to a three-legged African stool:

Wangari Maathai receiving honorary doctorate and delivering commencement speech at Le Moyne College, 1992.

LE MOYNE COLLEGE ARCHIVES

The first leg stands for democratic space, where rights are respected, whether they are human rights, women's rights, children's rights, or environmental rights. The second represents sustainable and equitable management of resources. And the third stands for cultures of peace that are deliberately cultivated within communities and nations. . . . Unless all three legs are in place, supporting the seat, no society can thrive.[10]

In awarding her the Nobel Peace prize in 2004, the first African woman and the first environmentalist to receive the honor, the committee highlighted her status as a moral exemplar: "She represents an example and a source of inspiration for everyone in Africa fighting for sustainable development, democracy and peace." Upon hearing about this award, Maathai faced Mt. Kenya, the sacred ground that was the source of inspiration throughout her life, which she felt was celebrating with her.

When asked whether it was religion or spirituality that motivated her actions, she indicated that her early focus was often pragmatic—a desire to work for justice and to restore the natural resources of her native Kenya. Yet upon reflection she realized that it was a deep and abiding affirmation of the spiritual over the material dimensions of life that shaped all that she did. She recognized that none of the core values of the Green Belt movement belongs to one faith tradition more than any other; indeed, someone can adhere to these values without being particularly religious or holding onto one particular creed. Rather, she came to the belief that these values were spiritual because they cultivated those dimensions of humanity that seek more than material comfort, power, or worldly success. They are what give our lives value and meaning, and inspire us. "We cannot tire or give up. We owe it to the present and future generations of all species to rise up and walk."[11]

SOCIAL ETHICS

Thus far, the discussion has focused on moral or ethical action for individuals seeking to be faithful to their religious tradition and to uphold or create the moral order within that tradition. Religious ethics, however, are also social ethics in that they relate to the way institutions and societies organize and structure themselves. Like interpersonal ethics, social ethics address the moral order within the community. Social ethics provide norms for both the ethical action and character of social institutions. Religious social ethics have become increasingly important as we have become a more global, interdependent world. Many of the ethical challenges that face us today are global in nature. Economic life—development, employment, income distributions, and so on—within and across nations is affected positively and negatively by changes in global financial, capital, and labor markets. Environmental degradation or accidents in one part of the globe—destruction of the Amazon rain forests, overfishing of the seas, oil and nuclear disasters in the Gulf of Mexico and Japan—can have ramifications for the health and well-being of human and non-human species. Disease and other health-related problems—the AIDS epidemic, the spread of the H1N1 virus, E. coli food contaminations—are more difficult to contain and require global solutions. Religious leaders within and in partnership with other religious communities are drawing upon their faith traditions to highlight and further develop ethical frameworks that address these and other social ethical concerns.

One of the more notable attempts at developing this ecumenical ethical framework is the interfaith declaration of a "global ethic," which was drafted by Catholic theologian Hans Küng and endorsed by more than two hundred religious leaders and forty faith communities at the 1993 Parliament of World Religions, sponsored by the Council for a Parliament of the World's Religions (CPWR), begun in 1893. The CPWR began as an effort to cultivate harmony among the world's religious communities. A fundamental way of doing this, it contends, is to draw from their traditions to foster their engagement with the world and its guiding institutions in order to achieve their vision of a just, peaceful, and sustainable world. There are four broad principles to this global ethic: (1) commitment to a culture of nonviolence and respect for life, (2) commitment to a culture of solidarity and a just economic order, (3) commitment to a culture of tolerance and a life of truthfulness, and (4) commitment to a culture of equal rights and partnership between men and women. Since this declaration hundreds of other religious leaders and communities have signed on to this global ethic.

As can be seen from their vision and principles, two key ethical principles are operative in this and any social ethic: a conception of justice and a vision of community. When we use the word *justice,* we are often unclear about its meaning. More often we are clearer about what is unjust more than what is just. Justice as a norm for social institutions often centers on the notion of distributive justice. Distributive justice refers to the proper distribution of the social benefits and burdens that society generates; because society has benefits and burdens to distribute, they have to be distributed fairly. Aristotle argued that distributive justice requires treating equals alike and treating unequals differently. For example, a community seeking to reduce the pollution produced by local manufacturing plants decides to enact an equal tax on those plants to encourage them to reduce the pollution they emit and to pay for the costs to the community such pollution generates. One plant, however, has invested in technology to reduce such pollutants, and so the community reduces its tax liability. Deciding what is a fair or just distribution requires that we understand the appropriate criteria by which the goods are distributed.

In Hindu caste society, and in European feudal society, a legitimate criterion for the distribution of society's benefits and burdens was ascription. What this means is that certain benefits and burdens follow one's station or status in the community. Recalling the Vedic creation account from Chapter 1, we see that certain rewards went with being born to the Brahman, or highest, caste. Members of the caste had certain privileges, opportunities, and responsibilities that went along with their position in society. The distribution of society's goods that favored them was considered just and fair because it was in keeping with the moral order inherent in the universe, an order that is hierarchical.

By contrast, the Jewish and Christian traditions speak about a distribution of goods based upon need and equality. The justice of a community or society depended upon all members of the community having their basic needs met, especially the poor and the marginalized. By providing equally for their needs, the community would undergird their basic equality before God and with other members of the community. A similar conception of justice is embedded in the global ethic espoused by the CPWR's emphasis on solidarity and a just economic order.

As with personal ethical obligations, the right action, justice as law, may be connected to a specific goal or end. For the many religious traditions that endorsed the global ethic, justice is connected to a vision of community, a community in which all members participate meaningfully in society and in which the well-being of all is assured. It is a vision of community that fully values all persons, particularly those who are marginalized. This collective sense of well-being is often referred to as the common good.

The common good has been a critical component of official Catholic social thought in recent times. The common good refers to the communal nature of human existence. Humans were created for community and not for isolation, and this means that the good of each person is bound up with the good of the community. Catholic teaching contends that the common good is a social reality in which all persons should share through their participation in it. On the one hand, participation means that each person should contribute to the common good to the best of his or her abilities, not simply attend to individual goods. It is a part of each person's moral obligation. On the other hand, participation means that all persons in the community should benefit from the enhancement of the common good. In his encyclical *Mater et magistra* (1961), Pope John XXIII (1881–1963) says that the common good is "the sum total of conditions of social living, whereby persons are enabled more fully and readily to achieve their own perfection" (no. 65). Unless everyone shares in the benefits of social advance, the common good can be a source of domination and exploitation. To keep this from happening, Catholic teaching advocates the guarantee of basic political and social rights for every citizen that specify basic levels of material and higher goods that no citizen is allowed to fall below, including food, water, shelter, health care, and education. Moreover, because the human community has become globally interdependent, efforts must be made to secure the

MARYKNOLL MISSION ARCHIVES

One of the most popular popes of modern times, John XXIII. His official portrait.

universal common good, not just the good of nations, a principle shared by the CPWR.

Catholic teaching on the common good does not limit itself to the boundaries of the human community, however. Pope John Paul II advocated including the protection of the environment in his discussion of the common good in his encyclical *Sollicitudo rei socialis* (1987). Human technology will have disastrous effects on the environment, and on humanity, unless it is guided by moral values or ends. Although including the biosphere in deliberations about the common good transcends the human community, it still does not go far enough. Ultimately, Catholic social teaching contends, the full common good is realized only in the communion of all God's creatures with God and with one another in God. This is the highest good for humanity and transcends any good that can be achieved politically, economically, or culturally. Likewise, the CPWR affirms a vision of the common good where the earth and all life are cherished, protected, and restored.

Whether or not a religious tradition has a social ethic depends on the attitudes of the tradition toward the world. If a religion affirms this world as good and urges its members to live within it, then there is the need for a social ethic and norms for life in the world. We have seen how this is true for the Catholic tradition in our discussion of Catholic social thought and the common good. This is also true for Islam, which holds that the world is a theater for human service to God. Not all religious traditions find significance in this world, however. As noted previously, historically Buddhists thought of this world as a place of suffering and sought release from this world. The goal of religious and moral action, then, is to eliminate desire, the craving for the things of this world. The goal is to reach nirvana, which, in Theravada Buddhism, is done through monastic withdrawal from this world. This rejection of the world can be seen in the following quotation from the Dhammapada, a classic text of early Buddhism: "Whoever looks upon this world as a bubble, as a mirage, is not seen by the King of Death. . . . Come, look at this world, like a painted royal chariot; fools sink in it, the knowing have no attachment to it."[12] As a result, some would contend, Buddhism has been slow to develop a social ethic (although the emergence of socially engaged Buddhism and the many Buddhist leaders who have signed onto the global ethic suggest this is changing).

THE RELATIONSHIP BETWEEN SYMBOLIC AND PRACTICAL RELIGIOUS ACTION

Most people have a keen sense of the intricate connection between ritual and ethics. Those of us who have a negative opinion of ritual often relate it to our feeling that many who engage in rituals fail to live up to the ethical norms of their religion. Like the biblical prophet **Amos**, we understand that the rituals we practice should correspond with our actions in our everyday lives. Without fully understanding the implications, we recognize that just as important as orthodoxy (right belief) is orthopraxy (right action). Moreover, we realize that orthopraxy encompasses both ritual and ethics. In the Jewish and Christian traditions this connection is reflected in the twofold commandment to love God and to love one's neighbor. Holding the two forms of action together fulfills all the law and the prophets. Thus, ritual and ethical action are mutually reinforcing. Rituals support a particular moral way of life, embody values and relationships, and remind us of our moral responsibilities and commitments. How religious rituals accomplish this is through their pedagogical, their redemptive, and their transformative functions.

RITUAL AND MORAL PEDAGOGY

Theodore Jennings, Jr., reminds us about the pedagogical character of ritual. Ritual's repetitive dimension teaches knowledge to its participants and invites our imitation or response. In the performance of ritual, we learn not only how to conduct a ritual but also how to conduct ourselves outside of the ritual act. This teaching provides a pattern of doing. Ritual is important "in forming a way of being and acting in the world." In fact, Jennings suggests, "ritual serves as a paradigm for all significant action."[13] We can see this pedagogical dimension of ritual in a variety of ways.

As part of the ethos—the acceptable ways of behaving and living—of an individual or community, a ritual action is often symbolically supportive of a particular moral way of life. For example, storytelling is ritualized in many cultures. On the one hand, the stories remind people of the significant events and people in the life of the community, thereby reinforcing the worldview. On the other hand, they hold up certain virtues or qualities that a person in the community should develop in order to live rightly within that community. This is especially true in stories about heroes. The heroes in the stories become moral exemplars, people who embody the moral character the community cherishes. For example, during the Jewish festival of Purim, the story of Esther is read in the synagogue. This story recounts how the Jews were saved from persecution and death by the courage and shrewdness of Esther and her cousin Mordecai.

Some rituals remind us of our moral commitments and responsibilities. The rituals associated with the holidays of Thanksgiving and Christmas remind people of the good fortune they have and prompt them to share it with others. The "giving tree" ritual developed in many Christian churches and by the Salvation Army reflects this connection. In the ritual activity of Christmas gift giving, the giving tree reminds people of the value of charity and meeting the needs of others and provides a formalized way of practicing that virtue. A similar ritual among the Oglala Sioux is the "giveaway ceremony." The ceremony is done in conjunction with a significant event in the life of the individual or family or as an attempt to find spiritual renewal. In this ceremony a family may give away some or most of its valued possessions to others, especially the poorest members of the community. This provides a ritualized way for practicing the value of sharing and for demonstrating concern for the well-being of others. It also inhibits concentrations of wealth.

Rituals also embody values and relationships. Having the "man of the house" sit at the head of the table and carve the turkey on Thanksgiving Day, even though he has no role in the preparation and cleanup of the meal, embodies certain values and gender roles. The Native American ritual of giving thanks to the animal for surrendering its life for the health and well-being of the tribe suggests the valuable place of all living creatures in the web of life and the importance placed on humanity's relationship with the rest of nature. Female circumcision rituals practiced in some African cultures reflect the historical belief that the value of sexuality for women is more for procreation than pleasure. They also point to the subordinate position of women.

The pedagogical significance of ritual can be seen in moral development. Rituals often include the recitation of myths, proverbs, or creeds that reinforce the moral worldview of the community. For example, schoolchildren in the United States often say the pledge of allegiance to the flag. The concluding phrase of that pledge is "with liberty and justice for all." Because these are moral norms that the community wishes all members of the community to abide by, they are included in their daily rituals. The repetition of this ritual suggests this ordering to the minds of the people. Rites of initiation in many religious traditions include training and instruction in moral behavior. The puberty rites of African Traditional Religions include lessons in the values of the society as well as special instructions on the roles the participants will have as adults and how they are expected to behave sexually.

In addition to the cognitive dimension, ritual action enables participants to perform actions of fellow feeling and social solidarity. Victor Turner's description of the transition or *liminal* phase in rites of passage is a good example. He suggests that participants in a rite, such as an initiation rite, experience a common bond or feeling of *communitas* that they do not encounter outside the ritual experience. As a result, there is a sense of community and social solidarity that takes place among the initiates that enables them to become aware of the interconnectedness and equality among them. This can be seen clearly in the pilgrimage experience associated with Islam. The people on the pilgrimage (hajj) wear a common white garment. All distinctions of rank and ethnic background are lost. Together they circumambulate (walk around) the Ka'ba in Mecca. In undergoing the ritual, the participants understand and feel the unity and solidarity that make up the Umma, the world community of Islam.

RITUAL AND MORAL REDEMPTION

The intricate relationship between ritual and ethics can also be seen in the redemptive character of ritual. When we act in ways contrary to the moral order affirmed by our religious traditions, we can experience a sense of guilt and confusion. Conscience may come into play here as we feel that our actions have become disruptive to the moral order. In some indigenous religious traditions, when the harmony in the universe is out of balance there is an assumption that someone or some group has acted contrary to the moral order of the universe. The only way to set things right, to restore the balance, is by means of ritual action, which may include some divination process as to the cause of the malaise.

Religions have provided people with a variety of rituals to help assuage their moral guilt and to restore them to community. Many indigenous religious traditions use the sacrifice of vegetables or animals as a way of appeasing the offended party, especially if that party is the deity or some other trans-human being. Other traditions, including Judaism and Christianity, affirm the importance of the private and public confession of wrongdoing. We have heard people say that confession is good for the soul. What they mean is that confession allows people to give voice to their wrongdoing, to take ownership of and responsibility for it, and to make amends. The Call to Confession liturgy and the Jewish holy day of Yom Kippur, discussed in detail in Chapter 11, are good examples of confession rituals that enable people to experience moral redemption.

Ritual and ethical action are also connected when there is moral ambiguity, such as is the case with the morality of abortion in many countries. The *mizuko kuyo* ritual in Japan highlights this redemptive function. Abortion has been legal in Japan since 1948. It is the most effective form of birth control in a nation where other forms of birth control are not discussed widely. Women seeking abortion feel it is the right thing to do, especially before they marry or after they have borne their complement of two children, because it accords with the norms of their society. Yet they cannot escape the fact that the unborn

Japanese statues of the Mizu-ko Jizo, protector of children, have children in various poses around them, clinging to their robes, holding on to the staff for support, or held securely in Jizo's arms.

child is still human life attested to by Buddhist religion. Women may still feel pangs of guilt and grief over the loss of the child, even though they willed it. They experience a form of spiritual malaise that needs healing.

The *mizuko kuyo* ritual means offering up prayers for the nourishment of the spirit of the unborn child. It also is a service intended to console the parents, especially the mother. There is a wide variety in the practice of the ritual because of the sectarian nature of Japanese Buddhism. The service may take place once, monthly, or on the anniversary of the death of the fetus. The service can be private, although mostly it is a service said for many *mizuko* at the same time. The priest conducts the service at the altar on behalf of those requesting the service. One or more names of the Buddha or bodhisattvas are invoked. Some parts of sutras (Buddhist scriptures) are chanted. During the service, offerings of food, flowers, incense, and the like are made to the Buddha on behalf of the child. Some sculpted representation of Jizo, a bodhisattva seen as the protector of young children, or an infant is left on the temple grounds. A Buddhist name is given to the child posthumously. A mortuary table is placed in the temple or placed in the family shrine. Sometimes a priest gives a sermon to place the experience in a wider context.

This ritual relates to Japanese Buddhist cosmology in two ways. First, *mizuko* literally means "water-child" or "child of the waters." To refer to a fetus as a child of the waters means that its status is fluid and in flux. This notion accords with the Buddhist notion of the impermanence of the self and its understanding of reality as becoming. If for some reason, such as having too many children or an inability to care for a newborn, a woman decides to abort a fetus, her decision means returning the child to the heavenly realm from which it came until it can be reborn into a better situation, a situation where the child is welcomed and nurtured instead of seen as a burden. Thus, abortion is viewed as a moral course of action, although recognizing the difficulties and the pain it brings to the woman who undertakes the action.

Second, Buddhist cosmology recognizes that there is ambiguity in all existence; anything can be malevolent, but it is not inherently so; these same forces can be turned into good for those who seek wisdom and goodness. In Buddhist doctrine there are various worlds for the dead, some of which are not pleasant. Without proper veneration there is potential that the spirit of the unborn child may become a demon. The *kuyo* service provides a means for transforming potentially dangerous or malevolent forces to helpful and beneficial forces for the living.

Thinking about Ritual and Moral Redemption

To explore the connection between ritual and moral redemption, think of a time when you did something wrong (or ask several friends to do so). What feelings, if any, did you experience as a result of your wrongdoing? How did you express those feelings? What activities did you find helpful in dealing with or channeling these feelings? What actions did you do to make amends for what you did? What did you do to help you feel good about yourself again? Thinking about those activities, do you find that you repeat them in other instances of wrongdoing?

Non-Japanese viewers of the *kuyo* ritual may see it as strange. But it deals with the issue of moral ambiguity and perplexity head on. It recognizes that what is at stake in many moral decisions is the quality of life versus life. No matter which choice we make, we experience guilt. This and similar rituals enable people to confront the dark side of human experience directly instead of glossing over its ambiguities and difficulties. It seeks to reestablish harmonious moral order, but only after the roots of disharmony have been confronted and displaced.

RITUAL AND MORAL TRANSFORMATION

A final dimension of the relationship between ritual and ethical action is in the transformative character of ritual. Not only does ritual action affirm the moral order, but sometimes it also reorders or recenters the moral universe, transforming the lives of participants. It is easy to see the transformative dimension of ritual. The performance of rituals associated with birth actually change the status of the participants. When people perform marriage ceremonies, their status is transformed from single to married, and that has communal significance. When individuals pray for healing, they want some state of affairs to be different. They hope that through their ritual action, some transformation will take place.

The question is how this transformative dimension is related to morality. How can ritual effect moral change in the lives of individuals and communities? At a basic level, ritual is *performative*. It enables us to see ourselves as agents, enacting some event or state of affairs. We bring something into being. For example, many students take advantage of weekend-retreat opportunities afforded to them by their colleges. Usually they go off campus to a quiet place away from the grind of college life and spend the time reflecting and meditating individually and communally. Many students return to campus feeling refreshed and renewed. Some students, however, experience far more. They speak of how the retreat allowed them time to rethink their goals, values, and priorities. They declare that they have a new outlook on life and that their actions and behaviors will take new directions. In other words, they have changed, a transformation has taken place.

Tom Driver suggests that "when we understand ourselves as agents active in a world made up of other purposive beings, our sense of self and responsibility is heightened."[14] His point is that the doing of ritual has a moral effect; it helps us to understand our connections with others and forces us to some moral action. A good example is the Islamic practice of almsgiving. The intent in this is not to ponder whether there is poverty. By giving alms, Muslims are doing something about poverty and inequality. Their actions are attempting to make a transformation in the world. They suggest that poverty and inequality are not acceptable, even though they are widely practiced and accepted in the world at large. Almsgiving also has the effect of helping people realize that their lives are more than material possessions.

The connection between ritual performance and the transformation of society can be seen in the Civil Rights movement in the United States. The marches, the sit-ins, and the singing were all ritualized actions, formal and repetitive, performed by the participants. These rituals were often preceded by worship and prayer. But these actions were not done to affirm the structures of segregation and injustice prevalent in society. Rather, they were geared toward the transformation of that society toward a vision in which all persons, regardless of race, would be treated with respect and dignity. Moreover, that vision, which Martin Luther King, Jr., called the "beloved community," included the oppressor as well as the oppressed. More important, the participants lived out that vision in their rituals. People of different races worshiped together, marched hand in hand, and refused to return violence with violence. As a result, these actions pricked the nation's collective conscience, forced the end of legal segregation, and led to a greater degree of social justice for all citizens.

It should be clear that sometimes the transformation that takes place through ritual can also affect the ritual itself. What this means is that as a result of moral transformation, people will attempt to transform the rituals. This is what occurs when people see the sense of community built into the Christian ritual of communion, and they redirect the rest of the service to reflect this new vision. Through participation in the ritual of communion, distinctions are broken down, a common humanity before God is affirmed and declared. In many traditions there is the passing of the peace before or following the communion ceremony, reaffirming this inherent equality before the eyes of God. This inherent equality has led many to argue for equality in other ways as well. When the ritual affirms the equality of all, it becomes difficult to justify the prominent place of men in the ritual, for example, or any division between the races.

Sometimes the moral transformations that occur can lead to challenges in relation to other rituals as well. The emerging affirmation of mutuality and equality among men and women globally has called into question the appropriateness of the ritual of female circumcision, which opponents refer to as female genital mutilation, and which continues to take place in some African and Middle Eastern contexts. They juxtapose the moral values of the well-being and flourishing of all humanity with the physical and health risks—such as infection, sterility, and death—and the loss of sexual pleasure and fulfillment this ritual has caused and continues to cause for countless women. It is important to note that this change is not coming simply from people outside of these cultural contexts but also from within them; they are developing other rituals that affirm the sexual and reproductive roles of women in their communities but without the negative connotations and devastating consequences associated with female circumcision.

SUMMARY

As you can see, ritual and ethical action help us to order our lives in meaningful ways individually and socially. Without such symbolic and practical actions, our lives would seem chaotic and confusing. The chaos impinging upon our lives, chaos that comes with changes in our lives, such as moving away from home, changing jobs, or going to college, has the potential to overwhelm us. Fortunately, we are able to gain control over this chaos and find meaning in our lives through the actions we take. As we have seen, however, many religious traditions use stories, metaphors, and myths to enable us to understand and to motivate us to perform the ritual and ethical actions critical to finding such meaning. They are a part of the language that makes up our religious traditions. Thus, we now turn our attention to language.

RESOURCES

ACTIVITIES

1. Do an analysis of a religious social justice organization. Visit a local religious organization seeking to promote social justice, gather information regarding the underlying values and beliefs of the organization, and analyze how well the structure (ethos) reflects the organization's purpose (worldview). Present your findings in a written, oral, or multimedia report.
2. Gather the moral questions of members of the class or study group. At the beginning of the session ask students to write questions regarding any ethical concerns they have. Place the questions in a brown paper bag. Periodically draw questions from the bag that the entire class will attempt to answer together using the materials from the text.
3. Interview eight to ten people about the ritual activities that help them cope with the moral difficulties they experience. Analyze the responses to discern the type of ritual activities respondents use to help deal with their moral issues.
4. Have a debate over the following statement: Morality without religion is impossible. Have teams research each position thoroughly and provide time for each group to make its case.
5. Watch several films that raise significant moral issues (*John Q*, *Crash*, and *The Kite Runner* are good examples). Analyze the films to discern the approach the film maker takes on the moral issue in question. Is the emphasis on moral conduct? Moral character? Both?

READINGS

Crawford, Cromwell S., Editor. *World Religions and Global Ethics*. New York: Paragon House, 1989. An excellent collection of essays on the ethical traditions of a variety of religions, including African Traditional Religion, Buddhism, Hinduism, Christianity, Confucianism, Judaism, and Islam.

Küng, Hans, and Karl-Josef Kuschel, ed. *A Global Ethic: The Declaration of the Parliament of the World's Religions*. New York: Continuum, 1993. This book contains the principles of a global ethic endorsed by the leaders of the world's religions with commentaries about the history and significance of the global ethic by Küng and Kuschel.

LaFleur, William R. *Liquid Life: Abortion and Buddhism in Japan*. Princeton, NJ: Princeton University Press, 1992. This book explores the meaning and practice of *mizuko kuyo*, the Buddhist abortion ritual in Japan.

Lovin, Robin W., and Frank E. Reynolds. *Cosmogony and Ethical Order*. Chicago: University of Chicago Press, 1985. A collection of essays that brings together religious ethicists and historians of religion in an attempt to further the discipline of comparative religious ethics by exploring the ethical orderings present in a variety of religious cosmogonies.

Reeder, John P., Jr. *Source, Sanction, and Salvation: Religion and Morality in Judaic and Christian Traditions.* Englewood Cliffs, NJ: Prentice-Hall, 1988. This book provides a framework for understanding religion as the source, sanction, and goal of religious ethics. Although restricted to the Jewish and Christian religious traditions, some of the themes are applicable to other religions as well.

Runzo, Joseph, and Nancy M. Martin, eds. *Ethics in the World Religions.* Oxford: Oneworld Publications, 2001. This volume is part of the Library of Global Ethics and Religion, which includes essays from various scholars who examine the role of ethics in all the major religious traditions. The other volumes in the series include *Love, Sex, and Gender*; *Meaning of Life*; and *Human Rights and Responsibilities.*

Schweiker, William, ed. *The Blackwell Companion to Religious Ethics.* Malden, MA: Wiley-Blackwell, 2008. Written by internationally renowned scholars, this book provides a thorough introduction to the moral teachings of the world's religions and also identifies new directions for those working in the field of religious ethics.

Wolfe, Regina W., and Christine Gudorf, eds. *Ethics and World Religions: Cross-Cultural Case Studies.* Maryknoll, NY: Orbis Books, 1999. This book provides a number of case studies and looks at them from various religious ethical perspectives. It is a great resource for teachers and students looking to understand ethical issues in context.

AUDIO-VISUALS

Religion, War, and Violence: The Ethics of War and Peace (2002). Available from Films for the Humanities and Sciences, 132 West 31st Street, 17th Floor, New York, NY 10001. This selection of stand-alone segments from *Religion and Ethics Newsweekly* brings together experts, scholars, and religious leaders from a variety of communities and faiths to discuss a wide range of related issues: war and peace, terrorism and its roots, fundamentalism, just war, holy war, pacifism, the use of force, and violence in the name of God.

The Great Religions and the Poor (1991). Available from Films for the Humanities and Sciences, 132 West 31st Street, 17th Floor, New York, NY 10001. Part of the Religions of the Book series, this film explores the beliefs of Judaism, Christianity, and Islam regarding the poor, taking a comparative look at the traditional concept of the poor.

A Spirituality of Co-Creation: Partnering with God (2007). Available from Films for the Humanities and Sciences, 132 West 31st Street, 17th

Floor, New York, NY 10001. This program questions the suitability of the traditional monotheistic, hierarchical model to the challenges of the twenty-first century. It presents the idea that humankind should step forward to accept greater responsibility for its own actions while becoming more attuned to the transpersonal creative energies at play in the universe.

A Congress of the World's Religions: Speaking Out for Peace and Unity (2007). Available from Films for the Humanities and Sciences, 132 West 31st Street, 17th Floor, New York, NY 10001. This program captures the wisdom of attendees at the 2006 congress in Montreal who addressed topics ranging from widespread religious fanaticism, the destabilizing action/reaction spiral of violence, and the misuse of religion for political ends to defusing alienation through acceptance, fighting the radical poverty that polarizes communities, and nurturing understanding through greater awareness of the oneness of humankind.

Wangari Maathai: For Our Land (2009). Available from Films for the Humanities and Sciences, 132 West 31st Street, 17th Floor, New York, NY 10001. This video highlights the work of Wangari Maathai—environmental activist, social justice advocate, and Nobel Peace Prize recipient—through her Green Belt movement of planting trees and democratic advocacy in Kenya.

NOTES

1. Joachim Wach, *The Comparative Study of Religions* (New York: Columbia University Press, 1958), 115.

2. John P. Reeder, Jr., *Source, Sanction, and Salvation* (Englewood Cliffs, NJ: Prenctice-Hall, 1988).

3. Walter E. Conn, *Conscience: Development and Self-Transcendence* (Birmingham, AL: Religious Education Press, 1981), 206.

4. *Trials of War Criminals before the Nuremberg Military Tribunals*, quoted in Edward Zukowski, "The 'Good Conscience' of Nazi Doctors," *The Annual of the Society of Christian Ethics* (1994): 56–57.

5. Martin Luther King, Jr., "Letter from Birmingham Jail," in *Why We Can't Wait* (New York: New American Library, 1964), 82–84.

6. Jonathan Haidt, "The Emotional Dog and Its Rational Tail: A Social Intuitionist Approach to Moral Judgment," *Psychological Review* 108 (2001): 814–34.

7. John K. Ansah, "The Ethics of African Religious Traditions," in *World Religions and Global Ethics*, ed. Cromwell S. Crawford (New York: Paragon House, 1989), 249.

8. See Robert Bellah et al., *Habits of the Heart* (Berkeley and Los Angeles: University of California Press, 1985), 223.

9. The following paragraphs are drawn from two books authored by Wangari Maathai, *Unbowed: A Memoir* (New York: Alfred A. Knopf, 2006), and *Replenishing the Earth: Spiritual Values for Healing Ourselves and the World* (New York: Doubleday, 2010).

10. Maathai, *Replenishing the Earth*, 294.

11. Ibid., 295.

12. *The Dhammapada*, trans. Thomas Cleary (New York: Bantam Books, 1995), 59–60.

13. Theodore W. Jennings, Jr., "On Ritual Knowledge," in *Readings in Ritual Studies*, ed. Ronald L. Grimes (Upper Saddle River, NJ: Prentice-Hall, 1996), 324–34.

14. Tom F. Driver, *The Magic of Ritual* (San Francisco: HarperCollins, 1991), 1974.

PART III

RELIGIOUS LANGUAGE

We humans are born storytellers. Out of our experiences we turn momentary setbacks into comedy as we explain to skeptical classmate that the new puppy mistook copies of a group report for a bowl of kibbles. When a sudden failure or unexpected tragedy bulldozes our world, we recount yesterday's triumphs in order to reassert our sense of self and to lend some coherence to a crumbling universe. Like the woman in the Wallace Stevens poem in Chapter 1, we use language to make sense of our experiences. Out of language we create and share stories that reveal who we are and how we fit into the world.

At the same time we inherit stories about the values and customs of our families, our religious traditions—even about our nation. Motion pictures and television programming shape our imaginations and provide narratives that challenge or reinforce individual and communal stories. Thanks to characters like Frodo Baggins and Sam Gamgee (*The Lord of the Rings* trilogy), and Harry Potter, Hermione Granger, and Professor Dumbledore (*Harry Potter* films), we participate, for a few hours at least, in stories where we practice justice and compassion toward those trapped in an unjust world. The stories of Saruman, Lord Voldemort, and the Joker, on the other hand, celebrate greed, instant gratification, and disdain for life. On the surface many contemporary stories seem to be nothing more than light entertainment. Others, whose popularity spans generations, contain powerful narrative structures that continue to question readers and viewers.

In European-based societies the Bible has influenced both cultural and individual stories. Hollywood cinema often draws on this material for themes and plots. Obvious examples are older films, favorite television fare around Christmas and Easter: Cecil B. DeMille's *The Ten Commandments* (1956), George Stevens's *The Greatest Story Ever Told* (1965), and Franco Zeffirelli's *Jesus of Nazareth* (1977), among others. More recent examples are Martin Scorsese's *The Last Temptation of Christ* (1988) and Mel Gibson's *The Passion of the Christ* (2004). US politicians and citizen groups rely on biblical morality for popular support of legislation, despite its tenuous connection to any biblical law code. Presidents frequently pepper major addresses with references to covenant and justice, in line with the popular story that the United States was founded as a Christian nation. While frequently ignored or distorted by Hollywood film makers, the religious literatures of non-European traditions (for example, Native American, Mesoamerican, African, Islamic, Buddhist, Hindu) offer valid ways of ordering the world.

Parts I and II of this book introduced the importance of storytelling in different religious traditions. We studied how creation stories help believers locate themselves within an ordered universe and how stories accompany ritual action to remind them about their ancestors and to set their history within the activity of the **sacred**. Now we look more specifically at religious language. In Chapter 6 we discover that language is more figurative than literal. We identify language as hyperbole, paradox, and negation; these aspects allow us to talk about mystery and power, a dimension we locate within and beyond human experience. Religious traditions use language to create myths, **parables**, and stories. We consider different types of myths and practice reading them responsibly. Because religious language includes physical actions (for example, gesture and dance), we also examine ways in which religions speak about the sacred nonverbally, how using calligraphy and basket weaving incorporate the sacred power into their cultures.

In Chapter 7 we consider the processes through which these narratives and stories have been preserved and handed down from one generation to another. Some of these stories have become canonical scripture, that is, normative for belief and practice. We explore what *scripture* means in both oral and written religious traditions. The ways in which many religions use their scriptures as standards to measure correct behavior and practices indicate the connections they have established between scripture and the sacred. Using the New Testament as a case study, we examine the formation of Christian canons. Finally, we consider how traditions construct the more formal, conceptual statements, such as creeds and doctrines, that practitioners use to order their behavior and beliefs.

Chapter 6

Talking about the Sacred

We live in a web of language. We use it to convey facts ("It's raining!"), to give directives ("Meet me at the mall!"), to express opinions ("I love football!"), to declare love ("I can't live without you!"). Language helps us convey our experiences, our ideas, and our perspectives on the world. It also stands between these experiences and us because any description is already an interpretation, an ordering, of experience. As we are well aware, the description is not the experience itself.

Far from being neutral and transparent, language both conveys and shapes our experience. According to novelist Iris Murdoch:

> We can no longer take language for granted as a medium of communication. Its transparency is gone. We are like people who for a long time looked out a window without noticing the glass—and then one day began to notice this too.[1]

In other words, language is the medium through which we experience the world. Language makes our experience available for reflection, sharing, and discovery. It is, however, limited because it is a human creation. We discover that it cannot contain all the meaning we perceive.

What we see and how we respond depends on the language we use to create the story, the "world" that mediates significance for us. If, for example, we use language that excludes some groups or individuals, we might eliminate them from our definitions of human being and citizen, convinced that they are invisible and unimportant; we may identify their differences as a threat and respond to them with anger and violence. In one way or another, language shapes and expresses our private and our public worlds. According to literary critic, Amos Wilder:

Language is the medium through which we experience our world and ourselves. We weave it into stories that shape or distort, cloud or illumine, what we believe to be real.

There is no "world" for us until we have named and languaged and storied whatever is. [What we take to be the nature of things has been shaped by calling it so.] This therefore is also a story-world. . . . Stories would not exist or even be heard through if human nature did not look to them avidly for illumination of its homelessness in time and circumstance. It is just because life is a labyrinth that we follow eagerly the clues and traces, the impasses and detours and open sesames of a myth or tale. The world of story is our own world in a higher register.[2]

RELIGIOUS LANGUAGE AND FIGURATIVE LANGUAGE: SIDES OF THE SAME COIN

Just as we often use religious vocabulary in everyday contexts, we use ordinary vocabulary in religious contexts. For example, we read about the "myth of progress," the "Church of Baseball," the "ritual of negotiation," in articles about economics or sports or labor relations. Such language, used in religious contexts (ritual, prayer, sacred narratives, and so on), however, concerns the ultimate; it suggests the vision the divine has for the world. In the Gospel of John, Jesus of Nazareth uses such language in his conversation with the Samaritan woman at the well (Jn 4). Her physical thirst for water is also a spiritual thirst; the fresh water that Jesus offers is also the "living water" that sustains eternal life. In Matthew's parable of judgment, the hungry and the naked, the homeless, and the imprisoned are the suffering Christ crying out for help (Mt 25:31–46). Religious language identifies the presence of God within human experience.

Language about the sacred is "speech about the unspeakable, speech at the limits of language."[3] Such language, like all language, is figurative, the language of metaphor. Some metaphors express analogy, that is, a similarity between two unlike entities. For example, the anonymous author of 1 John declares, "Whoever does not love does not know God, because God is love" (4:8). This metaphor suggests that some experiences of unconditional, self-giving love are similar to experiences of God's love, that the love binding a community together is, in fact, something like the presence of God. The use of such language asserts that there is some continuity between the human and the divine, that the human is a helpful, if inadequate, model for understanding and manifesting mystery. Buddhism has a similar understanding: "It is precisely the Original Face of Man—of any of us human beings—which is the True Buddha."[4]

Another kind of metaphor is paradox; it combines opposites in such a way that a new insight appears. Paradoxical metaphors insist that the sacred is simultaneously revealed and concealed. They reverse and upend the world as we know it. In describing the demands of discipleship, Jesus of Nazareth declares, "For those who want to save their life will lose it, and those who lose their life for my sake will find it" (Mt 16:25; cf. Mk 8:35; trans. K. Nash). Jesus tells parables that describe the reign of God, the social arrangement that he preaches, not as a place but as transformed seeing and acting: late-coming workers receive the same pay as those who showed up at daybreak ("So the last will be first, and the first will be last" [Mt 20:16]); a woman loses a gold coin and throws a party when she finds it ("Everyone who exalts herself will be humbled, but he who humbles himself will be exalted" [Lk 18:14b; trans. K. Nash]). "It is more blessed to give than to receive" (Acts 20:35b).

Faced with describing the saving action of Jesus the Christ, the apostle Paul uses paradox freely: "For those who were called in the Lord while slaves are free in the Lord; those who were called while free are Christ's slaves" (1 Cor 7:22; trans. K. Nash). "As unknown yet well-known, as dying yet alive; as punished yet not put to death, as sorrowful yet always rejoicing, as poor yet making many rich, as having nothing yet possessing all things" (2 Cor 6:9–10; trans. K. Nash). "For whenever I am weak, then I am strong" (2 Cor 12:10b).

Religious language also describes what mystery is not. Because we can speak about the sacred only indirectly, we gain some knowledge of the sacred by learning what it is not. Ancient Egyptian (1290–1224 BCE) hymns of praise to the sun-god Amon-Re deny that this god is like other gods and challenge any claims that humans can know him. Some Islamic thinkers from the ninth century CE insisted that they can make only negative assertions about Allah:

[Allah] is one; there is no thing like him. . . . He is not a body, not a form. Not flesh and blood, not an individual, no substance nor attribute . . . no movement, rest, or division. . . . He is not comparable with men and does not resemble creatures in any respect. . . . He is unlike whatever occurs to the mind or is pictured in the imagination.[5]

These statements from two different traditions represent the intuition that the sacred is truly mysterious, too dense for humans to grasp, too opaque for language to describe. Negative language (*via negativa* or the coincidence of opposites) is the most accurate way to

LINDY GLENNON

We often anthropomorphize or deify powerful natural forces. This project expresses the intuition that humanity, the divine, and nature are independent on and continuous with one another.

describe it. Religious language indicates that while the sacred may be described with human characteristics, it does not possess those characteristics, at least not in the way individual humans possess them. Analogy underscores similarity; negation emphasizes difference; paradox simultaneously affirms the "is" and the "is-not" aspects of any comparison.

RELIGIOUS METAPHORS: HERE ONE CENTURY, GONE THE NEXT

Each religious tradition has a signature understanding of one or other aspects of mystery or life: Allah, Krishna, Buddha, God, Great Spirit, the Lord, Adonai, Goddess, Gaia, Tao. This sacred is forever unfamiliar. We make it familiar by constructing metaphors that describe how our relationship to the sacred is like and not like ordinary, everyday relations. The metaphor is the lens through which we view mystery; it may sharpen or distort what we see. Like other figurative language its adequacy depends on culture, history, and experiences unique to some believers.

For example, God the Father is a metaphor that affirms that our experience of the sacred resembles our relationship to a male parent. It may create a safe, ordered world in which we are dependent upon a kind provider for our needs. It may also create a cold, chaotic world in which we must rely on a distant, harsh taskmaster. How we read the metaphor depends, in part, on our own experience of father. This metaphor does not, however, exhaust all potential ways for constructing the relationship between the sacred and the human worlds. We can insist that our experience of relating to God is like the experience of relating to a mother or a companion or lover or healer or liberator or friend. These are mutually enriching models or metaphors that we use to describe our experience of the holy.

Metaphors we use about the holy are culturally and politically conditioned. For example, for centuries in Christian Europe the metaphor of Christ as king was very popular. In the great chain of being, Christ the divine king governed the world and the universe; the pope, as Christ's earthly representative, conferred on secular rulers the authority to govern. The implication of that symbolic action is clear. Many earthly rulers took their orders from the pope or involved the pope in diplomatic decisions. Their Christian subjects were expected to be loyal subjects, even though their awareness of royal policies rested on demands to supply a greater percentage of crops, more young men to fight royal and religious battles, or impromptu raids on rural villages. Nonetheless, peasants, spurred on by local clergy, honored Christ as king, affirming their belief that Christ was in sure control of world events, even if the powers of evil seemed to be winning, and that one day the Christ would arrive to reveal his kingdom and reward his faithful followers. As political systems changed and monarchies disappeared, this metaphor of Christ as king gradually lost its power to mediate the holy to Christian cultures. While some believers still find the metaphor meaningful, especially in its reinterpretation of Christ the victorious warrior-king of the Book of Revelation, cultural worldviews to support it are fragmentary at best.

Many Native American peoples in the United States draw their metaphors for mystery or power from their lives as farmers and hunters. For examples, animals such as the bear, the deer, and the eagle represent power and wisdom encountered in individual visions. The Lenape People of Delaware tell a story about a deer who leads their ancestors from a place of darkness beneath a lake to the upper world. The animal instructs the tribal leader to kill it and share its flesh with the others. By eating the deer's flesh, the Lenape acquired the knowledge they needed to live in the forests.

Native American peoples also revere the earth with the title Mother. In some native stories of origin, the people emerge from the earth as from a womb. And like a mother, the earth nourishes her children, providing good crops for harvest and large herds for hunting. The farming and hunting contexts of these metaphors for mystery give them their power and meaning. Members of ecological movements use the metaphor to emphasize that pollution of air and water, along with the loss of wetlands and endangered species, destroy a sacred balance with nature. In a similar fashion some feminist theologians identify physical violence acted out on women's bodies and industrial pollution of the "body" of Mother Earth as related symptoms of a patriarchal society that knows too little about intimacy and collaboration and too much about domination and control. Metaphors and their interpretations are culturally conditioned; they draw their power from their contexts, from personal experience, and from the reality they mediate.

JESUS THE MOTHER

The impulse to use feminine language and imagery to describe the sacred has been part of religions from the very beginning. Human beings have generally peopled the realm of power with goddesses and female spirits as well as gods and male spirits. In much ancient mythology (Mesopotamian mythology, for example) goddesses possess cultural knowledge and teach human beings how to farm and weave, how to make music and pottery; they act as midwives for kings and heroes and control fertility. Many scholars point out that in the Jewish and Christian traditions, God often does what would have been regarded as woman's work. God sews clothes (Gen 3:21) and mothers Israel (Hos 11:3–4), loving the Israelites more than a human mother loves her child (Is 49:14–15). Moses suggests that God has conceived and given birth to the Israelites (Nm 11:10–15), while Isaiah declares that God comforts Israel as a mother comforts her child (Is 66:13). We find similar imagery in the Christian New Testament. Jesus likens himself to a mother hen in his desire to protect Jerusalem (Lk 13:34). One of his parables—the story of a woman losing money, searching energetically and throwing a party for her friends and neighbors when she finds it—describes God's delight at the return of a sinner (Lk 15:8–11).

Feminine imagery to describe God's relationship with believers threads its way through the Christian tradition. An early Christian writer, Clement of Alexandria (c. 150–220), speaks of "the Father's loving breasts" and "the milk of the Father." In the twelfth century some writers used "Mother Jesus" as a symbol of tenderness and supportive love. The English mystic Julian of Norwich (1342–c. 1423) writes about the "motherhood of Jesus."

Julian of Norwich lived a secluded life with her maid and, some say, her cat, in a tiny room attached to the village church in Norwich, England, during the late fourteenth and the early fifteenth centuries. She often prayed for the grace of a serious illness in order to imitate more closely the crucified Christ. During such an illness, she claimed that the crucified Christ visited her many times. She learned through experience about God's great love for each person and about the delight Christ takes in each human being. She first wrote down the content of these visions in a short collection. Later, after she had thought more about them, Julian wrote a second, longer version, *Showings*. In the following passage she describes her experience of the motherhood of Jesus:

> Our Mother in nature, our Mother in grace, because he [Jesus] wanted altogether to become our Mother in all things, made the foundation of his work most humbly and most mildly in the maiden's womb. . . . The mother's service is nearest, readiest and surest: nearest and surest because it is truest. No one ever might

MARYKNOLL MISSION ARCHIVES/E. WHEATER

To call God mother is to evoke the power of love in its fierce fight against death. To call God mother is to wait through death for the stirrings of life.

or could perform this office fully, except only him. We know that all our mothers bear us for pain and death. O, what is that? But our true Mother Jesus, he alone bears us for joy and for endless life, blessed may he be. So he carries us within him in love and travail, until the full time when he wanted to suffer the sharpest thorns and cruel pains that ever were or will be, and at the last he died. The mother can give her child to suck of her milk, but our precious Mother Jesus can feed us with himself, and does, most courteously and most tenderly with the blessed sacrament, which is the precious food of true life. . . . The mother can lay her child tenderly to her breast, but our tender Mother Jesus can lead us easily into his blessed breast through his sweet open side, and show us there a part of the godhead and of the joys of heaven with inner certainty of endless bliss.[6]

Thinking with Religious Metaphors

1. What are your **emotional** and **intellectual** reactions to Julian's use of maternal language about Christ?
2. How does Julian justify calling Christ mother? Throughout her writings Julian celebrates the great love Christ has for individuals. She seldom mentions sin or punishment for sin. How does this text reflect that attitude?
3. Julian's image of motherhood was influenced by her own experience of having been mothered and by her culture's understanding of mothering. What influences, do you think, affected Julian's understanding of motherhood? What images of mothering exist in your culture? Who mothers you? In what ways? Whom do you mother? In what ways?
4. Rewrite the passage to reflect your understanding and experience of mother.

EXTENDED METAPHORS: PARABLE AND MYTH

A **parable** is an extended metaphor, as well as a particular kind (genre) of literature; it contains a plot and characters and occurs in many religious traditions. It involves imagination and intuition, belief and revelation, and mediates the sacred even when it occurs in literature and cinema. Unlike a short story, a parable is an interactive narrative, much like an electronic game. It works only if the reader works with it, for "it leaves us in such doubt about its precise meaning that we are challenged into active thought." Like other Jewish rabbis (teachers) in first-century Palestine, Jesus of Nazareth used parables. "To what shall we compare the kingdom of God, or what parable can we use for it? It is like a mustard seed . . ." (Mk 4:30–31), a barren fig tree, a pearl of great price, among other things. What happens in these stories is like God's kingdom or reign. More specifically, parables are models for living within God's domain, a just earthly social-political system, not to be confused with an otherworldly "heaven."[7] They are not allegories that make sense only if the reader can figure out equivalents for the parable's important elements. Rather, they draw their audiences into the action of the story. Parables demand a careful analysis of all their parts since these parts are its meaning. They invite us to see differently and to imagine the sacred in unconventional ways.

Consider this parable about a wedding feast from the Gospel of Matthew (22:1–10) in the New Testament.

> Once more Jesus spoke to them in parables, saying: "The king-dom of heaven may be compared to a king who gave a wedding banquet for his son. He sent his slaves to call those who had been invited to the wedding banquet, but they would not come. Again he sent other slaves saying, 'Tell those who are invited: Look, I have prepared my dinner, my oxen, and my fat calves have been slaughtered, and everything is ready; come to the wedding ban-quet.' But they made light of it and went away, one to his farm, another to his business, while the rest seized his slaves, mistreated them, and killed them. The king was enraged. He sent his troops, destroyed those murderers and burned their city. Then he said to his slaves, 'The wedding is ready, but those invited were not wor-thy. Go therefore into the streets, and invite everyone you find to the wedding banquet.' Those slaves went out into the streets and gathered all whom they found, both bad and good, so the wedding hall was filled with guests." (Mt 22:1–10; cf. Lk 1:16–20)

Please read the parable at least once. Let it take up residence in your mind, heart, and your imagination as you become more familiar with its world. For example, what are the dynamics of that world? Does power shift from one character to another? Do unexpected events happen? Does anyone get special treatment?

In Matthew's parable the political setting is significant. A king invites influential subjects to his son's wedding banquet. No surprises yet; we expect this. Yet the guests refuse to honor the invitation once they hear that preparations are complete—once they arrive, the party will begin. What kind of guests are these? What kind of king tolerates such behavior? The king persists, hoping his elaborate menu will make them reconsider. Why does he appeal to their stomachs and not to their obligations or to his authority? Why does he beg them to attend? After all, he is the king! His guests answer his second summons by murdering his slaves. Why? Why does the king tolerate humiliation? Why does he humiliate himself, accepting rebuffs from those who should quickly obey him? Now pushed to his limit, the angry king orders their deaths; for a moment, he meets our expectation of a "real" ruler. Then he quickly reverts to previous behavior. Still eager to gather guests for his son's celebration, he sends his slaves out into the streets and highways to collect whomever they find, good and bad, stranger or subject, prepared or not; it doesn't matter.

This story is purposely open ended. Who finally accepts the invitation to come to the king's feast? What is the nature of this invitation? Who deserves it? What kind of ruler is this? There are many more questions to ask. Each reader deals with the questions personally in relation to the text. The temptation to read the parable as an **allegory** is appealing; we would identify the king as God, the son as Jesus, the slaves as the prophets, the first round of guests as first-century CE. Jews who reject Jesus as the **messiah**, and the second round as those Jews and Gentiles who accept him—but we still haven't gotten to its meaning and significance. The parable isn't a test of its listeners' grasp of Jewish and Christian history. After working through the parable, what is its effect on you intellectually and emotionally?

Think about parable as a paradigm, a model, of your worldview, your sense of yourself and your situation placed in a new context, like playing football on a baseball diamond—what new insights might you get into both football and baseball? Parables invite us into a familiar situation that is quickly turned upside down, posing unfamiliar questions and perhaps eliciting uncomfortable emotions. Parables are fine examples of paradox and metaphor extended into story; they scramble the sense and comfort we usually find in our worldviews.

MYTH

Myths raise "big" questions that continue to emerge as we move from one stage of life to another, are faced with tragedy, whether expected or unexpected, and so on. A myth is a symbolic story, not a literal account. Thus, creation myths do not describe the ordering of the universe; they describe the customs, practices, fears, and so on of the cultures in which they are embedded. They describe the ordered interrelationships among men, women, nature, and the sacred that must be maintained if order is to continue.

Sometimes we may think of myth as something false, something that facts can dispute. This is a popular (mis)understanding of myth. Based on the study of myths from various cultures, scholars in the field of religious studies have constructed a definition of myth that challenges popular understandings. Within a religious tradition a myth is a narrative that builds a worldview. We are not always able to express through factual statements what is trustworthy or genuine about the ordering of our world. While myth is not factual in the same way that news reports or personal memories are factual (if indeed they are), myth does embody helpful insights into the network of relationships that make up our world. It constructs the world or the universe in a certain way and offers this model as "the ways things really are" or "should be." Myth also shows us how to live in that world; it creates the structures we need to negotiate social relationships. Thus, it portrays gender in such a way that individuals learn how their culture expects them to be feminine or masculine. Such configurations are not universal norms; they promote specific value systems of specific cultures. They often establish power relationships that privilege groups at the center of social arrangements. Marginalized groups far from that center must depend on the politically and socially powerful to affirm their dignity as human beings and to grant access to basic resources (safe living spaces, food, quality education, jobs that pay at least living wages, and so on).

FUNCTIONS OF MYTH

Scholars continue to debate the function of myth. In Chapter 1 we met Mircea Eliade. He conjectured that some myths, especially myths of origin or creation, refer to an original condition outside time, a paradise to which we all wish to return. Perhaps that "paradise" represents a perfectly ordered world in the distant future that humanity could create through myths expressed in rituals with the power to realize that world. Eliade also argued that

> the foremost function of myth is to reveal the exemplary models for all human rites and all significant human activities: diet or marriage, work or education, art or wisdom. This idea is of no little importance for understanding the man of archaic and traditional societies.[8]

Eliade suggested that myths do more than record hierophanies (manifestations of the holy); they are the scripts that allow believers to participate in those manifestations.

Psychologist Carl Jung, once a protégé of Sigmund Freud, studied myth in cross-cultural contexts. He observed that mythic patterns occurred across different cultures in diverse geographic locations. To explain these phenomena, Jung theorized the existence of a collective unconscious, the spiritual heritage of the human community in which all individuals share. He also developed the idea of an archetype, the structure of the unconscious; its center is the self that emerges as the unconscious and the conscious are integrated:

> The collective unconscious—so far as we can say anything about it at all—appears to consist of mythological motifs or primordial images, for which reason the myths of all nations are its real exponents. In fact, the whole of mythology could be taken as a sort of projection of the collective unconscious. . . . We can therefore study the collective unconscious in two ways, either in mythology or in the analysis of the individual.[9]

Jung himself examined the themes of the divine child, Mother Earth, the hero, the self, and the shadow self. In the hero myth, for example, an individual, completely human or partially divine, frees people from all forms of evil, including death. Through a particular hero myth, the story of the death and resurrection of Jesus Christ, for example, individuals may identify with the hero and integrate this archetypal representation into their conscious selves, finding in it a pattern for their own experiences of death and rebirth. Jung insists that the loss of cultural myth has both psychological and moral implications—alienation from self, the loss of a sense of community, insensitivity to violence and brutality.

For Joseph Campbell, myths express cultural attitudes toward life, death, and the universe. Campbell found inspiration for his work in the writings of Carl Jung. In George Lucas's *Star Wars*, Campbell sees a modern version of the hero myth, suggesting that it might be relevant to a US society that no longer has a cohesive common myth. Scholars reject his anti-Semitic views and criticize his dismissal of differences in cultural myths in favor of a universal "mono-myth" of the hero.[10] They do, however, point out that Campbell's discussion of the individual and communal functions of myth remains helpful.

1. Like Rudolf Otto's *numinous*, described earlier, myths call forth feelings of fascination and dread as believers experience the presence of mystery. They are catalysts for experiences of mystery and address significant questions: Why are we here? What are our responsibilities? How can we maintain hope in the face of death? Like Eliade, Campbell agrees that through myth people experience the powerful feeling of the divine in their lives.
2. Myth describes an ordered universe (a cosmology) and locates humans within that universe. Its focus on order diminishes fear of chaos and anxiety about death. According to Campbell, cosmology and culture interpret each other. As understandings of cosmology change over time, so does myth; it reflects our changing relationships within a changing cosmos.
3. Like Jung, his major influence, Campbell argues that myth supports and validates the specific moral order in the society that it explains. This function and related rituals produce emotions that establish bonds among believers.
4. Finally, myths demonstrate how to live a human life under any circumstances. This pedagogical function carries the individual through the various stages and crises of life, from childhood dependency, to the responsibilities of maturity, to the reflection of old age, and finally, to death. They help people grasp the unfolding of life with integrity and guide them toward a sense of understanding and fulfillment.

TYPES OF MYTH

Many different kinds of myth exist in religious traditions and cultural groups. The most universal are myths of origin; that is, how the people came to live in this place; what their responsibilities are, and so on. Some founding myths declare that society emerged from separation, explaining why individuals are at odds with one another, with themselves, and with their gods. The Bantu people of Mozambique tell a story in which their god Mulungu has Spider spin a rope so that Mulungu and his court can climb up to the sky. Ancestors of the Bantu humans violated the sacred harmony of the earth by hunting, killing, and making fires to control and develop the environment, driving their gods away.

MYTHS OF ORIGIN

We have already noted that such myths often address continuing issues of order in the human world rather than establishing an eternal or sacred order. They represent the urge to discover meaning in or to impose meaning on the worlds of cosmos, *polis*, family, and self. Today, scholars understand them as symbolic narratives whose understanding depends on their cultural contexts. Creation myths orient human beings in the world, giving them a sense of their place in the world and the regard that they must have for humans and nature.

Hindu Creation Myths from the Chandogya Upanishad

The *Upanishads*, meaning "sessions with" or "sitting next to," record monologues and debates among Hindu teachers and their disciples about Vedic scriptures. They generally emphasize self-denial, the way of asceticism, as a means to religious truth and the absolute spiritual realty in and behind all the visible elements of the physical world. Hindus also refer to the Upanishads as Vedanta (end of the Veda) because they end the Vedic scriptures. Many Upanishads have survived; the most important date from 800 to 400 BCE. The Chandogya Upanishad is one of the earliest.

The following myth begins at a distant point. Like a film camera the narrative focuses on a faraway point on the horizon. Then it moves forward to earth and its inhabitants. Everything originates with nonbeing; nonbeing goes on to generate the universe and its inhabitants.

In the beginning, this universe was nonexistent. It became existent. It grew. It turned into an egg. The egg lay for the period of a year. Then it broke open. Of the two halves of the eggshell, one half was of silver, the other of gold. That which was of silver became the earth; that which was of gold, heaven. What was the thick membrane of the white became mountains; the thin membrane of the yolk, the mist and the clouds. The veins became rivers; the fluid in the bladder, the ocean. And what was born of it was younger Aditya, the sun. When it was born shouts of "Hurrah" arose, together with all beings and all objects of desire.

This Hindu story uses language on two levels. It first offers a hatching egg as a metaphor for the self-directed, systematic emergence of the universe. At the same time it constructs, from the very beginning, the reality of the One and the illusion of the many that Hinduism seeks to overcome. Present, too, is desire, which lures men and women to confuse the many with the One. Creation of the universe, then, becomes the backdrop for the story's main purpose, the construction of a Hindu view that explains the hard work of achieving union with the One.

In the second myth, Being, desiring to be many, releases fire. Procreation is neither violent nor painful. Desiring to be many, fire discharges water, which then emits food.

> It [Being] thought to itself: "Would that I were many! Let me procreate myself!" It emitted heat. Heat thought to itself: "Would that I were many! Let me procreate myself." It emitted water. Therefore, whenever peoples grieve or perspire from the heat, then water is produced. Water thought to itself: "Would that I were many! Let me reproduce myself." It emitted food. Therefore when it rains, then there is plenty of food. So food for eating is produced from water.

Like many creation myths, this one contains etiological elements, that is, it explains the origins of biological, meteorological, and geographic phenomena. Here, for example, human tears and perspiration are the result of heat's desire to reproduce. As the Upanishads indicate, a single tradition often has several foundational myths, one containing as much truth as the other. Truth, then, may "be an artifact whose fundamental design we often have to alter" rather than an unchanging order imposed by the gods or nature.[11]

MYTHS OR NARRATIVES OF ALIENATION

Many religious traditions also contain stories that introduce alienation into the relationship between the divine world and the human world, between the natural world and the human world, or between humans themselves. These figurative narratives often account for the problems and sufferings that men and women continue to experience. A story, called "The Fall" in most Christian Bibles, is a good example of this type of narrative.

> Now the serpent was more crafty than any other wild animal that the LORD God had made. He said to the woman, "Did God say, 'You shall not eat from any tree in the garden'?" The woman said to the serpent, "We may eat of the fruit of the trees in the garden; but God said, 'You shall not eat of the fruit of the tree that is in the middle of the garden, nor shall you touch it, or you shall die.'" But the serpent said to the woman, "You will not die; for God knows that when you eat of it your eyes will be opened,

Thinking with Myth

1. Cultural institutions other than religious traditions have foundation myths: the United Kingdom, the United States, Italy, and Israel are examples. Christopher Flood describes political foundation myths as a series of past, present, or predicted political events that a social group accepts as essentially valid.[12] Research two or three foundational stories to which politicians and elected officials refer for support from the majority of their audiences, for example, the United States as a city on a hill. Connect the story to its historical context. This activity involves some research; check the validity of your sources.

2. Compose a myth that accounts for your present world. What relationships and rituals govern this world? What contributions do the relationships make to recreating order within your world on a regular basis? What is your role within this world? How do you maintain it?

3. Comment on this observation: "Myths are maps and myth is symbolism, and for this reason myths are not to be taken literally. It is rather that when the dust falls from our eyes, human beings are themselves the gods and demons, acting out, not the piddling business on worldly life, but the great archetypal situations and dramas of the myths. The gods are the archetypes but they exist as perpetually incarnate in ourselves."[13]

and you will be like God, knowing good and evil." So when the woman saw that the tree was good for food, and that it was a delight to the eyes, and that the tree was to be desired to make one wise, she took of its fruit and ate; and she also gave some to her husband, who was with her, and he ate. Then the eyes of both were opened, and they knew that they were naked; and they sewed fig leaves together and made loincloths for themselves.

They heard the sound of the LORD God walking in the garden at the time of the evening breeze, and the man and his wife hid themselves from the presence of the LORD God among the trees of the garden. But the LORD God called to the man, and said to him, "Where are you?" He said, "I heard the sound of you in the garden, and I was afraid, because I was naked; and I hid myself." He said, "Who told you that you were naked? Have you eaten from the tree of which I commanded you not to eat?" The man said, "The woman whom you gave to be with me, she gave me fruit from the tree, and I ate." Then the LORD God said to the woman, "What is this that you have done?" The woman said, "The serpent tricked me, and I ate." The LORD God said to the serpent,

> "Because you have done this,
>   cursed are you among all animals
>   and among all wild creatures;
> upon your belly you shall go,
>   and dust you shall eat
>   all the days of your life.
> I will put enmity between you and the woman,
>   and between your offspring and hers;
> he will strike your head, and you will strike his heel."

To the woman he said,

> "I will greatly increase your pangs in childbearing;
>   in pain you shall bring forth children,
> yet your desire shall be for your husband,
>   and he shall rule over you."

And to the man he said,

> "Because you have listened to the voice of your wife,
>   and have eaten of the tree
> about which I commanded you,
>   'You shall not eat of it,'
> cursed is the ground because of you;
>   in toil you shall eat of it all the days of your life;
> thorns and thistles it shall bring forth for you;
>   and you shall eat the plants of the field.
> By the sweat of your face
>   you shall eat bread
> until you return to the ground,
>   for out of it you were taken;
> you are dust,
>   and to dust you shall return."

The man named his wife Eve, because she was the mother of all living. And the LORD God made garments of skins for the man and for his wife, and clothed them.

Then the LORD God said, "See, the man has become like one of us, knowing good and evil; and now, he might reach out his hand and take also from the tree of life, and eat, and live forever"—therefore the LORD God sent him forth from the garden of Eden, to till the ground from which he was taken. He drove out the man; and at the east of the garden of Eden he placed the cherubim, and a sword flaming and turning to guard the way to the tree of life. (Gn 3:1–24)

Notice the role of the serpent. In many cultures the serpent is associated with life or wisdom. Influenced by Zoroastrianism, early Christian and Jewish interpreters identified this serpent as the devil, although nothing in the text suggests that the serpent is evil. It is simply part

BROOKE CASTILLO

In Genesis 3, "knowledge of good and evil" represents all knowledge, once divine privilege. Knowledge is a powerful tool for naming oppressive situations. A first step toward taking control of one's life is learning to use language critically to detect when the powerful are lying.

of God's creation. The serpent asks the critical question that shakes Eden's harmony; it sparks the woman's curiosity, fuels her desire, and eventually thwarts the implicit divine plan. The woman reveals that she is already an interpreter of texts; she expands the divine command about the tree of the knowledge with the addition "nor shall you touch it," while the man silently observes (Gn 3:3).

Eating the fruit, of course, breaks one of the deity's commands, a command that sought to deny the couple access to knowledge. Once the first couple eats the fruit, "their eyes were opened"; they are suddenly self-conscious, aware that they are naked in the presence of the other. They become like gods, "knowing all things." They use that knowledge to make clothing to protect their new consciousness of self, a first step toward culture. At the end of the narrative the deity follows their example, making more durable clothing, realizing that they have shed their childish innocence and that, to preserve the integrity of the divine world, they can no longer live in the garden. The serpent's assertion is proven true; they do not die immediately. Only immortality separates them from the gods. The myth itself, not the action of Eve and Adam, may generate some alienation in its readers. This reading differs from the traditional Christian interpretation—among other things, the serpent implies that God has lied about the tree of knowledge. An uncomfortable thought. If so, what is the motivation? Are there details in the story to support such an interpretation?

Why does the woman desire the fruit? Curiosity? Rebellion? How we assess her action may reflect our own socioeconomic status and living situation as well as other privileges and advantages that we bring to reading the Bible. In *Thinking about God* theologian Dorothee Sölle recounts one experience that challenged the traditional reading of the story:

> A black woman pastor interrupted me and said: "But it's quite clear. Adam and Eve wanted to have more than others and so they ate the apple, and that is covetousness. Sin is the immeasurable greed of people who want to possess something, and everything else follows from this desire to possess."[14]

Sölle concludes: "The poor read the Bible and the tradition with different eyes than ours."

Many people live in socioeconomic systems where a few corporations control most resources. Perhaps we should read Genesis 3 as a story about the impact of individual greed on others rather than as a story about breaking a divine command and the entry of evil into the world through original sin.

That example suggests that Genesis 3 has several interpretations. The traditional Christian reading interprets Genesis 3 in light of the crucifixion of Jesus. The sin of the first couple created a huge gulf between God and humanity and so distorted human nature that no human could win God's forgiveness. In addition, the sin of the first couple, original sin, introduced evil and death into the world and became the birthright of every human being. Motivated by love, God sent his Son to free the world and its inhabitants from the grip of original sin and to win forgiveness for human beings. Jesus of Nazareth brought freedom from sin and death through his suffering and death.

Some biblical scholars and theologians break ranks with Christian tradition and read Genesis 3 as a "coming of age" narrative. Remember when you were struggling to establish your own identity, a task that meant separating yourself from your parents? Maybe it began with refusing to attend synagogue, getting a tattoo, deliberately breaking curfew, or rejecting your parents, or rejecting your parents' suggestions about college—a painful time for you and your parents but a necessary transition into adulthood.

The god figure draws a line in the sand: don't eat fruit from the tree of knowledge. If you do, you will die immediately. The woman wants to know how far she can push this god figure; eating the apple is a first step toward independence. She and the man quickly learn the cost of that independence. They acquire "knowledge of good and evil," that is, knowledge of everything, knowledge like the gods. They recognize their physical differences and make clothes; they hide from the god figure, thinking that God has come to exact punishment. Surprisingly, the serpent was right: they don't die. They have the status of adulthood: knowledge about the life they will find outside the garden, a life of hard work, painful childbirth, and sexual desire. The god figure will no longer take care of them; they are on their own. They lose the innocence of the garden; they gain all the knowledge they need to live outside the garden. That knowledge is the reason they must leave. In the divine court the god figure muses, "They have become like one of us, knowing good and evil. If they eat from the tree of life, they will live forever." In other words, they will become gods.

STORIES OF DESTINY

Unlike stories of origin, stories of destiny are meant to inspire hope in and fidelity to God. They are symbolic narratives, speculations about rewards awaiting the faithful. Such narratives do not predict twenty-first century events. They look for an earthly restoration of unity and recompense for the alienation and hostility once suffered by a particular group. They are metaphors of human hope: some day the deity they worship will make things right for the faithful, even if they must wait until after death.

Many myths or religious narratives recount a hero's life, patterning the way a culture thinks about life and providing a paradigm through which people can interpret their own experiences. We can think about the Christian gospels in this way or about the stories of Muhammad preserved in the *hadith*, narratives that demonstrate the Prophet's virtue and dedication to the Qur'an. Other myths concern quests on which the hero embarks to discover her identity or his life-task; these myths sometimes pattern the life stages through which we pass in the work of creating our identity. Some myths struggle with questions of evil, undeserved suffering, and the inevitability of death. Others push beyond the boundaries of death, suggesting that our lives continue.

Stories of Destiny in the Jewish and Christian Scriptures

Some of the most vivid images of future earthly restoration occur in the prophetic literature of the Tanakh. A first set of stories developed out of the destruction of Jerusalem and its Temple in 587–86 BCE to demonstrate that, in spite of those faith-shattering events, Israel's God would reestablish the city as a home for the divine presence. There are several versions of these stories. In each one the people of Israel are granted a secure, peaceful place. They enjoy agricultural and economic security. In the future age, God will be with the people, and that presence will protect and bless believers. Consequently, Israel and Jerusalem will be filled with joy and praise of their God.

The future of the nations who tried to destroy Israel accounts for variations in this story. They suffer various fates as one prophet or another modifies the plot. Sometimes they worship the God of Israel and become Israelites, traveling to Jerusalem in order to learn the Torah.

> Peoples shall stream to it,
>   and many nations shall come and say:
> "Come, let us go up to the mountain of the Lord,
>   to the house of the God of Jacob;
> that he may teach us his ways
>   and that we may walk in his paths." (Mi 4:1–2; see
>   also Is 2:1–3; 25:6–8)

Sometimes these nations are completely destroyed: their armies, their populations and their homelands.

> Egypt shall become a desolation
> and Edom a desolate wilderness,
> because of the violence done to the people of Judah
> in whose land they have shed innocent blood.
> (Jl 4:19).

Sometimes, these nations rebuild Jerusalem and serve the people of Israel as slaves (Is 60:10–12). This restoration is not otherworldly; it takes place in history, on a rejuvenated earth. Some of these narratives describe a new human leader who will occupy David's throne in Jerusalem or a high priest who will reestablish temple worship. Under his rule the people will live faithfully in covenant with one another and with Israel's God, protected from agricultural disasters and military invasions.

A second set of stories developed out of the oppressive governance (175–64 BCE) of the Hellenistic ruler Antiochus Epiphanies IV. Faithful Jews were being executed before they could experience the benefits of their religious devotion. Instead of experiencing the material rewards of covenant living according to God's law—a long life, many descendants, and economic prosperity—Palestinian Jews were bring tortured and executed because they defied Antiochus's ban on circumcision, Torah study, and Sabbath observance. Some storytellers reinterpreted the covenant blessing of long life as a resurrection that only faithful Jews would experience after death.

> Many of those who sleep
> in the dust of the earth will wake up;
> Some will live forever,
> others will be an everlasting horror and disgrace.
> But the wise shall shine brightly
> like the splendor of the heavens,
> And those who lead the many to justice
> will be like the stars forever. (Dn 12:2–3)

This story relocates the blessings of the faithful from this life to the other side of death. Israel's God will raise those wise enough to remain within the covenant to a place of honor. This new image allows the faithful to maintain their hope in God's faithfulness and probably reflects the evolution of the community's own belief and its dissatisfaction with its former model of religion (fidelity leads to blessings and life in the here and now). In a vision the prophet Daniel sees:

> One like a son of man coming, on the clouds of heaven; When he reached the Ancient One and was presented before him, He received dominion, glory, and kingship; nations and peoples of every language serve him. His dominion is an everlasting dominion that shall not be taken away, his kingship shall not be destroyed. (Dn 7:13–14)

Son of man is an important term. In the Tanakh it is a synonym for *person,* with emphasis on human mortality, and it is often used as an antonym for God. In Daniel's vision, "one like a son of man" represents as a group the Jews who remained faithful in spite of persecution; they will form the nucleus of God's kingdom on earth.

In the Gospel of Matthew the triumphal return of Jesus as the son of man is associated with an elaborate final judgment scene. When the Lord returns he will hold court, separating people "as a shepherd separates the sheep from the goats." The blessed, the sheep on his right, inherit the kingdom of heaven and eternal life. They are blessed because they cared for the most disadvantaged members of the Lord's family and, in doing so, ministered to the Lord. The accursed, the goats on his left, enter eternal, fiery punishment because they ignored the disadvantaged and, in so doing, ignored the Lord. Notice that the emphasis of this narrative is on acting justly toward those in need, both neighbor and stranger.

Some stories of destiny involve the abandonment or destruction of this world. Fundamentalist and evangelical Christians read the Book of Revelation in the New Testament in this way: The world as we know it is under the rule of Satan. Famine, wars, and disease mark its last days. Some believers cannot distinguish between Christ and the anti-Christ. This final time ends with a catastrophic battle between the forces of good, led by Christ, believers, and Jews who at the last minute become Christians, and the forces of evil, led by Satan. God and good triumph. Satan, the anti-Christ (who is not mentioned in the book), their followers, and Jews who have refused conversion burn in a lake of fire. (Note the anti-Semitism and the subjugation of Judaism to Christianity.) The earth is destroyed and replaced by the New Jerusalem, where the good live joyfully in God's presence.

I [John] also saw the holy city, a New Jerusalem, coming down out of heaven from God, prepared as a bride adorned for her husband. I heard a loud voice from the throne saying, "Behold, God's dwelling is with the human race. He will dwell with them and they will be his people and God himself will always be with them." (Rv 21:2–3)

Christian Stories of Heaven

Christianity offers stories of destiny for the faithful set in a place called heaven. In Christianity the dead await the return of the Christ and the final judgment that will settle their destiny for eternity. Catholicism extends that story to include a particular judgment immediately after death. Based on the results of the judgment, those who reject God's love head to hell; those who are not purified enough to enter heaven go to purgatory, where they achieve the holiness necessary for heaven; and those who die in God's grace go immediately to heaven and unity with God. When the Christ returns in glory, the dead will experience a bodily resurrection and appear before him for a final judgment, where all the good they have done is revealed. Those who had originally been in purgatory move on to heaven, and those who were already in heaven return there. In an atmosphere of harmony and order, individuals dwell in the presence of God, participating fully in the divine life. Other popular narratives, drawing on gospel stories of Jesus' post-resurrection appearances, emphasize resurrection of the faithful to a perfect physical body with the ability to know everything, reunion with family and friends, conversations with Jesus and Mary, opportunities to meet theologians and the four evangelists, direct accessibility to God, the ability to pass through walls, hobnobbing with all the choirs of angels and so on.[15]

Muslim Stories of Destiny

Like Christianity, Islam views the heavens as the dwelling place of God. Both traditions agree that only those who live according to divine will can gain entry. Since 9/11, one Qur'anic description of a martyr's life after death has garnered attention and commentary— the reward and one possible motive of the hijackers—immediate entry to the Garden of Eden where they will recline on couches, savoring meats and fruits, and enjoying dark-eyed *houris* (virgins) to the background music of flowing rivers. There they remain until the resurrection.

Commentators fail to mention that *martyr* refers to other Muslims who did not engage in killing non-Muslims and in defending Islam. In some Muslim traditions *martyr* includes Muslims who die by fire, by drowning, in the collapse of buildings, or in great physical suffering (including, then, civilian Muslims who are collateral damage in war). All martyrs go directly to the Garden of Eden described above.

Non-martyred Muslims have other things to anticipate. Before they are buried, their spirits return to their dead bodies, rendering them sensate corpses. In the grave, two ghastly angels conduct a trial to determine their next destination. The graves of faithful Muslims are transformed into a luxurious space where they enjoy the long wait for final judgment. For a Muslim whose faith is far from satisfactory or who has sinned, the grave becomes a brutal experience. Earth weighs heavily on the sentient corpse until its rib cage collapses, and worms nibble away at the body. This situation continues sporadically until the final judgment, when Allah sometimes forgives these wayward Muslims.

Native American Stories of Destiny

Some Native American traditions also have stories of destiny that describe a new age and the restoration of past tribal glories. In the late eighteenth and nineteenth centuries Jack Wilson, also known as Wovoka, a Nevada Paiute, told a story based on a vision the Great Spirit had shown him. The story and the dance that accompanied it quickly spread through the native population in the western Plains states. In the story Wovoka described a place he had seen in his vision where all Indians who had died were young and happy again. The land was theirs, and filled with buffalo. They eagerly followed the old ways of life. To transform the present world into this vision world, Wovoka urged Indians to learn and perform the Ghost Dance that he had learned during his vision. These performances were aimed at returning dead ancestors to earthly life and at sparking a peaceful revival of Native American culture.

Wovoka's story nourished the hopes of many Native peoples, and some suggested that the dance alone would drive white settlers off Indian lands and protect Indians from US cavalry bullets. While severe losses at Wounded Knee, South Dakota, in 1890, destroyed these immediate expectations, the Ghost Dance and its promise of revitalized

Native American cultures remain part of the Native imagination. Many Indians continue to search for signs that herald the revival of the Ghost Dance and the restoration of traditional ways.

In 1890 the Bureau of Indian Affairs issued a ban against the practice of Native spiritual rituals, fearing that such rituals, especially the Ghost Dance, were the first step toward a revival of Native American militancy and rampant violence against the US cavalry stationed in Indian territory, as well as violence against white settlers who had appropriated Indian land. The ban held for eighty-eight years, until the American Indian Religious Freedom Act became law in 1978, the second year of the presidency of Jimmy Carter.

Asian Traditions

Asian religions such as Hinduism and Buddhism do not have myths expressing their hopes for restoration or a new creation. Their stories about human destiny are more internal and abstract. In Hinduism, the soul *(atman)* is Brahman, an eternal perfect being. Human beings live in the changing world of appearances and in the immutable Brahman. The souls of individuals captivated by a love of life and an ignorance of true being migrate from one body to another in an endless cycle of reincarnation. Liberation from such reincarnation, the goal of Hinduism, is accomplished through a surrender of individuality in union with Brahman. The natural world is not part of this union.

While Buddhism rejects the existence of a permanent self, it does affirm a connection among the several lives a person may endure. Thus a life in this world is connected to other lives in the many worlds that Buddhists accept. Buddhists recognize desire as the root of all suffering. Their goal, achievable in this life, is nirvana, an indescribable void, a way of being characterized by the absence of desire and ignorance.

PROPHETS WHO CHALLENGE THE STATUS QUO

Not all religious narratives within a community are created equal. Because they create order and structure power relationships, myths carry with them potential for life or death. Therefore, each community must critically reflect to determine, on a regular basis, the adequacy of its underlying myths. If the community ignores or refuses this task, often men and women within it will challenge the community's predominant story. Dietrich Bonhoeffer was one such person. He lived in Germany during the rise of the Third Reich in the twentieth century. A pastor of a Lutheran church, he spoke out against the Reich's normative story, a story of Aryan superiority and Jewish inferiority. The alternate story of the dignity and value of each human person, the center of both Judaism and Christianity, held such power for Bonhoeffer that he joined others with similar views. This group worked together to unmask the fallacies of the myth of Aryan superiority. Because of his allegiance to Christianity's core story, he left the woman he was about to marry and continued to fight the Nazi government until Adolf Hitler's Schutzstaffel (the SS) arrested and executed him for participating in a plot to assassinate Hitler. Bonhoeffer lived a prophetic life; through his words and actions he dismantled a myth founded on the broken bodies of men, women, and children that it judged substandard.

In the 1960s the United States was challenged and eventually, albeit not completely, dealt with a long-standing civil myth for which supporters claimed biblical roots: racism. Rosa Parks opposed that prevailing cultural narrative in Montgomery, Alabama, in 1955. According to that narrative, whenever she, a black woman, boarded a bus, she was to take a seat in the back. One day she found the strength to act against the narrative. She was returning home after a long day of working at a downtown Birmingham department store. Being an African American woman, she was viewed by most white residents of Montgomery as marginally human. Like other blacks, she could not use public facilities reserved for white citizens. Black children were segregated and attended black schools, which often received little or no city or state public moneys. Too tired to stand for the long ride to the bus stop near her home, Rosa Parks chose a seat in the front of the bus. Despite attempts by several male passengers to remove her physically, she refused to surrender her seat.

Her quiet act of rebellion challenged the myth of order and led to her arrest. It also sparked the Montgomery Bus Boycott, a formative event in the African American community's fight for civil rights, headed by Dr. Martin Luther King, Jr., and other African American leaders. Her belief in her human dignity challenged Montgomery's racism. Like Bonhoeffer, she unmasked the inadequacy of a narrative whose power depended upon the white people who complied with it; most failed to question the dehumanization and exclusion of people of color. Bonhoeffer and Parks represent men and women who revealed and who continue to reveal the inadequate narratives that control US society. They include groups advocating nonviolent strategies instead of war, the abolition of nuclear weapons, and a ban on nuclear power plants, reproductive freedom, and unconventional definitions of marriage and family.

The Jewish scriptures include many stories of individuals who challenged the controlling stories of their societies. In the eighth century BCE the prophet Amos contested Israel's dominant story, which went something like this. The nation was enjoying prosperity and domestic security. Its political and religious leaders interpreted this as evidence that God was blessing the people, that their relationship with God was whole and operative. They congratulated themselves on their ability to please God with elaborate sacrifices on festival days. They anticipated the "Day of the Lord," when they expected the Lord to destroy all their national enemies and reward the Israelites with greater economic and political power. Amos, however, disagreed with that assessment. He looked at the situation and told another story. He paid attention to the silent voices. He told the story of a God concerned for the people who were suffering because of the prosperity of the upper classes: small farmers who had been forced to sell their land, and others who had sold themselves into slavery to pay their debts.

> For the three sins of Israel
>   and for four, I will not revoke the punishment;
> Because they sell the righteous for silver,
>   and the needy for a pair of sandals—
> they who trample the head of the poor
> into the dust of the earth,
>   and push the afflicted out of the way. (Am 2:6–7)

The prosperous had forgotten that Israel was one family, that the quality of its relationship with God was determined by the concern the people showed for the poor and homeless in their land. Amos maintained that the prosperity of the upper classes had nothing to do with God's blessing; rather, it was a lightning rod for divine displeasure. The Day of the Lord would blast them; it would bring destruction, not glory. Amos holds out little hope that God will change his mind and be gracious, even if the people "Seek good, not evil" (Am 5:14). Their excessive worship is a poor substitute for what their God desires:

> Let justice roll down like the waters,
>   and righteousness like an ever-flowing stream. (Am
>   5:24)

MANY TYPES OF RELIGIOUS LANGUAGE

In our discussion of religious language thus far, we have considered words spoken and words written. While words are an important aspect of talk about the sacred, we acknowledge that other modes of communication also exist. Feet pounding the earth in rhythmic patterns; heavy drumming, sometimes loud, sometimes soft; bodies swaying to the movements of spirits; arms raised in glad salute to the sun; space ordered with flowers and incense; quiet breathing in harmony with a beating heart; soaring cathedral spires and golden icons—gestures, art, dance, music, and architecture are also words about the sacred. In this final section we consider two such words: the word of Arabic calligraphy in the Islamic tradition and the word of basket weaving of the Yekuana tribe in the South American rain forest.

ISLAMIC CALLIGRAPHY

From its beginning Islam has banned statues, pictures, and other images of Allah and of Muhammad. Muslims developed other forms to honor Allah. Through Egypt, Syria, and Jordan, for example, geometric patterns of inlaid woods and mosaics generally decorate mosque ceilings and floors. As they catch the sun, lattice window coverings create intricate shadows and designs on bare walls. Editions of the Qur'an in Arabic script contain no illustrations; instead, intricate calligraphy (handwriting) draws the reader's intellect and imagination into the recitation of the text. It is not unusual to find framed verses of the Qur'an, in elaborate script highlighted with gold, for sale in tourist gift shops; a popular subject

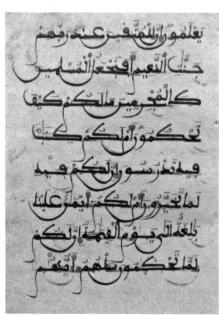

Mo Costandi

Calligraphy from an illuminated Koran, Egypt 1400–1500, in the Jameel Gallery at the Victoria & Albert Museum.

is the divine name Allah, which begins with *alif*, the first letter of the Arabic alphabet. Nor is it unusual to find, in museum displays in Aleppo or Amman, pen boxes and dinner plates from twelfth and fourteenth century CE decorated with calligraphy. This writing transforms these articles, once part of someone's daily life, into reminders of the God whom Muslims seek to remember throughout their day.

Allah used the Arabic alphabet to create cosmic order and natural space. Islamic calligraphy, then, makes visual the inner reality of Islamic revelation. For Muslims, the divine presence resides in the Qur'an. Through calligraphy and recitation, Muslims can "taste the reality of spiritual world."

For centuries Muslims have practiced calligraphy, not only to cultivate good handwriting, a sign of traditional culture, but also to discipline their souls. As they draw a line from right to left, the direction of Arabic writing, they move from the edge of themselves to their heart; through concentrating on writing words in beautiful forms, they gather together fragments of their souls. Meditation on the beauty of these forms leads them to the divine word flowing from beauty's source:

> for every *alif* cannot help but remind us that only the *alif* of Allah should occupy our heart and mind while every point brings about the recollection. . . . "God was and there was nothing with Him," and that furthermore "He is even as He was."[16]

BASKET WEAVING AND THE YEKUANA TRIBE

Muslims may detect the Invisible—discover the order Allah has written into the cosmos—through calligraphy and reestablish order within themselves. In a similar fashion the baskets the Yekuana basket makers weave for their villages daily recreate their world, imbuing it with light and order. The Yekuana, or Canoe People, located alongside two rivers in the South American rain forest, are hunters and farmers who live in self-contained autonomous villages.

The myths associated with the origins and designs of their baskets depict a deeply divided world filled with negativity and darkness; terrible monsters prey on the people themselves. In the myths not only must they drive death away but they must somehow incorporate it into their world and control it. For the Yekuana, weaving is the symbolic way in which they accomplish this. Weaving incorporates the wild cane into ordered, useful patterns. The basket makers, all men, are custodians of order in their villages, as they produce new baskets whose patterns embody myths in which ancestors gain control of hostile forces. The completion of each new basket asserts that these forces are still under control, held fast in the woven cane.

The Yekuana world is also a complex dual reality. It has an invisible double, both independent of it and eternal. Rituals negotiate between these worlds, weaving spirit world and visible world together into a coherent pattern and neutralizing the powers of the spirit world for the Yekuana. Just as new baskets are prepared for each ritual, rituals accompany each aspect of basket weaving, from collecting the raw cane, to preparing dye, to cleansing the completed baskets and inviting the spirits of the material it will hold to come fill it. At each stage of the process invisible spirits are met and disarmed, their powers incorporated into the basket.

Different kinds of baskets play significant roles in rituals of puberty, marriage, and fasting. Like the rituals, the weave and design of the baskets represent a successful resolution of opposites and the creation of integration. The baskets promise resolution at the ritual's beginning, assist in it, and then witness that it has occurred.

In addition to languages of myth and song, the Yekuana weave a language of baskets. The baskets assert that hostile powers are trapped in their weave and in their design; they assure the people that their world is secure and meaningful.[17]

MARY N. MacDonald

Weaving is a powerful symbol of our ability to create order out of chaos. The Hopi Spider Woman weaves a world; Yekuana men weave cosmic order into baskets; Dogon storytellers weave the ancestors into the memory of later generations. These women in Goroka, Papua New Guinea, carry bags that they have woven out of colorful yarn. The bags, useful for carrying babies, food, and daily necessities, are symbolic of women's lives. In their Kewa language the word for "string bag" also means "placenta."

SUMMARY

In this chapter we have considered different ways in which we talk about the sacred. We started with language and discovered that we use it in many ways. We most commonly use language figuratively. We use the language of metaphor to talk about the sacred. These metaphors are the products of our imagination, our experience, and our culture. No one metaphor exhausts the ways we can describe the holy. No single metaphor defines mystery.

In the second part of the chapter, we examined myth. A myth is a story that embodies a community's value systems and power structures. Although myths talk about origins of the universe, they are generally about the relationships that must be in place for the present community to function. Myths of destiny motivate religious people to remain faithful to their traditions in the hope of experiencing harmony and fulfillment after their death. Prophetic myths judge the accuracy of a community's foundational narrative in terms of a competing story. Finally, we looked at two types of religious language whose words are neither spoken nor written. Arabic calligraphy and Yekuana basket weaving speak words of order and protection to their respective communities; like myths, they too symbolize the order they create.

In Chapter 7 we continue to consider religious stories. Our categories, however, change. Many religious traditions have their own scriptures. We will study how scriptures are collected, how decisions are made about what material to include, and how religious traditions regard their scriptures. We will also read selections from different traditions. These scriptures are often the basis for doctrine, the normative beliefs of a community. Both doctrines and creeds, statements in which doctrines are sometimes expressed, are other versions of the community story. Like myth, their language is figurative, not literal. Like myth, they are metaphors that order our relationship with the sacred.

RESOURCES

ACTIVITIES

1. Ask several people from different age, ethnic, and social groups what metaphors they use to describe their relationship with the sacred. Where do they find these metaphors: scripture, ritual, personal reading, personal experiences or relationships, their imaginations? Are there metaphors that they no longer use? Why? What metaphors do you or someone you know use to describe a relationship with the sacred? What associations do you make with each metaphor? Where did you find these metaphors? Combine your data with other students who worked on this activity and present your findings to the class.

2. Consult a good translation of the New Testament (New Revised Standard Version or New Revised American Bible, for example) and read several parables about the kingdom of God/heaven. Identify and analyze the images these parables use. Rewrite one or two parables using contemporary language and images. Share your analysis of language and your rewrites with your group, with the whole class, or post this information in your class bulletin folder.

3. Read the book of Jonah in the Hebrew scriptures. When you have finished, think about the two major narratives that make up the story: Jonah has one narrative; God has another. You may want to include the narratives of the sailors and of the people of Nineveh. Describe these narratives and how they are in tension with each other. You may want to express your thinking in different media: pen and ink sketches, a song, a poem, a video, and so forth.

4. Interview the leader of a church, synagogue, or mosque in your neighborhood or city. Ask how that person understands the prophetic identity of the religious community. How does that identity direct its involvement in the neighbor or city? What social problems does it target? If one of the individuals discussed in the section on prophets were to accompany you on the interview, what questions would that person ask? How would the prophet respond to the minister, priest, rabbi, or imam?

5. Create your own anthology of sacred stories from several religious traditions. Use the categories in this chapter or create your own. Provide commentary for the stories you select and give information about the religious traditions in which they are found. Share your work with your group. You can find collections of religious myths in the library or on the Internet.

6. Joseph Campbell has argued that movies like the *Star Wars* trilogy are the best examples of contemporary mythologies. Were he alive

today, he would undoubtedly add *The Lord of the Rings* trilogy and the Harry Potter films. You might want to add others. Identify the mythic structure of one of the films—the views of humanity, the world, the sacred, and other themes that you think are important. You may want to do this as a group project and then present it to the class, using film clips to illustrate important points.

READINGS

Esack, Farid. *The Qur'an: A Beginner's Guide*. Oxford: One World, 2007.

Guss, David M. *To Weave and Sing: Art, Symbol, and Narrative in the South American Rain Forest*. Berkeley and Los Angeles: University of California Press, 1990. Guss describes a culture in which weaving is a metaphor for order-producing activities.

MacLeish, Archibald. *J.B.* A 1950s adaption of the biblical book of Job in which J.B., the main character, struggles to maintain faith and hope in the aftermath of terrible loss.

Nasr, Seyyed. *Islamic Art and Spirituality*. Albany: State University of New York, 1987.

Roncace, Mark, and Patrick Gray, eds. *Teaching the Bible through Popular Culture and the Arts*. Atlanta: Society of Bible Literature, 2007. This book suggests activities for collaborative learning integrating biblical themes and popular culture.

Sproul, Barbara. *Primal Myths: Creation Myths around the World*. Second edition. San Francisco: Harper, 1979. In addition to an extensive introductory essay on myth, Sproul presents myths of origin according to geographic area and provides background and commentary for each entry.

For additional examples of parables see, among others, Plato, "The Cave," in *The Republic*; Franz Kafka, *Metamorphosis, The Trial*.

AUDIO-VISUALS

Popol Vuh (1989). A PBS presentation of the Mayan creation myth, with animated images based on figures carved on Mayan architecture.

Joseph Campbell and the Power of Myth (2001). New York: Mystic Fire Video. Bill Moyers and Joseph Campbell discuss the themes and roots of human myth, which is seen as humanity's attempt to relate to the universe. Starting with various topics Campbell shows both how humanity creates its universe and is controlled by the myth it has created.

Pulp Fiction (1995). Miramax Films. A Quentin Tarentino film, the title is a reference to the inexpensive and sensational dime novels printed on cheap paper at the beginning of the twentieth century. Healing, forgiveness, and grace run through the film.

The Mythology of Star Wars with George Lucas and Bill Moyers (1999). Available from Films for the Humanities and Sciences, 132 West 31st Street, 17th Floor, New York, NY 10001. In this program George Lucas discusses his efforts to tell old myths in new ways, the role of faith in his own life, and the influence of his mentor, Joseph Campbell.

NOTES

1. Iris Murdoch in Sallie McFague, *Speaking in Parables: A Study in Metaphor and Theology* (Philadelphia: Fortress Press, 1975), 24.

2. Amos Wilder, *The Bible and the Literary Critic* (Minneapolis: Fortress Press, 1991), 143–44.

3. Paul van Buren, *The Edges of Language*, cited in James C. Livingston, *The Anatomy of the Sacred* (New York: Macmillan, 1989), 96.

4. Shin'ichi Hisamatsu, "Zen: Its Meaning for Modern Civilization," trans. R. DeMartino and Gishin Tokina, *The Eastern Buddhist* 1/1 (1965): 32.

5. W. M. Watt, *Islamic Philosophy and Theology* (Edinburgh: University Press), 246–47.

6. Julian of Norwich, *Showings: Revelations of Divine Love*, trans. Edmund Colledge and James Walsh, Classics of Western Spirituality (New York: Paulist Press, 1978), chap. 60.

7. C. H. Dodd, *The Parables of the Kingdom*, rev. ed. (New York: Scribners, 1961), 16.

8. Mircea Eliade, *Myth and Reality*, trans. W. R. Trask (New York: Harper and Row, 1963), 12–18.

9. C. J. Jung, *Man and His Symbols* (Garden City, NY: Doubleday, 1964); see also Wallace Clift, *Jung and Christianity* (New York: Crossroad, 1982).

10. Joseph Campbell, *Myths to Live By* (New York: Bantam/Viking, 1973); idem, with Bill Moyers, *The Power of Myth* (New York: Doubleday, 1988).

11. Kenneth Kramer, *World Scriptures: An Introduction to Comparative Religion* (New York: Paulist Press, 1986), 154–56.

12. Christopher Flood, *Political Myth* (New York: Routledge, 2001), 44.

13. Allan Watts, *The Two Hands of God* (New York: Macmillan Publishing Co., 1969), 13.

14. Dorothee Sölle, *Thinking about God: An Introduction to Theology* (Philadelphia: Trinity Press International, 1990), 61.

15. For changing interpretations of the symbol of heaven, see Colleen McDannell and Bernhard Lang, *Heaven: A History*, 2nd ed. (New Haven, CT: Yale University Press, 2001).

16. Seyyed Hussein Nasr, *Islamic Art and Spirituality* (Albany: State University of New York, 1987), 34. The discussion in this section is based on the book's second chapter, "The Spiritual Message of Islamic Calligraphy," 17–34.

17. This discussion of Yekuana basket weaving depends on David M. Guss, *To Weave and Sing: Art, Symbol, and Narrative in the South American Rain Forest* (Berkeley and Los Angeles: University of California, 1990).

Chapter 7

Scriptures, Canons, and Creeds

SCRIPTURE

Most religious traditions have a collection of stories, prayers, curses and blessings, incantations, and laws that they consider powerful and authoritative. Scripture, from the Latin scriptura, "a writing," is usually part or all of an oral tradition written down, whether on sheets of papyrus or palm leaves, in a scroll, or in a book. The word *scripture* is usually reserved for texts that, over time, a believing community has determined to be an authoritative support for belief and practice and a rich source of spiritual life. Its purpose is to preserve normative texts at certain times and in certain cultures while oral traditions may continue to develop. At one time the word was synonymous with the Jewish Tanakh and the Christian Bible. Today scholars of religion also use it to designate normative texts of other religious traditions, although practitioners might not appreciate such vocabulary. Whether oral or written, these collections shape the personal and communal lives of believers and, for some, their participation in the political process.

Christians use scripture in positive authentic ways: in ritual and other forms of communal prayer, and as a primary source of teachings and practice. They also turn to scripture for personal prayer, meditation, and transformation. Some Christians seek not only personal transformation but social transformation as well. Scripture calls them to action—to oppose legal and social institutions that, from their readings of scriptures, seem to violate human rights. For example, they might publicly oppose the death penalty because, in their estimation, the criminal justice system seldom delivers justice for people of color and people of lower economic status. Others support the death penalty, citing the Old Testament *lex talionis* passages, "An eye for an eye . . . a life for a life" (Ex 21:22–25; Lv 24:19–21; Dt 19:16–21).[1] Many Christians, including some Catholics, contend that the United States was founded as a Christian nation; therefore, a literalist interpretation of the Bible should inform federal and state laws as well as Supreme Court decisions. Proponents and opponents of almost any political issue can find texts to support their positions.

Members of other religious traditions appeal to their scriptures in similar ways. In Israel, religious practices about the Shabbat, the Sabbath, shape the lives of both religious and secular Jews. Public transportation on the Shabbat, especially in Jerusalem, ceases before the Shabbat begins Friday evening and resumes Saturday evening; shopping malls, restaurants, recreational facilities, and so on are closed; streets are silent while observant Jews walk to synagogue. Muslim leaders use the verses from the Qur'an and the Hadith to place constraints on the behavior and dress of Islamic women around the world, although the degree of restriction differs from group to group.

In addition, many practitioners across the religious spectrum question why a three-thousand-year-old book like the Bible should influence personal decisions about life issues that did not exist "back then." Religious leaders, they claim, use certain texts to control believers, threatening an eternity in hell if believers question, much less ignore, their directives. For whatever reasons, some leaders fail to model different methods of interpreting the text for their communities. Numerous questions surround scripture: How can it be the word of God? What makes scripture holy or sacred? Who decided which scriptures contain God's word? You probably have other questions about scripture or sacred religious texts, whatever your religious tradition. In the previous chapter we learned that the language of religion is symbolic and conditioned by history and culture. How do those insights influence the ways in which believers read and interpret such texts?

We consider some of these important questions in this chapter: how anonymous Christians shaped the four New Testament **gospels** out of existing materials; how individuals dealt with inconsistencies among those gospels; how the early church responded to questions about the significance of the Jewish Tanakh. Our discussion also provides tools to read scripture responsibly for understanding and meaning. Finally, we briefly examine doctrines and creeds and their relationship to scripture and other religious literature.

Space limitations preclude even brief discussions of the scriptures, religious writing, performances, and oral texts of all major world religions. We have selected Judaism for its influences on Christianity; Islam for its importance in today's world; and Hinduism for its challenge to Western notions of religion. Because we consider Christian scriptures in the case study later in this chapter, they are not part of the following discussion.

JEWISH SCRIPTURE

The sacred books of Judaism are the Tanakh, especially the Torah, and the **Talmud**. In addition to the Torah, the Tanakh contains the Nevi'im, the books of the prophets (Joshua to 2 Kings). This literature is a mix of social criticism and history. It relates the rise and fall of the Israelites from the Israelite takeover of Canaanite land, through the creation of the northern kingdom of Israel and the southern kingdom of Judah, to the destruction of the northern kingdom in 720 BCE and two hundred years later the sacking of Jerusalem and its Temple, and the exile of the royal family as well as the upper class and middle-class artisans to Babylon, the fifth-century BCE "Paris" of the Middle East. Also part of the Tanakh, the Writings contain a less unified body of literature: the lyrical and demanding psalms, the pessimistic book of the preacher (Qoheleth), the erotic Song of Songs, the righteous complaint of Job, assertive Ruth and Esther, legalistic Ezra and Nehemiah, the revisionist Chroniclers, and playful feminine Wisdom.

The Torah, the first five books of the Tanakh, and the Talmud (see discussion below) are the central and most important religious scriptures in Judaism. Frequently construed as Law, the Torah is better understood as "teaching" or "instruction." The titles of the books in the Torah are the first Hebrew words in each book.

1. *Bereshit* (Genesis)—the beginning of the social world as the Israelites knew it and the beginning of the Israelites as God's people.
2. *Shemot* (Exodus)—a list of the Israelites who traveled to Egypt to escape famine, and their subsequent enslavement. Moses leads them into the wilderness to worship the god of their ancestors, to make a covenant in which people choose that god as their god, and to become God's chosen people; they build a tent of meeting, resembling the Jerusalem Temple, where God's presence dwelt.
3. *V'yakra* (Leviticus)—the duties of the Levites; dietary laws; caring for the poor and non-Israelites; purity laws governing food and behavior; and duties of the priests and Levites who will minister in the yet-to-be-built Temple.

4. *B'midbar* (Numbers)—stories of Israelite's rebellion against Moses and their God, fearful they will starve and die of thirst in the wilderness; celebration of the first Passover; selection of Joshua as the successor to Moses; a delightful narrative of Balaam and his ass; and laws governing festivals while the Israelites gather on the bank of Jordan River, ready to enter Canaan.

5. *Devarim* (Deuteronomy)—Moses's final sermon; an account of the deeds of the Lord on the Israelites' behalf; command to teach their children about those deeds and to recite the **Shema**; laws regarding war, treatment of widows, orphans, and non-Israelites who live among them, and so on; Moses's death and Joshua's preparations to cross the Jordan River into the land of Canaan.

According to Jewish tradition, God dictated the written Torah and an oral Torah to Moses on Mount Sinai fifty days after the Exodus from Egypt into freedom. Observant Jews regard the Torah as a divine blueprint that demonstrates God's will on a daily basis. Among narratives, songs, and prayers, rabbis isolated 613 *mitzvoth* (commands). Many of the *mitzvoth* offer positive and negative versions of the same command. For example, *mitzvoth* 71 states that the newly married husband shall (be free) for one year to rejoice with his wife (Dt 24:5); and *mitzvoth* 72 states that a bridegroom shall be exempt for a whole year from taking part in any public labor, such as military service, guarding the wall, and similar duties (Dt 24:5). The *mitzvoth* have one major purpose: to erode excessive self-concern as Jews perform *mitzvoth* for others, thus growing in love of others and of the world. This purpose is related to the concept of *tikkun olam*, performing *mitzvoth* to perfect or heal the world and thereby hastening the arrival of the **messiah**.

Not only did the Lord dictate the written Torah, but he had Moses memorize an oral Torah to be handed down from one generation to another. Following Hadrian's final destruction of Jerusalem (140 CE), rabbis in Palestine feared that their community and its oral traditions might be destroyed. They agreed that the only way to preserve the oral Torah was to write it down. The project, later called the Mishnah, was completed around 200 CE. Gradually over the next four centuries in Israel and Babylon, the two centers of Jewish life, rabbis recorded their debates and discussions about the Mishnah; at different times those records were compiled into the Gemara (rabbinical debates about the Mishnah). The Mishnah (written oral law) and the Gemara were edited into the multi-volume work known as the Talmud around the late fourth century or early fifth century CE in Jerusalem. The Babylonian Talmud compiled in the late sixth century or early seventh century is preferred to the Jerusalem Talmud because its text is better preserved and it contains debates on more portions of the Mishnah. Most rabbinical schools use the Babylonian Talmud for debate and discussion.

ISLAMIC SCRIPTURE

The Islamic holy books are the records that most Muslims believe were dictated by God to various Jewish and Christian prophets. Muslims believe that Jews and Christians had falsified the divine message revealed to Adam, Islam's first prophet, to Abraham, to Moses (the Torah), to David (the Book of Psalms), and to Jesus, the Injil (gospel). To correct those distortions, God spoke one final and literal word, the Qur'an (reading or recitation). Through the angel Jibrîl (Gabriel), God revealed sections of the Qur'an to Muhammad, a non-literate Meccan merchant, beginning in 610 and ending in 632 CE, the year of his death. Muhammad memorized the verses *(ayat)* and recited them to his companions, who wrote down each revelation. At the same time these revelations became part of an oral tradition. After Muhammad's death, Abu Bakr, the first caliph, had all the written revelations standardized and edited into one book. Today, the Umma, the worldwide Islamic community, uses the Abu Bakr edition.

In its 114 surah (chapters), arranged from the longest to the shortest, the Qur'an represents Islam as the definitive religion, declaring that the essence of religion is submission to Allah in every aspect of life. The Qur'an has one purpose stated in multiple ways: to declare that God is one and sovereign. The first surah, part of the *salat*, the prayer that Muslims recite daily, is the heart of the Qur'an:

> In the name of Allah, filled with compassion and
>   mercy!
> Praise to Allah, Lord of Creation,
> The Compassionate, the Merciful King of Judgment
>   Day:
> You alone we worship and to you alone we pray for
>   help—
> Guide us to the straight path,
> The path of those whom you have favored;
> Not [the path] of those who have earned your anger,
> Nor [the path] of those who have gone astray.

Even though the sounds and shape of the Arabic letters of the Qur'an are valued more than the printed book itself, Muslims ritually wash their hands before reciting from the Qur'an. These Islamic women in Bangladesh follow the custom of resting the Qur'an on a small book stand so it does not touch the floor.

The Qur'an is intended for study, but more important, for chanting, memorizing, and reciting. Muslims believe that the Arabic language of the Qur'an and its contents, as well as its rhythm, figurative language, and rhetorical features, each reveal something of God's essence. So sacred is the Qur'an that Muslims consider translations into other languages as commentaries and not authentic versions of the Qur'an. Non-literate Muslims and non-Arabic speakers trace verses with their fingers and receive as much merit as those who chant or recite the Qur'an.

Because the Qur'an is the literal word of God, its meaning is crystal clear and critical interpretation has been discouraged. In the last two decades, however, American and European Muslim scholars, especially women, have taken on critical analysis of Qur'anic statements on women; other scholars are beginning to use historical criticism to unravel the contexts and applicability of the controversial "sword" *ayat*.

HINDU RELIGIOUS LITERATURE

Unlike Judaism, Christianity, and Islam, Hinduism does not have a central narrative. Its religious literature is divided into two categories: *shurti* literature and *smurti* literature. The gods revealed the *shurtis* to the earliest wise men; thus they are divine truths and earthly manifestations of the gods. The four Vedas are the oldest *shurti* texts. They include various creation stories (remember the Purusa Sukta discussed in Chapter 1), directions for making proper ritual sacrifices, and assorted prayers to the gods. Second in importance to the Vedas are the Upanishads. At one time they were considered secret texts handed on from wise teacher to a disciple.

Smurti literature, composed by wisdom teachers, is based on the Vedas and intended to explain their content to ordinary Hindus. Hindus memorize them and pass them from one generation to the next. Among *smurti* texts we find both epics and sutras. The Mahabharata, including the Bhagavad Gita, and the Ramayana are the oldest epics. Similar to Homer's *Iliad* and *Odyssey*, they are long poems recounting the heroic exploits of gods and human warriors. Krishna, an avatar of the god Vishnu, appears in the Bhagavad Gita; Rama, another avatar, has a central role in the second of these great epics. The sutras contain a number of important texts concerning subjects such as dharma, yoga and vedanta. The most important of these texts is the Manusmurti, the Laws of Manu, dealing with Hindu law and conduct.

Latin Bible, f.325r, thirteenth century.

The Mahabharata, India's national epic, tells the story of the five Pandava brothers whose father ruled a kingdom in the Himalayas. The oldest brother puts up his brothers and the kingdom to cover his losses in a dice game. His ploy is unsuccessful, and throughout the rest of the epic, the brothers struggle to win back their kingdom.

The Bhagavad Gita, the most popular epic, focuses on Arjuna, the greatest warrior among the Pandava brothers. Shortly before a major battle against family members, he freezes and tries to withdraw from battle, from action. He worries that he will be fighting relatives toe to toe. Would that be moral? Why must he kill them? At that point Krishna, Arjuna's chariot driver and an earthly manifestation of the god Vishnu, begins a dialogue with Arjuna, reminding him that as a warrior, his dharma is to fight. If he refuses, cosmic order will be undone. Krishna also instructs Arjuna (and the reader) about the paths of devotion, disinterested action, meditation, and knowledge, emphasizing that each is a valid way to attain *moksha* or enlightenment. Krishna convinces Arjuna to fulfill his dharma.

WHY SCRIPTURE AND NOT THE BIBLE?

Why scripture and not the Tanakh, the Bible, the Qur'an, or religious literature"? Here are several grossly simplified descriptions of the ways in which religious practitioners, in these examples Christians, and others distinguish between scripture and the Bible. They focus on Christians in preparation for the case study later in this chapter.

Many Christian practitioners believe that God, however they understand the concept of God, revealed their sacred writings and that they are God's word, which has been written down and handed on from one generation to the next. Some maintain that these writings are inerrant, that is, true in every possible way, and that they need no interpretation. Because they represent a literal timeless divine perspective on the meaning of reality, these texts are essentially different from secular writing and are most appropriately used for ritual, personal prayer, and public and personal moral and spiritual guidance. To distinguish its unique quality, this group conceives of the Bible as sacred or holy scripture. This approach, for example, pits creationism and intelligent design against scientific theories about the origin of Homo sapiens and Darwin's theory of evolution, for example.

Other Christians understand the Bible as the word of God in a figurative or metaphorical sense, inerrant (without mistakes) in matters that are necessary for salvation, but not in other areas mentioned above. This group maintains that critical analysis is necessary to understand the biblical text. They use such methods as historical and literary analyses to arrive at understanding. Their goal, however, is to grasp the theological meaning of the text and, in turn, to be grasped, transformed, by it. Thus they use the lens of their faith to move beyond the understandings reached through critical analyses to that meaning. To highlight this approach to the Bible, they refer to it as holy or sacred scripture used for ritual, private prayer, and moral and spiritual guidance.

A third group has little or no interest in considering a theological meaning of the biblical text. It regards the Bible as a secular cultural artifact, similar to other ancient Near Eastern literatures in its claims to truth and innocent of divine revelation. Members of this group exhibit a variety of legitimate interests: reconstructing and understanding the cultural, historical, and social background of texts; tracing the transition from oral tradition to written texts, both with multiple textual variants; studying the text as literature as one might study a modern short story, poem, or novel; uncovering ideologies that govern the text and privilege the voices and interests of one group over another. This group, sometimes disparagingly referred to as scholars, includes nonbelievers as well as religious practitioners. For the most part, members of the last group suspend their beliefs to distinguish their academic writings from the writings of those who seek not only understanding but also theological meaning—meaning grounded in the covenant between the Lord and Israel or in the saving event of Jesus the Christ.

SCRIPTURE AND CANON

Open your Bible and find the table of contents or the list of books contained in the Old Testament and the New Testament. Note that a Catholic edition of the Bible contains more Old Testament books than a Protestant edition.

Case Study: The Christian Canon

We generally refer to the first developmental stages of Christianity as early Christianity, as if the majority of Christian communities accepted the same teachings and practices. It would be more accurate to rename that period early Christianities or early Christian churches. Christian communities then were as creative and fractious as Protestant and Roman Catholic Christianities are today. Unity is not established by means of uniformity; rather, it results from interactions among diversity, pluralism, tradition, experience, and imagination.

The English word **canon** comes from the Greek *kanon*, itself a Hebrew loan word, *qanah* (reed). Straight reeds of an agreed-upon length are similar to today's measuring tape or yardstick. They were used to measure length or height (see "measuring rod" in Ez 40:3, 5). The apostle Paul is the only New Testament writer to use the Greek form to mean a "standard of true Christianity" (Phil 3:16; Gal 6:16). Later theologians used the word to describe authoritative teachings or laws (such as canon law) that are binding and then as the authoritative list of books in the Christian Bible.

The New Testament Gospels

Gospels are stories of victory, good news (in Greek, *euangelion*). Neither biography nor history, they are interpretations of the life and ministry and the death and resurrection of Jesus from particular points of view. Written for specific communities, they elaborate and strengthen the faith of community members. Some interpreters suggest that the Gospel of Mark, for example, presents Jesus as the perfect disciple who remains faithful to God through suffering and death. Using that as a clue, they suggest that Mark's community might have been facing persecution. His gospel, then, challenges his community to follow Jesus' example, to remain faithful and share in his victory over death.[2]

Of the four gospels, the Gospel of John is distinctive in language, style, and content; in fact, it bears little resemblance to the other three gospels. The gospels of Matthew, Mark, and Luke seem to view Jesus "with the same eye" (**synoptic**) and often contain similar material, sometimes word for word. At the same time, the Gospel of Matthew contains passages and events that are missing from the Gospel of Luke, and Luke contains material that does not appear in Matthew. How do we explain the sources of that material? Scholars describe that question as the **synoptic problem**. This next section presents one solution.

The Synoptic Gospels: From Oral Tradition to Canonical Texts[3]

How did the gospels originate? Did evangelists produce them as whole and complete manuscripts? In their search for answers scholars have created a variety of models using clues from the gospels and other New Testament texts, historical and cultural studies, intuition and imagination. The following model describes four broad and overlapping stages in the formation of the first three gospels.

Stage 1: The ministry of Jesus of Nazareth and the formation of his disciples to carry on that ministry in their preaching: According to the **Acts of the Apostles,** after his resurrection and ascension, the apostles and disciples began to interpret the words and deeds of Jesus, as they remembered them. As this oral tradition was developing, early Christian communities utilized the apostles' preaching to create hymns, prayers, and other aids to integrate new members. They also reinterpreted parts of the Jewish tradition to express their faith in Jesus.

Stage 2: Creation of written collections of the sayings of Jesus as well as parables, miracles, and healing stories; stories of confrontation and controversy with Jewish religious leaders, and so on: Scholars call one collection of sayings **Q** (from the German word **Quelle,** "source"). This source, some suggest, accounts for the material present in the gospels of Matthew and Luke but absent from the Gospel of Mark. Proponents of Q use Matthew and Luke to reconstruct Q, sometimes generating lists that differ. Opponents point out that no physical evidence for Q exists, suggesting that it might be more imaginary than real. These collections, both oral and written, were circulated among the Christian communities. Preachers and teachers modified or expanded oral sources to emphasize different points of view and to accommodate specific audiences, thus diverging at times from the written collections.

Stage 3: Development of apologetic material, defending the claim that Jesus is the Messiah. Preachers and teachers generated new material for Jewish audiences, drawing on the Septuagint (an expanded Greek version of the Tanakh) to support their assertion that Jesus was God's anointed, the Messiah. This declaration would not have been evident to first-century Jews because Jesus had been rejected by the religious leaders in Jerusalem and had died a criminal's death. In a letter to the Corinthian community, Paul, for example, calls the cross a "scandal" or "stumbling block" (in Greek, *skandalon)* for the Jews (1 Cor 1:23). To address that concern, the first continuous narrative about Jesus, the passion and resurrection narrative, is created. It places the passion and death in the context of a divine plan. Such a narrative may have formed the core of the Gospel of Mark, which is sometimes described as a **passion narrative** with a long introduction.

Stage 4: Writing of the gospels. Each gospel was written for a specific community in a specific historical setting. Working from some (but not all) written and oral collections mentioned above, individuals wrote narratives that celebrated the victory of Jesus over the powers of death and sin. This was a process rather than a one-time event. Later editors, for example, added material based on oral traditions and material to bring a narrative more in line with others. The Gospel of Mark is a good example. Look at Mark 16. Notice that editors at different times added different endings. Read Mark 16:1–8 (Mark's original ending) and the added endings. How are they different? Also notice that neither added ending has a parallel in Matthew and Luke. What does that indicate?

Even though the four gospels in the New Testament are traditionally linked with Matthew, Mark, Luke, and John, the authors actually are unknown. Their acquaintance with Jesus probably came from their religious experiences in response to preachers and teachers who used second- and third-stage materials. In antiquity, authors often attached names of well-known or revered people to claim authenticity for their writings.

The four gospels that were included in the New Testament (the canonical gospels) were not the only gospels written in the early days of Christianity. Others circulated, often providing information about the life of Jesus of Nazareth ignored by or unknown to the authors of the canonical gospels. The boyhood of Jesus was a favorite topic of such narratives, some bordering on legend. One gospel, for example, tells of the boy Jesus molding birds out of clay, breathing on them, and letting them fly away. Another recounts a story of Jesus playing with his friends. One boy knocked Jesus down, and in retaliation Jesus struck his playmate dead; only when their mothers call them to supper does Jesus restore the boy to life. As problematic as we may find this material, it reminds us that the gospel narratives are symbolic stories. Because we may be so accustomed to viewing the canonical gospels as factual accounts of what really happened, we forget that they are interpretations in narrative form. They express insight, not fact.[4]

The Gospel of Thomas is an important non-canonical gospel. Originally written in Greek, it is a compilation of 114 sayings, proverbs, parables, and prophecies that Jesus secretly taught to a small inner group of followers. While some of the teachings have a **Gnostic** flavor, many sayings parallel those found in the canonical gospels. Compare, for example, "Let the little children come to me; do not stop them. For it is to such as these that the kingdom of God belongs. Whoever does not receive the kingdom of God as a little child will never enter it" (Mk 10:14–15) with "Jesus saw infants being suckled. He said to his disciples, 'These infants being suckled are like those who enter the kingdom'" (Thomas 22a.). The Gospel of Thomas may preserve an older form of Jesus' words, along with authentic sayings not found in Matthew, Mark, Luke, or John. Its existence offers some support for the existence of other collections (Q, discussed in Stage 2, for example). Some scholars, convinced of its authenticity, call the Gospel of Thomas "the fifth [canonical] gospel."[5]

The Christian Canon: The Four Gospels

Most church historians agree that the list of the four gospels in the New Testament developed in response to several crises. The first of these crises was the appearance of Tatian's **Diatessaron**, produced in Syria in approximately 165 CE. In addition to heretical teachings, **Tatian** edited the four gospels into one harmonious biography of Jesus of Nazareth, omitting inconsistencies and contradictions found among the four gospels. His work raised questions about the nature of a gospel. Was it a historical document or a faith statement? What did the lack of harmony among the gospels on some issues mean? Did Christianity need four gospels?

By 180 CE we have the first documentation for the canon of four gospels in the Muratorian Fragment.[6] In response to Tatian's Diatessaron and the proliferation of gospels circulating among Christian communities, church leaders established the criteria for texts to be recognized as official gospels:

1. They eliminated **heresy**.
2. They encouraged martyrdom in response to the mandate to "take up your cross and follow me."
3. They were connected with the original apostles, however tenuously.
4. And, perhaps most significant, local Christian communities were using them for teaching and preaching.

Directed by the Holy Spirit, church leaders were astute enough to recognize the four gospels of Matthew, Mark, Luke, and John; all of them met the newly established criteria.

The **Council of Chalcedon** (452 CE) established the current New Testament canon with twenty-seven books. Some books made it onto the list after considerable politicking. For example, as a compromise the Letter to the Hebrews was allowed into the canon on the condition that the Book of Revelation was also declared canonical. To meet established criteria, participants assigned apostolic authorship to them: the Book of Revelation was attributed to the apostle John and the Letter to the Hebrews to Paul.

The Christian Canon: The Old Testament

Many early theologians contended that the Tanakh offered great legitimacy for Christianity because, in their estimation, the Tanakh foreshadowed the coming of Jesus the Christ and his identity as Messiah, thus establishing his life and particularly his execution as a "rabble rouser" and "blasphemer" as part of God's plan. Others argued that the focus of the Old Testament was a covenant between Israel and that its God had been replaced by a new covenant between Jesus the Christ and the church. As a result, some Christian thinkers dismissed the Tanakh, arguing that Christians were now the "new Israel" (Rom 11, for example).

Marcion, a Christian scholar living in Rome (and the son of a bishop) is probably the most notorious representative of the latter group. Marcion was convinced that the Old Testament God was not the God whom Jesus of Nazareth addressed as Father. The forgiving, loving God that Jesus preached had replaced the angry vengeful God of the Old Testament. This New Testament God, revealed in Jesus' ministry, wanted to free human beings from the tyranny of the Old Testament God. To buy their freedom, this God offered his Son as a sacrifice. Insistent that the authentic writings of the apostle Paul had primacy over other early Christian texts, Marcion proposed a very short canon: ten letters attributed to Paul and an edited version of the Gospel of Luke. He selected that gospel because its author also wrote the Acts of the Apostles and apparently accompanied Paul on some of his missionary journeys.

Church leadership condemned Marcion's canon and its interpretative principle and struggled with the challenges it represented: What was the relationship between the Tanakh and the New Testament? Should the Christian Old Testament follow the canon of the Jewish Bible or the canon of the Greek Septuagint (the Greek translation of the Tanakh for Greek-speaking Jewish communities in the Diaspora)?

The Councils of Hippo (393 CE) and Carthage (397 and 419 CE) addressed that challenge. Most Christian communities were already using the Septuagint. Furthermore, authors of some of the canonical gospels had relied on versions of the Septuagint for Old Testament citations, an indication, perhaps, that early communities in Syro-Palestine used the Septuagint to emphasize their separation from Judaism. Also included in the Septuagint canon were Tobit, Judith, the Wisdom of Solomon, Sirach (then named Ecclesiaticus), 1 and 2 Maccabees, 1 and 2 Esdras, the Letter of Jeremiah, and additions to the books of Esther and Daniel. By selecting the canon of the Septuagint as the

Old Testament canon, the councils recognized the faith and practice of local communities.

Conclusion of Canon Controversy—Almost!

For more than a thousand years a relative peace reigned regarding the Christian canon. Then the cleric Martin Luther nailed his ninety-five theses to the door of All Saints, the castle church in Wittenberg. His agenda included ridding the church of the excesses acquired since its founding. He chose the canon of the Tanakh as the proper Old Testament canon for the Christian church. Then the sixteenth-century **Council of Trent** opposed Luther's Old Testament canon. It reaffirmed the decision of third- and fourth-century church councils to accept the Septuagint as the Christian Old Testament canon. It also officially defined that the Roman Catholic canon included the books of the New Testament as well as the books of the Jewish Bible. It also included the books of the Septuagint not included in the Tanakh, asserting, against Luther, that they too were the inspired word of God.

The Icing on the Cake

Vatican II made no declarations about the Roman Catholic canon. It did, however, say something important about truth and scripture. It affirmed that scripture has limited inerrancy; in other words, it contains no errors in teaching what is necessary for salvation. The somewhat ambiguous statement reads:

> We must acknowledge that the books of Scripture firmly, faithfully, and without error teach that truth which God, for the sake of our salvation, wished to see confided to the Sacred Scriptures. (*Constitution on Divine Revelation*, no. 11)

Commenting on this statement, New Testament scholar Raymond E. Brown writes: "In this long journey of thought the concept of inerrancy was not rejected but was seriously modified to fit the evidence of biblical criticism which showed that the Bible was not inerrant in questions of science, of history and even of time-conditioned religious beliefs."[7] Most Protestant evangelical denominations stand by the doctrine of inerrancy, arguing that God would not have inspired human authors of scripture to write what is false, even in areas such as history and science. Some Catholic groups also cling to inerrancy of scripture.

MARY N. MACDONALD

Prayer group in Papua New Guinea.

READING RELIGIOUS LITERATURE

Reading religious literature is a challenge for both believers and non-believers. This section focuses on reading Christian scriptures as a case study. To some extent, however, you can apply many principles of the art of reading scripture to the religious literatures of other religious traditions. Religious traditions usually consider their sacred literature to be divine revelation, communication in symbolic form, about norms for believing how they should think and live in union with their god or gods. Most scriptures also share other common elements:

1. They include different types (**genres**) of literature. Identifying the genre is an important first step in reading. Genre governs the questions we ask. Questions about plot or character development, who speaks and who is silent, and so on are appropriate for narratives. For the legal codes in the Torah, our concerns are about the group or individual subject to a particular law and group or individuals whom the law protects; what its language reveals about the law's sociopolitical setting (urban or agricultural, war or peace; family, tribal or monarchy); the relationship between the law and its immediate literary context.

2. They first existed as oral literature. Storytellers often varied details, using personal names and locales familiar to specific audiences. After they were written down, oral versions continued to develop. Present-day scriptures often contain multiple versions of a narrative or a teaching. For example, the Book of Genesis includes three versions of a narrative about a tribal ancestor putting his wife in a threatening situation to protect himself. In the Gospel of Mark there are two versions of a narrative about Jesus feeding a large group with a few pieces of bread and some fishes.

3. They combine the insights and perspectives of different authors and editors from different historical periods. They are rarely homogenous documents, that is, they contain inconsistencies, inaccuracies, and contradictions.

4. They are sometimes self-reflective and self-critical: a later document may expand an earlier teaching, change it, or even mock it. In the Tanakh, for example, the Book of Job debunks covenant theology: If you walk in the ways of the Lord, you will live a long and prosperous life in the land the Lord has given you and will see your descendants to the third and the fourth generations. If you do not walk in the ways of the Lord, you will be "cut off from the land of the living." Job has walked in the ways of the Lord, yet he lost his material wealth; his children died; and he suffers a disfiguring skin condition, all the while claiming that he has done nothing to deserve such suffering. He demands that the Lord appear in court and accuse him face to face. In the Book of Qoheleth, the narrator is skeptical whether humanity can know what the Lord demands. The final editor of the Tanakh honors those texts and does not try to bring them into agreement with Deuteronomy's dominate covenant theology.

5. They reflect several historical and cultural contexts, none of which is the historical and cultural context of present-day readers or audiences. First-world Jews, Christians, and Muslims generally live in highly mobile societies, in families of choice rather than families of birth, with access to technology and social media, and so on. Even believers frequently question the relevance of scripture and its meaning as a divine word.

6. They are available, for the most part, as literature in translation. Some translations try to retain as much of the grammar, sentence formation, and so on as possible; other translations are so free that they miss the sense of the original text.

All these elements work together to transform reading into a challenging multi-layered experience.

Even when we read for entertainment, we discover opportunities to understand our humanity, our world, and our place in it in new ways. Sometimes we find our worldview affirmed; other times, we are brought up short by the realization that meanness or jealousy may be the cause of dissatisfaction with our lives. When we read religious literature as insiders of a religious tradition, we deliberately read for meaning, with the belief that we are reading God's self-revelation expressed in human language. What exactly is meaning? Where is it located? How do we find it?

Texts alone do not communicate meaning. In response to students who claimed that interpretation is unnecessary because "all you have to do" is to listen to the text, a professor began class by placing an open Bible before the students. Five minutes into the class students had stowed cell phones and opened notebooks. Several minutes later they were whispering, "Where did she say we're beginning today?" Fifteen minutes into the class, students were shifting in their desks, rifling through papers for the syllabus, rolling their eyes. Finally the professor picked up the Bible and asked: "What did you hear this text saying?" Her students got the point: texts do not send out messages to whoever is listening.[8]

Meaning is an event; it happens as we engage and integrate the multiple worlds of a text with an open mind, heart, and imagination. Associated with each text is the world or worldview of the author who produced the text (the world behind the text), the world or worldview of the text (the world within the text), and the world or worldview in front of the text (the world of the reader). Once we have engaged and integrated those multiple worlds with mind, heart, and imagination, meaning happens. It is an event or process with the power to transform readers, their attitudes about and relationships with others and their world.

One caveat: We might conclude that some texts are morally wrong and therefore should not be treated as scripture. The story of Jephthah's daughter in the Book of Judges is a good example (Jgs 11:29–40). Jephthah's brothers drive him from home because he is the bastard son of their father. Later, when the Ammonites have invaded Gilead's territory (Gilead was the tribe to which the brothers and Jephthah belonged), the brothers plead with Jephthah, promising to anoint him as leader of Gilead if he will accept leadership of the army against the Ammonites. Once he is commander, he tries unsuccessfully to convince the Ammonite king to withdraw to the original borders.

Then "the spirit of God rushes upon Jephthah," investing him with divine power. To make sure that the Lord grants him victory, Jephthah vows to sacrifice whoever or whatever first greets him when he returns home. Jephthah defeats the Ammonites and returns home. His unnamed daughter rushes to greet him. She urges him to fulfill his vow despite his reluctance. All she asks is time to spend with her friends, mourning that she will die as a virgin with neither husband nor sons. She returns home to be sacrificed by her father. As reward for being a good daughter, Israelite virgins lament her for four days each year.

This horrifying story demonstrates women's low status in biblical Israel. Jephthah receives no censure for killing his daughter. He continues to enjoy military victories, defeating the Ephramites. He dies peacefully and is praised for his actions as a judge in Israel. His reputation survives: Samuel declares to the assembled Israelites that the Lord sent Jephthah to free them from their enemies' oppression (1 Sm 12:1–7, 11). The author of the New Testament Letter to the Hebrews praises Jephthah for doing great things through faith (Heb 11:22–24). Jephthah's sacrificial murder of his daughter, apparently condoned by the Lord, goes unmentioned and unpunished.

The particularly vexing narrative of Isaac and his near-sacrificial death, a test of Abraham's loyalty to the Lord (Gn 22), is a parallel. Note, first, that the narrator calls Isaac by name, allowing him visibility and gravitas. Jephthah's daughter is anonymous; only her actions make her visible. In a sense, by encouraging her father to fulfill his vow, she engineers her own death. At the same time, her acquiescence indicates how thoroughly she has internalized the patriarchal code; she is the "good daughter" who accepts her father's authority over her. Isaac is the "good son"; the few questions he asks are about technicalities—where is the sacrificial victim, for example? He has also internalized the patriarchal code, allowing his father to bind him for sacrifice. However, as Abraham positions the knife to slit his son's throat, a divine messenger intervenes and suggests that a ram caught in the underbrush would be a suitable substitute for Isaac. Abraham then earns praise for his dreadful willingness to sacrifice his son, and the Lord reiterates the promise of land and numerous descendants. No divine messenger intervenes on behalf of Jephthah's daughter. The annual custom of young women mourning her for four days seems bittersweet. The only name she has is the name of her murderer. Both the Jewish and the Christian traditions proclaim Isaac's story regularly in their rituals. The story of Jephthah's daughter escapes their attention.

CRITICAL READING FOR MEANING
INSIDE AND OUTSIDE A RELIGIOUS TRADITION

Many Christians approach the Bible as if they are its primary and original audience, and as if it were factually true. For example, on the basis of Genesis 1:28, some argue that the purpose of sexual intercourse is reproduction. They ignore the verse's multiple contexts: for the narrator, the small group of Judahites who had returned from exile in Babylon; for the narrative, the newly created world with only a male and a female; for a twenty-first-century reader, a world in which thousands of children die every day. They seldom question what those contexts might mean for Genesis 1:28 in the our century. Does it have the same meaning today that it had in its original context? How do we read that text responsibly?

THE WORLD OF READERS[9]

Our reading of a biblical text begins with our *social location,* a term borrowed from sociology. Social location identifies the groups to which we belong on the basis of race, economic class, gender, ethnicity, age, religion, education, attitudes toward authority, and so on. It also includes attitudes toward local, national, and global events and their impact, such as local unemployment, threats to national security, or a nuclear accident in Japan. Social location determines social roles and rules, power, and privilege (or lack of), all of which influence our identity and how we see the world. Social location shapes our reading of a biblical text. It informs the questions we ask and the details we notice. An awareness of what we bring to the text is important to acknowledge.

After you've described your social location, read Matthew 15:21–28. What are your first impressions about the characters? Of the narrative as a whole? What attracts you? What repels you? Jot down your thoughts; you will return to them as we work through the passage.

THE WORLD BEHIND THE TEXT

To construct this world, we ask two types of questions: (1) questions about the author of the text, the reason or occasion for the text, and its original audience; about the historical and cultural context and so on; and (2) questions about sources the author might have used, the author's use of those sources, the influence of a later editor or editors on the text, its form (a prophetic speech, an ancestral narrative, a judgment against a ruler, and so on), and its original setting (outdoors, in the Temple, at the city gate, and so on). We look for details in the text for help in answering these questions and consult biblical commentaries. We might discover that we must sort through multiple answers.

Write down what you have discovered about the narrative. These examples will get you started:

1. The Gospel of Matthew was written after the Gospel of Mark. My Bible text has Mark 7:24–30 in parentheses. Matthew probably used Mark's narrative as a source. Differences between them: Matthew adds "and Sidon" but omits that Jesus was staying at someone's house." (You can find a list of similarities and differences between the two narratives in a synopsis of the gospels. You will be more familiar with them, however, if you work them out for yourself.)

2. Matthew's audience (not the same as the audience inside the text) is probably his faith community who might be suspicious of people of other backgrounds and reluctant to welcome them into the community.

THE WORLD WITHIN THE TEXT

Pay attention to the story. What do you need to know about Matthew? To answer this question, you should read the introduction to the gospel in your Bible and consult a recent commentary on the Bible as a whole. What is the larger context of the narrative? What material precedes and follows it? In this narrative what does "unclean" mean? What is considered unclean in the story? What is the story's plot? Who is the protagonist? The antagonist? What titles does the narrator have the woman use to address Jesus? Why? (Note: *Lord* can mean "Mr." or "Sir" as well as "God.") How does Matthew show the tension between Jesus and the Canaanite woman? What does he do and what does he say? Does he answer her question directly? What details show the woman's persistence? What images occur in verse 26? Has Jesus' attitude toward the woman changed? How? What does the woman do with Jesus' response in verse 27? What is the purpose of her response, for example, why does the narrator have her say what she says? How does the narrative end? Why does Jesus heal the woman's daughter? Having read this narrative, how would you describe the narrator's notion of faith?

Now you can return to the differences you noted between Matthew's version of this narrative and Mark's version. Do any of the details make a difference in your understanding of Matthew's narrative? Explain how they make a difference. If you were reading the text only for a critical understanding, you could stop here and write a unified version of your understanding. You might also consider whether and how your social location influenced your understanding, as well as what you learned about the world behind the text.

THE WORLD IN FRONT OF THE TEXT REVISITED

If you are reading for meaning as well as for understanding, you have one more world to think about. This step takes you back to the first step, the world before the text. In speaking about meaning, we are not attempting to discover what the author of the text or even God intended to communicate. As we noted earlier, meaning happens in dialogue, even confrontation, between reader and text. The big question to think about here is: What kind of world does the text create and invite readers to inhabit? For whom is this life-giving world created? Why?

A possible response of a feminist might be to rail against the stereotypical portrayal of the Canaanite woman: groveling to get what she wants; putting up with Jesus' silence; allowing him to call her "dog," an unclean animal, thus reinforcing her status as unclean because she is not a Jewish woman. All those observations are correct; however, the narrative turns them around. This unclean woman reminds Jesus that even dogs eat the crumbs that fall from the table. She challenges Jesus, teaches him, to expand his mission. She opens his eyes to see that the *goyim* (a disparaging word for those who are not Jews) are as needy as the people of Israel. And most striking of all, her demonstration of faith amazes him.

Second, a woman whose race, economic status, or ethnicity shames her in the eyes of others might draw strength from the Canaanite woman, who refuses to allow her social location and the labels of others define her. And third, a literalist reader might cringe at the suggestion that the narrative presents Jesus as imperfect, with something yet to learn, and that his teacher is a Canaanite woman, loaded down with all the contempt of first-century Jews. Then again, the reader might not notice how Jesus changes.

These are merely suggestions and are not meant to close off ways in which the text affects you. What transformations does the text offer? This process takes time to complete. In addition, working through a text in a group is recommended, especially a group that asks critical questions about one another's understanding. We need such a context to push us toward meaning and keep us honest.

THINKING WITH SCRIPTURES

We have read how different religious traditions interpret their scriptures. We have also looked at ways in which scholars of religion interpret texts. We saw that interpretation is necessary because the language of texts is figurative language. It is also necessary because the scriptures of individual traditions often contain contradictory texts or texts that challenge the presuppositions of the religion itself. Now would be a good time to apply some of the methods we have explored.

Religious traditions often contain stories that challenge the main beliefs of the tradition. For example, the major story line of the Tanakh is presented in the Book of Deuteronomy. In its simplest form, that story line is "Obey the Lord, you will prosper [that is, you will enjoy a long prosperous life in the land with many blessings]." The opposite is also true: "Disregard the Lord and you will suffer the loss of the land along with every possible misfortune." The authors of Deuteronomy insist that Israel's God selected Israel as his own special people, promising to protect them from misfortune if they are faithful to him. A "good things happen to good people" scenario. If the people suffer loss individually or collectively, they have only themselves to blame. One story challenges this view; it is about a good man, Job, who faithfully keeps the Lord's commands.

The book is unsettling, for it presents a God who seems to care no more for his human creatures than he does for the animals that roam the wild. It challenges Deuteronomy's simplistic formula and suggests that there is little correlation between one's behavior and what happens in one's life. It is also challenging, for it models a commitment to God and to right living that expects no reward or blessing except the relationship itself.

Through history, people have sought explanations and understanding to resolve Job's paradox. Like the character in Archibald MacLeish's modern play, *J.B.*, they bellow, "What I can't bear is the blindness. If I only knew why!"[10] Others, like Kurt Vonnegut in his novel *Cat's Cradle*, wonder whether suffering has any meaning or purpose.

Man blinked. "What is the purpose of this?" he asked politely. "Everything must have a purpose?" asked God. "Certainly," said man. "Then I leave it to you to think of one for all this," said God. And he went away.[11]

Thinking with Job

1. Read the first two chapters of the Book of Job in the Tanakh. What kind of a person is Job? According to Deuteronomy, what can Job expect in his life? What does the Satan (a member of God's court, charged with prosecuting God's causes; not the devil) have against Job? Why does God cooperate with the Satan?

2. How does Job respond to the losses he experiences? What advice does his wife give him? Why? What notion/s about woman might be at work here? Where is Job at the end of chapter 2?

3. Friends arrive to comfort Job. Like him, they are well educated in their religious tradition; these are teachers of wisdom. They are so overwhelmed with horror when they see him that they keep silent for a week. Why do they react this way?

4. Read through chapters 3–37, a series of speeches. How does Job describe his situation? What advice do his friends give him? How do they rationalize what has happened to him? What do you think of their responses? Whose interests do they serve? How does Job respond to his friends? What emotions does he experience? What does he demand?

5. God does eventually address Job in chapters 38–42. What is his speech about? What challenges does he lay down for Job? Does he do what Job has demanded?

6. How does God explain Job's losses? What is his opinion of Job's friends? What has happened to Job's wife? Now that you have read the whole book, re-evaluate her advice, independent of Job's response. What would have happened to Job had he followed her advice?

7. Think of a time of loss or grief in your life. What, if anything, helped you make sense of it? In a reflective essay, poem, or short story, articulate your understanding of suffering in life.

8. Psychologist Carl Jung wrote *Answer to Job,* in which he argues that the God of Job is, in fact, God's shadow self.[12] Thus God acts out his own doubts about himself and Job's loyalty to him by making Job suffer. Using poetry, song, or art, compose your own "answer" to Job's question about why he is suffering.

If I speak, my pain does not lessen; if I keep silent, how much of it disappears? God has worn me out, . . . rushing at me like a warrior. My face glistens with my tears, shadows weight down my eyelids. (Jb 16:6–17, trans. K. Nash).

DOCTRINES AND CREEDS

By this time the following statement should not come as a surprise. Religion is story: a story acted in ritual, lived in ethical action, proclaimed in figurative language; a story with the potential as much for alienation as for reconciliation, renewing itself and being renewed in conversation with history and culture. There are two final dialects of religious language to consider: doctrines and creeds. Both grow out of a community's reflection upon its story.

DOCTRINE

Doctrines (literally, teachings) are formal and authoritative statements that articulate a religion's beliefs. For example, the central Christian **kerygma** or teaching is the death and resurrection of Jesus the Christ (1 Cor 15:3–4); acceptance of this teaching marks a person as Christian. In our discussion of scripture and canon we saw that already in the first century Christians were struggling to understand and interpret this central belief for their communities. Out of that struggle came the gospels and the letters, as well as numerous treatises and letters written by the earliest theologians. All these works, along with their interpretations, are part of the doctrine of the Christian church; they represent efforts to assist the church in remaining faithful to its central teaching. In the Roman Catholic Church this body of teaching and interpretation is called **tradition**.

Doctrines are rooted in history as well as in mystery, and for Christians that mystery is Jesus the Christ, his words and deeds. Each doctrine articulates truth and meaning, but no doctrine exhausts either truth or meaning; thus new doctrines, in response to the recurring questions, may be formulated again and again. In each historical age the community has the privilege and the responsibility to participate in the development of doctrine by bringing it into conversation with the experiences of individuals and with the insights of philosophy, psychology, literary theory, and science. Moreover, the language, thought patterns, and concerns of a particular community and historical era shape the language of doctrine.

This language is figurative language that, too, requires interpretation and reformulation. Over the last two centuries Christian theologians have reformulated doctrines on such topics as the sacraments of baptism and Eucharist, the nature of the church, the role of the Spirit, and grace. While one function of doctrine is to promote right thinking, a far more important function is the creation of a religious worldview. Christian doctrine, for example, establishes a world in which Christians may understand themselves in their relationship to the God of Jesus Christ and to each other.[13]

CREEDS

The word *creed* derives from Latin *credo*, "I believe." However, the action of believing is more than an intellectual exercise. *Credo* also has the sense of committing one's heart or self to someone or something. A creed is a statement in verbal form of the faith of an individual or a community. By means of its creed, a religion both defines and teaches the beliefs its members must accept.

The **Shema** Yisrael, the heart of Judaism and the source of its beliefs and customs, unites Jews throughout the world. Many Jewish scholars recognize the Shema as the Jewish creed. Others argue that Judaism emphasizes religious practices *(mitzvoth)* rather than right belief, other than that God is one and Israel, the chosen people. If they had to select a creed, many congregations would probably select the thirteen principles that Maimonides (1138–1204) considered binding on every Jew: the existence, absolute unity, spiritual nature, and eternity of God; God alone deserves worship; God gave the Torah, itself unchangeable, and spoke through the prophets of whom Moses is the greatest; divine providence, divine punishment, and divine reward exist; a Messiah will come, and the dead will be resurrected.

In a similar fashion Muslims recite the **Shahadah**, "There is no God but Allah, and Muhammad is Allah's prophet," when they pray. The one action required of anyone who wishes to enter the Umma, the Islamic community, is the recitation of the Shahadah privately or publicly. The Arabic word for creed is *aqīdah*. While religious scholars don't generally see the Shahadah as a creed, they agree that it is the beginning point for later creeds. Buddhists identify the Four Noble Truths and the Eightfold Path, along with the three jewels of Buddhism, as essential teachings of the Buddha, material that fits easily into the category of creed. As mentioned above, belief in the death and resurrection of Jesus the Christ and the affirmation that Jesus the Christ is the source of all truth are essential for Christians.

The earliest Christian creed was the simple affirmation, "Jesus Christ is Lord" (Phil 2:11). The questioning of candidates at baptism about Jesus, Father, and Spirit led to the development of a trinitarian creed, with separate sections describing the saving work of the Creator, the Redeemer, and the Sanctifier. These creeds sprang up all over the Christian world; the Apostles' Creed, in wide use today among

Christians, was based on one of the oldest such creeds used by the community in Rome.

A second important Christian creed is the Nicene Creed, adopted by the Council of Constantinople (381) and promulgated by the Council of Chalcedon (451). Catholics, Orthodox, and many Protestant denominations affirm this creed.

Thinking with Creeds

The Apostles' Creed

I believe in God, the Father almighty, creator of heaven and earth. I believe in Jesus Christ, his only Son, our Lord. He was conceived by the power of the Holy Spirit and born of the Virgin Mary. He suffered under Pontius Pilate, was crucified, died, and was buried. He descended to the dead. On the third day he rose again. He ascended into heaven, and is seated at the right hand of the Father. He will come again to judge the living and the dead.

I believe in the Holy Spirit, the holy catholic Church, the communion of saints, the forgiveness of sins, the resurrection of the body, and the life everlasting. Amen.

The Nicene Creed

We believe in one God, the Father, the Almighty, maker of heaven and earth, of all that is, seen and unseen.

We believe in one Lord, Jesus Christ, the only Son of God, eternally begotten of the Father, God from God, Light from Light, true God from true God, begotten, not made, of one Being with the Father. Through him all things were made. For us and for our salvation he came down from heaven: by the power of the Holy Spirit he became incarnate from the Virgin Mary, and became human. For our sake he was crucified under Pontius Pilate; he suffered death and was buried. On the third day he rose again in accordance with the Scriptures; he ascended into heaven and is seated at the right hand of the Father. He will come again in glory to judge the living and the dead, and his kingdom will have no end.

We believe in the Holy Spirit, the Lord, the giver of life, who proceeds from the Father and the Son. With the Father and the Son he is worshiped and glorified. He has spoken through the Prophets. We believe in one holy, catholic, and apostolic Church. We acknowledge one baptism for the forgiveness of sins. We look for the resurrection of the dead, and the life of the world to come. Amen.

1. With your group, write a creed or faith statement to which you all can subscribe. Your creed does not have to be religious. You could construct a creed of basic beliefs that someone would have to affirm in order to become part of your learning group or your social group.
2. Go through each creed above statement by statement. How does the Nicene Creed expand on statements in the Apostles' Creed?
3. Compare the statements in each creed with what we learn about Christian belief from the Gospel of Mark. What are the differences? How do you account for them?

SUMMARY

In this section, we have grappled with the complexity and ambiguity of language. In the world of language things are rarely as they appear. Most language, including language that we think is most objective and factual, is figurative; it is the model through which we experience others and ourselves. In many ways language is like a computer simulation program. Students in an archeology class may work through a virtual dig—constructing hypotheses, "excavating" sites, analyzing data, modifying assumptions, and formulating a final report—without leaving their computer terminals. In an analogous fashion, we rely on language, and its propensity for metaphor, hyperbole, paradox, and ambiguity, to build and inhabit worlds in which we negotiate relationships and dialogue with one another and with texts to create meaning betwixt and among our dialogue partners.

Out of language religious traditions create their distinctive models for interaction with ultimate Reality. In myths of origin and destiny, parables, and stories of challenge, we experience both the ordering and the disordering aspects of power and the transformative experience of pursuing justice. Religious traditions also use art and architecture to order their worlds. Calligraphy and basket weaving are only two of the many artifacts that speak to us about the holy and assure us that order endures from one day to the next.

Narratives about the sacred are generally canonical, normative for faith and living, and they become holy in relationship to a believing community. As we have observed, there are many scriptures, many articulations of truth and meaning. No one formulation is intrinsically absolute or more accurate than the next. Every sacred story is "true."

Its truth does not reside within the story, but within the lived experience of practitioners of the religious tradition. Its truth derives from personal experiences of the holy, from the manner in which we hear them. Paul Ricoeur has observed that "forgetfulness and restoration" characterize our relationship with scripture and symbol. We distance ourselves from sacred narratives when they do not resonate with our expectations or provide adequate answers to wrenching questions; we return to them with the humble realization that they are our best tools for recreating order and remembering the holy.

When the great Rabbi Israel Baal-Shem-Tov saw misfortune threatening the Jews, it was his custom to go into a certain part of the forest to meditate. There he would light a fire, say a special prayer, and the miracle would be accomplished and the misfortune averted. Later, when his disciple, the celebrated Magid of Mezritch, had occasion to intercede with heaven for the same reason, he would go to the same place in the forest and say: "Master of the Universe, listen! I do not know how to light the fire, but I am still able to say the prayer," and again the miracle would be accomplished. Still later, Rabbi Moshe-Leib of Sasov, in order to save his people once more, would go into the forest and say: "I do not know how to light the fire, I do not know the prayer, but I know the place and this must be sufficient." It was sufficient and the miracle was accomplished. Then it fell to Rabbi Israel of Rizhyn to overcome misfortune. Sitting in his armchair, his head in his hands, he spoke to God: "I am unable to light the fire and I do not know the prayer; I cannot even find the place in the forest. All I can do is to tell the story, and this must be sufficient." And it was sufficient.[14]

Religious traditions look within their sacred stories and scriptures to rediscover the path to the forest place and to remember the words that kindle holy fire. If they cannot do that, they tell their stories—and it will be sufficient.

The next section introduces the concept of religious change and development within the lives of individuals and communities. This change may sometimes occur as a dramatic reversal, but it may also appear as the natural progression and development of one's life. Within religious communities changes herald renewed creativity and angry division. However change occurs, whatever its consequences, it alters existing order and reinterprets foundational stories.

RESOURCES

ACTIVITIES

1. Many contemporary theologians are using the life experiences of women as well as the customary practices and scriptures of their religious traditions to retell their communities' stories. Find examples of this in the work of African American, Latino/a, Native American, US, and Asian theologians. Share your findings with your group or class. Lead a discussion on how these interpretations may influence how different traditions understand the sacred and relate to it. Summarize the discussion in a short paper or post the summary on the class bulletin board and invite additional comments.

2. The scripture of a tradition often becomes the source of a group's prayers and hymns, even when that scripture is the scripture of the oppressor. Bereft of their indigenous African religions, slaves found comfort and hope in stories from the scriptures of their white owners. They claimed the stories that mirrored their own experiences of suffering and death that nurtured their desires for freedom and release. Such stories became the basis for the spirituals. Find texts and recordings of these songs. How do they use the language of Christian scripture to interpret the slave experience? How does the slave experience interpret the scripture? Present your findings to the class, using multimedia if possible.

3. The New Testament gospels include four different accounts of the suffering and death of Jesus of Nazareth. Using a synopsis, list the differences in events and in details. Since each gospel presents its own unique interpretation of Jesus, what do the differences among the passion narratives contribute to each gospel's understanding of Jesus? You may wish to consult a good introductory text on the New Testament for an overview of the four differing presentations of Jesus.

4. Watch one of the segments of Bill Moyers's *Genesis: A Living Conversation*. Describe the participants' attitudes toward the Book of Genesis. With your group, plan a similar discussion on some text in Genesis or another book of the Bible. Provide time for your classmates to react to your group's discussion and to add their own insights.

5. Select passages from the Qur'an, for example, surah 15:16–48, 16:1–17 (Creation); surah 2:28–27 (Adam, his Wife, and the Fall); surah 4:1–10 (Women and Orphans). Read them carefully. What do you learn about the values of Islam from these few passages? Compose a letter to a Muslim friend in which you share what you have learned about Islam.

6. Read through the Gospel of Mark in the New Testament. Select a passage that interests you. Find three commentaries on the gospel.

How do the authors of these commentaries discuss the passage? What method or methods of interpretation do they use? What understandings and beliefs do they bring to the text? Which interpretation do you like best? Why?

7. Describe the creeds of Judaism, Islam, and Buddhism, the beliefs central to each tradition. You may need to consult some introductory texts to these religions. Then describe your understanding of creed in Christianity. You may wish to formulate your own creed. Compare it with the Apostles' Creed and the Nicene Creed. Explain the symbolic language of these creeds to a Buddhist friend.

8. The 2006 publication of an English translation of the Gospel of Judas ignited much discussion. You can find a copy online or at your library. Read the translation. Then have a small-group discussion about the text.

READINGS

Denny, Frederick M., and Rodney L. Taylor. *The Holy Book in Comparative Perspective.* Columbia: University of South Carolina Press, 1985. Critical essays on the scriptures of Judaism, Christianity, the Latter Day Saints, Islam, **Zoroastrianism**, Hinduism, Buddhism, Confucianism, Taoism, and indigenous oral traditions (Sam Gill on Native American traditions).

Gunn, David M., and Danna N. Fewell. *Narrative in the Hebrew Bible.* New York: Oxford University Press, 1993. In this literary analysis of Genesis to 2 Kings of the Tanakh, the authors discuss literary theory, character, and plot, as well as the construction of meaning and responsible reading. An extensive bibliography for each section of the text is included.

Harris, Stephen L. *Understanding the Bible.* Mountain View, CA: Mayfield Publishing, 1997. This text is a substantive introduction to the Bible, historical-critical and theological in scope. It is well illustrated and has a comprehensive glossary.

Newsom, Carol A., and Sharon H. Ringe, eds. *The Women's Bible Commentary.* Louisville, KY: Westminster/John Knox, 1992. Contributors discuss texts and issues within each biblical book that touch women's lives. The text also includes essays on women's lives in biblical times and on **feminist hermeneutics** (interpretation).

Stowasser, B. *Women in the Qur'an: Traditions, and Commentaries.* New York: Oxford University Press, 1994. The book provides an excellent treatment of the status and role of women in the different levels of Islamic literature.

Van Vorst, Robert E. *Anthology of World Scriptures.* Second edition. Belmont, CA: Wadsworth Publishing, 1997. Good introductory material on major world traditions and excerpts from most scriptures in the categories of teachings, ethics, ritual and worship, and organization.

Young, Serenity. *An Anthology of Sacred Texts by and about Women*. New York: Crossroad, 1993. Wide-ranging selections of scriptures and other significant writings from Judaism, Christianity, Islam, Hinduism, Buddhism, Confucianism, Taoism, ancient European and Near Eastern religions, shamanism and indigenous religions, and new religions of modern times.

AUDIOVISUALS

Three Faces of Protestantism (1977). BBC-TV. Part of the Long Search series, this film, although dated, provides a good portrait of how a mainline Christian church in the suburbs, a fundamentalist Christian church in the Bible Belt, and a store-front African American Pentecostal church in the inner city interpret the same gospel.

The following videos are available from Films for the Humanities and Sciences. Order online or from 132 West 31st Street, 17th Floor, New York, NY 10001.

Genesis: A Living Conversation with PBS journalist Bill Moyers (2003). A ten-part series. In each one-hour segment Moyers speaks with religious scholars, psychologists, theologians, academics, and performers about major themes in the Book of Genesis, for example, God's image, temptation, the first murder, call and promise, deception, God wrestling, exile.

The Bible's Buried Secrets: Beyond Fact or Fiction (2009). This video explores the relationships among science, scripture, and scholarship and examines the most pressing issues in biblical archeology.

What Is Truth? The Gospels and Their Authors (2003). This program focuses on accounts and theories pertaining to the identities of the four evangelists, as well as the authenticity of the texts attributed to them.

Too Close to Heaven: The History of Gospel Music (1996). This three-part series traces the two-hundred-year history of gospel music from black churches to the Civil Rights movement to its influence on modern music.

Whose Truth Is the Truth? New Testament Apocrypha and Codification of the Canon (2003). This program surveys many of these texts and their adherents, and traces the course of the New Testament's codification.

NOTES

1. Not all New Testament letters are addressed to local communities. The pastoral letters (1 and 2 Timothy and Titus) are about church structure and order; their audience was church leaders. The letters of James, 1 and 2 Peter,

1 and 3 John, and Jude are called catholic epistles; that is, they were intended for public reading in many different communities. The intended audience of the anonymous Letter to the Hebrews is unknown.

2. This discussion depends on Joseph Fitzmyer, SJ's explication "The [Pontifical] Biblical Commission's Instruction on the Historical Truth of the Gospels," *Theological Studies* 25 (1964): 386–408. See also Christopher M. Tuckett, "Synoptic Problem," in *The Anchor Bible Dictionary*, ed. David Noel Freedman (New York: Doubleday, 1992), 6:263–70.

3. According to Eusebius, a fourth-century church historian, Papias (second century) identified the authors of canonical gospels in this way: Matthew, a tax collector and one of the twelve apostles; John Mark, a companion of Paul for a time and a confidant of Peter; Luke, Paul's traveling companion in Acts of the Apostles; John, the beloved disciple and close associate of Jesus. Thus Mark and Luke, while not apostles, had authoritative sources in Peter and Paul.

4. Among these texts are the Infancy Gospel of Thomas (mid-second century) and the Protoevangelium of James. Supposedly authored by James, the brother of Jesus, the Protoevangelium is the source for legendary material about Mary, the mother of Jesus. It recounts, for example, that from the age of three she was raised by priests in the Jerusalem Temple until she was engaged to a much older Joseph, a widower with children, who acted as her guardian and respected her virginity. See Robert J. Miller, ed., *The Complete Gospels*, Annotated Scholars Version (Sonoma, CA: Polebridge Press, 1992). Texts of these and other noncanonical gospels are available on the Internet.

5. This document is part of the "Nag Hammadi Library," named for the Egyptian village near where it was found. It was attributed to "Didymos [the twin] Judas Thomas," sometimes identified as Jesus' twin brother. It now survives only in a Coptic translation. See Elaine Pagels, The *Gnostic Gospels* (New York: Random House, 1979); and James M. Robinson, ed., *The Nag Hammadi Library* (San Francisco: Harper and Row, 1988).

6. In 1740, Lodovico Antonio Muratori discovered this fragment, which bears his name, in Milan's Ambrosian Library in a **codex** dating to the seventh or eighth century. The fragment contains only eighty-five lines and begins in midsentence.

7. Raymond E. Brown, *The Virginal Conception and Bodily Resurrection of Jesus* (New York: Paulist Press, 1973), 9.

8. Gordon Fee and Stuart Douglas, *How to Read the Bible for Its Worth* (1981; Grand Rapids, MI: Zondervan, 1995), 17.

9. This discussion depends on Sandra Schneiders, *The Revelatory Text: Interpreting the New Testament as Sacred Scripture*, 2nd ed. (Collegeville, MN: Liturgical Press, 1999).

10. Archibald MacLeish, *J.B.* (Boston: Houghton Mifflin, 1958), 108.

11. Kurt Vonnegut, Jr., *Cat's Cradle* (New York: Dell, 1965), 177.

12. Carl Jung, *Answer to Job* (Princeton, NJ: Princeton University Press, 1973).

13. This discussion relies on Nancy C. Ring, "Doctrine," in *The New Dictionary of Theology*, ed. Joseph A. Komonchak et al. (Wilmington, DE: Michael Glazier, 1987), 291–93.

14. Elie Wiesel, *The Gates of the Forest* (New York: Holt, Rinehart and Winston, 1966), preface.

PART IV

RELIGIOUS CHANGE

Through their symbolic processes, religions bring order into our lives, both personal and communal. They help us establish and maintain relationships. We often use religious teachings to decide how to conduct our lives. Religious myths help us understand our roles in our families, our communities, the natural environment, and even the unfolding of history. Through ritual and storytelling we pass on our religious traditions to anther generation. When we think of religion in these terms, we are describing it as a symbol system, that is, a system of symbolic actions and symbolic narratives that help maintain a certain worldview. To describe a religion in these terms is like looking at a snapshot. We can describe the elements in the picture and the relations among those elements at a particular moment. Scholars of religion label this approach to the study of patterns of religious thought and action synchronic (see pages 20–21).

A snapshot, however, is static. It does not allow us to see how time alters the individual elements of the snapshot or their relationship to one another. If we understand the study of religion as watching a movie, we will understand better that religion is not only a system, but also a process. Since religions are embedded in human culture, they are also embedded in history; to omit this element is to ignore an important part of what it means to be human. Therefore, along with our *synchronic* study of religion, we also want to include *diachronic* study of religion—study of the ways in which patterns of religious thought and action change over time. This approach is important in the study of religious biography as well as in the study of religious communities.

Perhaps you have had the experience of returning to your hometown after an extended absence. Although friends and family who have remained there assure you that over the years nothing has changed, you find much that is different: your favorite stores are gone, houses are abandoned and boarded up, apartment complexes sprawl alongside malls, new highways crisscross the area. For those who still live there, these changes have been so gradual that they were hardly noticed, but for you the changes appear dramatic.

Or maybe you have returned to your elementary school years after graduation. Although the structure is physically the same, the building seems smaller and shabbier, the playground equipment barely adequate, and the playing fields no longer stretch on forever as they once seemed to do. Because you have changed and matured, you see this environment with new eyes.

We live in a world that is constantly changing. As we move through this world, we both instigate change and are affected by it. In this uncertain world people frequently cling to their religious traditions as insurance against instability. Christians, for example, who call on God as "the one who was, and is, and is to come," expect their religious communities and practices to endure without appreciable change through their lives and beyond. Religion, however, is a human institution, subject to the same forces of change as other human institutions.

In Chapter 8 we consider the process of change in the lives of individuals. Some undergo personal crises and leave the practices and beliefs of their youth for new modes of religious action and knowledge. Others, once indifferent practitioners of religion, may become fervent and influential promoters of the faith. For still others, religious change may happen more slowly, as a matter of personal development over a lifetime.

Chapter 9 investigates the process of religious change in communities. Thinking about religion (particularly one's own religion) in terms of process may provoke feelings of insecurity and uncertainty. Indeed, as we will see, living through a period of religious change can be challenging, confusing, even alienating. Often religious change occurs so subtly that members of a community are hardly aware of the process of change. In other cases communities deliberately decide to adopt new beliefs and practices. Such changes in the structure of religious thought and habit often accompany shifting social, political, and economic contexts.

Finally, we focus on the effects of religious change. Does such change inhibit or promote human flourishing? The answer, of course, is that, depending on the circumstances, change can be harmful or beneficial. However, even when a community experiences change as a breath of fresh air, some individuals within that community may resist it; that is, an experience of change that enables a community to function more fully in the world may nonetheless alienate members within that community.

Chapter 8

Personal Religious Change

Christians remember the words of the apostle Paul to the first-century Christians in Corinth, "When I was a child, I spoke like a child, I thought like a child, I reasoned like a child; when I became an adult, I put an end to childish ways" (1 Cor 13:11). He implies that the present knowledge of mature Christians, while more complete than it was when they joined the Christian community, cannot compare to the knowledge God will reveal at the end of time. "For now we see in a mirror, dimly, but then we will see face to face. Now I know only in part; then I will know fully, even as I have been fully known" (1 Cor 13:12). These words evoke the spectrum of change that is possible in the lives of religiously observant persons. In the life of an individual, religious change may occur almost as a natural process, part of maturing from infancy to childhood through young adulthood. The process of religious change continues in adulthood, as an individual moves through various life crises and stages of maturity. For Christians, however, the notion of religious change is not confined to an organic process but holds the potential for ultimate transformation at the finale of all things: " . . . in a moment, in the twinkling of an eye, at the last trumpet. For the trumpet will sound, and the dead will be raised imperishable, and we will all be changed" (1 Cor 15:52). Thus, for Christians, the notion of religious change has theological importance, for it implies God's ongoing work of bringing creation to fulfillment.

As we consider religious change in the lives of individuals, we encounter examples both of gradual maturation and of sudden conversion and drastic changes in life. We can see these as two patterns of religious change (growth and conversion), yet each person's biography offers a unique story of change. A woman may have an experience of enlightenment or conversion whose significance she understands more deeply as the years pass; a man may live a life of quiet unfolding of faithfulness yet welcome moments of keener awareness of God's presence. Furthermore, not all personal religious change tends toward heightened faith or closer observance. A man whose ties to family and childhood community diminish over time may find that his faith is also gradually eroding in the absence of external structures to support it. A woman may confront catastrophic personal loss or illness only to realize that she can no longer believe that this chaotic and frightening world is in the hands of a loving God.

PERSONAL RELIGIOUS CHANGE AS DEVELOPMENT

For some religious traditions, the notion of a lifelong maturing into one's tradition is valued far more than the experience of a conversion that causes a break with a personal or communal past. In the Confucian tradition, which has been historically important in China, the notion of the good life includes an education in virtue that begins in the cradle and extends to the grave. Confucius (551–479 BCE), remembered as the founder of the Confucian tradition, passed on to his many students his understanding of the principles of the good life. The goal of the Confucian life is to become fully human, a goal that is always just beyond the grasp of the wise man. According to the Confucian idea of selfhood, a person is not a freestanding individual; a person, a self, represents an intersection of relationships. Most classical Confucian texts focus on the roles of men. A man sees himself as a son, a brother, a friend, and a loyal subject of the state. With characteristic humility, Confucius said:

> There are four things in the Way of the profound person, none of which I have been able to do. To serve my father as I would expect my son to serve me; that I have not been able to do. To serve my ruler as I would expect my ministers to serve me; that I have not been able to do. To serve my elder brother, as I would expect my younger brother to serve me; that I have not been able to do. To be the first to treat friends, as I would expect them to treat me; that I have not been able to do.[1]

An emphasis on conversion is foreign to the Confucian tradition. An intense experience that might cause a person to reevaluate or even to renounce former ties to family and community would betray the Confucian ideal of jen (or ren), the highest Confucian virtue; no single

English word offers a satisfactory translation. We could translate *jen* as "love" or as "human-heartedness." It implies empathy and self-respect as well as an appreciation for the dignity of humanity. A man does not achieve *jen* by shedding his earlier ways. Rather, in the Confucian tradition personal religious change involves a painstaking education and detailed attention to ritual from youth. One Confucian tradition invites the eldest grandson to take the most honored seat, even when he is a young boy. This is the seat of the deceased ancestors. When the boy is thus seated, the older men of the family bow before him because he represents their departed fathers and grandfathers. The boy learns what it is like to receive honor and respect, and so he finds it easier to show honor and respect to others. In this and other ways he cultivates *jen*. As an old man, a Confucian would not describe his life as a series of new beginnings and fresh starts. Rather, the Confucian views his life as a careful cultivation of an original virtue, a virtue that encompasses his dutiful attentions to others in his personal network of relations and his equally dutiful acceptance of the respect and honor due him. Development, not conversion, is the model for personal religious change in the Confucian tradition.

Although the notions of conversion and repentance are central to many Christian biographies, the lives of other Christians are marked more by continuity than by discontinuity. Religious change occurs along with emotional, moral, and intellectual development. For example, a Christian child who grows up in a stable home situation may have little reason to struggle with the question of how to reconcile the reality of human suffering with belief in a loving and powerful deity.

As we grow to adulthood, however, we inevitably confront some of the evils of the world: lives lost to warfare and random violence, the untimely death of a parent, the injustices suffered by those living in poverty, the random assaults of cancer or AIDS. We learn that belief in God and faithfulness to religious demands will not protect us or those we love from pain or loss. If we are open to growth in our faith life, we may still pray the prayers of our youth, but we pray them in a new way. As children we may have heard the words of Psalm 23 as a promise of safety from all harm:

> Even though I walk through the darkest valley,
> I fear no evil;
> for you are with me (v. 4).

As adults who have walked through the dark valleys of job loss, death of loved ones, and human cruelty, we understand these verses not as a promise that God will protect us from all harm, but as a promise that God will be with us in moments of crisis. In such a life, religious change does not take place through moments of dramatic conversion; rather, religious change is manifest in gradual insights, deepening faith, and eventually a mature religious vision.

The life of Saint Catherine of Siena (1347–80) is a story of one woman's intellectual, moral, and spiritual development. Although Catherine had visions and other intense religious experiences, she never underwent a major conversion experience in which she dramatically renounced her earlier ways to follow a new path. Rather, her mature spiritual writings represent the culmination of her life-long faith. As a young girl she had her first vision in which a radiant Jesus smiled at her. On another occasion she prayed to the Virgin Mary that she might enter into a mystical marriage with Jesus. She then had a vision in which Mary and Jesus appeared to her, and she received a ring from Jesus marking her as his bride.

Catherine's family did not approve of her religiosity; they wanted her to marry, and they exerted pressure on her to do so. However, she persisted in her personal ascetic practices, denying herself both luxuries and necessities, and was finally accepted as a Dominican tertiary. That is, she affiliated herself with the Dominican order although she did not formally become a nun. Only then did she have the opportunity to learn to read. She came to believe that God wanted her to take an active public role that included preaching. As a woman assuming such an unusual role, she became a controversial figure. Her personal prayer life included a variety of mystical experiences; in her public role she even influenced Pope Gregory XI's decision to return from Avignon to Rome. Although she spent her young life secluded in her parents' home, she ultimately traveled to Rome, where she recorded her visions and served as an adviser to Pope Urban VI. Catherine was one of the most influential women in medieval Europe, and her story includes her dramatic rise from conventional beginnings into the confidences of the pope. Although she died at thirty-three, her writings are marked by rare spiritual maturity. In Catherine's story religious change appears not as renunciation of former ways accompanying a dramatic conversion but as a deepening of an intense personal faith she already enjoyed in her childhood.

ANTMOOSE

Tomb of Saint Catherine of Siena.

PERSONAL RELIGIOUS CHANGE AS CONVERSION

In the lives of individuals, religious change can follow a developmental model, or it can redirect the course of a person's life. At the turn of the twentieth century the pioneering psychologist William James wrote *Varieties of Religious Experience: A Study in Human Nature.* This volume was one of the first scholarly treatments to break with theological concerns and to examine religion as a human institution from a social-science perspective. James's analysis of the conversion experience has been especially influential:

> To be converted, to be regenerated, to receive grace, to experience religion, to gain an assurance, are so many phrases which denote the process, gradual or sudden, by which a self hitherto divided, and consciously wrong, inferior and unhappy, becomes unified and consciously right, superior and happy, in consequence of its firmer hold upon religious realities. This at least is what conversion signifies in general terms, whether or not we believe

that a direct divine operation is needed to bring such a moral change about.[2]

James argued that religious beliefs or ideas are true if they "work," that is, if they are useful. Thus, he claims that we should neither arbitrarily privilege nor dismiss religion; we should, however, judge it according to how well it achieves some valued goal or purpose. Religious experiences and beliefs, in James's words, should be judged "by their fruits . . . not by their roots."

To James, then, beliefs, religious beliefs as well as other beliefs, are conditional, fallible, and subject to experimental testing. In the preface to *The Will to Believe*, James maintains:

> If religious hypotheses about the universe be in order at all, then the active faiths of individuals in them, freely expressing themselves in life, are the experimental tests by which they are verified, and the only means by which their truth or falsehood can be wrought out. The truest scientific hypothesis is that which, as we say, "works" best; and it can be no otherwise with religious hypotheses.[3]

James found the greatest "fruits of the religious life," and therefore the greatest justification for religion, in *saintliness*. Typical of the individual "regenerated character" and indicated by charity, modesty, piety, and happiness, saintliness is "present in all religions." James viewed saintliness as a key insight into human nature, the possibility that religious experience might regenerate the original "rightness" of human being.

We rely on James's framework as we analyze a variety of stories of conversion. Many cases of conversion experiences substantiate his claims, although there are certainly exceptions. For example, people who undergo a conversion experience often live first through a period of difficulty or even despair, a period of an "unhappy self"; however, as we will see, such unhappiness is not a necessary first step in the conversion process. While we may notice typical features in these narratives, each story is unique.

The story of the apostle Paul is an archetype for later Christian stories of conversion. Saul, more frequently identified by the Roman version of his name, was a **Pharisee**, a Jew committed to strict observance of the Law of Moses. He was also an archenemy of the earliest Christian community. According to the Acts of the Apostles he was present at and approved of the stoning of Stephen, the first Christian martyr (Acts 6:8—7:60, esp. v. 58; 22:20). We read Paul's recollections of those days in his letter to the Galatian Christian community: "You have heard, no doubt, of my earlier life in Judaism. I was violently persecuting the church of God and was trying to destroy it" (Gal 1:13).

The Acts of the Apostles supplies the famous story of his moment of conversion (Acts 9:1–19; 22:6–16; 26:12–18). Saul was traveling with some companions to Damascus on a mission against members of the church residing there. A bright heavenly light suddenly knocked him to the ground: "[He] heard a voice saying to him, 'Saul, Saul, why do you persecute me?' He asked, 'Who are you, Lord?' The reply came, 'I am Jesus, whom you are persecuting. Now go into the city, and you will be told what to do'" (Acts 9:4b-6).

For three days Saul prayed and fasted at the house of Judas. Meanwhile, a disciple named Ananias received a directive from the Lord: "Go to the street called Straight and ask at the house of Judas for a man from Tarsus named Saul. He is there praying and [in a vision] he has seen a man named Ananias come in and lay [his] hands on him, that he may regain his sight." Ananias was understandably reluctant to obey because he had heard about Saul's persecution of the Lord's "holy ones" and his authority to imprison "all who call upon [the Lord's] name." He is assured, however, that the Lord has chosen Saul "to carry [his] name before Gentiles, kings, and Israelites." Ananias goes to Saul, lays his hands on him, and tells him, "Saul, my brother, the Lord has sent me, Jesus who appeared to you on the way by which you came, that you may regain your sight and be filled with the holy Spirit." Immediately, "things like scales fell from his eyes," and he regained his sight. Saul was then baptized and became the greatest of the early Christian missionaries to the Gentiles.

In his writings Paul does not offer anything like this vivid story of conversion. He writes simply that "God, who had set me apart before I was born and called me through his grace, was pleased to reveal his Son to me, so that I might proclaim him among the Gentiles" (Gal 1:15–16).

To later Christians the important element in Paul's call is its suddenness and completeness. The Pharisees had a special commitment to observance of the Torah, or Jewish Law. As a Pharisaic Jew, Paul had perceived his attempts to destroy the fledgling Christian community as fidelity to the Torah. Paul turns (or is turned) 180 degrees to promote this very church. He describes how "coming to know Christ" has redefined his understanding of profit (gain) and loss. At one time he might have identified gains as "proud to be a Pharisee," "obedient to the Torah," and the "worst nightmare for the followers of Jesus."

Those qualities enhanced his reputation throughout Syro-Palestine and won the trust of Jerusalem's Jewish leadership. His conversion experience turned those qualities into losses. Now Paul counted as gain the opposite of those qualities: knowledge of Christ, the life of an itinerant preacher of the gospel to Gentile communities in Asia Minor, concern about communities he had founded, threats on his life, alienation and hostility from Jewish synagogues, opposition from Gentile idol makers, house arrest. Those were the riches of his new life in Christ.

> Yet whatever gains I had, these I have come to regard as loss because of Christ. More than that, I regard everything as loss because of the surpassing value of knowing Christ Jesus my Lord. For his sake I have suffered the loss of all things, and I regard them as rubbish, in order that I may gain Christ. (Phil 3:7–8)

Jews and Gentiles who did not know Christ would have rolled their eyes and wondered about Paul's connection with the real world. His words, however, have influenced subsequent generations of new Christians, challenging them to regard their "old lives" as loss and their "new lives" in Christ as gain. In the words of a popular hymn,

> Amazing grace, how sweet the sound
>   that saved a wretch like me.
> I once was lost, but now am found,
>   was blind, but now I see.

In Paul's generation all Christians were converts, because Christianity had not existed in the previous generation. Centuries would pass before infant baptism was commonly accepted. Paul did not view conversion to Christianity as an individual, solitary experience. In his understanding, being a Christian meant belonging to the community, the body of Christ. Therefore, conversion was not only cognitive, coming to hold a new set of beliefs, but conversion also entailed a new identity as a member of the Christian community. Paul linked the conversion experience to baptism into the community: "As many of you as were baptized into Christ have clothed yourself with Christ. There is no longer Jew or Greek, there is no longer slave or free, there is no longer male and female; for all of you are one in Christ Jesus" (Gal 3:27–28).

An early Christian legend tells the story of Thecla, a young woman whom Paul converted to Christianity. Thecla had agreed to marry,

Thinking about Personal Religious Change

These questions ask you to think about the process of change in the religious faith and practice of individuals. You might address these questions to someone you know who is comfortable about talking about his or her religious autobiography or you might think through these questions with respect to your own life.

1. In what ways have your religious practices changed in the past ten years? In the past twenty years? Since childhood?
2. What caused these changes? Did they occur gradually or rapidly?
3. Were these changes major or minor? In what ways?
4. What continuities link your religious beliefs and practices as a child with those of your adulthood?
5. Would you categorize your religious autobiography as a story of growth, a story of conversion, or a story of growth and conversion? Or is your religious autobiography a story of erosion or sudden loss of faith? Please give examples or reasons.

but when she heard Paul preach she abandoned her plans so that she might fully live her Christian calling. Despite her mother and her fiance's public opposition, she persisted in her newly found path and was sentenced to the gladiatorial arena. In full sight of the crowd Thecla baptized herself in a ditch of water. Miraculously, the beasts fought for instead of against her. Finally, her wealthy friend Tryphaena intervened to save her. Thecla converted Tryphaena and the majority of her female slaves to Christianity, but she wanted to rejoin Paul. She dressed in men's clothing and met up with Paul, who at last blessed her teaching mission.

Although most (if not all) elements of Thecla's story are legendary, we can see several aspects of Paul's influence in the tale. When Thecla chooses to wear men's clothing, she is living in the sphere defined by Paul in Galatians: for those who are in Christ, there is no division between male and female. New clothing also symbolizes the new journey on which she embarks. Furthermore, Thecla's conversion is linked with the conversion of a number of other women, notably Tryphaena and her slaves. Although her conversion means the loss of her family, particularly her mother, she gains a new family: Tryphaena, Paul, and other Christians.

We find another important conversion story from Christian antiquity in *The Confessions* of Saint Augustine of Hippo. Augustine spent his youth seeking meaning and truth, often in dubious places. His various searches exemplify William James's divided consciousness, the unhappy soul. Augustine first sought consolation in sexual relationships and philosophy: "Being in love with love I looked for something to love" (III.1). He established a long-term relationship with a woman whose name he does not record, and with her he has a son. He falls under the intellectual sway of Manichaeism, a popular dualistic philosophy. Neither sex nor philosophy satisfies him. In *The Confessions* he records his struggles to maintain his old pursuits and to begin anew as a Christian:

> I hesitated to die to death and to live to life; inveterate evil had more power over me than the novelty of good, and as that very moment of time in which I was to become something else drew nearer and nearer, it struck me with more and more horror. (VIII.12)

The moment finally arrives when he becomes "something else." In a moment of anguish he hears a child's voice singing to him, "Take it and read it." He picks up the Bible and chances upon a passage that alleviates any uncertainty about this new way of life: "It was as though my heart was filled with a light of confidence and all the shadows of my doubts were swept away" (VIII.12). A lifetime of searching culminates in a conversion that brought him clarity, security, and peace.

> This was just what I longed for myself, but I was held back, and I was held back not by fetters put on me by someone else, but by the iron bondage of my own will. The enemy held my will and made a chain out of it and bound me with it. From a perverse will came lust, and slavery to lust became a habit, and the habit, being constantly yielded to, became a necessity. These were like links, hanging each to each (which is why I called it a chain), and they held me fast in a hard slavery. And the new will which I was beginning to have and which urged me to worship you in freedom and to enjoy you, God, the only certain joy, was not yet strong enough to overpower the old will which by its oldness had grown hard in me. So my two wills, one old, one new, one carnal, one spiritual, were in conflict, and they wasted my soul by their discord (VIII.6).

Saint Francis, from a plaque based on the Giotto frescoes in Assisi.

Francis of Assisi (1182–1226), the son of a prosperous business-man, experienced a conversion that led him to a life of service to the poor and to the establishment of major religious orders for men and women. In his youth Francis led a carefree life, spending his father's money and running with a fast crowd. Even before the dramatic moment of his conversion, however, he had begun searching for greater meaning in his life. After a serious illness he exhibited what William James calls a "divided and unhappy self." He sought solitude for prayer and had visions he did not yet understand. Once, when he was praying in a dilapidated old church, he heard a voice from the cross say, "Francis, repair my house, which is falling into ruin." Francis assumed that the voice was referring to the physical decay of that church. Only after his conversion did he realize that God was calling him to the work of healing the spiritual corruption of the medieval church.

Francis often dressed in the clothes of the poor and donated the proceeds of his father's business to them. According to legend, such behavior resulted in the dramatic scene of his conversion. His father summoned Francis to court before the bishop of Assisi to account for the money he had transferred from the family business to the poor. Francis responded by renouncing his family ties, stripping off his expensive clothes, and returning them to his father, symbolically severing connections with his past life. From that day forward Francis was committed to forming a community whose members would live together in poverty and service to the poor in witness to the gospel. Although Francis's father and the bishop of Assisi may have regarded Francis's response as sudden and impulsive, his conversion had been gradual; he had sought various ways to ease his troubled soul.

Augustine and Francis provide stories of two men with misspent youths whose dramatic conversions led to lives of devotion to God's will. We find a more contemporary example of such a conversion in *The Autobiography of Malcolm X* (as told to Alex Haley). In

Malcolm X's own words, as a young man he lived "like a predatory animal," supporting himself with robbery and living for a nightlife centered on drugs. The police apprehended him when he tried to have a stolen watch repaired. Reflecting on his life story years later, Malcolm X acknowledged:

> I want to say before I go on that I have never previously told anyone my sordid past in detail. I haven't done it now to sound as though I might be proud of how bad, how evil, I was. . . . The full story is the best way that I know to have it seen, and understood, that I had sunk to the very bottom of the American white man's society when—soon now, in prison—I found Allah and the religion of Islam and it completely transformed my life.

Prison afforded him time to further his education and to decide the future direction of his life. Although he had at first resisted his family's enthusiasm for Elijah Muhammad's Nation of Islam (NOI), a black American branch of Islam, their persistence eventually convinced him to write to its founder. The latter's prompt and warm response encouraged Malcolm to move forward and to contact him when Malcolm's prison sentence ended. He began praying to Allah and became a Muslim. When he left prison, Malcolm X progressed

ROBERT ELLSBERG

Malcolm X, a poster for a rally in Harlem.

from convicted criminal to one of Elijah Muhammad's trusted advisors and a popular NOI leader.

The dramatic conversion from savvy criminal to devout Muslim was not the only transformation of Malcolm's life. Tension between Elijah Muhammad and Malcolm X developed over the years, until Elijah Muhammad ousted him from the NOI movement. At the same time, Malcolm yearned to become more involved with Islam worldwide. The Nation of Islam taught that the white man was the devil, not to be trusted under any circumstances. Malcolm's prominence (or notoriety) had brought him into contact with some white people who supported him and did not seem to him to embody the devil. He also began to realize that the religious practices of the NOI were out of step with the practices of traditional Islam:

> At one or another college or university, usually in the informal gatherings after I had spoken, perhaps a dozen generally white-complexioned people would come up to me, identifying themselves as Arabian, Middle Eastern or North African Muslims. . . . They had said to me that, my white-indicting statements not withstanding, they felt that I was sincere in considering myself a Muslim—and they felt if I was exposed to what they always called "true Islam," I would "understand it, and embrace it."

When he turned to orthodox Islam for instruction, he found that the Muslim community eagerly welcomed him as one of their own.

Malcolm X decided to make the hajj, one of the five pillars of Islam and the pilgrimage to Mecca required of all physically and financially able Muslims at least once in their lives. His experience was transformative. He found himself in the company of Muslims from around the world, of every racial and ethnic background, whom he discovered to be brothers and sisters in their submission to Allah. Prominent Muslims heard that he was on the hajj and offered him hospitality and support. On the hajj he was treated with the honor and respect long denied him in his native land. More important was the recognition that all hajjis accorded one another similar honor and respect. From that time forward he endeavored to live as a Muslim according to the classical traditions. Furthermore, although he was still damning in his indictment of white America, he no longer preached that the white man is the devil. The problem, he insisted, was neither the complexion nor the genetic makeup of white people, but their attitudes and actions toward African Americans and other people of non-European descent.

On February 21, 1965, less than a year after returning from the hajj a changed man, Malcolm X arrived at the Audubon Ballroom in Harlem to speak. As he began his address, some members of the Nation of Islam assassinated him. He had betrayed Elijah Muhammad, they claimed, and founded the Organization of Afro-American Unity to undermine the NOI. Malcolm X did not survive long enough to build on the momentum of his hajj. However, his life story exemplifies the power of conversion in an individual life.

As in Confucianism, the language of conversion is foreign to Islam. It perceives the experience we have been calling conversion as a homecoming and insists that we are all born Muslim: each newborn baby submits to Allah in response to the Shahadah its mother whispers in its ear. As our personalities develop, our innate stubbornness emerges; we find ways to resist Allah's will, that is, we refuse to submit our wills to him. When adults turn in submission to Allah, they are in fact coming home, returning to the state into which they were born. The transition that Malcolm X began on the hajj developed from his existing faith, part of a long homecoming that dominated his adult life.

DEVELOPMENT AND CONVERSION
IN AN INDIVIDUAL LIFE

Although we are trying to distinguish personal religious change as *development* from personal religious change as *conversion*, such a distinction is difficult to maintain. The life of the martyred Archbishop Oscar Romero of El Salvador has often been narrated as a mature and public conversion, yet Romero resisted that description.

Romero was a native of El Salvador, a man of humble origins whose piety had directed him early in life to the priesthood. He was widely known as a traditionalist resistant to change in the Latin American church when he was ordained bishop in 1970, a few years after **Vatican II**. In response to that vibrant and exciting time, the Latin American church developed new ministries that brought lay people, religious women and men, and clergy into closer contact with the daily struggles and longings of the poorest sectors of society. Early on, Romero was at best lukewarm toward these innovative ministries.

As editor of the archdiocesan newspaper, he published attacks on progressive efforts of the church. He helped oust the Jesuits from the archdiocesan seminary because, in his view, they were initiating radical reforms and disregarding traditional church practices too quickly.

To ensure the orthodoxy of future priests, Romero took over as rector of the seminary. Confronted with human rights atrocities, including the brutal murder of members of his diocese by national security forces, he refused to hold national leaders accountable. When Romero was installed as archbishop, the most conservative sectors of the Salvadoran church, government, and society applauded the event, certain he would protect their interests by maintaining the status quo.

Within weeks of becoming archbishop a number of incidents forced Romero to rethink his earlier assumptions. After the murder of the Jesuit Rutilio

MARYKNOLL MISSION ARCHIVES/O. DURAN

Archbishop Oscar Romero, El Salvador.

Grande, Romero asked Arturo Molina, the president of El Salvador, to investigate the circumstances surrounding the priest's death; Molina agreed but never followed through. Grande had worked in a very poor parish, where he encouraged his parishioners to recognize and resist injustice and economic exploitation, a message powerful landowners and government officials considered subversive. Romero's reaction to Molina's failure to investigate Grande's death put him at odds with the Salvadoran government and with many Salvadoran bishops. The archbishop could no longer ignore the government's disregard for the legitimate concerns of the indigenous people in order to protect the interests of El Salvador's wealthy class and many members of the Roman Catholic hierarchy.

By the time members of the military murdered Romero as he celebrated mass on March 24, 1980, the world recognized the traditionally conservative archbishop for his unshakable belief that the gospel was good news for the poor but a goad for their oppressors. In weekly radio addresses Romero begged Salvadoran soldiers to put down their weapons and join their sisters and brothers in a nonviolent quest for justice. Romero also challenged leaders of the local churches to become more Christlike by acting in solidarity with the marginalized, oppressed, and persecuted, thereby sharing the sufferings of the poor as Christ continues to share the sufferings of the world (Rom 18:17). Romero wrote:

> The church is persecuted because it wants to be truly the church of Christ. As long as the church preaches an eternal salvation without involving itself in the real problems of our world, the church is respected and praised and is even given privileges. But if it is faithful to its mission of pointing out the sin that puts many in misery, and if it proclaims the hope of a more just and human world, then it is persecuted and slandered and called subversive and communist.

Supporters celebrated and opponents condemned Romero's so-called conversion. Romero, however, insisted that his conversion was one more step in his lifelong journey of following Christ. He viewed his appointment to the ministry of archbishop as Christ's call to identify more profoundly with the poor. He stated, "What happened in my priestly life, I have tried to explain for myself as an evolution of the same desire that I have always had to be faithful to what God asks of me." Until his death Romero remained a conservative Catholic, observing traditional Catholic practices such as devotions to Mary. At the same time he recognized that change within the church might mean new life, beyond the scope of tradition.

Although we have focused on Romero as an exemplar of personal religious change, his story is part of the larger story of religious renewal in Latin America. It exemplifies the necessary interconnections between individual and communal religious change. In his own words:

> To keep oneself anchored, out of ignorance or selfish interest, in a traditionalism without evolution is to lose even the notion of the true Christian tradition. The tradition that Christ confided to his church is not a museum of souvenirs to preserve. It comes, indeed, from the past and is to be loved and preserved faithfully, but always with a look to the future. It is a tradition that makes the church fresh, up-to-date, and effective in each epoch of history. It is a tradition that nourishes the church's hope and its faith so that it can keep on proclaiming and inviting all toward

the "new heaven and new earth" that God has promised (Rv 21:1; Is 65:17)[4]

Romero's life continues to challenge Christian communities to abandon their anxieties about orthodoxy and to embrace the praxis of justice both within the world and within church structures and teachings.

PERSONAL CONVERSION AND NEW RELIGIONS

A story of personal conversion often introduces the story of the birth of a world religion. A Jewish legend suggests that Abraham was the son of an idol maker. Convinced that idols were worthless, he smashed the contents of his father's shop. In Genesis 12:1–3, Genesis 15:15–21, and Genesis 17:1–16, God calls Abraham to be the ancestor of the people we know as the Israelites. Christianity represents Abraham as a prototype of obedience and trust as seen, for example, in his unquestioning willingness to sacrifice Isaac, his long-awaited son. One interpretation of the New Testament narrative understands the Genesis story as a foreshadowing of God the Father's suffering at the death of Jesus on the cross. The Qur'an considers Abraham a prophet of Islam and the ancestor of Muhammad through his firstborn son, Ishmael. Muslims further honor him in their reference to Islam as *millat Ibrahim* (religion of Abraham). Because Judaism, Islam, and Christianity share close connections, real or constructed, with Abraham, some believers describe them as "Abrahamic religions" and Abraham as their eponymous ancestor.

As interesting as the story of Abraham sounds, the story of the enlightenment of Siddhartha Gautama of the Sakyas—the Buddha—provides a more elaborate example of a personal religious conversion in an Asian context that produced a new religious movement.

Siddhartha was born in India in the sixth century BCE, the favored son of a wealthy aristocratic family. According to tradition, an oracle at his birth predicted that he would become either a political leader who would unite all India or a man whose renunciation of the world would lead to its redemption. Because his father had political ambitions, he raised Siddhartha to promote his attachments to the world, to wealth, and to power. He surrounded his son with beauty and luxury, creating an environment in which Siddhartha would not encounter ugliness, pain, destitution, or death. Despite his father's efforts, Siddhartha did see such sights as he traveled outside his father's palace. On one ride Siddhartha saw an aged man; on another ride he saw a disease-ridden man at the side of the road; on a third ride he saw a corpse. Perhaps, the story hints, these visions were incarnations or avatars of gods committed to Siddhartha's enlightenment. When Siddhartha saw a monk in simple robes carrying his begging bowl, he realized that the path of world renunciation might bring about enlightenment.

Although this version of Siddhartha's early life may not be historically accurate, we do know that as a young man Siddhartha grew dissatisfied with his life of luxury and comfort and its lack of meaning. He left his beautiful wife and their young son to discover a meaning in life that could satisfy him. Dressed in rags, he first apprenticed himself to two Hindu masters who instructed him in the way of **raja yoga**, a mental, physical, and spiritual discipline central to advanced Hindu piety. He appreciated their instruction, but it did not satisfy him. He next joined a group of ascetics and spent years engaged in fasting and other austere practices. From these masters he learned the practices of asceticism, but enlightenment eluded him. Siddhartha drew on those ascetic principles as well as his earlier life of luxury to articulate the Middle Way, one of his key teachings as the Buddha; those who choose moderation and reject both unbridled physical pleasure and harsh bodily discipline will achieve enlightenment.

As a last resort Siddhartha tried the way of mystical contemplation. He sat under a tree, later known as the Bo Tree, and decided to remain there until he was enlightened. Demonic powers tried to tempt him from his course, but he had already reached a stage of enlightenment that protected him from their attacks. Then, absorbed in meditation, Siddhartha entered enlightenment. According to Siddhartha, he "woke up." He had become the Buddha, the enlightened one, who awoke out of the illusory world of change into the reality of Brahma. From the Buddha's spiritual awakening and his subsequent decision to teach his companions the way to enlightenment emerged the new religion of Buddhism.

Siddhartha's story exemplifies the way of conversion outlined by William James. People who are seeking truth and wholeness, who are unhappy because that goal is just beyond their grasp, one day realize that they have been blessed with wisdom and the unification of self. The conversions of the Buddha and of Francis of Assisi have parallel outcomes; both men established monastic communities to share their life and work along with their visions for the world. Members of both communities discovered that this purposeful commonality strengthened their personal conversion experiences.

FROM PERSONAL
TO COMMUNAL RELIGIOUS DEVELOPMENT

We have been considering religious change as it develops in individual lives. We cannot, however, separate models of individual change from models of communal change. As hinted in our discussion of Archbishop Romero, changes within the Latin American Roman Catholic Church influenced the direction of his personal religious growth. Alternately, as we noticed with figures as diverse as Francis of Assisi and the Buddha, individuals often reinforce their conversions by founding religious communities or by joining likeminded others in communal religious life. In this section we are especially interested in the intertwining of personal and communal religious change during the Great Awakenings (1730–60 and 1810–30) in the United States. In a sense, these moments of societal change were collections of individual conversion stories. In another sense, individuals might not have experienced those conversions if they had not lived in communities where emerging styles of preaching and personal piety were generating considerable spiritual excitement.

The Puritan settlers of the earliest New England colonies planned to establish a religiously based society. Social power was originally linked to church membership, and church membership was restricted to those whose wealth testified that God had marked them for salvation. Soon, however, the availability of land allowed many colonists to gain wealth and power through their own efforts rather than through a divine call to salvation. By the early eighteenth century the initial spiritual intensity had degenerated into a routinized and bureaucratic church life. At that time several waves of Christian renewal swept through the Protestant colonies. This societal religious change continues to influence the shape of religious experience in the United States in nondenominational evangelical communities and the fundamentalist movements in major religions.

The First Great Awakening (1730–60), a resurgence of evangelical religion taking place simultaneously in Europe, challenged the Enlightenment's emphasis on human reason. It also valued emotional displays of religiosity over intellectual ascent to doctrine, and it prized the Bible as the inerrant source of truth. Social and cultural changes left believers on both sides of the Atlantic worried and anxious that such changes were signs of divine displeasure. For example, in the United States, industrialization was creating a class of manual laborers who were exploited, overworked, and underpaid. Then the Irish potato famine drove hundreds of thousands of Catholic immigrants to this country. "Nativists" often used violence to secure their needs for jobs and housing. As land along the Mississippi River became available, settlers contended with crop failure, death, and isolation from family and friends, as well as attacks from Native Americans, whose lands they had confiscated. As a response to this personal and cultural upheaval, preachers of the First Great Awakening offered the experience of God's transforming love for personal regeneration and conversion.

The Tennent family of Pennsylvania—the Reverend William Tennent and his four clergy sons—began religious revivals during the 1730s, relying on their enthusiastic preaching to attract more sinners to experience evangelical conversions. Ten years later ministers were conducting revivals throughout the eastern colonies. George Whitefield, an ordained minister in the Anglican Church, joined with other Anglican clergymen, especially John and Charles Wesley, to reform the Church of England. That effort encouraged the Wesley brothers to establish the Methodist Church in 1770. Whitefield's message was familiar Calvinist theology: sinners who desired salvation had to depend on the mercy of an all-powerful God. His dramatic gestures, public weeping, and threats of damnation stirred his audiences to emotional expressions of personal conversion. While the public welcomed Whitefield, conservative and moderate clergymen questioned the emotionalism of evangelicals and charged that revivals confused audiences. They particularly objected to the often undereducated itinerant ministers who traveled from town to town to spread the good news of being born again and, at the same time, criticized local clergy for their book learning. Pastors were doubly exercised when some white women and African Americans preached at religious gatherings.

While Whitefield gained his reputation as an itinerant preacher, others, like Jonathan Edwards of Northampton, Massachusetts, the best-known preacher of the Great Awakening, ministered to particular congregations. Edwards evoked vivid, terrifying images of the corruption of human nature and the terrors awaiting the unrepentant in hell. His description of sinners dangling by a slender thread over a fiery pit from his best-known sermon, "Sinners in the Hands of an Angry God," provides powerful examples:

> The God that holds you over the pit of hell, much as one holds a spider or some loathsome insect over the fire, abhors you, and is dreadfully provoked. . . . You have offended him infinitely more than ever a stubborn rebel did his prince; and yet it is nothing but his hand that holds you from falling into the fire every moment. . . . And there is no other reason to be given, why you

have not dropped into hell since you arose in the morning, but that God's hand has held you up in the morning.

Edwards urged individuals to repent and experience God's transforming love. As he urged individuals to open their hearts to this experience, he deliberately evoked the renewal movement sweeping the colonies:

> And now you have an extraordinary opportunity, a day wherein Christ has thrown the door of mercy wide open, and stands calling and crying with a loud voice to poor sinners; a day wherein many are flocking to him, and pressing into the kingdom of God. Many are daily coming from the east, west, north and south; many that were very lately in the same miserable condition that you are in, are now in a happy state, with their hearts filled with love to him who has loved them, and washed them from their sins in his own blood, and rejoicing in hope of the glory of God. How awful is it to be left behind at such a day! Are not your souls as precious as the souls of the people at Suffield [a nearby town], where they are flocking from day to day to Christ?

Edwards instigated the personal crises that led to highly individual renewal by challenging new converters to participate in a societal awakening. He needled one congregation, "Will you be content to be the children of the devil when so many other children in the land are converted, and are become the holy and happy children of the King of kings?"[5] Some converts took up his challenge and became missionaries to the southern colonies.

Thinking about Being "Born Again"

Are you born again? How do you know?

Have you been saved? How do you know?

Have you worked, studied, or socialized with individuals who posed those questions? Why do you think they are compelled to ask those questions?

Are you comfortable or uncomfortable with these questions? Why or why not?

The phrasing of these questions, with their emphasis on profound individual conversion as essential to personal salvation, is part of the legacy of the Second Great Awakening (see the discussion in

Chapter 9). Protestants of the Reformed traditions, the majority of northern European colonists, believed that God had chosen an "elect" group for salvation. One could not choose to be in that number but had to be invited and singled out by God for salvation. During the Second Great Awakening (1810–30) preachers assured their congregations that they could choose to be saved, marking a major break with earlier Reformed theology. The hallmark of someone "born again" frequently was an emotional conversion in which the person claimed Jesus as personal savior and witnessed to nonbelievers that they too could choose salvation. The Second Great Awakening left other important legacies to the young republic, for example, a heightened social consciousness that promoted the nascent anti-slavery movement.

The next time anyone asks if you have been saved, or you reflect on a personal experience of being saved, you might recall the ways that a larger social movement shaped this uniquely personal mode of spiritual expression.

As a final example of the interdependence between personal spiritual growth and conversion and social context, we consider the twentieth-century emergence of Alcoholics Anonymous (AA) and other twelve-step programs modeled on it. AA is a secular organization that emphasizes personal spiritual awakening as a significant element of sobriety. It originated in the spiritual awakening of its co-founder, Bill Wilson (1897–1971). For more than seventeen years Wilson drank to alleviate feelings of worthlessness and to escape chronic depression. About his spiritual awakening, he wrote:

My depression deepened unbearably and finally it seemed to me as though I were at the very bottom of the pit. I still gagged very badly on the notion of a Power greater than myself, but finally, just for the moment, the last vestige of my proud obstinacy was crushed. All at once I found myself crying out, "If there is a God, let Him show Himself! I am ready to do anything, anything!" Suddenly the room lit up with a great white light. I was caught up in an ecstasy, which there are no words to describe. . . . And then it burst upon me that I was a free man . . . for a time I was in another world, a new world of consciousness. All about me and through me there was a wonderful feeling of Presence [and peace]. . . . I thought to myself, "So this is the God of the preachers! No matter how wrong things may seem to be, they are still all right. Things are all right with God and His world."[6]

To support his sobriety, Wilson sought fellowship with other alcoholics in meetings of the Oxford Group. Concerned that the group did not minister to members who relapsed into drinking, Wilson and his friend, Dr. Bob Smith, founded AA upon the principles that emphasize that alcoholics could achieve and maintain sobriety one day at a time by surrendering to a Higher Power and by helping other alcoholics. They maintained that "once an alcoholic, always an alcoholic" and described recovery as a lifelong process, a series of beginnings sometimes interrupted by relapse.

Wilson and Smith developed twelve steps to guide AA members to a spiritual awakening. Many AA members acknowledge that the steps helped them give birth to a new self, not only sober but spiritually awake. The first step encourages alcoholics to recognize that they are powerless over alcohol. The remaining steps invite them to rely on a Higher Power (God, however they understand God); to make an inventory of how their drinking has wronged others and to make amends; to seek to know and to follow God's will in all ways; and to share this healing word with other alcoholics. Those who find strength in the program experience spiritual growth and conversion of heart, along with an unexpected and rewarding closeness to God (as they understood God).

Conversion stories of alcoholics who finally realized that they could not "fix" their lives alone pepper AA literature. They share their stories anonymously or use only their first names. Members represent the spectrum of society: an executive whose drinking destroys her marriage, a student whose binge drinking ends his academic career, a father estranged from his teenage children, a homeless couple. William James's description of the unhappy or divided self seeking unification applies to many of these individuals. Through the twelve steps and fellowship with other alcoholics, they find peace and meaning as they work toward unity of self and strive to live honestly in relationship with others.

These dramatic individual conversions occur within the fellowship of Alcoholics Anonymous. Without the program, many "friends of Bill W." say they might never have acknowledged alcohol's hold on them or looked to a Higher Power for help. Each individual's story is unique, yet without AA many stories might have ended in despair and death. AA is a good example of a larger social movement that fosters, promotes, and sustains highly personal experiences of religious growth and conversion. Without the individuals who live the twelve steps, there would be no AA; without AA, few of these individuals would have spiritual awakenings to narrate.

SUMMARY

In this chapter we have studied different types of personal conversion stories: conversion as the gradual deepening or development of personal faith; conversion as a sudden and dramatic break with one's past life; conversion as the catalyst for new religious movements; and conversion as part of a broader social or cultural renewal. Despite the unique character of each narrative, together they exhibit certain commonalities. Whether sudden or gradual, conversion deepens or awakens an intimate relationship with a Higher Power. It facilitates a growing self-knowledge along with the humility to recognize the usefulness of both weakness and strength in ministry to others. Conversion creates a new sense of peace and internal strength so that individuals, despite their fears, find the courage to defy social, religious, or familial constraints. In conversion's aftermath, individuals transcend self-interest to address and change social and religious violation of human rights and social injustice. They seek out likeminded individuals for support; from their spiritual awakening they distill general principles to guide others to similar transformative experiences. Even though individual religious change is personal, it is seldom private; it has an impact on the wider community.

In Chapter 9 we consider religious change within communities and discuss the different ways in which members of these communities negotiate the challenges and uncertainties that accompany such change. We note the interrelationship between shifts in religious thought and practice, on the one hand, and shifts in social, political and economic contexts on the other. At the end of the chapter we focus on the effects of religious change.

RESOURCES

ACTIVITIES

1. We have relied on a classic work by William James, *The Varieties of Religious Experience*, in our discussion of conversion. James's work has been influential in defining categories in the academic study of religion. Read the volume and summarize the main

topics for the class. Such a summary could serve as a catalyst for a class discussion on the psychology of individual religious experience.

2. Make a scrapbook of your family's religious history. You could include a genealogy highlighting the religious affiliations (or lack of such affiliations) of family members, photos of family members involved in religious rituals, a list of religious artifacts in your home and/or dorm room (noting if those artifacts have been passed down through generations), and other relevant memorabilia. Then analyze the trends that appeared from one generation to the next in light of discussions in this chapter.

3. Two recommended films, *Dead Man Walking* and *The Rapture*, tell very different stories of religious conversion. View one of these films and write an analysis using William James's description of the conversion process.

4. Assign Augustine's *Confessions*, *The Autobiography of Malcolm X*, Apuleius's *The Golden Ass*, and *The Book of Margery Kempe* to various class members. Organize a presentation highlighting aspects of conversion common to these four accounts, and aspects of conversion unique to each narrative.

5. Research the life of Archbishop Oscar Romero. Organize a class presentation connecting changes in his personal theology with larger social shifts in El Salvador and the Roman Catholic Church. Perhaps you could include film clips from the film *Romero* in your presentation.

6. The effects of the First Great Awakening continue to influence religious experience and culture in the US today. People have left mainline denominations for evangelical churches. Why do you think this is so?

READINGS

Apuleius, *The Golden Ass* (available in a variety of translations). This Latin novel of the second century relays the comical adventures of Lucius, a well-born young man who falls into a series of mishaps, is accidentally transformed into an ass, and ultimately finds redemption through conversion to the cult of the goddess Isis.

Augustine, *Confessions* (available in a variety of translations). Augustine's spiritual autobiography is a classic of Western spirituality.

The Sermons of Jonathan Edwards (available in a variety of editions and anthologies). Vivid imagery accompanies Edwards's message of human depravity and divine sovereignty. Considered by many to be a highlight of early American literature.

Fowler, James W. *Stages of Faith: The Psychology of Human Development and the Quest for Meaning.* San Francisco: Harper and Row, 1981.

A scholarly discussion of the intersection between spirituality and developmental psychology.

James, William. *The Varieties of Religious Experience* (available in a variety of editions). James's work was a pioneering attempt in the field of psychology and remains essential for the study of individual experience of religion.

Kempe, Margery. *The Book of Margery Kempe* (available in a variety of editions and anthologies). A late medieval woman's tumultuous spiritual autobiography.

Malcolm X. *The Autobiography of Malcolm X*, with the assistance of Alex Haley. New York: Ballantine Books, 1992. The dramatic tale of Malcolm X's disadvantaged childhood, troubled youth, discovery of Islam, and development as a major international figure.

McLoughlin, William. *Revivals, Awakenings, and Reform: An Essay on Religion and Social Change in America*. Chicago: University of Chicago Press, 1978. A scholarly account that situates a variety of American religious reform movements in their social and political contexts.

AUDIO-VISUALS

Dead Man Walking (1995). Tim Robbins, director. Based on the experiences of Sister Helen Prejean as chaplain on death row in Louisiana's Angola Prison; conversion stories of prisoners on death row and Prejean's mission to eliminate the death penalty in the United States.

The Rapture (1991). Michael Tolkin, director. A challenging drama of personal conversion and theological disenchantment.

Malcolm X (1992). Spike Lee, director. A somewhat sanitized interpretation of *The Autobiography of Malcolm* X (as told to Alex Haley).

Romero (1989). John Duigan, director. Follows the life of Romero from his appointment as archbishop, through his advocacy for indigenous Salvadorans, to his murder by government forces.

The Buddha (2010). PBS. David Grubin, director. Tells the Buddha's story through ancient artwork, contemporary animation, and footage of northern India, where many ancient Buddhist rituals are still practiced.

My Name Is Bill W. (VHS, 1989; DVD, 2007). The story of Bill Wilson and Alcoholics Anonymous.

Lightning Rod of the Great Awakening. Brief portrait of British evangelist George Whitefield, whose preaching ignited a spiritual revival in the early nineteenth century.

NOTES

1. Huston Smith, *The World's Religions: Our Greatest Wisdom Traditions* (New York: HarperCollins, 1991), 157.

2. William James, *The Varieties of Religious Experience: A Study in Human Nature* (New York: Modern Library, 1902, 1929), 186.

3. William James, *The Will to Believe and Other Essays in Popular Philosophy* (New York: Longmans Greene and Co., 1907), xii.

4. Quotations from James R. Brockman, *Romero: A Life* (Maryknoll, NY: Orbis Books, 1990).

5. The above quotations are from Jonathan Edwards, "Sinners in the Hands of an Angry God," a sermon preached July 8, 1741, in Enfield, Connecticut. The text is available online.

6. Bill Wilson, *Alcoholics Anonymous Comes of Age: A Brief History of A.A.* (Alcoholics Anonymous World Services, 1957), 63.

Chapter 9

Communal Religious Change

As we have seen, religious change in the life of an individual can be incremental, marked by a gradual deepening (or erosion) of faith; or it can be dramatic, marked by a sudden and life-changing conversion experience. Similarly, religious change in the life of a community can occur incrementally, almost imperceptibly, over the lifetimes of its practitioners; or it can occur dramatically, so that the face of a religion changes in a single generation or less. We begin our consideration of communal religious change with a discussion of two "new religions," that is, with the origins of Islam and Christianity.

Muhammad was born in 570 in Mecca, a city that is in present-day Saudi Arabia. Arabia was a tribal society where rival family groups were constantly fighting one another not only for political power but also for economic gain. When Muslims recall this period prior to Islam, they label it ignorant. Arabia was a **polytheistic** society; people lived in fear of the demons who were said to inhabit the vast sandy reaches of the desert. Mecca itself was a religious attraction, home to hundreds of shrines to the vast pantheon of Arabian deities. Mecca's role as a pilgrimage center helped solidify its place as a regional economic power.

Muhammad, an orphan, was adopted by his uncle. The young Muhammad shared both love and hard economic times with his new family. When he was twenty-five, he married his first wife, Khadija, a forty-year-old widow. Although after her death Muhammad married multiple wives, while she lived Muhammad had no other wife. Muhammad spent years engaged in the caravan business, years that were also a time of spiritual searching. A small number of people who lived around Mecca worshiped one god exclusively, a god known as Allah, meaning "the God." Muhammad was among this number, and he spent many long nights in prayer and contemplation of Allah. Sometime around 610 he had an experience in which he heard a voice speaking to him from heaven, calling him to the service of Allah. After a long night of wrestling with the call, Muhammad returned to Khadija and told her about the experience. She became the first convert to Islam. From the Islamic point of view, though, as was discussed in Chapter 8, one does not so much "convert" to Islam as "come home" to Islam.

In the years that followed Muhammad preached the message of Allah around Mecca. At first he was the object of mockery; however, as he began to win converts, he became the object of hostility and violence. His message of one God named Allah threatened the economic livelihood of the city, which was based on its position as a center of polytheistic pilgrimage. Furthermore, his strongly moral message threatened the hedonism and corruption of the city.

A turning point came in 622, when the city of Medina invited Muhammad to bring the message of Islam there. Medina, like the rest of Arabia, was in severe turmoil because of tribal and other rivalries. A number of residents of Medina who had traveled to Mecca returned to their city speaking of Muhammad and his unifying and righteous message. They decided to invite Muhammad to take up residence, and he agreed to do so when they agreed to accept an uncompromising version of the message he bore—a message of complete submission to the one God, Allah. Muhammad proved himself an exceptional administrator. Although he continued to live a humble life, he united the city of Medina under his rule, and the message of Islam took hold.

Ten years after Muhammad arrived in Medina, he died. In those ten years Medina and Mecca engaged in a series of battles. First, Islamic Medina won, but then power reverted to the larger and better equipped Mecca. However, Medina won the next round, and eventually Muhammad returned in triumph to the city that had rejected him. At his death Islam had spread not only to Mecca and Medina but to virtually all of Arabia. Within a century the Islamic empire spread still further, as far as Spain. The struggle for the spread of Islam was called jihad and those who engaged in it were called mujahideen, meaning "those who struggle or exert themselves." These terms are employed today by militant Islamists, such as members of al Qaeda (the base), a group founded by Osama bin Laden in 1988 or 1989 that engages in a global struggle against Western capitalism. Many Muslims who oppose the militancy of the jihadists consider Islam to be first of all a struggle to conform oneself to the will of Allah and to live according to the Five Pillars (outlined in Chapter 1).

To a Muslim, only one explanation is needed for the unprecedented spread of Islam: God was with Muhammad, who was truly the greatest prophet of Allah. Scholars of religion must be careful to respect the belief systems they are studying; however, they often go beyond those belief systems to offer a variety of other explanations for religious phenomena. Islam was born in a chaotic and violent world and brought a great measure of order and morality to that world. It served an important political function and helped people make sense of their difficult lives. The spiritual success of Islam is perhaps inseparable from its political success. Furthermore, like many new religious movements, Islam built on elements of earlier traditions. For example, Islam builds on insights of Judaism and Christianity, which Islam respects as flawed attempts to articulate a monotheistic faith. After the birth of Islam, Mecca was no longer the home of hundreds of shrines dedicated to tribal deities. However, it became a greater pilgrimage site than could have been imagined by its earlier residents; all Muslims are bound (if it is possible) to make at least one pilgrimage to Mecca to retrace some of the steps of Muhammad's route of revelation. In the previous chapter we noted the importance of this pilgrimage, the hajj, to one Muslim, Malcolm X.

Like Islam, the story of Christianity originates in the story of one man, Jesus of Nazareth. What we can confirm historically about Jesus is slight. He was born in Palestine, probably about 4 BCE and grew up in Nazareth. In adulthood he came into contact with John the Baptist, who was leading a movement of repentance and renewal within Judaism. Following this encounter, Jesus began his own ministry: preaching the imminence of God's reign, reaching out to heal those who were ill, and extending a welcome to those who were marginalized by first-century social structures. He gathered about himself a core group of followers, including not only the group of men known as the Twelve but others, including women such as Mary Magdalene. As his ministry began to attract greater attention, political and religious leaders in Jerusalem sought to eliminate his influence. They executed Jesus by death on the cross, a disgraceful death generally reserved for slaves.

Although Jesus gathered a number of followers, or disciples, during his lifetime, we do not speak about "the church" until after Jesus' death, when his followers began to proclaim the resurrection. (Contrast this with the foundation of Islam, which clearly develops within Muhammad's lifetime.) The Acts of the Apostles tells the story of the emergence of the church under the power of God's spirit after Jesus' death and resurrection. Jesus' followers began to proclaim that the

Crucified One had been raised, and that God had therefore vindicated his beloved Son and anointed one; Jesus was the messiah.

It can be difficult for us today to realize that this declaration that Jesus was the Messiah did not mean that Peter and other early members of the Christian church ceased to be Jews. In fact, the New Testament document known as Acts of the Apostles indicates that they continued to gather for prayer at the Jerusalem Temple, the center of Jewish ritual practice (Acts 2:46; 3:1). Yet today, we certainly think of Judaism and Christianity as distinct religious movements. How Judaism and Christianity come to define themselves in mutually exclusive terms is an important study in religious change.

A partial and misleading insight is that when Peter and the others called Jesus the messiah, they marked themselves as Christian. We have to remember that they did not stop being Jews when they made this declaration; they were simply Jews who believed that the messiah had come. First-century Jews entertained a variety of ideas of who the messiah—the anointed one—would be. Perhaps he would be a political leader who would restore Israel as a sovereign nation, or a priest who would purify the corrupt leadership of the Temple cult. However, the ideas and terminology of messianism were distinctively Jewish.

In the course of Jewish history other Jews have been declared messiah, yet their followers did not cease to be Jews. In the seventeenth century over half the Jews in Europe declared that Sabbatai Zevi was the messiah. Jews who disagreed did not think those who identified Sabbatai Zevi as the messiah had severed their ties to Judaism. (This messianic movement came to an abrupt end when Sabbatai Zevi converted to Islam in 1666.) More recently, a small group of Hasidic Jews claimed that the messiah had come in the person of the late Rebbe Menachenem Schneerson (1902–94) and even after his death there are some who continue to await his return as messiah. While the vast majority of Jews doubt that he will return, they do not declare that those who view Schneerson as the messiah are no longer Jews. Neither should we assume that Jesus' followers destroyed their Jewish identities by acknowledging him as messiah.

What, then, prompted the separation of the early Christians from their parent religion of Judaism? We can identify three major factors that led to this significant religious change. First, the Jewish War of 67–70 was a political event that caused Judaism to look at itself more critically and to draw clearer lines to demarcate the boundaries of Judaism. Second, the increasing numbers of Gentiles entering the church caused a marked lessening in Jewish identity of the church as a whole. Third, the development of the idea that Jesus was not only the

Thinking about the Historical Jesus

Regardless of their religious affiliation, scholars agree on certain historical claims about Jesus. However, from the perspective of faith, Christians affirm many other things about Jesus of Nazareth. For many Christians it is important to note that tradition claims that Jesus' mother, Mary, was a virgin at the time of his conception and birth. The gospels suggest that during Jesus' ministry God acknowledged Jesus as his own Son. An important foundation of later Christian faith is the belief that after Jesus died on the cross God vindicated him by raising him from the dead. Christian tradition includes the further claim that the resurrected Jesus ascended to heaven and sits at God's right hand until the end of the world, when he will come again in judgment. All these claims are matters of faith shared by Christian believers. An agnostic historian who recognizes that Jesus of Nazareth suffered capital punishment in Roman-occupied Jerusalem does not accept as a necessary corollary that God raised this Jesus from the dead.

Survey some people you know about their beliefs about Jesus. After you compile a list of commonly held beliefs (you may include your own beliefs, if you like), categorize those beliefs as matters of historical fact or items of faith.

Is it always possible to separate what we consider to be "historical fact" and what we consider to be an item of faith?

messiah but God challenged the limits of Jewish monotheistic faith. Each of these factors deserves further comment.

The church emerged in Roman-occupied Jerusalem at a time when Judaism was highly factionalized. A small group of Jews who proclaimed that the messiah had come was easily incorporated into the pluralistic picture. The political context changed in 67–70 with the outbreak of the Jewish War, a bloody war for liberation from Rome that the Jews lost. Apparently, many Christians refused to fight, perhaps on the basis of pacifist principles, a position that seems to have alienated them from many compatriot Jews. Perhaps more important, the Romans demolished the Jerusalem Temple, causing Judaism to undergo one of its most significant periods of self-examination. Political circumstances forced the Jewish community to articulate more carefully what it meant to be a Jew, and this process of self-definition resulted in the demise of various sects that had existed before the war.

In such a political climate early Christianity's demise as a messianic Jewish sect may have been inevitable.

A second factor in the separation between Judaism and Christianity was the increasingly large number of Gentiles entering the Christian community, along with their marked indifference to the observance of Jewish law. Some early Christian missionaries who preached to the Gentiles insisted that conversion to the Jewish covenant must accompany conversion to a belief in Jesus as messiah. However, the church eventually decided to baptize Gentiles without insisting on circumcision and the observance of food laws. This decision was important in the history of the separation of Judaism and Christianity for two reasons. First, as greater numbers of Gentiles entered the community, the church ceased to be an ethnically and culturally Jewish movement. Second, from a Jewish perspective, when Christians decided not to insist on Torah observance, they ultimately defined themselves as outside the boundaries of Judaism.

We have seen that Jews who proclaimed Jesus as messiah did not thereby end their ties to Judaism. However, as Christians began to proclaim that Jesus was God, they made a theological claim that almost all Jews would recognize as incompatible with a Jewish interpretation of monotheism. Centuries of Christians have acknowledged Jesus both as messiah and as God, so it may be hard to recognize that before the Christian movement Jews did not expect their messiah to be divine; there is little if any precedent in Judaism for the notion of a messianic figure who is himself God. While the claim that Jesus was the messiah was not theologically problematic, an emerging Christian belief that Jesus was the incarnation or embodiment of God proved impossible for Judaism to accept.

The emergence of Christianity as a religion separate from its parent religion of Judaism is a dramatic example of communal religious change. We could see this development as the culmination of a large number of individual conversion stories, as Jews who acknowledged Jesus as the messiah began to act and believe in ways that were incompatible with their Jewish heritage. We have seen that it is also the result of a political context that forced Judaism to reexamine and redefine itself in new ways. What is perhaps most important is that Christianity did not simply emerge overnight as a distinct religious tradition, but that over the course of several generations a number of factors precipitated a division between the synagogue and the church. The shame of this situation is that Christians over the centuries have forgotten the enormous debt they owe to Judaism, the religious movement that gave them birth.

RENEWAL AND REFORM WITHIN A RELIGION

At what point do we say that a new religion is born? At what point did Christianity cease to be a reform movement within Judaism and become a distinct religion? Certainly, religions can sustain major reform movements and still retain their identities. The Protestant Reformation is an important example of a movement that greatly altered the contours of a religion without effecting a split into a new religion. (Although some confusion prevails on this point, Roman Catholicism, Protestantism, and Orthodoxy are all branches of a single religion, Christianity.)

At the end of the European Middle Ages the Roman Church wielded broad cultural influence and great political power. The popes were important patrons of the arts. Julius II, for example, who was pope in the early 1500s, commissioned such great Vatican art works as the Sistine Chapel. Julius II was also a warrior-pope, leading troops into battle in order to claim northern Italian lands for the papacy. Because of its sometimes self-interested involvement with secular matters, the church had begun to attract criticism from a number of quarters, both political and theological. Although there were a number of minor attempts at reform, not until Martin Luther (1483–1546) did the process of reform really grip Europe.

Luther was a German monk steeped in the theological world of the late Middle Ages. He came to public attention in 1517 when he posted a list of criticisms, his Ninety-Five Theses, on a church door in the German city of Wittenberg, where he resided. (The tradition that he nailed them to the door of the Wittenberg castle church has been questioned.) Luther intended the list to spark discussion; in university towns such as Wittenberg posting such lists was a relatively common practice. (Think of the use of bulletin boards and electronic media for public announcements in colleges and universities today.) The criticisms focused on the sale of indulgences. An indulgence was essentially a reprieve from penitential time in purgatory, where Catholics believed that the souls of those who were forgiven but not entirely purified went after death. In the theses posted in Wittenberg, Luther emphasized the corruption of selling such indulgences, a practice that would imply that God would release the souls of the rich sooner than the souls of the poor. Luther thought that the church preyed on people's vulnerabilities in its teaching that one could buy relief for loved ones who had died and were suffering in purgatory. In his words, "There is no divine authority for preaching that the soul flies out of purgatory immediately [as] the money clinks in the bottom of the chest."

Luther was certainly not the first Catholic to voice such criticisms; however, for a variety of political and social reasons his articulation of theological concerns triggered an unusually strong response from ecclesial authorities. Leaders of the church asked Luther to take back his criticisms. He considered this. He did not want to see division in the church that he loved. However, the more he thought about the situation, the more disturbed he became. Pushed to his limits, he dug in his heels and argued his position even more strongly than he had at first. His meditations on church teachings about purgatory and indulgences led him to articulate his understanding of "justification by faith." Influenced by the letters of the apostle Paul to the Romans and the Galatians, Luther came to believe that human beings would not be rectified before God because of their own deeds, and particularly not by participating in the ritual system of the church. Rather, Luther believed that salvation was a free gift of God, freely given to those of faith. He stood against the church on grounds of conscience, always hoping that the breach between him and the hierarchy would be mended. It was not. By the end of his life, Luther was aware that his words had initiated a process of both reform and division that resulted in the birth of Protestant churches.

A number of factors contributed to the growth of the Lutheran Reformation, as well as other branches of the Protestant Reformation. Luther appeared on the scene at a time of growing nationalism, when the various nation states of Europe had begun to resist the political control of the papacy. His writings offered some theological rationale for ending one's allegiance to the pope. At least initially, the Protestant churches seemed to be free from the overtly corrupt practices of the late medieval church, such as the sale of church offices and the propensity of certain priests to live openly with women to whom they were not married. Ministers in Protestant churches were allowed to marry. Luther promoted popular reading of the Bible, translating it himself into a lucid German edition; he wrote popular hymns that taught aspects of the faith. Perhaps most important, though, the interpretation he offered of the gospel, the teaching of Jesus, convinced many Christians throughout Europe that they were hearing the good news for the first time.

Other religious traditions have gone through significant moments of reform that redefine the tradition without marking a definitive break from it. Native American tradition provides another example of this phenomenon. From 1799 to 1815 a Seneca prophet named Handsome Lake preached to the people of the Six Nations of the Haudenosaunee (the Iroquois Confederacy). At this time the westward expansion of people of European descent threatened the ways and the existence of the Six Nations. Threats to their well-being were both overt and insidious. Not only were there political threats to their sovereignty, but internal problems had arisen as contact with outsiders introduced new problems into their communities. Alcoholism, for example, was rampant. Many women chose to have abortions because they did not believe that the world was hospitable to new life. Handsome Lake's message recalled older traditions but also included a number of directives necessary for sustaining the health of the communities. Avoid alcohol, remain faithful and loving to your spouse, don't be afraid to bring children into this world, care for the elderly—these are among the messages Handsome Lake delivered to his people, conveying messages from the Creator.

The message of Handsome Lake was pivotal in the development of the thought and practice of the Six Nations. Every fall the nations still gather in their longhouses to recite his prophecies. At the time of his death, however, Handsome Lake does not seem to have been held in great honor. One tradition even reports that he had been expelled from the reservation where he was living because he seduced a young woman who had come to him to heal her illness. How does one move from the tarnished reputation of a dying man to the commemoration of a significant moment of religious renewal? Political and social circumstances are certainly factors; the Iroquois nations needed Handsome Lake's message of spirituality and caring for one another in order to sustain the life of their people. Nonetheless, acceptance of his message was not automatic. It took the hard work of his followers to keep his prophecies alive in the years and decades after his death.

Approximately a decade after Handsome Lake's death, around 1825, women who remembered his message despaired as they viewed the problems that still beset the Six Nations. Furthermore, they realized that those who remembered his prophecies vividly were declining in number. They therefore invited a descendant of Handsome Lake to recall publicly Handsome Lake's words. Thus began the annual recitation of Handsome Lake's prophecies. It seems that at first the recitation of the prophecies took place at only a few longhouses, but as time passed the practice spread throughout the confederacy. Strangely, we can say that the Handsome Lake revival among the Six Nations of the Iroquois Confederacy dates not to the lifetime of Handsome Lake but to the preaching of his grandson a decade after his death.[1]

SOCIAL CHANGE AS A CATALYST
FOR RELIGIOUS CHANGE

Social change often accompanies religious change; indeed, distinguishing the two is often impossible. In the nineteenth century, when scholars began to study religion as a system or an institution, they offered a variety of explanations for the relationship between religious and other social phenomena. Karl Marx, for example, saw religious beliefs and actions primarily as symptoms or manifestations of underlying social conditions. According to this view religious change would always follow fundamental social change; religious change could not cause a reordering of the larger relations of society. Max Weber, on the other hand, believed that religious thought and practice play more complex roles in the structuring of society. Weber referred to "elective affinity" between religious and other social change. That is, he noted that religious change often accompanied social change, and that social change often accompanied religious change. However, he thought that it was overly simplistic to separate religious change from other kinds of social change and to identify one set of changes as causes and the other set of changes as effects.

MARYKNOLL MISSION ARCHIVES

A Marian procession in Chile. The large statue of Mary (behind and to the left of the cross) is being carried by a group of men.

In some cases alterations in social and political circumstances prompt changes in patterns of religious thought, practice, and community life. In many agricultural areas, for example, festivals of planting and harvesting dominate the ritual calendar. When factories replace farms, some communities abandon their rituals, others reinterpret them, and still others continue to preserve seasonal rituals but no longer as the organizing aspects of community life. As changing circumstances alter the totality of a community's worldview, religious beliefs and practices are also likely to evolve.

When Roman Catholics arrived in large numbers on American shores in the late nineteenth century, they often settled in ethnic neighborhoods where they maintained traditions familiar to them from the old country: Polish families brought baskets of paschal bread and eggs to church to be blessed on Holy Saturday (the day before Easter), and Italian immigrants organized large festivals in honor of the Virgin Mary and other saints. As the decades passed, immigrants increasingly integrated into American culture, often marrying members of other ethnic groups and otherwise reducing their exclusive reliance on ethnic networks of support. By the 1960s and 1970s, large numbers of Catholics had moved from ethnic urban clusters to live in suburban communities. The slow process of cultural change included diminishing attachment to older religious practices. At no point did ethnic communities consciously decide to alter their practices. Customs were abandoned one at a time as family members moved away or as upwardly mobile generations began to feel at home in suburban parishes. There was no definitive break with the past. Nonetheless, American Catholicism had assumed a new face.

Thinking about Ethnicity and Religion

Do you or your immediate family have traditions associated with your ethnic heritage(s)? Do you consider these traditions religious?

Do your parents or grandparents remember participating as children in religious traditions associated with their ethnic heritages that they have not passed on to your generation?

When and why did your family abandon these traditional practices?

If your family retains significant aspects of an ethnic religious heritage, what do you think accounts for this attachment?

What does this suggest about the process of change in the religious heritage(s) of your family?

Trying to grasp the moment when religious change happens is often impossible. Change is a process. At times we may single out a moment as crucial in the unfolding of change. However, as we look more deeply we will undoubtedly realize that a variety of circumstances have led to the symbolically important moment, and that a variety of consequences result from it. One key moment in the recent development of American Christian history was the controversial ordination of fifteen women to the priesthood of the Episcopal Church in Philadelphia on July 29, 1974. We can pinpoint the moment at which the ordination occurred, but to understand its significance we need to understand the historical context in which it took place.

The women and their supporters were involved in the women's liberation movement, which in turn had been largely influenced by the Civil Rights movement. The preacher at the ordination was Dr. Charles Willie, an African American professor at Harvard who was an Episcopal lay man (that is, not a member of the clergy) and vice president of the Episcopal Church's House of Deputies. Dr. Willie's sermon explicitly linked the women's ordination to these two movements:

> There are parallels between the Civil Rights Movement and the Women's Movement and this is what we are witnessing today. . . . As blacks refused to participate in their own oppression by going to the back of the bus in 1955 in Montgomery, women are refusing to cooperate in their own oppression by remaining on the periphery of full participation in the Church in 1974 in Philadelphia.[2]

Dr. Willie, the women priests, and the Episcopal bishops who broke ranks with their brother bishops to participate in the ordination were aware that developments in American society over the previous twenty years had created a social climate in which the ordination of women was conceivable. Nor were the ordinations the end of the story. Since then, the Episcopal Church has been trying to understand what it means to have women as well as men as priests and even as bishops. To those involved in the ordinations, the action was a way of honoring more fully several biblical insights: that both women and men are formed in God's image, and that in Christ there is neither male nor female. The ordination of women and of gays and lesbians in several denominations also reflects changing social mores. While we can focus on key scenes in various dramas of religious change, in order to understand their significance we will need to examine the larger settings in which they are enacted.

As we discussed in Chapter 1, people around the world were shocked on September 11, 2001, at the coordinated attacks upon the United States by terrorists from the militant Islamist group al Qaeda. In the aftermath of the attacks it became clear that the attackers perceived the West, led by the United States, as the enemy of Islam and Islamic values, a view not shared by the majority of Muslims. Initially the leader of al Qaeda, Osama bin Laden, denied involvement in the attacks, but then he claimed responsibility for them. As motivation, he cited US support of Israel, the presence of US troops in Saudi Arabia, and US sanctions against Iraq. In response to the attacks, the United States launched a "war on terrorism," invading Afghanistan to depose the Taliban, an Islamist political group that had ruled parts of Afghanistan from 1996 and harbored al Qaeda members. The Taliban was notorious for its strict interpretation of *shari'ah* law and for its punitive treatment of women. The events of 9/11 have caused many people to reflect on the relationship of religion and terrorism and also on the global inequities that foster resentment of the West.

In 1979, too, America was shocked when Islamic militants overthrew the Shah of Iran, who had been a staunch American ally. This event, which symbolizes the explosive growth of Islamic fundamentalism in the 1970s and 1980s, leading to the events of 9/11, appears much less surprising when viewed against the backdrop of the changing political and social circumstances of Islam in the twentieth century. As the century began, the Turkish Empire still survived as a testament to the potential of Islamic political power. Although considerably diminished from the height of its power—in 1683 the Turkish Empire had come close to annexing Vienna—other Islamic nations considered the empire's persistence evidence of Islam's ultimate domination of the world. Turkey allied itself to Germany during the First World War, and Germany's loss in that war meant the end of the Turkish Empire in 1918. This was a traumatic blow to the worldview of the Islamic world, especially when the founder of the Republic of Turkey, Mustafa Kemal Atatürk, began to rebuild Turkey's power as an entirely secular nation, excluding Islamic law and tradition from the nation's political and social structure.

In succeeding decades technological differences exacerbated the gap between the largely Christian countries of Europe and North America and the Islamic nations of East Asia and North Africa; living conditions, economic influence, military might, and international political sway all varied widely. In order to close the gap a number of Islamic nations began to adopt a variety of Western ways. In Iran the ruling Pahlavi family tried especially hard to "modernize" the nation. Although the real goal of the effort was to help Iran catch up to Europe and the United States in economic, military, and political strength, the Pahlavi family also focused on other symbolic aspects of Iranian Muslim practice as targets for change. In 1935 the shah forbade woman to wear the chador, the traditional heavy black cloak, which to him was a visible expression of his country's "backwardness." This decree was painful to Iranian women, most of whom had never left their houses without this clothing that they felt protected them from male eyes. Even the shah's wife wept when she left home without the chador. In 1941, the shah decreed that it was again legal to wear the chador, although he continued in a variety of ways to discourage it.

The Pahlavis' position on the chador served as a symbol of their plan for Iran's restoration to a position of political and economic power, a plan that relied largely on adaptation to Western ways. Many Muslims in Iran and other nations rejected this response to Islam's diminished role in world affairs. They believed that Islam would again rise in the world in historical importance not by rejecting traditional ways but by following them more closely than ever, not by emulating the West but by distancing itself from it.

The rise of fundamentalist Islam took a distinctive course in Iran. Iran has a religious tradition in which a particular form of Islam known as Shi'ism is dominant. In Shi'ite Islam clergy mediate between believers and Allah. In the 1979 revolution against the last of

FRED GLENNON

Muslim woman in microbiology class.

the Pahlavi shahs, the **Ayatollah** Khomeini achieved an international reputation first as a critic of the Pahlavi regime and then as a leader in the new Islamic republic. Predictably, early legislation mandated that women wear modest dress (loose clothing and a head scarf), and a national campaign emerged to encourage (or coerce) women to wear the **chador** that successive Pahlavi shahs had tried to eliminate from the nation's wardrobe. The revolutionary government responded to the various crises of the country not by adapting Western ways but by reinterpreting the *shari'ah*, the traditional Islamic code of law, to fit the complex realities of late-twentieth-century life. The existence of an Islamic Republic in Iran since 1979 has been a constant reminder that certain social, economic, and political conditions can be fertile ground for growth of a religious sensibility that seeks its own way of ordering the world.

What we are calling Islamic fundamentalism takes a variety of forms, depending on the particular economic and political situations of various nations. In Egypt, for example, as the Westernizing policies of a succession of leaders accompanied a growing gap between the wealthy and poor, a fundamentalist group known as the Muslim Brotherhood worked to enact laws in conformity with their interpretation of the duties of Islam. As Americans applauded official Egyptian efforts to work for peace with Israel, members of the Muslim Brotherhood interpreted these efforts as capitulation to the decadent foes of Islam. Perceptions of political and economic vulnerability thus fostered growth in one form of Islamic fundamentalism.

Al Qaeda, the more recent terrorist group responsible for the 9/11 attacks, is a global Sunni Muslim movement calling for worldwide jihad and advocating a destruction of Western influences in the Islamic world. It is particularly sensitive to the inequities fostered by Western exploitation of global resources. As Muslim communities establish themselves in religiously plural countries around the world al Qaeda worries that Islam will become allied with other religions and with Western capitalism. It looks for the unification of global Islam and the imposition of *shari'ah* law.

CULTURAL CONTACT AND RELIGIOUS CHANGE

Contact between two or more cultures is a social circumstance that often catalyzes religious change. When two worldviews collide, individuals and communities may begin to challenge aspects of their traditional ways of seeing and acting in the world. The history of

European exploration in Asia, Africa, and the Americas affords many examples of such encounters.

Economic advantage was a goal in European exploration, perhaps the major goal. Missionaries often followed and sometimes even accompanied the traders. At times, missionary efforts offered a justification for the aggressive actions of the explorers. Bartolomé de Las Casas (1484–1566), a Spaniard who was the first priest ordained in the Americas, was an early critic of the practices of Europeans in the lands they had newly encountered. After many years in the recently established colonies, Las Casas returned to Spain where he published a blistering attack on what he saw as the savagery of the Christians. Las Casas identified gold as the motivation for his fellow Europeans to travel to the Americas, despite the claims of many that they were attempting to convert the natives. He described one such attempt. As a band of explorers approached a local village, they read—in a language the villagers could not comprehend—statements demanding conversion to Christianity. Naturally, no villagers came forward to convert. Their supposed resistance to the gospel was the alleged reason for destroying their village, killing many inhabitants, and capturing others to sell as slaves. In fact, Las Casas suggests, the real goal was not to convert the inhabitants but to eliminate them so their gold could be stolen. Las Casas tells of an indigenous leader who was about to be executed. His captors told him that if he would convert to Christianity he was assured of going to heaven after death, but if he resisted he would go straight to hell, which they described in terrifying terms. The leader asked whether all Christians went to heaven, and those about to execute him said yes. Then, said the man, he would prefer to go to hell. Las Casas concludes, "Such is the fame and honor that God and our Faith have earned through the Christians who have gone out to the Indies."[3]

As Las Casas noted, the Spanish wanted to acquire the land and resources of the peoples of Latin America. Such has been the case with settlers and colonizers in many parts of the world. A notion associated with the conquest of the land of indigenous peoples by European nations is called the Doctrine of Discovery. The name relates to the Age of Discovery, a period of some two centuries, beginning in the early fifteenth century, during which European explorers and colonizers established contacts with Africa, the Americas, Asia, and Oceania. However, the underlying rationale is earlier. For instance, in Roman law the idea that colonizing powers could take land that was not being used as a "civilized" Roman would use it was termed *terra*

A portrayal of the encounter between Bartolomé de Las Casas and Cortes in a portion of a mural by Diego Rivera.

nullius (empty land). *Terra nullius* came to be cited as justification for the British acquisition of land in Australia.

The Doctrine of Discovery and *terra nullius* are now established concepts in international law. The Doctrine of Discovery was expounded by the United States Supreme Court in a series of decisions, particularly in Johnson *v.* M'Intosh in 1823, a case in which Chief Justice John Marshall justified the ways that colonial powers claimed lands belonging to indigenous peoples during the Age of Discovery. Under the Doctrine of Discovery title to lands lay with the government whose subjects occupied a region whose indigenous inhabitants were not the subjects of a European Christian monarch. The lack of "civilization" of the indigenous peoples and their lack of "religion" were given as reasons for conquering them and their lands. Some trace the doctrine to Pope Nicholas's bull *Romanus Pontifex* in 1452, a decree that approved the Portuguese acquisition of lands in West Africa, and to Pope Alexander VI's bull *Inter Caetera* of 1493 that gave approval to Spain to conquer lands in South America. (A bull, in this sense, is a solemn papal letter sealed with a *bulla*, a lead seal, or with a red-ink imprint of the device on the *bulla*.) We must remember that these bulls come from a time when the pope was not only a spiritual leader but also an arbiter among the Christian monarchs of Europe. Thomas Jefferson's idea of "a wall of separation between Church and State" was articulated in a letter in 1802 and first quoted in the United States Supreme Court in 1878.

Alliances between traders and missionaries have continued to be common not only in the Americas but also in Africa and the Pacific. Las Casas demonstrates the ambiguity of such alliances. Himself a missionary, he was a vehement critic of missionary practices, raising the awareness of Europeans about the activities of their compatriots in the Americas. His grounds for criticism were religious. He expected God's eternal condemnation of those Christians who exploited and killed native peoples. Conversion was a high priority for Las Casas. He worked to teach the gospel peacefully to the peoples of the Americas, insisting that such a method was far more efficacious than forced baptisms leading to enslavement. We could also say that he worked and prayed for the conversion of Christian Europe to an attitude of compassion and love.

If we focus only on the horror stories narrated by Las Casas we will be surprised to learn that Christian missionaries ever succeeded in winning the hearts of people they encountered. Of course, most missionaries have been far from the cynical opportunists Las Casas portrayed. In Papua New Guinea, a large island northeast of Australia, missionaries followed traders in the late nineteenth century. At first the inhabitants of New Guinea were suspicious of the missionaries, and indeed killed some of them. In time, however, many islanders came to accept the missionaries. Islanders offered a variety of reasons to explain their acceptance of the Christian message. Some believed that the hymns the missionaries taught were powerful. Others said that, unlike the traders, the missionaries "walked softly." According to one story, a missionary intervened in a risky situation to save a woman's life. Other island women were amazed. In their worldview, one typically acted on behalf of family members, and the woman obviously was not kin to the missionary. The incident led local people to think about the possible benefits of the message they were hearing.

Whether Christian teachings are ultimately embraced or rejected, those who have had contact with outsiders never see the world precisely as they did prior to the encounter. On the one hand, the colonial and missionary encounter may broaden their notion of community. On the other hand, it may cause people to despair at the disparities between their communities and those of the outsiders. In Papua New Guinea, according to the 2000 census, 96 percent of respondents identified themselves as Christians. Their Christianity links them to the worldwide Christian community, yet it is distinctive to their region as it draws on the ways and the wisdoms of their ancestors. Today, scholars speak of "global Christianity" in referring to the varying qualities of Christianity among diverse populations.

In 1965 the Kenyan writer Ngugi wa Thiong'o published a novel entitled *The River Between* that dramatizes the pain inherent in cultural struggles between Christianity and indigenous traditions. Waiyaki is the protagonist of the novel. His father, who is committed to the tribal ways, reveals to him that ancient prophecies foretell a role for Waiyaki in saving his people. However, European Christians have come to the area, and the father understands that the people cannot ignore these new influences. He orders Waiyaki: "Arise. Heed the prophecy. Go to the Mission place. Learn all the wisdom and all the secrets of the white man. But do not follow his vices. Be true to your people and the ancient rites." Waiyaki struggles to follow his father's advice. He goes to the Christian school and then returns to his village. He starts a school that will teach the children reading, writing, and other skills he thinks are necessary to cope in the modern world. However, the school does not teach Christianity; it teaches tribal traditions. Waiyaki's larger goal is to organize the people so they will be able to resist the political and economic compromises that accompany their expanded interactions with the white man.

Even as Waiyaki's mission gains momentum he falls in love with Nyambura, the daughter of a local Christian preacher. Because her father has rejected the ancestral ways, Nyambura is not circumcised. Waiyaki exemplifies the contradictions between traditional religions and contact with the West. Educated at a Christian school, Waiyaki longs to be a teacher of traditional ways. An adherent of ancestral practices, his attachment to an uncircumcised woman renders him suspect in the eyes of his peers. Ngugi expands on Waiyaki's dilemma:

> For Waiyaki knew that not all the ways of the white man were bad. Even his religion was not essentially bad. Some good, some truth shone through it. But the religion, the faith, needed washing, cleaning away all the dirt, leaving only the eternal. And that eternal that was the truth had to be reconciled to the traditions of the people. A people's traditions could not be swept away overnight. That way lay disintegration. Such a tribe would have no roots, for a people's roots were in their traditions going back to the past, the very beginning.[4]

Waiyaki understands that his people will lose themselves if they lose their ancestral ways, but that their life after contact with the Christian missionaries will never be what it was before.

Study of the contact between two or more cultures dramatically reveals what is true of all religions: human institutions are not static but dynamic. We cannot capture the essence of a religion with a snapshot; we need the metaphor of the movie to help us understand how religious life changes as communities move, disintegrate, regroup, absorb foreign influences, or otherwise confront altered circumstances. Early in this chapter we referred to the situation of enslaved Africans who arrived on American shores. Now that we have considered in greater depth the ways that social and political changes trigger religious evolution, we can better appreciate the religious changes that followed the upheaval and involuntary relocation of hundreds of thousands of Africans.

The enormity of the dislocation experienced by the enslaved Africans is hard to imagine. They were forcibly removed from their own shores to travel to an unknown land, to speak a language they had never heard, never to see family or familiar places again. One newly arrived slave said, "As every object was new to me, everything I saw filled me with surprise."[5] Once on American shores the experiences of the enslaved varied considerably. Until about 1800 slavery was legal throughout the English-speaking colonies/states, even in the North. Some slave traders sold African slaves in northern ports, although in most northern areas the concentrations of African Americans remained small. Smaller communities of African slaves meant greater contact between slaves and Americans of European heritage, and more rapid acculturation into the larger society.

Phillis Wheatley offers an extreme example of such adjustment. Born in West Africa and sold into slavery as a child, she arrived in Boston and learned not only English but also Greek and Latin. In 1773, at the age of eighteen, she published a learned book of poetry. Although Phillis Wheatley seems to have moved into the dominant culture with unusual rapidity—and one may wonder what memories of her African childhood she nurtured without committing them to the language of her captors—her story points to wide opportunities for contact between black and white residents of Boston in the late eighteenth century. Such contact extended to Christian education and worship. By the end of the eighteenth century a number of important northern congregations were integrated, and some autonomous black churches had developed whose worship styles closely resembled those of neighboring white institutions.

Africans sold onto southern shores had a very different experience. Particularly in the coastal areas of the Carolinas, many slaves continued to live in communities that were predominantly African.

Living in enclaves of other Africans and their descendants, slaves continued to draw on traditional African medicine, agricultural and fishing techniques, and crafts styles. In many ways these communities continued to transmit an African religious heritage, emphasizing belief in a world of good and bad spirits that influence the course of the world and of human events. However, African traditions suggested that spirits permeated particular places and objects, and that after death the ancestors returned to the people and territories they had known in life. The Middle Passage across the Atlantic in the holds of the slave ships had twisted and broken many of the connections the slaves held to the world of spirits and ancestors. Thus, their removal to American shores necessitated some measure of religious change.

Only slowly did slave owners begin to instruct the slaves in Christianity. Their reluctance stemmed from their belief that baptism into Christianity would cause slaves to become arrogant and perhaps to demand their freedom. When the slave owners did begin Christian instruction, the gospel they taught was this: Obey your master and your mistress if you want a reward in heaven after death. Understandably, this message was not especially appealing in slave quarters. However, other Christian messengers got through to many slaves, and the Christian message was sufficiently multi-layered that the slaves were able to develop their own interpretations of the gospel. We have already discussed the First and Second Great Awakenings of the eighteenth and early nineteenth centuries, which emphasized spirited preaching and intense personal conversion experiences. Missionaries of these periods sought opportunities to preach to slaves, who often responded fervently to the message of God's love and renewal of life.

The Christianity the slaves came to practice was different in many respects from the Christianity practiced by their white neighbors. When two cultures come into contact with each other, it is unlikely that either culture will remain unaffected. When African slaves came to these shores, their traditional patterns of belief and habit altered; when they embraced Christianity, the scope of Christian thought and action also altered. The slaves became Christian, but their Christianity in turn became "Africanized." One way that slaves were able to connect to Christian thought was to find areas of similarity between their old ways and the new message they were hearing. So, for example, the benevolent and loving God of the Protestant missionaries might remind them of the benevolent and loving high God of West African religions. Evangelical Christian preaching emphasized that God was taking possession of the body and spirit of the convert, and this experience resonated with West African understandings of spirit possession.

Visitors (including African American visitors from staid northern congregations) commented on many African elements that remained in the Christian worship of southern blacks, such as a communal circle dance. The development of unique forms of Christianity among the slaves, incorporating both remnants of African thought and practice and missionary influences, is evidence of the tremendous power of religious traditions to adapt as they conform to new circumstances.

RELIGION AS A CATALYST FOR SOCIAL CHANGE

Social change triggers religious change, and contacts among various cultures spark new religious configurations. If we stop our analysis here, religious worldviews will appear merely as byproducts of the material arrangements of people's lives. While social and political circumstances certainly affect the development of worldviews, the religious imagination also shapes visions of the kinds of life people want to lead. As a result, shifting religious perspectives can alter social and political landscapes.

As previously noted, the Second Great Awakening (1810–30) was a period in American religious history when waves of renewal swept through the new republic. This time of religious regeneration precipitated the movement for the abolition of slavery. A shifting theological perspective thus engendered change in the social and political arrangements of the nation. Understanding the theological innovations of the Second Great Awakening will help us see how those involved extended their concerns to encompass the situation of American slaves.

American Protestantism had strong Calvinist roots. John Calvin, an early French Protestant reformer, was active only a few years after Luther's actions instigated the Protestant Reformation. Many colonial churches—especially in New England, New York, and New Jersey—followed Calvin's teaching that God had chosen in advance certain people for salvation and others for damnation. Those predestined for salvation were known as the elect, those for whom Jesus had died. This scheme leaves little scope for the operation of free will, since it implies that human beings cannot choose to act in a way that will gain salvation. During the eighteenth century another view of human nature, the Enlightenment, became popular among intellectuals in Europe and America. It was a philosophical movement that emphasized the rationality of human nature and the importance of free will in the ethical decision-making process. Enlightenment teachings about human power to define and shape the world formed the intellectual background for the American and French revolutions.

This reevaluation of human nature eventually began to affect the ways religious people saw the world. In the early nineteenth century evangelical preachers began to minimize or omit the role of predestination in salvation. The excitement of living in a new nation fostered a climate in which many came to believe that human nature could bring itself to perfection, freely vanquishing the powers of sin. According to the theology that swept the nation, human beings have the capacity to will a conversion to new life in the gospel. This teaching offered a markedly more optimistic view of human nature than the older Calvinist view. Around 1830 two evangelical preachers, Charles Grandison Finney and Theodore Weld, began organizing church-based abolitionist societies that called for an immediate end to slavery. Finney, in particular, believed that this goal could be reached by preaching conversion to slave owners, who would on their own reject the sin of slave owning. Finney, of course, was wrong; the nation went through a long and bloody struggle before the abolition of slavery. However, in the decades leading to the Civil War, leaders of the abolition movement continued to arise from the ranks of evangelical Christians influenced by the Second Great Awakening.

Churches provided not only a theological but also an institutional base for the abolition movement. Black churches in particular were often the location for anti-slavery societies and activities. In Boston, for example, both black and white abolitionists assembled in black churches to hear prominent anti-slavery speakers. Pastors preached against slavery from the pulpits, and congregations worked together to give safe refuge to runaway slaves, an increasingly dangerous ministry. African American churches even developed rituals to commemorate key moments in the struggle against slavery, for example, the abolition of the trans-Atlantic slave trade and the end of slavery in Britain and its territories.

The black church has remained a force in shaping black communities and hence the national fabric. During the civil rights era black churches offered an institutional base and religious inspiration in the struggle for human dignity. Martin Luther King Jr.'s dream for America was based on a biblical vision of peace and justice. Countless preachers proclaimed from their pulpits that God was on the side of those working for justice. White America was slow to comprehend the power of the church to shape political opinion in the black community. An incident from the Montgomery, Alabama, bus boycott

(1955–56) illustrates both the influence of the black church and the lack of white comprehension.

The boycott began when a respected woman named Rosa Parks refused to move to the back of the bus, as the law required. The subsequent refusal of blacks to ride segregated buses—instead walking miles upon miles and organizing elaborate car pools—was an economic blow to the city of Montgomery. One weekend the leaders of the city hatched a plan to restore black ridership. They wrote an article to appear in the Sunday paper saying that black leaders had negotiated an end to the boycott. Somehow, the story was leaked to King on Saturday night, and he organized all the black ministers in Montgomery to denounce the story in their sermons. When Monday morning arrived, white Montgomery was stunned as empty buses continued to roll by. They had underestimated the efficacy of the black church network and the degree to which the black church was a factor in shaping black opinion and community life.

Just as the black churches played a significant role in the Civil Rights movement, so too they were influential in getting out the vote in the 2008 election in which Barack Hussein Obama II was elected as the first African American to hold the office of president of the United States. Obama, who was born in Honolulu and lived as a child in Indonesia as well as in Hawaii, represents the multi-ethnicity of many Americans today. The child of a Kenyan father and white American mother, educated at Columbia University and Harvard Law School, he worked as a civil rights attorney in Chicago, taught constitutional law at the University of Chicago Law School, served in the Illinois Senate and was a US senator before running for president. During the election campaign there was speculation about Obama's religious beliefs. The picture that emerged is multifaceted and in keeping with the religious experience of many Americans today. His mother was the daughter of non-practicing Christians; his father was raised a Muslim but had become an atheist before he married Obama's mother. Obama's Indonesian stepfather was also Muslim and acquainted, too, with indigenous and Hindu beliefs. Although neither Obama nor his mother were ever atheists, she raised him in a relatively secular household; it was only as an adult that he became an active Christian. The president, it seems, is comfortable with the religious pluralism of his own background and of the world today.

A final example of the influence of religious factors on social and political structures is the role that Christianization has played in the emergence of new nation-states in the postcolonial era (roughly, since the Second World War). Papua New Guinea, for example, achieved independence from nearby Australia in 1975. The constitution of the new nation acknowledges both "our noble traditions" (local religions) and "Christian principles." This dual recognition encapsulates the past century of local history and the intertwining of ancestral ways with the new Christian religion. Papua New Guinea is a relatively small country. Its population in 2010 was six million. Nonetheless, more than eight hundred languages are spoken there. Its various communities have sustained separate identities both through warfare and exchange alliances. Christianity has forged a new understanding of neighboring peoples as brothers and sisters in Christ, helping to create an ideological configuration in which national loyalties can emerge. In Africa as well, the spread of Christianity and Islam created the common languages, educational opportunities, and wider loyalties necessary for the apparatus of statehood in the countries that won independence from colonial powers in the 1960s and that face problems in the global economy of the twenty-first century. Even as social and political circumstances help shape a people's religious vision, the religious imagination is a powerful instrument in shaping people's understanding of the potential for social and political growth.

RESISTANCE TO CHANGE

Change is not always easy to accept. Even if we choose to move to a new town or to enroll in a new school, we may be unsettled by unanticipated circumstances. We may find ourselves lonely as we lose touch with people we were convinced were friends for life. When change is involuntary, we may be overwhelmed by it. When parents announce that a family is relocating, for example, children and teenagers may be angry and resentful. It can be difficult to imagine that one will find another soccer team quite as supportive as one's current team, or that a current boyfriend or girlfriend will be easily forgotten in a new romance. Societal change can also be as slow, painful, and uneven. For example, decades ago American government and industry began to discuss switching over to the metric system of measurement used by most of the rest of the world. Although Americans often buy beverages by the liter rather than the quart, a mile is still the standard measure of distance, and weights are reported in pounds rather than kilograms.

Thinking about the Difficulty of Change

Take a minute to think about two major changes you have made in your lifetime. Choose one major change that was voluntary and another that was involuntary.

For the voluntary change: Were there problems with it that you had not anticipated? What were your expectations when you made the change? Did it live up to your expectations? Were you happy with your decision?

For the involuntary change: Did you have fears? Were they justified? Were there unexpected benefits that came with the change? In the end, did you come to accept the change, or do you still wish things could be as they were?

Have these experiences encouraged you to seek change in your life, or have you become more resistant to it?

Because religious issues are so central to people's worldviews and self-definitions, religious change can be especially painful. Both individuals and communities resist innovations that are accepted by others as healthy. Not all change promotes human well-being, of course, nor do all people agree on the nature of human flourishing. Fear of change itself, however, or at least a strong attachment to what is familiar, can lead religious individuals and communities to cling tenaciously to the past. Congregations that introduce a new hymnal, for example, find that at first many members are critical of both words and music. They miss those hymns that have been dropped, and they belittle hymns recently introduced. After a period of use, however, such criticisms are often forgotten. In the 1950s the release of the Revised Standard Version (RSV), an important translation of the Bible, attracted much negative publicity. Pastors condemned it, and religious writers found fault with its theological tendencies. (Every translation involves some measure of interpretation.) What was most disturbing to many about the RSV, though, was that it replaced a translation that was much closer to the King James version, familiar in the English-speaking Protestant world since the 1600s. The RSV was problematic to many simply because it was unfamiliar. In 1989 a new version of the RSV, known as the New Revised Standard Version (NRSV), was released in the United States. Changes in language and advances in biblical scholarship make such new translations an ongoing necessity.

Resistance to religious and cultural change in the early twentieth century was a major factor in the rise of Protestant fundamentalism. Fundamentalists accept the Bible as the literal word of God and resist many aspects of modern value systems. Contemporary fundamentalism is a complex phenomenon, and there is neither a single profile that adequately describes all Protestant fundamentalists,, nor even complete agreement on the question of who qualifies as a fundamentalist. We can make better sense of the rise of fundamentalism by discussing its wider historical context.

A number of cultural factors affected the religious landscape in the late nineteenth and early twentieth centuries. The writings of Charles Darwin (1809–82) on evolution were influential. Many liberal church leaders accepted the scientific theory of evolution and suggested that the creation accounts in Genesis should be read as metaphor rather than as scientific or journalistic reporting. The Jesuit paleontologist Pierre Teilhard de Chardin, whom we met in Chapter 3, was of this bent. He embraced Darwin's theory of evolution in writings such as *The Human Phenomenon* and *The Divine Milieu* and tried to demonstrate that belief in evolution was compatible with Christian faith. However, the Vatican forbade publication of most of his nonscientific work and it was only after Teilhard's death that his more theological and philosophical writings became widely available.

In the twentieth century intellectuals in Europe and the United States gave serious consideration to communism and other forms of socialism. Many watched hopefully to see the direction the newly established communist government in Russia would take after the Bolshevik Revolution of 1917. Again, many liberal church leaders were receptive to socialist ideas, which they believed were in keeping with Jesus' declaration that he had come to proclaim good news to the poor. While this was a period of excitement for many, the fundamentalists were among those who saw these new teachings as threats to the values with which they had been raised.

World War I (1914–18) was unsettling to all who lived through it. The introduction of weapons of mass destruction, such as chemical agents, shocked and frightened much of the world. As the 1920s began, many believed that the world had been irrevocably changed by the bloody conflict. In 1921 Irish poet William B. Yeats published "The Second Coming," a poem that invoked the climate of the postwar era. Two lines read:

> Things fall apart; the centre cannot hold;
> Mere anarchy is loosed upon the world.

A year later American-born poet T. S. Eliot published a long poem called "The Waste Land" that reflected his sense of the disarray of European culture in the aftermath of the war. Throughout the poem he includes fragments of earlier literary works, and toward the end of the poem he declares,

> These fragments I have shored against my ruins.

Nostalgia for the past was not confined to the fundamentalist movement.

While others greeted the future with a mixture of hopeful anticipation and mourning for a world that seemed to have died, fundamentalists refused to accept change as inevitable. They responded to cultural and religious change by resisting it. In doing so they constructed a worldview in which those who disagreed with them were seen as evil influences. One issue that particularly vexed them was the teaching of evolution. This involved them in arguments with both secular intellectuals and liberal Christians. Their disagreement with other Christians was interpretive in nature. A prevailing question was how to interpret the opening chapters of Genesis. Fundamentalists insisted that Genesis proved that God had created the world in seven days. Liberal Christians not only embraced the idea of evolution but also advocated "scientific" methods of Bible study. So, for example, liberal scholars focused on the differences between the two versions of the Genesis creation accounts, while fundamentalists refused to acknowledge discrepancies between the two accounts. More broadly, fundamentalists started with the words of the Bible, on the basis of which they evaluated modern thought and practice. Liberal Christians often started with insights and methods derived from secular criticism and applied them to the Bible. There was little common ground.

The conflict between fundamentalists and liberal forces within church and society came to a symbolic climax in the 1925 "Monkey Trial" of John Scopes. Scopes, a biology teacher in a small town in Tennessee, angered local fundamentalists when he taught his students about evolution. Fundamentalists had worked for the passage of a Tennessee law that forbade the teaching of evolution, which they saw as a blasphemous contradiction of God's words in Genesis. The trial became a symbol for those on both sides in a debate and still resonates in the current political landscape. For Scopes's supporters, major issues included the credibility of modern science and the separation of church and state. For fundamentalists, the overriding concern was to resist any accommodation to the corrosive forces of the modern world.

In a sense the Scopes trial has been continued into the twenty-first century in the United States by those who espouse various forms of creationism and make a case in the courts for its teaching in the public schools. Creationism is the belief that the earth, all forms of life, and humankind are the direct creation of a supernatural being (God). Among the many forms of creationism, creation science (which attempts to provide scientific support for the creation narrative in Genesis) and intelligent design (which posits an intelligent first cause rather than a process of natural selection) are frequently in the news.

As we evaluate fundamentalists and their resistance to cultural and religious change, we should consider not only what they stand for but also what they stand against. Fundamentalism develops as resistance to aspects of the modern world that may be confusing or even alienating. The twentieth century brought changes that sometimes seem beyond the individual's control. Because of economic demands, people move more than they used to. Family members are likely to live hundreds of miles apart. Shifting employment patterns and "downsizing" make people worry that their futures are not secure. In the United States the 2008/2009 recession and its aftermath saw private consumption fall drastically for the first time in twenty years, while many people lost jobs. At the same time rising costs of health care have restricted the options of young families. In such an uncertain climate people crave security and constancy. The rock-solid claims of fundamentalism can be very appealing to those who seek stability in a rapidly changing world.

Following World War II, scientists began to voice concern about environmental changes such as depletion of the protective ozone layer, global warming on an unprecedented scale, the destruction of forests, the loss of biodiversity, the use of toxic products, and rapid growth of the human population on a planet with depleting resources. Religions were slow to show concern for the environment, but by the mid-century prophetic figures like Lutheran theologian Joseph Sittler (1904–87) began to speak of the religious responsibility for steward-ship of the earth and of nature as a theatre of grace. More recently, historian of religions Mary Evelyn Tucker has spoken and written of religions entering their ecological phase. She asserts that religions are increasingly becoming aware of their role in planetary life and are accepting the challenge to see the human as part of the sacred story of the universe.[6] In the liturgy and teaching of religious communities we see an increasing emphasis on the environment with congregations building on their traditions as they assume responsibility for caring for creation. For example, in Judaism the eco-kosher movement builds on Jewish dietary laws as it grapples with concerns about industrial agriculture, the just treatment of workers, and global warming. Just as in traditional Judaism, some foods are kosher (proper) and some are not kosher, so those who embrace an eco-kosher lifestyle consider it improper to consume on a regular basis foods whose production is detrimental to the planet.

SUMMARY

On both an individual and a communal level, religious change can either enhance or diminish human lives. We close this chapter with a brief discussion of alienating and reconciling elements of religious change.

Joining a religious movement can bring painful breaks with one's past. The first Christians, for example, often found themselves alienated from families and communities when they joined the church. No wonder they treasured Jesus' saying that anyone who left father and mother, sister and brother, would receive a hundredfold return. From the perspective of their peers, the early Christians probably seemed to be members of a strange cult that encouraged giving away possessions to the poor and leaving familiar surroundings to live in a community of other cult members. Jerusalem officials saw the movement as dangerous and tried to suppress it. One rabbi named Gamaliel argued that the authorities should leave the cult alone. He said that if the Christian community was not of God, then it would not survive. On the other hand, he said, if this movement is of God, you do not want to interfere with it. Later generations of Christians have always believed that the first followers of Jesus had found an authentic way of reconciling themselves to God, the world, and themselves. However, from the perspective of their contemporaries, they seemed to have chosen an alien way.

New religious movements are particularly likely to be seen by outsiders as evidence of alienation from the larger society; this may in fact be true. Nonetheless, many of those who join what are often called cults believe that they have found peace in a community setting. In the decades since World War II, Japan has witnessed the development of many new religious movements. A number of factors contribute to the popularity of these sects. For example, young people who must continue to live at home because land and housing are in chronically short supply can find a community of likeminded peers an important outlet. Some sects require great devotion; others require only casual, nonexclusive allegiance. The vast majority of Japanese who experiment with membership in a new religious sect find the experience either temporarily or permanently beneficial; if not, they leave. However, the experience of one religious group, Aum Shinrikyo, illustrates the dynamic by which an entire community can become alienated from the larger society in a destructive manner.

Aum Shinrikyo means "the true teaching of **Om.**" Shoko Asahara, the founder of the movement, based his teachings largely on Buddhism, although he also included Christian and Jewish elements. His followers typically gave their property to Aum Shinrikyo and lived with other members of the religious community. Cult members usually severed ties with their families. They sought spiritual insight through practices ranging from meditation to drugs. Although many who joined found what they wanted, others tried to leave the cult. Asahara coerced them into staying and may have ordered the murders of some who tried to leave. Most Aum Shinrikyo members did not realize that Asahara was using the money they brought to the movement to finance the development of sarin, a nerve gas so deadly that the greatest challenge in its manufacture is to prevent killing those who synthesize it. In March 1995, Asahara ordered his followers to release sarin gas in the crowded Tokyo subway system at rush hour. Eleven people died; thousands were hospitalized.

The Aum Shinrikyo experience exemplifies one tragic dynamic that can unfold as a religious group that perceives itself to be misunderstood cuts itself off from society. Because personal conversion experiences are so powerful, those who undergo them are often unquestioning of the movement to which they have converted. The members of Aum Shinrikyo surrendered themselves so thoroughly to a new and powerful experience that they were unable to assess the terrible power they were giving their leader.

On the other hand, religious change can be life giving to those who brave it. Vatican II was such an adventure in religious change. Pope John XXIII called for Vatican II, which was a global council of the Roman Catholic Church that met from 1962 to1965. Church councils are an ancient tradition of the Catholic Church, and council decisions are binding even on the pope. To this council John XXIII invited not only Roman Catholics but also observers from a variety of faith traditions, a move typical of the openness of the council. For many Roman Catholics, Vatican II was a fresh breeze blowing through open windows; it marked a new openness to engagement with the world.

MARY N. MACDONALD

The contemporary architecture of a Baptist church contrasts with the traditional architecture of a Methodist church on a city street.

The council declared in one of its document, the *Pastoral Constitution on the Church in the Modern World*: "The joys and the hopes, the griefs and the anxieties of the men of this age, especially those who are poor or in any way afflicted, these too are the joys and hopes, the griefs and anxieties of the followers of Christ. Indeed, nothing genuinely human fails to raise an echo in their hearts" (no. 1). With these words the Roman Catholic Church announced its willingness to align itself in closer solidarity with all the peoples of the world. The council reminded the world that "the Church has always had the duty of scrutinizing the signs of the times and of interpreting them in the light of the gospel" (no. 4). By emphasizing the church's duty to respond to the "signs of the times," Vatican II cleared the way for lasting reforms of church teachings and practices.

The legacy of Vatican II is rich. The council emphasized the biblical insight that the church is the people of God, thus empowering the entire membership of the church to share in the ministries of the gospel. In order to guarantee full understanding of the **mass**, the central Catholic rite, Vatican II ended the centuries-long practice of conducting the mass in Latin and introduced the use of local languages for its celebration. Even church architecture and music changed after Vatican II. Different kinds of worship spaces have different benefits;

many people prefer to pray or meditate in old, quiet, churches. However, the lighter, more airy style of architecture seemed to embody the spirit of change. After Vatican II many congregations began to substitute guitars for organs and folk-style hymns for more traditional service music. (Acoustic guitars and folk music were very popular in the 1960s.) Because the church had begun to understand itself as the people, its life grew closer to the daily rhythms of ordinary life.

Nevertheless, by the early twenty-first century many Catholics, particularly in Europe and North America, were expressing disappointment at the failure of the church to respond to the insights of Vatican II. For example, in public life they could see women as senators and prime ministers and in their sister churches they could see women working as priests and bishops, but the pope still refused to ordain women as priests. They felt that their bishops lacked compassion in dealing with issues such as homosexuality and birth control. Disappointed in the hierarchy, which seemed out of touch with the modern world, and despairing of changing the church, many Catholics were leaving it.

Few complex human experiences can be simply categorized in positive or negative terms. Even many of those who welcomed and promoted the changes of Vatican II had some nostalgia for older ways, some of which have been reintroduced. Elderly people who had worshiped in Latin their entire lives were denied the consolation of hearing that language again in communal prayer. Change, even healthy change, can be painful. Developments that help many reconcile themselves to God, community, and world may leave others feeling alone and alienated. We turn in the next chapter to a more thorough examination of reconciliation, alienation, and the search for authenticity in religious experience.

RESOURCES

ACTIVITIES

1. Organize a multimedia class presentation on the impact of the Reformation on art, architecture, and music.
2. Research fundamentalist movements in contemporary Islam, Protestantism, Catholicism, and Judaism. What are the common elements of these movements? How is each movement unique? Do you think that *fundamentalism* is a useful or adequate term for describing these movements?

3. How would you describe the al Qaeda movement? To what extent is it a religious movement, and to what extent is it a political movement?

4. Religions affect (and even effect) political change. Organize a debate on the merits and liabilities of religious influence on the political sphere.

5. Research the impact of the Holocaust on the development of Jewish thought and life, both religious and secular.

6. Analyze the dynamics of cultural contact represented in one of the following: the film *The Mission,* Ngugi wa Thing'o's novel *The River Between,* or Bharati Mukherjee's novel *Jasmine.*

7. Organize a panel discussion on the impact of shifting cultural and religious patterns on women's roles. (You may want to include reports on Mary Gordon's *Final Payments* or Anzia Yezierska's *The Bread Givers.*)

READINGS

The Acts of the Apostles. The New Testament book that records the history of the new religious movement that came to be called Christianity.

Aczel, Amir D. *The Jesuit and the Skull: Teilhard de Chardin, Evolution, and the Search for Peking Man.* New York: Riverhead Books, 2007. An account of Teilhard de Chardin's work to reconcile faith with science.

Bainton, Roland. *The Reformation of the Sixteenth Century.* Boston: Beacon Press, 1952. Still a useful scholarly treatment of the Protestant Reformation.

de Las Casas, Bartolomé. *The Devastation of the Indies: A Brief Account.* Translated by Herma Briffault. Baltimore: Johns Hopkins University Press, 1992. A brutal account of the actions of Europeans in colonizing the Americas.

Gordon, Mary. *Final Payments.* New York: Random House, 1978. A novel of a young Catholic woman caught between family obligations and a changing world.

Mukherjee, Bharati. *Jasmine.* New York: Grove Weidenfeld, 1989. The story of a young woman named Jyoti who is born in a village in India. She travels to the United States and makes a new life for herself on an Iowa farm.

Thiong'o, Ngugi wa. *The River Between.* London: Heinemann, 1978. This powerful novel follows a young man from a traditional African family who attempts to mediate between the ways of the Christian missionaries and his people's customs.

Weber, Max. *The Protestant Ethic and the Spirit of Capitalism.* Translated by Talcott Parsons. New York: Scribner, 1958. A classic work in the sociology of religion.

Yezierska, Anzia. *The Bread Givers.* New York: Persea Books, 1975. A novel of Jewish life in New York in the early twentieth century and the conflicts faced by a young Jewish woman who wants to study.

AUDIO-VISUALS

The Mission (1986). Dramatizes two styles of cultural contact and change in the encounter of European Christian missionaries with indigenous peoples in the Americas.

Faith and Doubt at Ground Zero (2002). Frontline. Co-written, produced, and directed by Helen Whitney. Religious responses to 9/11 a year later. The film includes interviews with priests, rabbis, an Islamic scholar, a Middle East expert, an English professor, a British novelist, a psychoanalyst, and a photographer who documented Ground Zero. Available on the pbs.org website.

Vatican II: The Faithful Revolution (1996). This five-part video series includes interviews with key participants and observers of Vatican II with the hope of portraying a balanced view of the impact of the council and how it changed the church.

NOTES

1. Elisabeth Tooker, "On the Development of the Handsome Lake Religion," *Proceedings of the American Philosophical Society* 133 (1989): 35–50.

2. Dr. Charles Willie, quoted in Alla Bozarth-Campbell, *Womanpriest: A Personal Odyssey* (New York: Paulist Press, 1978), 134–36.

3. Bartolomé de Las Casas, "A Brief Account of the Devastation of the Indies" (1552).

4. Ngugi wa Thiong'o, *The River Between* (London: Heinemann, 1978), 141.

5. William E. Montgomery, *Under Their Own Vine and Fig Tree: The African-American Church in the South, 1865–1900* (Baton Rouge: Louisiana State University Press, 1993), 14.

6. See Jospeh Sittler, *The Care of the Earth and Other University Sermons* (Minneapolis: Fortress Press, 1964); and Mary Evelyn Tucker, *Worldly Wonder: Religions Enter Their Ecological Phase* (Chicago: Open Court, 2003).

PART V

RELIGIOUS AUTHENTICITY

In the previous chapters we suggested that religion is one way in which we structure our lives. Religions are systems of symbols that help us to organize our experiences meaningfully. One way in which religions assist us in organizing our lives is through ritual activity. Rituals set apart certain times and spaces as special or sacred. Rituals help us to find a meaningful place in our cosmos, one that relates us to ourselves, others, and to the ultimate Principle(s) in our lives. Rituals such as Sabbath observances help us to maintain our place in the community. Other rituals such as marriage ceremonies announce that our place within the community has changed. Rituals also embody norms of behavior that assist a person to live well.

Religious texts orient us to issues larger than ourselves and connect us to others whose lives have also been shaped by these same texts. Together, rituals and texts combine to situate us in the world, to provide us with a position from which we make decisions and order our lives. We have seen that even those religions considered to be most traditional change due to the influences of history and the changing demands and customs of the society in which the religion is practiced.

From our study of religion, then, it would seem that participating in a religion would contribute to our happiness and well-being. Many times it does. Sometimes, though, the practice of religion tends to alienate or distance us from ourselves and the world around us. When we talk about the effect that institutional religion has on a particular person, we speak of religion as reconciling or as alienating.

When we say that religion is reconciling, we mean that practicing a religion helps us to grow and develop into responsible and free persons and to contribute to the society in which we live. It means that we find our place within a particular religion's worldview or cosmology, and that this adds meaning and purpose to our lives. In religions such as

Islam, Christianity, and Judaism, it means that we live in harmonious relation to the divine Mystery that is the source of all that is good and life giving. People who experience religion as reconciling say that their religion contributes greatly to their feeling at ease with themselves and the world. This feeling of being at home with oneself usually results in an openness to others and a concern for their welfare. Many of the world's social activists are motivated by religious traditions that consider every person who lives as a brother or sister.

Religion, however, sometimes has an alienating effect on people. When we say that religion is alienating, we mean that religious traditions require us to abdicate responsible decision-making, that they impede our freedom to think freely, and that they may contribute very little to the society in which we live. Rather than nourishing our imaginations and offering us challenges, they seem to require unthinking observance of outdated practices. Their ritualism keeps us from coming into contact with the deepest parts of ourselves. The practices of alienating religion leave us feeling "out of kilter." We soon feel adrift in the world. When we experience religion as alienating, we find little meaning in the religion's cosmology; we find its rituals suffocating, and its God either oppressive or meaningless. Often, people experience religion as ambiguous, at times reconciling and at times alienating.

Although the reconciling and alienating dimensions of religion nearly always coexist, Chapter 10 emphasizes the alienating features of religion, discussing both personal and social forms of alienation.

In Chapter 11 we investigate the reasons that contribute to the reconciling qualities of religion. Part I treated the interrelation that exists between religion and culture. Chapter 10 develops this point further by showing that many cultural norms, such as patriarchy, homophobia, and sexism, contribute to the religious alienation we experience. Chapter 10 also discusses the correlation that exists between religious and psychological maturity. Finally, we discuss cults as one response to alienating religion.

Although we can conceptualize and discuss religion as either reconciling or alienating, in most people's experience religion is neither completely one or the other. This should not surprise us, because in real life we seldom experience anything as completely good or completely bad. For example, we are glad we live in the United States, Canada, or some other country. But for one reason or another we may hesitate to give that country our total allegiance. We see its weaknesses as well as its strengths. We are not prepared to overlook its weaknesses, but neither do we want to deny its strengths. In such a case we say that our attitude toward our country is equivocal or ambiguous.

In the same way, many people are ambivalent toward institutional religion. They see its strengths but cannot deny its weaknesses. If we have been raised to think of religion as totally good, we may hesitate to underscore its limitations. On the other hand, unless we are aware of the limitations and weaknesses of an institution, including the institutions of religion, there is no incentive to improve it. More important, we will not be able to discriminate between reconciling and alienating religious practices and understandings of religion. Consequently, we will be unable to separate those that help us to live meaningful and authentic lives from those aspects that are insignificant and even detrimental to our flourishing. Now, we will discuss in more detail religion as alienating, as reconciling, and as ambiguous.

Chapter 10

Alienation

Recall that in Part 1 we differentiated between the search for meaning, the religious impulse, and institutional religion. The religious impulse is not always supported by the rules and practices of institutionalized religions. We often discover a contradiction or discrepancy between the ideals proposed by a religion and our personal religious impulse. Even when we accept the values of a particular worldview, we are at times disconcerted that so few people, including designated religious leaders, live according to the proposed ideals. We become aware of religious leaders who drink too much, of rabbis who eat non-kosher foods, of ministers who are unfaithful spouses, of Hindu leaders who promote violence against Muslims, and of Catholic priests engaged in pedophilia. We meet people who scrupulously observe the laws of their religion but are racists or are intolerant of the differences among religions.

These realizations about religious leaders often come during adolescence. At times during this period of our lives, it seems that our minds are flooded by new information. Further, we not only observe that religious leaders have failings, but we recognize that our parents are not perfect either. For that matter, we recognize that other authority figures—for example, teachers, police, and lawmakers—have their shortcomings, some of them grave.

These realizations about the weaknesses and even depravity of religious leaders and parents often cause us to question the value of some of the religious beliefs and practices they have taught us. For example, it is not unusual for parents to tell their sons and daughters that if they follow the rules of the family and of their religion, God will bless them and look after them. Perhaps we believe that God answers our prayers or that if we have enough faith we can move mountains. Then, disaster strikes. Perhaps a parent or much-loved relative dies a dreadful and painful death. Prayer seems to make no difference. We discover that people who manipulate and cheat are often the students or workers who reap rewards and get ahead in life. We have done all the right things, but our lives don't seem much different from the lives of those who appear to live with no regard for the well-being of other people. Additionally, adolescence is generally a time when, developmentally, **idealism** unfolds. Idealism, the conviction that the ambiguities of life are not to be tolerated, is often very pronounced during adolescence. This may compound the discomfort we experience because the more idealistic we are, the more clearly we see hypocrisy and the other inconsistencies between what religious people say and what they do.

These experiences of discomfort, doubt, and disillusionment frequently result in a feeling of alienation. Although such experiences may disconcert us and are never pleasant, they may also help us to sort out what we really believe. They may prompt us to rethink on a more mature level the meaning of such values as honesty and compassion as well as the meaningfulness of prayer. Even when these experiences of estrangement or disorientation prove to be catalysts for growth, they nevertheless cause us pain. The distress may be occasional and brief or constant and lasting. Whatever the degree of dislocation that we experience, it often has several causes that occur singly or in combination. Some of the more common causes of alienation are: (1) religion, as an institution, very often legitimates cultural biases that are themselves sources of alienation to certain groups within the religion; (2) images of God are proposed and passed down that have no connection with contemporary cultural or historical development; (3) religious authorities may use their power to control the lives of members; and (4) in the face of evil or of profound suffering, religion too often provides facile or glib reassurances such as "it is God's will" or "only have faith and everything will be all right," instead of remaining silent before the inexplicable.

Even when these institutional sources of alienation are not present to a great extent in people's lives, some people may still have ambivalent feelings toward religious institutions. This may not be due to the imperfections of the institutions, but may arise because these persons have not yet attained psychological, social, or religious maturity. Consequently, they are incapable of relating in an appropriate way to religious or other types of institutions. Some of these personal sources of ambivalence may be (1) fear of personal freedom and responsibility, (2) a legalistic mentality, and (3) fixation at a particular stage of psychological development. Usually, several institutional and personal factors combine to precipitate and determine the degree of alienation someone experiences.

THE RELIGIOUS LEGITIMATION
OF CULTURAL BIASES

HIERARCHY

Look around your classroom or church, the shopping mall, or your place of employment. Notice how things are ordered. Where is your attention directed? Where are the best stores or offices? In most cases the people and stores considered most important are situated where they are the center of attention. In the traditional classroom the teacher's desk is located in front of the classroom, sometimes even on a platform. In the malls the most important stores have the best locations. In church and synagogue our attention is focused on the priest or cantor. These are everyday examples of a way of ordering called hierarchy.

Some people would argue that hierarchy is natural, that it is rooted in nature, and therefore is the order established by the deity. After all, we observe hierarchy in the animal kingdom. There are dominant and submissive animals; the dominant animals direct the hunt, take

LE MOYNE COLLEGE ARCHIVES

In this image, sacred ritual is enacted by an all-male group of priests. Attention is focused on their actions.

the best food, and in some cases determine which females will be impregnated. By analogy, many societies are structured so that certain people, either because of some natural characteristic or because of the position they hold in the community, possess rights and privileges that others in the community do not have. They not only lead and instruct others, but they make decisions about what is to be learned, what is to be believed, and how things are to be organized. Hierarchy is a mode of authority very compatible with autocratic or monarchical forms of government. It is akin to the medieval concept of the divine right of kings.

Not all religious groups acknowledge that hierarchal administration originates from a divinely established sacred order. Anglican, Roman Catholic, Episcopalian, Russian and Greek Orthodox, Methodist, and Lutheran churches are among those denominations with the most formally articulated hierarchical structures. Notice that these churches also have the most elaborate and highly organized public worship services. In a hierarchical understanding of reality, only some members possess the God-given power to administer sacraments such as the Lord's Supper. According to this manner of thinking, if a person who did not have this power to execute the sacraments *did* perform a sacramental ritual, there would be no sacrament, because that person did not have the intrinsic power to bring it about.

Baptist and Pentecostal churches, on the other hand, have governing bodies, but they are not hierarchical. There are leadership positions within the community, but no one person has more intrinsic power than another. Usually, these churches have less formal public worship and fewer nonbiblical dogmas that believers are expected to accept.

In religions that have their origins in Asia, hierarchy is evident more in the rights of groups than of individuals. Hinduism, for example, has four castes: the Brahman, from which the priests come; the Kshatriya, the warrior and the governing class; the Vaishya, the class of merchants and farmers; and finally, the Sudras, the peasants and serfs. This way of understanding the world is portrayed in the Purusa Sukta, the creation account of the first man, which we read in Chapter 1. There are also the "untouchables," those who belong to no caste. Only members of the highest caste, the Brahmans, can be religious leaders. Gandhi, among others, tried to eradicate this system, but it is deeply rooted in the Indian approach to order, and it prevails in spite of legislation against it.

Throughout the world hierarchy is often linked to patriarchy and androcentrism, two cultural patterns that various religions legitimate and that we discuss next. When this is the case, males are dominant within each caste or group and the dominant group becomes even more elitist.

Many members of the hierarchy are leaders in service to others and are exemplary models of religious authority. The Dalai Lama, the leader of Tibetan Buddhism, is universally admired by religious people. Many people throughout the world, however, consider hierarchy to be intrinsically unfair, because people acquire position or dominance either by birth or by office. Those who object to hierarchy do so on the basis that possession of the qualities necessary to govern well is a secondary concern in a hierarchical system. Prayerful and talented persons well educated in their religious traditions often occupy a subservient position to members of the hierarchy who are less well developed religiously and psychologically. This is often a source of deep alienation, especially when combined with androcentrism or patriarchy.

ANDROCENTRISM

Androcentrism is a cultural pattern that attributes normativity to the male of the species; that is, the most accomplished males provide the standard by which everyone is measured.

Let us begin our discussion of this cultural attitude with an everyday example. In most sports, gymnastics and figure skating being notable exceptions, the men's events are considered to be more interesting and more skillfully played than the women's events in the same sport. "March Madness" focuses on male teams more than on women's teams. This results in much greater attendance at the men's games than at the women's. If you ask sports enthusiasts which teams had won the NCAA championship for the last five years, nearly everyone could quickly list the men's teams that had won. Yet women's teams also play in the NCAA tournament. Could the same people who named the winning men's teams also name the winning women's teams? Can you?

Let us now consider how androcentrism plays a role in the way we read, view movies, or enjoy art. Many times, when we read a book, watch a movie, or go to a museum, we spontaneously "read" or "see" from the point of view of the male. We do this automatically and spontaneously because this attitude permeates our cultural environment.

When we think of the portrayal in sculpture or art of the perfect human body, what comes to mind? Is it Michelangelo's David? Perhaps it is the figure of Adam receiving life from God as this is portrayed, again by Michelangelo, on the ceiling of the Sistine Chapel in the Vatican. For some of us, it may be the Venus de Milo. But even if the Venus de Milo comes to mind, we must remember it represents the male vision of the perfect female body. If none of these classic examples leaps to mind, perhaps more contemporary examples of the ideal body based on current celebrities do. If so, we can draw the same conclusions. In contemporary Western society the ideal of the human body is either male or the male notion of the ideal female figure. Why else would so many young women starve themselves nearly to death? Why else would those trying to alter their eating habits describe their successes and lapses in moral terms: I've been "good"; I've been "bad"?

Androcentrism pervades literature, also. In Shakespeare's *Macbeth* our sympathies are usually with Macbeth. If only Lady Macbeth were not so ambitious. A closer reading of the text shows that Macbeth is equally responsible for the heinous act of murdering Duncan while he slept in their castle. It is true that Shakespeare depicts Macbeth as the weaker member of the couple; perhaps that in itself is why we so despise Lady Macbeth. As she herself says, she is unwomanly. She is not supposed to be the strong partner. If only the woman had not led her man into harm's way!

Thinking with Movies and Novels

Call to mind one of your favorite movies, novels, or short stories. Reflect on these questions: With which character do I identify? What are the character traits I attribute to the male character? to the female character? To which character am I willing to extend forgiveness (if it is necessary)? Would the predicament posed by the plot be resolved if the female character would change her attitude or approach to the male character? Finally, with which character do your sympathies lie? Now, compare your responses with those of other members of your class or reading group. What conclusions do you draw?

What is noteworthy about these examples of androcentrism is that we are usually seeing or reading from the viewpoint of male normativity because our imaginations have been formed to see and read in this manner. It is not a conscious choice. The unquestioned and spontaneous nature of this pattern of thinking gives us a clue to its cultural pervasiveness. The conclusion that androcentrism is deeply rooted in cultures and the collective unconscious is well documented.

MARYKNOLL MISSION ARCHIVES/J. TOWLE, MM

Two Peruvian girls celebrate Mary's feast by dancing at a fiesta. For them, Mary is a reason to celebrate life.

People are born into this milieu of androcentrism and are affected by it. We must ask ourselves questions if we want to determine the shape of our own imagination: When I read, do I spontaneously adopt a masculine perspective? From where do I derive the norms by which I judge the excellence and beauty of the human body? If we never consciously reflect on such questions, we contribute to the perpetuation of this cultural attitude. Both females and males are responsible for this.

When we recall that religions are always practiced within a particular culture, and that all cultures are to some degree androcentric, it is easy to understand why religions themselves have developed and promoted androcentric attitudes.

Let us consider the alienating effects androcentrism has in various religions. A study of androcentrism enables the reader to more easily understand the connection between the manner in which *Macbeth* and Genesis 2—3 are traditionally read. Reread the section in Chapters 6 and 7 concerning the interpretation of Genesis 2—3. You will see that the biblical text does not support the traditional androcentric reading. Many of the traditional interpretations of Genesis 2—3 have more to do with the androcentric imagination reading the text than with the text itself. We are so used to reading the text through an androcentric lens that it is very difficult for us to arrive at an interpretation in which Eve is not the culprit and Adam the victim of so-called feminine wiles.

Some Christian denominations honor Mary, the mother of Jesus, in a special way. In these religions Mary is proposed as a model for all Christian women. The image of Mary that is proposed for emulation, though, is often an image of a woman who is the ideal of an androcentric culture: subservient, without passion, tending to household duties. The Mary about whom we read in the New Testament does not fit this description at all. It is no wonder that strong, articulate, decisive women feel alienated by this androcentrically shaped image of womanhood.

PATRIARCHY

Another cultural phenomenon that influences our patterns of relationship is patriarchy. Patriarchy is a social arrangement that legitimates the concept that in a family unit, or any social unit analogous to the family, such as a business or a nation-state, the dominant male has authority over those males who have no power and over all females and children. In the Western world this tradition comes to us through the Roman Empire and is known as *pater familias*. We see how this idea of *pater familias* is enacted in mosques, synagogues, and churches. Although culture is in transition and all institutions have been affected by the women's movement, most religious institutions are still headed by dominant males. The fact that we use the expression "a woman rabbi" or "a woman minister" shows us the novelty of that

---

Thinking about Patriarchy

To satisfy your curiosity about the extent of patriarchy, investigate and/or discuss these areas. In your school, business, or place of worship is the power structure patriarchal? If a woman occupies the dominant position, do people think of her as a man? Do they say she is as aggressive as or as hard working as any male CEO? What words are used to describe her? What is the meaning of the expression *glass ceiling*? How many women hold office in the legislature of the United States? When the Constitution was written, who qualified as a voter?

---

reality. We never hear the expressions "a male minister" or "a male rabbi." Indeed, in Islam and Roman Catholicism, patriarchy is viewed as divinely legitimated by either the Qur'an or the New Testament.

These attitudes of androcentrism and patriarchy have subtle but nonetheless profound effects on how both women and men relate to themselves, to one another, to religious institutions, and to divine Mystery. Although what you have just read concerning androcentrism and patriarchy may appear to be solely a women's issue, this is certainly not the case. Rather, it is a human issue. It is true that men and women experience androcentrism and patriarchy differently, but both genders are alienated by these cultural phenomena.

Having explored the pervasiveness of androcentrism and patriarchy generally, let us now see how these attitudes permeate institutional religions and the effects they often have on people who are affiliated with these institutions.

Several important distinctions must be kept in mind. First, if you, the reader, are female, you may not consciously consider that you are less than a male simply because divine Mystery is nearly universally referred to in male images. Images, however, do work on our psyches at a less-than-conscious level. It is a fact that a higher percentage of women seek treatment for depression than men do. Certainly this phenomenon cannot be reduced to a single cause. However, In androcentric religions women often become alienated or separated from their deepest desires. This is because they have been taught not to overreach by desiring positions in church, synagogue, or mosque that are thought to be more suitable for men, because women lack the qualities that leadership demands, or because divine Mystery mandates their exclusion. Karl Marx once made the statement that at times we are so alienated from ourselves that we don't realize we are alienated. He named this situation "falsification of consciousness." By this he meant that the shape of our imaginations coincides with dominant cultural expressions like androcentrism and patriarchy. We have become so adapted to our culture that it is impossible to perceive that things could be otherwise. That is one reason we may have come to believe that God is actually a male, not simply imaged as one.

Many women in androcentric and patriarchal religions declare that they have never desired to be ordained into the ranks of the clergy. They add that they are very grateful for this because they can't imagine the frustration a Roman Catholic woman would experience who wanted to be ordained but for whom it was considered to be against divine mandate. Then they sometimes acknowledge that—as a defense mechanism—perhaps they will simply not allow into consciousness a desire that might result in such frustration. When vocational choices are denied women by religions that legitimate androcentrism and patriarchy, they may never know what they truly desire. To be separated from our deepest desires, especially those involving religious orientation, can be profoundly alienating and result in chronic malaise.

We must not forget, moreover, that males can be alienated by religiously legitimated androcentrism. All of us have various public personae—the faces we show publicly. Teachers, for example, assume the persona of a teacher when in a classroom or when meeting with students in the role of teacher. This is fitting. But if teachers were to become totally identified with that persona or role, they would no longer know who they were other than teachers. They could relate to themselves and others only as teachers. Consequently, their capacity for intimacy would be greatly hindered.

Now, think of the male who has been burdened with being the image par excellence of the Divine. Think further of the male clergy in androcentric religions such as Christianity, Islam, orthodox Judaism, and Confucianism. They, more than other men, are burdened by androcentrism's need to symbolize the Divine. Many such men become so identified with the normative role they play in religion—even to being assimilated to the Divine—that they become alienated, unable to relate to themselves or others as people with desires, hopes, and failings.

Religions that legitimate patriarchy confer power on the dominant male (minister, pope, imam, tribal leader) to regulate the lives of less powerful men and all women and children in the particular religion. Often this way of organizing the religious polity is viewed as a reflection of the way things occur in nature and, therefore, as the way affairs are most properly organized. Hierarchy is also frequently viewed as divinely ordained. People, clergy or not, are usually reluctant to give up power voluntarily. If we are in a position of power or dominance, we instinctively seek to legitimate that authority by an appeal to cultural or religious theories. Some people who hold positions of power become identified with that power. When this occurs, self-worth depends on retaining dominance. The result is a vicious circle. Theoretically, only those who hold office can change the rules. But why would a person want to change the rules when one believes—even mistakenly—that his position is legitimated by the status quo?

Now we can begin to appreciate how alienating religious patriarchy can be for those who do not occupy positions of dominance. Women and men without power are excluded from governance, even when they might have a better understanding of the ways in which the church, synagogue, or mosque could be organized to assure greater participation of adherents. They are excluded from the decision-making process even when the decisions made are ordinances about how they are expected to live their lives. Once the patriarch or religious head has spoken, neither recourse to reason nor to a variant interpretation of a religion's story makes any difference. To those who lack participation in the power of the father or patriarch, the system appears to enact laws and interpret religious texts that ensure the continuation of the patriarchal system.

For some people patriarchy is alienating at so fundamental a level of their being that they choose to align themselves with another religious institution. They make this choice in order to remain authentic to themselves, to remain in harmony and reconciliation with themselves, and to feel at peace. Mary Daly (1928–2010), a former Roman Catholic, was among the first women to bring to light the alienating effects of patriarchy in two of her earlier books, *The Church and the Second Sex* (1968), and *Beyond God the Father: Toward a Philosophy of Women's Liberation* (1973). She had received the highest degree that is granted by Roman Catholic schools of theology, the Doctor of Sacred Theology (STD). Eventually, however, she decided that patriarchy was so central to the biblical message as well as to the governance of Christian denominations that she extricated herself completely from Christianity in order to maintain a sense of her own integrity.

Thinking with Mary Daly

Mary Daly left the United States to study Roman Catholic theology in Europe. It was necessary for her to leave the United States because at that time there was no place in the United States, where women were allowed to study for advanced degrees in theology. Mary Daly received her doctorate and returned to the United States where she was quite coldly received by male clerics. Her alienation was profound. In 1971, she preached at Harvard Memorial Church. She was the first woman to preach there in its 336–year history. This excerpt from that sermon shows that her profound and scholarly acquaintance with the Jewish and Christian scriptures allowed her to critique the patriarchy within the churches:

> Sisters and Other Esteemed Members of the Congregation: There is a problem. It is this: There exists a world-wide phenomenon of sexual caste, which is to be found not only in Saudi Arabia but also in Sweden. This planetary sexual caste system involves birth-ascribed, hierarchically ordered groups whose members have unequal access to goods, services, prestige, and physical and mental well-being. . . .
>
> Theology which is overtly and explicitly oppressive to women is by no means a thing of the past. Exclusively masculine symbolism for God, for the notion of divine "incarnation" in human nature, and for the human relationship to God reinforces sexual hierarchy. Tremendous damage is done, particularly in ethics, when theologians construct one-dimensional arguments that fail to take women's experience into account. . . . The entire conceptual apparatus of theology, developed under the conditions of patriarchy, has been the product of males and serves the interests of sexist society. . . .
>
> Sisterhood is also functioning as church, proclaiming . . . for the first time in history, the liberation of women—first. . . . The sisterhood of man cannot happen without a real exodus. We have to go out from the land of our fathers into an unknown place.[1]

Others also feel alienated but not at such a profound level. Many men and women decide that patriarchal religions, in spite of the alienating aspects of governance, provide worldviews and traditions of spirituality that are life giving and reconciling. Elizabeth Johnson, CSJ, an outstanding contemporary feminist theologian, shows how patriarchy can corrupt the interpretation of the Christian message. She also believes, however, that resourcing oneself in the texts of the Christian tradition offers an authentic way to critique the tradition and to reinterpret it from a contemporary perspective. Both Mary Daly and Elizabeth Johnson value authenticity. This does not mean, though, that they have been compelled to make identical choices in order to remain faithful to their insights.

The majority of religious feminists are women who have had the advantages that education offers. Their education has sensitized them to the social construction of knowledge, which we studied in Part 1. When these women applied this concept to religious institutions, they realized that hierarchy, androcentrism, and patriarchy are social concepts that privilege the male. Religions had simply assumed that male privilege was due to nature. Initially, religious feminists were Caucasian Jewish and Christian women who called into question the religious legitimation of androcentrism and patriarchy. Soon, however, African American women and Latin American Christians, whose issues were somewhat different, entered the ranks of those seeking to separate religious worldviews from outdated social constructs. Emilie Townes, an ordained American Baptist clergy person and professor of African American religion and theology at Yale University, draws deeply from the experiences of African American women to challenge theological and ethical paradigms generated by a patriarchal, Eurocentric culture. Similarly, the late Ada María Isasi-Díaz (1943–2012), who was a professor of ethics and theology at Drew Theological School, tapped into the struggles of Latina women to develop a *mujerista* theology, a theology that makes a preferential option for Latina women in their struggle for liberation in the hopes of altering radically the normative theological constructs in the church and society. There is even a developing feminist movement among Muslim women.

Men also have espoused the cause of women's religious liberation. Among them are North American theologian David Tracy, Dutch theologian Edward Schillebeeckx (1914–2009), and Indonesian theologian Tissa Balasuriya. Father Roy Bourgeois, an activist for social causes who publicly promotes the ordination of women in the

Catholic Church, has endured censure for his position. Such men join their sisters in seeking to lessen the alienation engendered by hierarchy, androcentrism, and patriarchy.

ALIENATING IMAGES OF GOD

As we have tried to understand how hierarchy, androcentrism, and patriarchy function in religious institutions, we have mentioned in passing how these cultural features influence our idea or concept of God. Androcentrism and patriarchy are so ingrained in our culture that we often come to think that maleness and fatherhood are actual attributes of God rather than metaphors that point in the direction of God. For example, we talk and act as if God *were* a male; as if God *were* literally a father. Imaging God in this way can alienate us from the whole notion of God by limiting our idea of God. If, as the various religions propose, the word *God* refers to whatever one conceives to be ultimate in the cosmos, for oneself, for the community; or if it refers to whatever makes us believe that life is at some level trustworthy; or if it refers to the depth and the height of our life, then we need as many metaphors as possible to point us in the direction of this Mystery. We learned in Chapter 6 that language influences action. Now, we consider how images, specifically images of God, can also be effective in alienating us from our centers. We need to examine how some images of God function to alienate us from divine Mystery, nature, our brothers and sisters, and ourselves.

Many years ago, Saint Thomas Aquinas (1225–74), who is among the most influential theologians of Christianity, made the statement,

Thinking with God Images

Write the first words that come to mind when you hear the word *God*. If *all powerful* or *judge* are among them, try to imagine what you mean by that term. Is "God" like a judge? How does "he" use power? If words such as *spirit* or *life* come to mind, try to form an image of that spirit or life. What are its characteristics? Now refer to your own experience. How does your image of God influence the way you think and act; how you view your job or career; how you view your relationship to the earth and to your brothers and sisters? Would you say your image of God is reconciling, alienating, or neutral? What conclusions do you draw from this exercise?

"Everything is received according to the mode of the receiver." Let us examine what this means using contemporary concepts. Throughout this book the authors have shown how we read and understand contextually. The geographical space that we inhabit influences our choice of religious symbols. We saw this in the first chapter in the discussion of how fish are portrayed in the cultures of New England fishing villages and in the Solomon Islands. We have seen how historical circumstances as well as our personal and collective development influence our reading of a text. All of these circumstances and conditions shape the "receiver," our psyches. When we read a religious text like the Muslim Qur'an, the Hindu Vedas, or the Christian scriptures, or when we hear an exhortation from a religious source, we read and understand it according to the "the mode of the receiver," that is, according to how our understanding or our psyches have been shaped.

Imagine mixing cake batter. Until we put the batter into a cake pan, it is a shapeless, amorphous mass. When we pour the batter into a pan, it takes the shape of the pan. It can be formed into the shape of a rectangle, a square, an angel, a heart, or an automobile. In the same way, our psyches have been shaped by our cultural patterns. In this example our psyches are analogous to cake pans. New perceptual and sensory data that we experience are received by our psyches and take their shape. That is why it is so difficult to read the story of Adam and Eve except through the lens of patriarchy.

Of course, it is not quite so simple because the boundaries of our psyches also change. Imaginations, though, have varying degrees of elasticity. Some people's imaginations have rigid boundaries with very little flexibility; such people find change very difficult and usually change very little. When change does occur, it is often dramatic, like some of the conversions discussed in Chapter 8. Other people's imaginations are more flexible. For them, change usually occurs more continuously, and the changes in their ways of thinking are seldom dramatic. Now let us apply this concept to various alienating images of God.

GOD AS SUPERMAN

Throughout the chapters in this book we have repeatedly explored the nature and function of myth, metaphor, image, and imagination. We have seen that religious language is closely allied with poetry, that it seeks to denote realities that can only be described metaphorically. People who think seriously about religious questions understand that the realities they are trying to describe can only be hinted at. That is, we know *mystery* in a different way than we know *book*. Our metaphors point us in a direction, but they are not that reality itself.

When we forget that the deity is not a human being, even when imaged as one, the deity often becomes Superman. Then, when this deity does not act in our lives in the same way as Superman, when he does not rush in to snatch us from danger, we lose trust. We begin to ask questions: Why didn't God move the car off the track before it was hit by the train? Why didn't God snatch the toddler out of the swimming pool before he drowned? Superman would never have let the car remain on the track or allowed the toddler to drown. You can see that if we hold such an image of God, we risk becoming alienated or at least we begin to think that God is ineffective.

THE STOP-GAP GOD

Many times people think of God as providing what human beings do not know how to provide. In ancient times, as well as modern, people believed that God controlled fertility. If a couple were childless, they prayed that God would make the woman fertile. (It was presumed that infertility was a defect in the woman.) Now, most couples who want to conceive a child but cannot seem to do so often visit fertility clinics. Many of these women do become pregnant, thanks to the advances of modern science. So, in a sense, God becomes a little smaller, a little less important in people's lives. Examples can be multiplied. If the snowfall is insufficient to provide good skiing, ski resorts make artificial snow. If a friend needs surgery, we try to find the best doctor. If there is a drought, farmers irrigate. If one's image of God is that God does what we need done, then every time human beings learn to do what they had previously depended upon God for, then God becomes a little smaller, a bit more peripheral to life.

Most religious traditions value prayer and often include in their rituals petitions to the deity. These petitions request—at times demand—the fulfillment of the petitioner's desires. Even when farmers irrigate during a drought and couples visit fertility clinics when they cannot conceive, they still pray for rain or for conception. We quite naturally ask, then, whether such people pray out of habit or from a superstitious mindset. The response such people often give is this: We experience that God does not intervene in the historical process to answer our individual prayers. Yet we pray because the act of petition symbolizes our belief that human beings are not in this world alone. God is with us. God expects us to use our intellects to solve problems for farmers and for infertile couples. Yet we are not totally autonomous; we live in relationship with God.

THE ABSENT GOD

Many times God is viewed as entirely removed from the human scene and totally disinterested in human concerns. Greek philosophers such as Plato and Aristotle ascribed reason to God and described "him" philosophically, as the source of all being or as the undivided one and source of all within the cosmos. It was understood that this God existed in utter isolation from humans and that our troubles and concerns were of no intrinsic importance to God.

The inception of the Age of Science in the seventeenth century provided us with a modern version of the absent God. The discoveries and methodologies of empirical scientists during this century contributed to the establishment of a new worldview. No longer was God understood to be directly responsible for the governance of the universe; God simply established the rules of nature and left them to work themselves out without intervening. According to this worldview the cosmos was envisioned as a machine, and the rules of mechanics prevailed. One image that was frequently used for the cosmos was a clock, with God the clockmaker. God wound up the clock and then forgot about it. Governed by this image of God, people could live their whole lives with little involvement with the deity.

THE ARBITRARY GOD

The arbitrary god possesses many of the characteristics of the Greek gods and goddesses who were thought to live on Mount Olympus. The mythic actions of these gods often incorporated the loves, passions, and jealousies we humans experience. These gods could be bribed and placated by humanity. They were willful. Sometimes they would respond positively to human entreaties, but oftentimes they responded in a spiteful or negative manner, for no apparent reason, and there was nothing that humans could do about it.

This image of an arbitrary and capricious God is very much operative in the contemporary world. Even though Christians, Jews, and Muslims do not claim the worldview of the ancient Greeks, many attribute these same characteristics to their deity. Uninterpreted and literally read biblical stories, such as that of Abraham and Isaac, contribute to our understanding of God as arbitrary. As a result, many live in fear of offending this God, not because they act unjustly but because they are not sure how this all-powerful God "thinks." Their concern to stay on the "right" side of this God sometimes prevents them from assuming responsibility for their own lives. This may have alienating results.

THE AMBIGUITY OF GOD IMAGES

The images of God just described are not alienating for everyone. There exists neither a universally reconciling nor an alienating image of God. We are all at different stages of personal development and live within various worldviews. These worldviews often propose divergent understandings of God that affect how we view particular portrayals of the Divine. Also, an image that may be alienating at a particular period in life may be found reconciling at a later stage. Women have reported that the image of God as father was alienating at one period in their lives, but at a later time they found it reconciling. They attribute this to the fact that they began to differentiate the images of God as father from the image of their biological father.

In Hindu mythology there is the saying that there are 333 million gods. Many understand this to mean that Hinduism is a polytheistic religion. Another view understands this statement to mean that there is an infinite variety of ways in which God is experienced and understood. It is unusual for a person to find the same image of God satisfactory throughout an entire lifetime.

THE TENDENCIES
OF RELIGIOUS AUTHORITIES TO CONTROL

Those who assume positions of religious leadership, whether they are **imams**, rabbis, **mullahs**, or priests, share the same human condition that we all do. They experience the same tendencies toward goodness and the same unscrupulous inclinations that all people do. Even though we know this, we sometimes project onto our religious leaders ideals of perfection that they accept. If such leaders are unsure of themselves or if they develop an unrealistic and inflated understanding of their importance, they often try to control the lives of their co-religionists. Religious authorities exercise control by mandating how people are to organize and manage various aspects of their lives: financial, intellectual, temporal, sexual.

Typically, religions involve their members in good works. This requires investments of money and time on their part. Often, these are freely given and flow from a generous spirit. At times, though, religious leaders manipulate members to contribute beyond their means or to spend more time in church activities than their family and work obligations allow. They are able to do this by speaking in the name of God; that is, they preach and speak as if they know, unambiguously, the mind of God. When they speak in this way, they may provoke feelings of fear and guilt that make it difficult for people to refuse unreasonable demands on their financial and temporal resources. Eventually, people become alienated and may equate religion itself with control and with constant demands for money. When this happens, they become disillusioned with or alienated from religion generally.

Similarly, our minds are made to seek knowledge and truth. It is true that each religious worldview or tradition has parameters that establish the boundaries of that tradition. If people follow a path that goes outside the tradition's parameters, then it is proper for religious authorities to declare that such people are no longer members of the community. As we saw in Part IV, however, every person and every group is always in the process of developing. Some people are more concerned than others that a community's teachings be expressed in ways compatible with the language of the prevailing culture. Their investigations uncover the disconcerting fact that language has changed and the cultural mind set has changed to such an extent that to continue using the same exact words to express a particular religious teaching would, in fact, be unfaithful to the meaning embedded in the teaching itself. So these scholars enter into the process of explaining or interpreting the tradition in new terms.

A striking example of this phenomenon in the Roman Catholic Church was the controversy know as the Modernist heresy. At the turn of the twentieth century many Catholic theologians, such as George Tyrrel (1861–1909), an Anglican convert to Catholicism who became a Jesuit priest, and Alfred Loisy (1857–1940), a French biblical scholar, attempted to bring the results of modern scholarship to bear on biblical and theological studies. They saw that the philosophical milieu had changed, and they desired to bring their church up to date. Because the language they used was new, it disconcerted many and made them uncomfortable. As a result of a religious leadership that sought unquestioning obedience, many of these men were declared heretics and were **excommunicated**. Many of them died alienated from the church that they so much wanted to serve. But not all religious leadership is controlling. A half century later, Pope John XXIII, about whom we read earlier, called a worldwide council of the Roman Catholic Church for the expressed purpose of bringing it up to date.

Finally, many religious traditions throughout the world seek to control their members through restrictions on sexuality and procreation. Religious traditions consider marriage and procreation to be important and sacred tasks. Indeed, the sexual instinct is among the most powerful forces in the animal kingdom. Indiscriminate sexual expression can have devastating effects on individuals and on society. So it is understandable that religions regulate sexual conduct and procreation. Still, religions may promulgate laws in these domains that go far beyond what is necessary to ensure the importance and sanctity of these areas of human experience.

Even though the rules of sexual conduct include both men and women, it is often the case that women bear a disproportionate burden of the law. This is true in Hinduism, where, until recently, it was expected that a widow immolate herself on her husband's funeral pyre. It is also true in Islam, where divorce is much easier for a man to obtain than it is for a woman. It is true in Judaism and some Christian denominations, where marriage with a person of another faith—if not absolutely forbidden—is discouraged and frowned upon.

RELIGIOUS RESPONSES IN THE FACE OF SUFFERING

Every religious tradition deals with suffering and death. When the various traditions are true to their ideals, they deal with suffering and death through rituals and reflection on scriptures that support the people affected. Profound loss is a mystery that calls into question our most basic convictions and apparent certitudes about good and evil and reward and punishment, as well as about the image of the deity that informs our living. Truly, nothing will ever explain suffering, death, and loss in a rationally satisfying way. The study of Job in Chapter 7 emphasizes this realization.

We are often told as we grow up that suffering and disease are punishments for sin. This is what the friends of Job believed, and that way of thinking persists even to this day. The inference of such a statement is that if we live honestly, study hard, and are faithful to our commitments, then we will live happy lives relatively untouched by suffering. At the end of a long, fruitful, and happy life, we will die peacefully amid the comfort of family and friends. Sometimes this happens. It is rare, though, that people live into old age unaffected by suffering. How can we maintain that suffering is punishment for sin when we read every day of innocent children who die from incurable diseases, inexplicable acts of violence, and neglect? In the novel

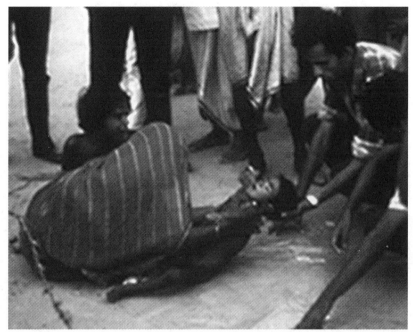

MARYKNOLL MISSION ARCHIVES/J. PADULA

An image of a death in India. What can be said in the face of such suffering?

The Plague, French existentialist Albert Camus (1913–60) wrote very movingly and courageously of the questions posed to religion by the suffering of innocent children. When all is said and done, when we have tried to relieve suffering and prevent death to the best of our knowledge and ability, perhaps the wisest response is to join Job before this impenetrable mystery.

Even though this may be the wisest response, many times religious leaders give facile and superficial answers to explain people's agony and grief. We hear sermons or read books that declare that God knows best or that this is the will of God. Yet Irving Greenberg, a conservative rabbi who has written extensively on the challenges to religious images of God posed by the Holocaust, asks us, "Can you say these things in the presence of a burning child?" If you can, what kind of monster have we made God to be?

When we suffer the effects of evil or even of natural catastrophes, we know intuitively that such responses are too facile and superficial and that, ultimately, they destroy connections between our unconscious and our conscious lives. This separation is alienating. Even when we have not thought through the implications of these facile answers to the extent that persons like Rabbi Greenberg have, we find them repugnant.

Modern psychology has formulated theories that legitimate and verify our intuitive rejection of the facile answers. Psychologists theorize that we must not repress our experiences of suffering and evil. When we do, the feelings attached to these experiences live a subterranean life and affect our consciousness in a debilitating way. We do not need to explain or completely resolve these experiences; in fact, we cannot. We can, however, bring them to the full light of day and find a place for them. Then these feelings of powerlessness and frustration lose their power over us. Religions do not serve us well by offering us easy answers or repeating platitudes when we suffer. Consequently, when this occurs we sometimes withdraw our allegiance from some part of that religion's worldview.

PERSONAL SOURCES OF ALIENATION

Up to this point we have investigated sources of religious alienation that are extrinsic to individuals and originate in our culture, in our society, or with religious leaders. But alienation can also result from psychological causes. Before we enter into this discussion, we do well to remind ourselves that none of us is a perfect psychological specimen. We all have our idiosyncrasies and areas of immaturity. The discussion that follows, though, can help us to understand more completely that authenticity is never completely achieved and that inauthenticity cannot be reduced to a single factor, whether social, cultural, or personal.

We assume that as human beings fulfill various life tasks, they develop into increasingly mature persons. But let us add to that understanding the fact that development is never simply linear; it is cyclical. We complete a developmental task appropriate to a two-year-old, for example, but we repeat that task at a deeper level during adolescence. Consider: One of the tasks of the two-year-old is to develop a sense of identity. The toddler does this by saying, "No." The purpose of this *no* is to discover the boundaries between self and parents. This task recurs during the teenage years. At a deeper, more mature level than the toddler, the teenager is faced with questions of identity and must work these out. The implication of this for religion is that we cannot arrive at a religious maturity sooner than we arrive at psychological

MINDS-EYE KKK RALLY IN GEORGIA

Members of the KKK feel they are superior to other groups such as African Americans, Catholics, and Jews, and they use religion to legitimate their belief. Members of the KKK separate themselves from others. What is their source of alienation?

maturity. Religious and psychological maturity are separate but not distinct. They are intrinsically related. If we are "stuck" at a particular level of psychological development, we will also be "stuck" at that level in our religious development.

When we are very young, we learn what we need to do to gain approval and rewards from authorities such as our parents. We also learn what to do to avoid punishment. Even though we may at times throw tantrums to gain attention, we also know how to act like "good" boys and girls to receive approval. In like manner, in the initial stages of religious development we transfer this need of approval to the deity. We act to please God in order to be rewarded. Of course, the stakes are very high—heaven or hell! As we mature psychologically, we learn that approval must come from within. In our corresponding religious development we are asked to leave behind seeking "God's approval," because this attitude often alienates us from our deepest wishes and desires. If we are not in touch with what is deeply satisfying to us, our lives will be constricted and barren. We will be alienated from God, even as we try to fulfill "his" demands. We need not draw the conclusion that God does not enter into our decision-making, but we do need to consider how we can be true to ourselves, our worldview, and God. People who remain in the stage of seeking approval outside themselves often become very legalistic. Fulfilling religious laws in order to please another relieves one of responsibility. It also contributes to profound alienation from oneself.

As we continue maturing, we reach a stage where we romanticize or idealize our parents and the institutions to which we belong. There is no school like ours, no pet as perfect as ours, no friend as perfect as ours, no religion more true than ours. Gradually, though, we begin to notice that there is no perfect school, parent, friend, or religion. Then we either accept this in ourselves and others, or we become disillusioned and begin a search for perfect replacements. One sign of maturity is that we acknowledge the ambiguity of life, the give-and-take of friendships, and the lack of perfection in people and institutions. We can see the implications for religious development. We go through stages when we think God is perfect—according to our conception of the perfect God. At this stage it is often said that human beings make God into their image and likeness. We project onto God our needs, much as we project our ideals onto friends, lovers, and spouses. In the case of both God and friends, the time comes when we realize they are different from us. We must allow them to be themselves, not who we want them to be.

RESPONSES TO ALIENATION

When we begin to leave the romantic or idealized stage of religious development—when the realization begins to dawn that our particular religious tradition has shortcomings, inconsistencies, and errors—we often feel we are not in step with our friends, with our families, with the worldviews of the religious traditions in which we were raised or about which we have read. We begin to feel a dissatisfaction with the way things are. The values and practices that had helped us find our place in the world no longer seem to fulfill that function.

Many writers have described this situation. If it were not for this restlessness, this dissatisfaction with our situation, many of the good things people have accomplished over the ages would have been left undone. Health care for the indigent, free education for all children, the abolition of child labor and slavery (if not of prejudice)—all this would not have been achieved if some individuals and groups had not looked around and said to themselves and to one another, "I am ill at ease with this situation. This is not the way things ought to be." Although those who set about making these reforms may have felt somewhat "outside" their immediate religious communities and families, they often felt deeply integrated with their religious story. In fact, it is from these stories that they received nurture and sustenance for actualizing their insights, even when this took years. Stories, because they appeal to the imagination and touch us on many levels, have the power to direct and sustain our orientation for long periods of time. Elizabeth Johnson makes this very point when she considers her motivation for doing feminist theology. She claims that the Christian story as appropriated in Catholicism has provided her with the very principles she employs to critique the inequities and injustices within Catholicism. Relying on their religious traditions for legitimation, reformers proceeded to rectify situations they viewed as incompatible with human living.

CULTS

People sometimes experience an even deeper, more profound alienation. It is an alienation that causes individuals to feel that their story no longer works and, in fact, is totally useless in orienting them in the world or in helping them find meaning.

We have seen that religions are ambiguous. They provide us with suggestions of how to live a reconciled or authentic life. We have seen, also, that because religions never exist in the abstract—they are always inherently cultural and social, affected by historical circumstances—they have within them sources of alienation. At times religions promote inauthentic living. Most people agree that everyone has a tremendous magnitude of psychic energy. Since this energy is immaterial, it is often named spiritual energy. Like any type of energy, it is useful only when it is focused or directed toward a goal—when it is ordered. When religions are perceived as misdirecting this energy toward inauthentic living, many people seek alternate ways of directing it. Some participate in political groups and direct this energy toward achieving the goal of the group. Others direct their energy toward accomplishing a particular social good, like securing a better education for the forgotten children of our various cultures.

Adolescents and young adults who are alienated by traditional religions often direct this spiritual energy within a cult. The word *cult* has many connotations. In its most general sense, it represents a minority religious movement, one that separates itself from the mainstream religions to which this text has often referred. If we accept that definition, we can say that—in its beginning stages—Christianity was a cult in relation to Judaism. If, over a period of time, a particular cult grows and becomes the dominant religious group in a particular region, it is no longer a cult. It may, however, give rise to other cults.

The Shakers (the United Society of Believers in Christ's Second Coming) were an English community formed about 1750, when its members seceded from the Society of Friends (Quakers). So intense was their prayer that their bodies actually shook when they were involved in community worship—thus their popular name. Under the leadership of Ann Lee, whom the Shakers regarded as the female incarnation of Christ, a group of Shakers established themselves in Massachusetts. They promoted the ideals of simple living: hard work, good food that was simply prepared, and good furniture that was simple in style. They cared for orphans and accepted new members, and all members practiced celibacy. Over time, these communities died off. Americans, however, still admire Shaker design in furniture and use Shaker recipes in preparing good, nutritious food.

In the contemporary world the word *cult* is often used in a derogatory or negative manner. This is not surprising, because the members of a cult deviate from general, more widespread beliefs. Whenever people begin to question the beliefs and practices of the dominant group, members of the dominant group often become defensive. We still see this in regard to the Vietnam War. Although that war forever changed American attitudes toward war, the patriotism of those young men and women who opposed the war remains in question to this very day, forty or more years later.

In the religious realm cults of the goddess often are viewed pejoratively. At first, referring to whatever is ultimate in a person's life as goddess rather than god seems strange and deviant. It is resisted. However, when we reflect that God is also a metaphor for ultimacy and spiritual focus, then goddess cults do not seem as threatening. The principal difference between the God of Christianity and the goddess of cults is the constellation of values that each perceives as ultimate.

There are, however, valid reasons that some cults provoke negative reactions. While some cults are benign or beneficial to their members, others, such as various satanic cults, are destructive not only toward those outside the cult but to the members of the cult themselves. Implied in that statement are criteria according to which we make that judgment. Strangely enough, the criteria are as psychological as they are specifically religious.

This book is based on several assumptions that are generally accepted but that cannot be conclusively proven. Included among these assumptions are the following: we human beings seek to live meaningful and authentic lives; we live meaningfully and authentically when we try to live justly and honorably with our brothers and sisters; as we mature, we assume responsibility for our decisions and our vision broadens so that we are able to appreciate our own cultures with their benefits and liabilities and to understand the benefits and liabilities of other cultures. When either religions or cults help us to achieve our humanity, they are deemed "good" for us, or beneficial. When they cause us to narrow our vision, to give responsibility for decision-making over to an extrinsic authority, to see nothing good in the religions and cults of others, then they are viewed as destructive or dangerous. Hitler's cult of Aryan supremacy was a destructive cult, destructive almost beyond imagining.

Why are adolescents and young adults often the ones who are attracted to cults? This is a complex question, and there is no single answer to it. The following characteristics, though, exist in some combination in every cultist. First, cultists are idealists; they have little tolerance for hypocrisy and ambiguity and so become disillusioned with traditional religions and other social arrangements when the participants, especially the leaders, do not always live up to the tradition's ideal. Second, cultists have often grown up in families that were either extremely controlling or exerted no control at all. In either case these young people received little or no assistance in discovering and nurturing their uniqueness or personal identity. In fact, the prospect of participating in the creation of their own destiny is often overwhelming. Third, cultists are naive; they believe there exists on this earth a group of people with neither guile nor malice who love simply, purely, and unambiguously. They are willing to follow unquestioningly the leader of such a group in order to take on the identity of the cult and live in this idealized state.

The reasons that cults are attractive are not only personal but social as well. In our contemporary world the stories and rituals, the myths and values that have traditionally helped young people find their place in the world, are falling apart. English poet Matthew Arnold (1822–88) poignantly expresses this sense of philosophical despair and dislocation in the poem "Stanzas from the Grande Chartreuse":

> Wandering between two worlds, one dead,
> The other powerless to be born,
> With nowhere yet to rest my head
> Like these, on earth I wait forlorn.

The religious and social stories that have provided a way of centering our lives are falling apart all around us. In the interim, when new stories are developing, it is sometimes attractive to throw our lot in with any group that promises "salvation."

The center of a cult is always the cult leader. This leader responds to the needs of young people by providing them with instruction on the rules and regulations for living in this ideal state. Often, to promote the formation of a new identity, young cultists are forbidden to have contact with parents or friends or anyone else who would tempt them to return to their former way of life. Many times they are deprived of sleep or other sense stimuli because this makes them more receptive to the instruction of the leader and his aides. Often, sacrifices—such as remaining celibate, giving material resources to the community, and rendering absolute obedience to the leader—are also demanded.

Thinking with Cults

Muhammad, Jesus, and Siddhartha Gautama (the Buddha) were religious leaders whose charismatic preaching attracted groups of followers. In the beginning each of these religious movements could have been called a cult. These cults developed into religions that have members in nearly every nation on earth. Generally, we think of these religions benefiting our attempts to live authentically. What characteristics do these religious innovators share with the cult leaders described above? What might make you hesitant to compare them with such cult leaders?

There have always been cults. People who have joined cults, for whatever reason, have always been viewed as living on the margin. Today, cults appear to have become increasingly attractive for the reasons we have just discussed, such as disillusionment with well-established tradition, extreme idealism, social disintegration, and the government itself. Two historically significant examples are the Branch Davidians of Waco, Texas, and Heaven's Gate of southern California.

The members of the Heaven's Gate cult believed that in order to prepare themselves to be born again in a new, higher level of being, they had to give up their belongings, end personal relationships, and renounce sensual pleasures. Periodically, when cult members were prepared to move to a higher level of existence, a heavenly body would come to facilitate their journey. The thirty-nine members of the cult who committed suicide in 1997 apparently believed that the Hale-Bopp comet was the signal that heavenly beings were coming to lead them to a new plane of existence.

There are cults that help us to live well and those that are destructive. Cults provide some members with a way of filling their emotional needs or their need for identity. Often when these needs are filled, the members become uninterested in the cult and leave it.

RELIGION UNDERSTOOD AS TOTALLY ALIENATING

Some people, including Karl Marx (1818–83) and Sigmund Freud (1856–1939), claim that religion totally alienates individuals from their humanity. Karl Marx, who along with Friedrich Engels wrote the *Communist Manifesto*, believed that all historical institutions—economic and political as well as religious—represented human self-alienation. Marx believed that the practice of religion was symptomatic of an unreal or illusory way of perceiving the world. Everything that humans gave to religion—the praise of God, the belief in an afterlife—distanced them from their own selfhood. Further, Marx taught that secular patterns of life, such as the conventional understanding of family, had religious underpinnings and were also alienating. For

PUBLIC DOMAIN   CAMBODIA4KIDS.ORG

Karl Marx (left) and Sigmund Freud (right) both found religion to be totally alienating. How do you evaluate their reasons for this alienation?

people to become reconciled to themselves, Marx thought, all existing systems or institutions, including religion, needed to be critiqued.

One example will show why Marx thought religion was a source of alienation. Marx observed the misery of the factory worker in the wake of the Industrial Revolution and judged that the comfort proffered to these workers in the name of religion was only an illusion. It did nothing to question the fundamental falsity of the economic situation itself. Rather, religion reinforced the status quo. Often, pastors preached that a person was born into the situation God willed for them. Therefore, poor people were poor and rich people were rich because God wanted it that way. The marginalized and disadvantaged people should endure their situation, placing their hope in the life to come. The powerful and advantaged people should give thanks for their blessings. Religion was certainly not viewed as a help to alleviate material suffering. As a consequence, both rich and poor were confirmed in their illusions about the nature of reality.

Sigmund Freud, the father of depth psychology, was not overly concerned about people's material situation, but he was concerned with their psychological condition. He understood religion to be an illusion. In his medical practice Freud treated primarily the middle class of Viennese society. Listening to their stories and analyzing their dreams led him to believe that institutional religions promoted repressive practices that frequently caused grave psychological damage in his patients. He observed that many people avoided assuming responsibility for personal decision-making by abdicating this obligation to institutional Judaism or Christianity. He further noticed that when these same people violated religious taboos, they were consumed by a destructive guilt. Certainly, neither Karl Marx nor Sigmund Freud regarded religion as a blessing.

Christopher Hitchens (1949–2011) is a contemporary example of a person who found religion to be totally alienating. An Anglo-American, he was a prolific journalist and described himself as an antitheist. He embraced and disseminated the position that God, understood as a Supreme Being, is a totalitarian belief that destroys individual freedom.

THE AMBIGUITY OF RELIGION

Marx, Freud, and Hitchens offer valuable critiques of religion, and Judaism and Christianity have benefited most from their critiques. **Liberation theologians** who work in less-developed countries have often acknowledged the astuteness of Marx's economic analysis of class conflict. Jewish and Christian psychologists who are assisting their clients to establish a healthy sexuality agree with Freud that religious authorities have often contributed to unhealthy sexual repression. Hitchens's position urges people to question whether one can be both authentically human and religious.

SUMMARY

The human journey is a search for authenticity. We have seen that religion is one way that may help us establish a meaningful way of life, a life that promotes our personal growth and our concern for others. In this chapter we also learned that established religious traditions, in distinction from our spiritual impulses, do not always assist us in living meaningful lives. This is true whether we are talking about Native American traditions, Buddhist cosmologies, or Christian religions. Each may foster responsibility or dependence, spiritual freedom or subservience, maturity or infantilism. But even these neat distinctions, although true, are misleading. Our development and human flourishing also depend on what we as individuals are looking for in a religion. It is not an easy task to live freely and responsibly, and although our religion may urge us to live in such a manner, we may choose to live a legalistic life in order to satisfy our own needs. Then we interpret our tradition's stories in ways that fulfill these psychological needs. Alienation, however, need not be permanent. The final conversation of this book discusses the topic of religion as a possible resource for alleviating alienation.

RESOURCES

ACTIVITIES

1. As people mature, they assess situations differently than they did when they were younger. Describe a personal, biographical, or fictional situation in which alienation was transformed into reconciliation. To what factors do you attribute this change?
2. For one week, keep a log of TV programs that you watch or works of fiction that you read. Decide which characters you think are alienated and why? Which are reconciled? Which characters accept the ambiguity of life? Explain and give reasons for your judgments.

3. List ten words or phrases that describe authenticity. List ten words or phrases that describe inauthenticity. Which was easier to do? Why do you think this is so?

4. Listen to the music and lyrics of a currently popular musical group in which the theme of alienation is prominent. How is alienation imaged? Put these lyrics into our current historical context. Given the historical context, do you think reconciliation is possible? What would it require?

5. Hare Krishna, Heaven's Gate, Branch Davidians (Waco), The Unification Church, and The Church of Scientology are cults that often appear in the media. Choose one of these cults and surf the Internet to discover the range of material that is available. Then critique the reports that you find to determine which are more reliable than others. Give reasons for your critique.

6. Choreograph a dance, create lyrics, or write a series of poems that portray the themes of alienation and reconciliation.

READINGS

Camus, Albert. *The Plague*. New York: Penguin Classics, 2008. This novel asks: Where is God in the face of innocent suffering?

Daly, Mary. *Beyond God the Father: Toward a Philosophy of Women's Liberation*. Boston: Beacon, 1985. One of the books that initiated the feminist movement within Christianity, it presents a philosophy of women's liberation.

Toni Morrison. *Beloved*. New York: Knopf, 1987. This is the profoundly moving story of various levels of alienation experienced in the life of a former slave.

Spiegelman, Art. *Maus I: A Survivor's Tale: My Father Bleeds History*. New York: Pantheon, 1973. The story of how Vladek Spiegelman, a Polish Jew, and his wife survived the Holocaust.

———. *Maus II: A Survivor's Tale: And Here My Troubles Began*. New York: Pantheon, 1986. This account takes up the story from the end of World War II, when Spiegelman and his wife left Germany and settled in New York. Told in cartoons by Vladek's son, the cartoonist Art Spiegelman explores with humor and pathos the tortured relationship in the lives of survivors and their children. The use of the cartoon genre is shocking but immensely effective. *Maus II* won the 1992 Pulitzer Prize.

Wiesel, Elie. *Night*. New York: Bantam, 1982. With this book the 1986 Nobel Peace Prize recipient broke ten years of silence following his liberation from a Nazi concentration camp. It is autobiographical and is the first in a series of books by this author that depict his struggles with religious alienation.

AUDIO-VISUALS

The Shakers in America (1991). Port Washington, NY: Applause Video. This video shows the history of the Shakers and the influence of their culture in the United States.

Night and Fog (1955). Chicago: Films, Inc. French film with English subtitles. This documentary is acclaimed as one of the most worthwhile among the many that have tried to come to grips with the Holocaust.

The Business of Paradigms (1990). Burnsville, MN: Charterhouse International Learning Corporation. Although the examples are drawn primarily from the field of business, this video provides an excellent portrayal of how we think in paradigms. It is easily applicable to the field of religion, especially such topics as images of God.

Religions of the Book: Women Serving Religion (1991). Available from Films for the Humanities and Sciences, 132 West 31st Street, 17th Floor, New York, NY 10001. This film traces contemporary women's roles in Judaism, Islam, and Christianity; it also explores the question of ordination in these religions.

A Conversation with Toni Morrison (1992). San Francisco: California Newsreel. This interview was given as commentary on the alienating themes in her book *Beloved*.

American Beauty (1999). Los Angeles: Dreamworks Pictures. This is an award-winning feature film that portrays various levels of alienation in the lives of a middle-class family.

NOTE

1. Mary Daly, "The Women's Movement: An Exodus Community," *Religious Education* 67 (September/October 1972): 327–33.

Chapter 11

Reconciling Religion

PERSONAL RECONCILIATION
WITHIN THE COMMUNITY

We need some degree of order in our lives. This order is at least partially realized by virtue of being born into a culture that has been handed on to us from our parents and grandparents, a cultural worldview that was passed on to them from their parents and grandparents. To a great extent, then, we are raised in a world that has already been ordered for us by our ancestors. With broad strokes, their cultural and religious stories tell us what is important and direct us to order our personal lives with these values as guidelines. In this way we are taught how to order our lives according to cultural and religious values. A worldview is not static, however. As it was passed on from generation to generation, it was modified, even if unconsciously, to accommodate new insights, attitudes, and discoveries. We, in our turn, are also adjusting this worldview to our particular circumstances. Nevertheless, being born in societies characterized by industry and technology shapes people differently from those born in societies that are less industrialized. The former generally appreciate values associated with individualism more than those associated with community. The latter seem to value the good of the community more highly than individual achievement.

The values embedded in worldviews are usually transmitted through the literary genre of myth. Initially, these myths are transmitted orally At a later time some of them may be committed to writing. Relying on the cultural and religious myths within which we live, we find our place in relation to one another, to nature, and to God (or to the source of life that we consider to be Ultimate). So, living in accordance with a particular cosmology (worldview, myth) provides us with a sense of being connected with the world rather than being cosmic orphans, unrelated even to ourselves, in a free fall, totally at the whim of chaotic forces.

TWO EXAMPLES OF LIVING WITHIN A WORLDVIEW

Two persons whose religion motivated them to seek peace and justice for marginalized peoples were Martin Luther King, Jr. (1929–68), and Mohandas Gandhi (1869–1948). Gandhi, an Indian Hindu, is remembered for his struggle for the civil rights of Indians living in South Africa, for leading the Indian struggle for independence from Great Britain, and for advocating the elimination of the caste system from Hindu life. Raised in a deeply religious family, Gandhi's spirit was nurtured by the Bhagavad Gita, a text of his religious tradition.

Gandhi studied law in England and was sent by his Indian firm to represent them in South Africa. The twenty years Gandhi spent in South Africa influenced him greatly. He experienced an appalling degree of discrimination toward Indians, which served to sensitize him to the plight of the politically powerless. Through the Russian writer Tolstoy he came to know Christianity and was inspired by the figure of Jesus, especially as he was portrayed delivering his **Sermon on the Mount** (Mt 5—7). The spirit of one of the beatitudes from that sermon, "Blessed are the peacemakers, for they shall see God," reso- nated with and strengthened his Hindu affinity for nonviolence. From a Hindu worldview, reinforced by his reading of another tradition, Gandhi conducted his liberation movements in a nonviolent manner. His Indian countrymen and women gave him the name Mahatma, which means "great soul."

Martin Luther King, Jr., born in Georgia, was a Baptist minister, the son of a Baptist minister. He discovered within his Christian tradition the resources to lead his fellow African Americans in their struggles for civil rights during the 1960s. In his studies and travels King became deeply affected by the peaceful, nonviolent revolution brought about by the leadership of Gandhi. Today, we remember King for his belief that to achieve positive change, violence must be met with nonvio- lence. Both Gandhi and King exemplify persons whose fundamental religious orientation served both to anchor their lives and to open them to respond to others' needs. Further, each was attuned to finding wisdom in traditions other than his own.

Since we are born into an already existing culture and religious worldview, it may seem that we have no choice in how we situate ourselves in relation to others. Although this may be true in the very

Thinking about Reconciliation

Recall a time when you felt at peace with yourself, in harmony with your environment, and in kinship with others. Such an experience is akin to reconciliation. Can you identify a tradition or practice that helps you maintain this feeling of being reconciled and in harmony with life? Did this experience of reconciliation make you more attentive to the lives of others.

earliest years of our life, we begin testing this worldview as soon as we learn to say no. As early as the "terrible twos," we test boundaries. This continues in various ways until we are satisfied (or dissatisfied) that living the values of our received worldview, for the most part, results in an interesting, meaningful, and fulfilling way of life, one that is humanly satisfying. We experience also that living outside these patterns sometimes causes feelings of dislocation. Although we may choose to live within the general contours of an inherited worldview, we continue to explore various ways of living within it, exploring

BEN SUTHERLAND

People who reconcile with one another often express this in a bodily manner. "Reconciliation" by Josefina de Vasconcellos in Saint Michael's Cathedral in Coventry.

its boundaries, learning whether the boundaries as they have been transmitted to us are pliable or rigid.

This type of exploration and interpretation is the reason Jews, Christians, and Muslims can share the creation narratives and the stories of the ancestors (such as those of Abraham and Sarah) that we find in the Book of Genesis. Because they share these sacred texts, the three religions embrace a worldview in which God is the fundamental reality and human beings live in a world of God's making. Yet further interpretation of these same texts results in religions that differ greatly from one another. Adding to the complexity of this situation is the fact that there are people within each of these religion who interpret these Genesis myths literally and others who interpret them symbolically.

Regardless of how people interpret the religious worldview within which they live, they will at times violate the value and belief system that they have embraced. Perhaps a religious orientation places a great deal of emphasis on living in harmony with nature and observing good ecological practices. Although the person has willingly embraced this value and finds it meaningful, it is conceivable that he or she may be lured by a business deal to ignore sound ecological practices for the sake of profit. Or those whose worldview demands that justice and a regard for the dignity of each person structure relationships may act in a mean-spirited or demeaning manner toward people whom they find irritating. Saint Paul knew this experience of struggling with opposing tendencies and inclinations. In Romans 7:15 he writes, "I do the things I do not want to do, and I don't do those things I want to do." How often we have experienced this state of affairs. "I want to stop smoking, but I'll finish this pack first." "I want to spend more time studying, but tonight I want to go out with my friends."

CONFLICTING WORLDVIEWS

At times it is not only our personal values and actions that are in conflict with our religious or cultural worldview, but the cultural and religious values we have embraced may come into conflict with each other and, consequently, put us in conflict. Consider these two cases. During World War II the German cultural myth was that of Aryan supremacy. This cultural myth shaped the consciousness of the German people to believe that they were racially superior to others, especially Jews. Of course, many Germans were also Christian. The Christian story teaches people to value all people as if they were other Christs. The values of these two worldviews clearly were in conflict.

Some German Protestant groups tried to accommodate themselves to National Socialism, Hitler's Party. Other Protestants found they could not accommodate themselves, and they formed the Confessing Church, which resisted Hitler's efforts to enlist the churches in his totalitarian endeavors. The Confessing Church supported the Barmen Declaration, issued in 1934 by church people from various traditions, which defined Christian opposition to National Socialism. Dietrich Bonhoeffer (1906–45), an influential Lutheran pastor, was imprisoned and eventually executed one month before the end of the war for resisting Hitler and his views to the extent that he became involved in various plots to assassinate Hitler. As we learned in Chapter 2, worldviews do have consequences.

The practice of burning witches that swept Europe between the fourteenth and sixteenth centuries is another example of the conflict between personal and religious values. In medieval Europe cultural and religious worldviews coincided, for the most part. This is the phenomenon often referred to as Christendom. During this period church officials often classified as witches those women who did not conform to the usual cultural norms. Among such women were those who chose neither to marry nor to enter a convent or who practiced traditional forms of healing. From one point of view, we can say that these women were put to death because they did not conform to the worldview of Christendom. From another point of view, we can say that the horror of this witch hunt led to a new understanding of the Christian message. The beloved French saint, Joan of Arc (1412–31), is a symbol for such women. As a young girl Joan believed she received messages from heavenly voices that urged her to lead France in battle against the English. She donned armor and led the French army to a decisive victory. In a later battle, however, she was captured. In a church trial in the king of England's military headquarters in Rouen, Joan was convicted of witchcraft for wearing masculine clothes and of heresy for claiming that she was compelled to follow her "voices" even when doing so put her at odds with the Roman Catholic Church. At the age of nineteen Joan, also known as the Maid of Orleans, was burned at the stake. Twenty-five years after her death, she was cleared of all charges of **sorcery** and heresy. Religious worldviews, although in one sense normative, are always in the process of reformation.

THE CONFESSION OF TRANSGRESSIONS

When we have disconnected ourselves from meaningful patterns of relationship, participation in public rituals can help us to reestablish and maintain these connections. Such rites and rituals are reconciling. They have the effect of healing dislocation and of revitalizing individuals and communities. We will investigate some of these practices of reconciliation. Ritual practices that include the confession or acknowledgment of sin, transgressions, defilements, or the breaking of taboos are practiced in many religions. Most Christian denominations include within their order of public worship a rite of confession in which the community participates. This rite is an acknowledgment that relationships have been broken and need to be repaired. It is the belief of these religions that such acknowledgment, if entered into sincerely, reconciles one to the community.

Religions recognize that all personal transgressions affect the community by weakening the bonds that unite its members. This social aspect of personal reconciliation can be seen very graphically in the early practices of the Christian Church. At that time the norm for reconciliation was public confession. Those seeking reconciliation confessed their sins in the midst of the assembly. The presiding minister, usually a bishop, imposed a penance in the name of the community. Often the penance was also public, such as wearing distinctive garb, performing good deeds, or even being excluded from the community for a certain period of time. Today, this seems very harsh, and we may wonder if people would submit to this discipline. Still, the traces of this understanding of the social nature of even our most private acts are found in the contemporary rites of various religions. Let us consider some of these public rites.

In Judaism the notion of reconciliation plays a major role. Yom Kippur, the holiest day of the year for Jews, is a Day of Atonement, a day when Jews align themselves anew with the community and with the community's worldview. Between Rosh Hashana, the day observed by Jews as New Year's, and Yom Kippur, which occurs ten days later, observant Jews reflect on how they have lived during the previous year. If they admit to themselves that they have held a grudge against someone or have acted unjustly, they make amends to those involved. On Yom Kippur itself observant Jews fast from sunset to sunset. They gather in their synagogues or temples and spend the day in prayer. This attitude toward reconciliation is a development of the prophetic insight that the quality of people's relationships with others mirrors the quality of their relationship to God. At the conclusion of Yom Kippur, they participate in a celebratory meal. Reconciliation engenders joy and good comradeship, which demands social expression. The sharing of food is among the most deeply symbolic and reconciling

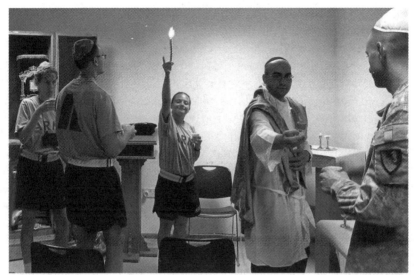

ROBERT COUSE-BAKER

Military personnel observing Havdalah at the end of Yom Kippur while stationed in Baghdad, Iraq.

rituals known to humankind. We don't eat with our enemies, and if we do, they usually do not remain enemies.

FROM THE JEWISH PRAYER *BOOK FOR THE DAYS OF AWE*

Our God and God of our fathers, forgive our sins on this Yom Kippur. Blot out and pass over our transgressions, as Isaiah declared in Your name: "I alone blot out your transgressions, for My sake; your sins I shall not recall. I have swept away your transgressions like a cloud, your sins like mist. Return to Me, for I have redeemed you." And the Torah promises: "For on this day atonement shall be made for you, to cleanse you; of all your sins before the Lord shall you be cleansed."

Rites of reconciliation reflect the cosmology, culture, and geographical context of a particular community. The Navajo are a Native American tribe who live in the arid lands of the Southwest where there is an abundance of sand. Within the Navajo cosmology, physical illness is understood to be a symptom of spiritual dislocation from the community. Therefore, the restoration of health is a function of becoming reconciled with the community. In order to achieve this restoration, the Navajo singer who is the traditional healer calls upon the mythic ancestors or holy people and mediates their healing power to the sick person. On the floor of the ceremonial **hogan**, in the sand, the singer draws mythic figures who bear some relation to the type of illness from which the person is suffering. When the sand painting is completed, corn pollen is sprinkled on both the painting and the afflicted person. The sprinkling of the pollen creates a connection between the mythic figures and the one who seeks healing. Then the one seeking healing sits in the middle of the painting. The singer, hands moistened with medicine, transfers sand from the faces of the various figures to the face of the suffering one. Next, the healer transfers sand from the feet of the figures to the feet of the one for whom the ritual is being performed. This pattern continues until the person, through the transfer of sand, has become totally identified with the holy persons represented in the sand painting. By this means the spiritual power of the ancestors has been mediated to the sick person. Through this rite the person is reconciled with the community, and thus healed in spirit even though perhaps not cured in body.

The realization that one's physical well-being is in some way tied to one's spiritual well-being is not limited to the Navajo conceptualization of the world. This understanding is widespread in both religious and secular settings. Modern medicine, as deeply embedded in science as it is, acknowledges that headaches and stomach aches—in fact, aches of all kinds—are often signs of something askew in the spiritual or psychological dimensions of our lives. Even cancer, which is certainly an organic disease, sometimes appears to be triggered by stress.

The use of substances such as sand, spittle, and oils to anoint the sick person's body is also a widespread practice. The New Testament recounts the story of Jesus applying spittle to the eyes of a blind man in order that he be healed (Jn 9:6). Among the Highlanders of Papua New Guinea, various oils obtained from trees are often used in healing rites.

In Christianity as well as in Judaism and among the Navajo, the ordinary place of personal reconciliation is within the context of public worship or of community. Each Eucharist in the Roman Catholic Church begins with a rite of reconciliation. In the *Presbyterian Order of Worship, The Service for the Lord's Day* includes the *Call to Confession* and the *Confession of Sin*. The directives for the Presbyterian service offer several options for this rite of reconciliation, but each minister is also at liberty to call the congregation to repentance in his or her own words. It is significant that after the congregation has acknowledged its sinfulness, the members are invited to extend a greeting of peace to one another.

CALL TO CONFESSION

If we say we have no sin,
we deceive ourselves, and the truth is not in us.
But if we confess our sins,
God who is faithful and just
will forgive us our sins
and cleanse us from all unrighteousness.
In humility and faith
let us confess our sin to God.

CONFESSION OF SIN

Merciful God,
you pardon all who truly repent and turn to you.
We humbly confess our sins and ask your mercy.
We have not loved you with a pure heart,
nor have we loved our neighbor as ourselves.
We have not done justice, loved kindness,
or walked humbly with you, our God.
Have mercy on us, O God, in your loving kindness.
In your great compassion, cleanse us from our sin.
Create in us a clean heart, O God,
and renew a right spirit within us.
Do not cast us from your presence, or take your Holy
    Spirit from us.
Restore to us the joy of your salvation
and sustain us with your bountiful Spirit.

Many people never participate in a formal ritual of reconciliation such as those just described. Everyone, however, has experienced the need to acknowledge failures and weaknesses. This need appears to be rooted in the human situation and to express a universal need to live in proper relationship. Recall a time, for example, when a friend offended you. Connections were broken. The next time you saw your friend, there was tension or unease between you. It was impossible for the two of you to proceed with your relationship as if nothing had happened. One of you had to break the ice. Either you had to acknowledge that you had been hurt, or your friend had to acknowledge that he or she had disrupted your relationship. Recall with what relief you resumed your friendship. Sometimes people describe this experience as having had a load lifted from their shoulders. Religious practices of confession are, basically, a ritualization of this human need to live a life reconciled to one's environment and all that is included within it.

Religions teach that there is no such thing as a purely private offense, one that affects only the transgressor. If a person tells a lie, it has the social effect of lowering the level of trust among the members of the community. If a person steals, others become very cautious to ensure that they are not victimized. Residence-hall directors counsel students to lock the doors to their rooms even if they are simply going to get a soda from the vending machine. College cafeterias check the card of each person who enters. This level of caution has developed gradually over the span of a few generations. Among other reasons, this distrust developed because an increasing numbers of individuals became dislocated from the community and initiated an avalanche of distrust. In the previous chapter we examined possible reasons for this dislocation or alienation from the community. The purpose of these examples, though, is to illustrate that the personal and the social effects of transgressions are always intertwined.

Because every transgression has social consequences, the ordinary place for rites of confession or of reconciliation is within the context of social or public worship. Acting upon this understanding, we have seen that Jews celebrate Yom Kippur in the synagogue, the Navajo enacts the sand-painting ceremony in the ceremonial hogan, and the Christian confesses in a house of worship.

There are some Christian denominations, such as Anglicans and Roman Catholics, whose practice of reconciliation includes private confession. In such a case the individual acknowledges his or her personal transgressions to a minister or priest, who gives verbal assurance that the person has, indeed, been reconciled. However, even this practice of individual confession emphasizes the social consequences of transgression, because the priest or minister reconciles the penitent in the name of the community.

God the Father of Mercies, through the death and resurrection of Jesus His Son, has reconciled the world to Himself and has sent the Holy Spirit among us for the forgiveness of our sins. Through the ministry of the church may God grant you pardon and peace and I absolve you in the Name of the Father, the Son, and the Holy Spirit.

RECONCILIATION BETWEEN RELIGIOUS GROUPS

Thus far, the emphasis in our discussion has been on the dynamics of personal reconciliation to the community. Intimately related to this, however, is the necessity for religious communities to acknowledge or confess publicly their transgressions. An example of such a corporate transgression would be a community's complicity in dehumanizing individuals either within or outside their religious group so that those devalued feel worthless or insignificant. In such cases the community needs to confess publicly its wrongdoing for two reasons. The group needs to remain connected to its own worldview, and it needs to maintain connections with other religious bodies.

Whereas religious traditions generally include prescribed rites and ceremonies for the reconciliation of the individual to the community, communal gestures of reconciliation are usually initiated and expressed in the name of the community by the community's leadership. Such corporate confessions of repentance occur much more rarely than personal expressions of transgressions. There are many reasons for this, but the principal reason is that Western modernity seems to lack an adequate understanding of the many and intricate ways that groups of human beings are connected. Another reason that leaders are reluctant to voice the shortcomings and sins of their religious groups is the fear that such admissions will lower the level of confidence that members have in the religious community. Still, there are such admissions of corporate guilt, and we need to pay attention to their significance. Instances of such gestures of communal or corporate attempts at reconciliation are illustrated by the following examples.

Pope John XXIII, who was pope from 1958 to 1963, was referred to by Catholics and non-Catholics alike as Good Pope John. He brought to the papacy an openness to new ideas, a trust in ecumenical and interfaith dialogue, and confidence in the goodness of the world. Because he wanted to bring the Roman Catholic Church into conversation with the contemporary world, he convened the Second Vatican Council (Vatican II), which met from 1962 to1965. This council is considered one of the most important religious events of the twentieth century. It was important for non-Catholics as well as for Catholics, because it brought to an end a period of isolation, defensiveness, and triumphalism in the Catholic Church.

Pope John XXIII seemed to understand more than any previous pope in modern times the deep bonds that unite Judaism and Christianity. While he was pope, he was visited by a delegation of

Jewish leaders. He greeted them, "I am your brother, Joseph." Pope John knew there were several levels of meaning present in his simple greeting. First, although his name was Angelo Giuseppe (Joseph), he had always been called Giuseppe. Immediately, by this greeting, he showed that their common humanity bound them together as equals. Then, of course, brothers have a common ancestry. Pope John thus acknowledged the ancestral history shared by Jews and Christians. Finally, within this greeting was an allusion to the story of reconciliation between Joseph, the son of the ancestor Jacob, and his brothers (Gn 45). To these leaders of Judaism, immersed in the common ancestral history of Judaism and Christianity, this simple phrase had profound resonances and was heard as an acknowledgment of the desire of Christians to be reconciled with their Jewish brothers and sisters.

Although that encounter was only a quasi-official acknowledgment of kinship, the same pope set the stage for the revisions following Vatican II of the Good Friday liturgy of the Roman Catholic Church. In the liturgy for Good Friday the church prays for many groups of people. Among those groups are the Catholic Church, the pope, those in government, and the Jews. In the pre–Vatican II liturgy the Jews, because they did not accept Catholic teachings concerning Jesus, were described as having a veil over their hearts, a veil that needed to be removed. After they were described in that manner, this prayer was made for them:

> Almighty and everlasting God, you drive not even the Jews from your mercy; hear our prayers, which we offer for the blindness of that people, that, acknowledging the light of your truth, which is Christ, they may be rescued from their darkness.

In the liturgical renewal that took place under Pope Paul VI in 1970, that Good Friday prayer was replaced with this one:

> Almighty and eternal God, you made the promises to Abraham and his descendants. In your goodness, hear the prayers of your church so that the people whom from of old you made your own may come to the fullness of redemption.

In changing the public rite of the entire Roman Catholic Church, its leadership acknowledged it had wrongly and insensitively understood its relationship to the Jews and had attributed bad faith to them. Consequently, the Christian-Jewish relationship had become marked by an alienation so extreme that the Holocaust could be tolerated by Christian people.

Expressions of reconciliation and alienation have results within our everyday world. As we saw in Part III words are effective in shaping our imaginations. The imaginations of countless generations of Christians had been formed so as to interpret Jewish motivations, actions, desires, and worship as "blind." The untold suffering and persecution of Jews over the centuries at the hands of Christians were partly the result of such alienating language. Although the persecution of the Jews by Christians cannot be reduced solely to the use of language, this example does show us how large a part language actually plays in shaping imaginations and effecting action.

The change in the prayers of the Roman Catholic liturgy is akin to an official acknowledgment that throughout the centuries untold harm has been done to Jews by Christians. The new language, although relatively recent, has been effective in furthering the process of reconciliation between Roman Catholics and Jews.

From the viewpoint of an observer outside the Roman Catholic tradition, and even for some within that tradition, the change of language in the Good Friday ritual did not go far enough. That may be. Yet, it remains significant that the language no longer is that of hostility and alienation. Sadly, it must be noted that the promise of further reconciliation heralded by the immediate aftermath of Vatican II has not occurred. Jewish-Catholic relations have basically reached an impasse.

A second example of the corporate acknowledgment of wrongdoing and repentance is that of the **Southern Baptist Convention**'s admission of racism. This admission of guilt is even more striking when we consider that Southern Baptists came into existence because they seceded from the American Baptist Church, which opposed slavery. In June 1995, more than a century after it was founded in order to legitimate the owning of slaves, the convention issued the "Resolution on Racial Reconciliation." The resolution states: "We apologize to all African-Americans for condoning and/or perpetuating individual and systemic racism in our lifetime; and we genuinely repent of racism of which we have been guilty, whether consciously or unconsciously."

This acknowledgment by the Southern Baptist Convention of its complicity in supporting the institution of slavery in the United States provides another instance in which a religious community seeks reconciliation with those whom its practices have harmed. It is also an example of the necessity every institution has to interpret continually its worldview in the light of personal, corporate, and historical developments. As the resolution correctly points out, some of the alienating attitudes and beliefs that we hold may be unconsciously held. Yet, we are bound to reflect consciously upon our religious worldviews and to reinterpret them as we ourselves become more mature and as knowledge in all fields, not only religion, advances.

RECONCILIATION TO ONESELF

Understanding ourselves within the context of worldviews, religious and nonreligious, and living in harmony with the values proposed by these worldviews would be easier if the connections among ourselves, institutions, nature, and other people were more neatly drawn. Neat and exact distinctions, however, can exist only in our minds. Although it is important to be able to think conceptually and theoretically about reconciliation and alienation, we must never forget that life blurs these theoretical distinctions. In everyday living, nothing is as clear cut and precise as it may appear to be in our thoughts.

For example, conscious participation in public rites of reconciliation such as Yom Kippur or in Navajo sand painting often helps a person reestablish inner harmony. But there is nothing automatic about it. Some people attend these rituals and they either feel no greater peace than before they attended or feel even more ill at ease. However, these same people may experience that the closeness with nature that occurs in activities as simple as gardening or hiking can result in a more genuine concern for their neighbor or a more receptive attitude to themselves. Sometimes the starting point of the reconciliation process begins with the attempt to realign or evaluate one's priorities in respect to how one is actually living. At other times achieving harmony and balance within ourselves may mean reevaluating the merits of our currently held viewpoints to determine if they continue to be meaningful.

People who continue to find their religious worldview meaningful frequently appeal to the spiritual traditions within their religion to nourish their religious development. Through these spiritual practices they reestablish harmony or meaning within their life and keep in touch with who they really are, who they want to become, and what they value. In contrast to the rites that reconcile us to the community, however, the exercises that foster personal reconciliation tend to be practiced privately rather than publicly. Examples of private rituals are personal prayer, meditation, retreats, fasting, and works of charity. Although these particular practices differ depending on whether they are shaped by Hindu, Christian, Muslim, Native American, or other traditions, they are similar in this respect: those who engage in these practices over a period of time report that they are quite effective in fostering in them an authentic way of living.

PERSONAL PRAYER AND MEDITATION

Personal prayer has many shades and hues. It can take the form of the simple repetition of a phrase or sound such as the phrase, "Jesus, Lord, have mercy upon me," or the *Om* of the Hindus and Buddhist monks. The Jesus Prayer has traditionally been more widely practiced by members of the Greek and Russian Orthodox churches than by other Christian denominations. Because people have become more open to investigating religious traditions beyond their own, this is now changing. People of other Christian traditions practice this chant and discover its value. It has often been referred to as a centering prayer, since its purpose is to gather and focus on God the energies of heart and mind. For Hindus, the chanting of the Sanskrit word *Om* is similar. For the Hindu, *Om* is the most sacred of sounds. It contains the whole meaning and power of the universe. As we learned in Chapter 9, the person who chants it with full realization will contemplate the ultimate reality and will be freed from the karmic effect of previous lives. *Om* may be recited privately or in communal prayer.

Prayer can also take the form of a heartfelt outpouring of our deepest emotions and feelings to the Mystery that surrounds us. Those who practice this type of prayer report that this manner of praying opens them to possibilities they have not imagined, and that it often transforms the way they look at the circumstances of their lives. They also report that it takes courage to engage in this type of prayer, because when we allow our deepest feelings to emerge, feelings that we may have covered over for a long period of time, this may initially disconcert us. What if we discover we have feelings of hatred toward our spouse or our children? If we are the caregivers for aging parents, our feelings may reveal that there are times when we wish they were dead. Perhaps we feel that God is absolutely no help in our lives. If or when this occurs, we are likely to experience discomfort. After all, we probably have been raised since infancy to believe that good people love their children unconditionally, that we should want our parents to live forever, and that we should never wander from loving God, trusting that God has a purpose for everything.

The **suppression** or **repression** of such feelings, however, results in blocks to intimacy with the divine Mystery. When we want to be intimate with another, whether that other is our spouse or God, it is necessary for the two parties to reveal themselves to one another.

At times, communication is blocked by unexpressed feelings, usually negative feelings of anger, inadequacy, or rebellion. Communicating these feelings both dissipates the power they have over us and establishes communication with the source of our being.

People who practice this model of prayer make the claim that prayer, by putting them in touch with feelings that are often suppressed during the course of daily activities, keeps them in touch with their center. In other words, prayer is effective in discovering or rediscovering within themselves that which is meaningful. That is why the expression of feeling is so important. Feelings are an indicator of who we really are at a particular moment, rather than who we think we should be or who we may want to be. Remember Augustine's heartfelt prayer: "Lord, make me chaste, but not now"! That prayer revealed the complexity and confusion of his feelings at that particular moment. But it is an honest prayer wherein he reveals himself to the other.

Because prayer is understood as communication with a holy One, we can also expect some sort of response. People report that this response takes many forms. Sometimes it is a change in feelings. A particular situation may not have changed, but we are more at peace with it. We experience an increase of energy or creativity. We become clearer about what we really value. We begin to understand God in a different way, to express ourselves more openly to our spouses, to acknowledge our own lovableness. The **psalms** of the Hebrew Bible are moving illustrations of this type of prayer. Listen to the Israelite psalmist and notice the range and depth of emotion poured out to Israel's God.

Psalm 137

By the rivers of Babylon—
  there we sat down and there we wept
  when we remembered Zion.
On the willows there
  we hung up our harps.
For there our captors
  asked us for songs,
and our tormentors asked for mirth, saying,
  "Sing us one of the songs of Zion!"

How could we sing the Lord's song
  in a foreign land?

If I forget you, O Jerusalem,
   let my right hand wither!
Let my tongue cling to the roof of my mouth,
   if I do not remember you,
if I do not set Jerusalem
   above my highest joy.

Remember, O Lord, against the Edomites
   the day of Jerusalem's fall,
how they said, "Tear it down! Tear it down!
   Down to its foundations!"
O daughter Babylon, you devastator!
   Happy shall they be who pay you back
   what you have done to us!
Happy shall they be who take your little ones
   and dash them against the rock!

Not all prayer, though, takes the form of words. If you think about your relationships with your closest friends or your spouse, you will remember times when it was enough simply to be in the presence of the person whom you cherish. It seemed inappropriate to disturb your presence to one another with words. So, you remained silent. Some people remark that simple presence in the company of a loved one is not a lack of communication but is, in reality, the deepest kind of communication. Prayer also has its wordless form of expression. Although the prayer itself is wordless, those who reflect on this experience describe it in lyrical language.

Jalal al-Din Rumi, who lived from 604 to 672 AH (1207 to 1273 CE), was a renowned spiritual teacher of Islam. In the following selection, this holy person of Islam describes living in the presence of Allah:

When I start from the beginning, He is my leader;
   when I seek my heart, He is its ravisher.
When I strive for peace, He intercedes for me; when
   I go to war, He is my dagger.
When I come to the gathering, He is the wine and
   sweetmeats; when I enter the garden, He is the
   narcissus.
When I go down to the mine, He is the ruby and car-
   nelian; when I dive into the sea, He is the pearl.

When I cross the desert, He is the oasis; when I ascend
the spheres, He is the star.

. . .

When I awaken, He is my new awareness; when I go
to bed, He enters my dreams.

When I seek a rhyme for my poetry, he eases the way
for my mind.

He stands above whatever form you can picture, like
painter and pen.

No matter how much higher you look, He is still
higher than that "higher" of yours.

Go, abandon speaking and books—much better it is
to let Him be your book.

Be silent! For all six directions are His Light; and
when you pass beyond the directions, He Himself is the Ruler.[1]

MYSTICISM

Many of the world's religions include mystical traditions of prayer.
People who follow the mystical path of prayer seek experiential union
with the source of life and power in their religions. Nevertheless,
people who adopt this way of prayer tell us that the mystic advances
through various stages of purification until at last union is achieved.
The *Om* of Hindus, the Jesus Prayer of Christians, and the Vision
Quest of Native Americans, as well as the wordless prayer of many
other traditions, foster this experience of union.

In *Varieties of Religious Experience* William James states that mystical prayer has four characteristics: it is noetic (gives knowledge or
insight), ineffable (cannot be put into words), transitory, and passive.
Because what is considered Ultimate differs from religion to religion,
there are differences in how this union is perceived. Consequently, all
four characteristics are not always present in any one experience of
mystical union. Yet, at least two always seem to be present, regardless
of the religious tradition of the mystic.

Some persons who attain mystical union state that they arrive at a
new knowledge or understanding of divinity (noetic). They describe
the knowledge as similar to the knowledge parents have of their
children or spouses have of each other. It is a knowledge born of
love. Often, spousal language is used to image the reality they have

FRED GLENNON

Prayer takes many forms.

experienced. The mystic experience is described as ineffable; there are no words that can adequately describe this prayerful experience. It is transitory; it comes and goes. This sort of prayerful union is sustained only for short periods of time. Finally, such prayer is passive. Individuals can prepare themselves for this experience by practicing the Jesus Prayer, **yoga**, or impassioned dancing such as the **Sufis** do (practices that foster self-forgetfulness). Mystics report, however, that the experience of intimacy is given to them. They are recipients of a gift.

Whatever form of prayer persons practice or whatever spiritual tradition gives shape to the prayer, people who pray generally share a common assumption. Antoine de Saint-Exupéry, a twentieth-century French author, expresses this quite well through the principal character in *The Little Prince*: "What is essential is invisible to the eye." People who practice personal prayer and meditation feel the need to focus their attention on the essentials of life, to clarify their needs and desires, to live life deeply rather than to move superficially from day to day. They feel there is more to life and reality than what they presently experience, and they want to explore this more deeply. It is true that not all people who experience this need to touch more deeply the sources of life do so by prayer and meditation. But people who live within a religious worldview often employ these means.

RETREATS

People who have had profound experiences often feel compelled to spend time reflecting upon the experience or attempting to make some sense of it. Notable religious figures who exemplify this basic human tendency are Siddhartha Gautama (the Buddha), Muhammad, and Jesus. Accounts of their lives record that a profound spiritual experience was followed by a period of silence and reflection, a retreat. When these religious figures emerged from their period of reflection, they seemed confirmed in the direction they wanted to take with their lives.

We know about the stories of these men because their lives and teachings influenced subsequent generations of people. Yet, for as long as history has been recorded, there are accounts of ordinary men and women who regularly take time to get in touch with themselves by spending shorter or longer periods in silent reflection. Retreats are simply extended periods of personal prayer.

College students sometimes put aside their studies and ordinary social activities and physically separate themselves from the places associated with their day-to-day activities. They reflect on their lives and often find it useful to share their insights with one another. Dialogue is frequently an important part of a retreat, because those participating value the community that dialogue engenders and profit from the support that the community provides. One college junior described what a retreat experience meant to her:

> I can hardly express what a gift these retreat weekends have been to me. They offer a time for reflection in addition to a break from busy campus life. I have come from the retreats with an enhanced and unbreakable relationship with God, and a community of faith that provides fellowship and support. We meet throughout the year to pray and share with each other, celebrate the liturgy and welcome new members to the retreat community. The retreat program truly offers more than just a weekend of peace and quiet, but a community that fosters faith and an experience that will change your life.

Why is silence important to self-discovery? All of us have good days and bad, times when our spirits are high, and times when we feel

Thinking with Silence

What did the biographer mean to convey about the value of a reflective life in his description of Antony when he emerged from the cave after twenty years? Although it is very unlikely that any of us would undertake such an extensive period of reflection, some reflection—an hour or two, a day, or a weekend—has proven to be a means by which we become or remain reconciled to ourselves. Describe your experiences with silence and reflection.

low. We also have periods when life is going well, and we don't want to be bothered with ethical questions such as those with which we dealt in Chapter 5. We can sometimes keep the "demons" at bay, or ethical and other personal questions at arm's length, if we keep ourselves involved and active. It is the silence of night we fear, when we have only ourselves to keep us company. Retreats provoke reflection by removing us from the busyness of everyday life. Like the Buddha, people emerge from such periods of reflection with new insight into or deeper commitment to that which gives their lives meaning.

A very moving story—probably only partially factual—captures the dynamics of silence and retreats. It was written in the fourth century by Saint Athanasius, the spiritual biographer of Saint Antony. Athanasius recounts that when Antony was a young man, he was inspired to remove himself from his usual concerns and from the company of his friends. He went outside the town and lived in a cave where he fought with the "demons," those conscious and unconscious worries and self-doubts that rob us of peace. From time to time his friends would leave him some bread or other types of food. After twenty years Antony left the cave and rejoined his friends and entered a daily routine. According to Athanasius, when Antony emerged from the cave, he had the appearance of a strong young man, vigorous, energetic, and very much alive!

FASTING

Fasting is the practice of reducing our intake of food in order to make us more focused or more alert to what is going on in our lives. Fundamentally, its purpose is the same as surrounding ourselves by silence. Siddhartha (the Buddha) found that too restrictive fasting, however, defeated his purpose of self-knowledge. The fasting became an end in itself rather than a means to an end. It was only after he had moderated his fasting that he had his profound and transformative experience of enlightenment. Still, fasting remains an important spiritual discipline fostered in many religions.

Islam, like some other religions, prescribes periods of public fasting. In Islam, during the month of Ramadan, the ninth lunar month, Muslims for whom it would not be too great a burden abstain from eating, drinking, tobacco, and sexual activity from sunup until sundown.

We human beings are very capable of making ourselves the center of our lives, in which case we focus on satisfying our physical needs and desires. Muslims believe that material desires are quite valid, but that the desire for God should dominate all other desires. The fast reminds the Muslim that humans need to order their desires so that bodily satisfactions do not eclipse the desire for God. Abstaining, temporarily, from fulfilling bodily desires is an aid to achieving this attitude. An eleventh-century Islamic theologian and mystic named Al-Ghazzali observed that unless the fast results in a positive interior focus on the Lord and the hereafter, those fasting are left with only hunger and thirst for their pains.

Besides emphasizing the highest dimension of life, fasting reminds Muslims of the plight of the countless humans living in destitution who have no choice about fasting. Their fasting is extreme, involuntary, and seldom interrupted. Experiencing the pangs of hunger and thirst, even in a mitigated way, reminds Muslims of the suffering of others. This experience of hunger and thirst may motivate Muslims to relieve the suffering of their fellows. Fasting is thought to promote inner or personal reconciliation for those who fast. If those who fast become more conscious of other people and reach out to them, it could also enable the poor and disenfranchised to become less alienated from the community. It is in these ways that fasting reminds Muslims of two central tenets of Islam: the transcendence of Allah and their bond with all other people.

WORKS OF CHARITY

Since biblical times, hospitality, particularly the sharing of food, has been a fundamental value for Jews. In particular, the stranger was to receive hospitality. The Hebrew scriptures contain many stories about hospitality and the significance of sharing food, but one particularly moving story is that of the prophet Elijah, who was fed by a widow during a time of drought and famine.

As the story is narrated (1 Kgs 17:8–16), a drought came over the land. Elijah, instructed by Yahweh, went to the land east of the Jordan River where he drank from the stream and ate food that ravens brought. Eventually, however, the water dried up, and Yahweh instructed him to go to Sidon, where he would be fed by a widow. When he reached the city gate, he met a widow who was gathering firewood. Elijah asked her to bring him water and a bit of baked bread. The widow replied: "As Yahweh your God lives, I have no baked bread, but only a handful of meal in a jar and a little oil in a jug; I am just gathering a stick or two to go and prepare this for myself and my son to eat, and then we shall die." However, Elijah assured her that the Lord would ensure that until the next rain neither her supply of flour nor her oil would diminish. In that way the widow, who from her meager supply fed a stranger, was rewarded by having a supply of meal and oil during the time when there was no rain to water vineyards or wheat fields.

The Jewish attitude toward hospitality is a particular instance of the view that the world belongs to everyone, and that everyone is entitled to enough of its goods to live with some degree of dignity. Jewish prophets such as Amos and **Micah**, who lived in the eighth century BCE reminded the people that the quality of their relationship with God was determined by the quality of their relationship with the least and poorest among them. Listen to the intense and powerful words of Micah:

> "With what shall I come before the Lord,
>   and bow myself before God on high?
> Shall I come before him with burnt offerings,
>   with calves a year old?
> Will the Lord be pleased with thousands of rams,
>   with ten thousands of rivers of oil?
> Shall I give my firstborn for my transgression,
>   the fruit of my body for the sin of my soul?"
> He has told you, O mortal, what is good:
>   and what does the Lord require of you
> but to do justice, and to love kindness,
>   and to walk humbly with your God? (Mi 6:6–8)

Christians recognize that their understanding of justice comes from the prophetic insights of Judaism. They also emphasize the reconciling value of sharing material, intellectual, or spiritual goods with others. The Gospel of Matthew expresses this perspective in a striking manner. Matthew includes a moving scene of the Last Judgment. Jesus has come again to judge who will enter into the presence of his Father and who will be banished from the divine Presence into everlasting fire. Jesus' criterion for deciding this is neither arbitrary nor obscure. It arises from the prophetic tradition of the Hebrew scriptures such as the one from Micah above, and it would have been well known to Matthew's audience. In the Last Judgment scene that follows, the king (Jesus) suggests that righteous people practice works of mercy toward all those with whom they come in contact. They do not differentiate between the deserving and the undeserving; everyone, in fact, is deserving of food and shelter. These are the words Matthew attributes to Jesus:

> Then the king will say to those at his right hand, "Come, you that are blessed by my Father, inherit the kingdom prepared for you from the foundation of the world; for I was hungry and you gave me food, I was thirsty and you gave me something to drink, I was a stranger and you welcomed me, I was naked and you gave me clothing, I was sick and you took care of me, I was in prison and you visited me." Then the righteous will answer him, "Lord, when was it that we saw you hungry and gave you food, or thirsty and gave you something to drink? And when was it that we saw you a stranger and welcomed you, or naked and gave you clothing? And when was it that we saw you sick or in prison and visited you?" And the king will answer them, "Truly I tell you, just as you did it to one of the least of these who are members of my family, you did it to me." (Mt 25:34–40).

The story of Zacchaeus recorded in the Gospel of Luke (19:1–10) is among the most appealing and engaging stories found in the Christian scriptures. It, too, illustrates the covenantal requirements of justice and community. As the story goes, Zacchaeus was a Jewish tax-collector; he collected taxes from his fellow Jews for the occupying Roman government. Being a tax-collector was in itself enough to distance him from most faithful Jews. Additionally, however, tax-collectors usually defrauded the people from whom they collected taxes. One day, Jesus came to the neighborhood in which Zacchaeus lived and began to teach. Zacchaeus was curious, and being a short man, he climbed up a sycamore tree to get a better view of the itinerant teacher about whom he had heard many tales. The scriptures are silent concerning the words Jesus spoke that day. Whatever they were, Zacchaeus was

Maryknoll Sister Mary Annel, M.D., visits a prisoner in El Salvador.

moved to reconcile himself with his community and the worldview of Judaism. He responded to Jesus with an exuberance that belied his former greedy ways. He invited Jesus to dinner and vowed to repay fourfold whomever he had cheated and to give half of his possessions to the poor. Jesus affirmed Zacchaeus's decision by assuring him that salvation had come to him that day. Indeed, Zacchaeus had not only fulfilled the demands of justice but far exceeded them.

The fourth of the five pillars of Islam is the obligation to share material goods with others. With Muslims, as with Jews, the fundamental reason for sharing material goods is the belief that the world belongs to all, and that there are many gratuitous and arbitrary reasons why some women and men prosper and others do not. One gives, therefore, not because one is more virtuous than other people, but because those who lack necessary material goods have a right to them. As stated in the Qur'an:

> They will question thee concerning what they should expend [for charity]. Say: "Whatsoever good you expend is for parents and kinsmen, orphans, the needy, and the traveler; and whatever good you may do, God has knowledge of it." (2:211)[2]

In reply to the question, How much is enough? the Qur'an suggests that the question itself betrays a mindset at variance with the intention of the command and with the Islamic worldview. The injunction demands the development of an attitude of sharing the world's goods. A legalistic mentality—one that asks, What is my strict obligation?—

tends to inhibit the cultivation of a generous spirit that the practice of almsgiving is intended to foster.

At the beginning of this chapter we observed that our actions always have social effects. Personal sins, such as lying, lessen the bonds of trust within the community. Now, when we consider some of the spiritual practices and disciplines found useful by various religions to promote reconciliation, we notice that they too have social effects. When we pray, meditate, fast, or perform good works in order to live in right relation to ourselves and to our worldview, there are social results. Although we can talk about public and personal reconciliation as if they were distinct realities, they are not. In day-to-day life they occur in a relationship of reciprocity; when we practice one, we are also practicing the other. One aspect of reconciliation—personal or communal—may be the one emphasized in a particular action, but both aspects of reconciliation are always present. Personal and communal reconciliation are not exactly the same thing because there are distinctions between them that can be made; neither are they totally unrelated to or entirely separate from each other.

Judaism, Christianity, and Islam, the three religions we have considered in our discussion of good works, are often referred to as religions of the Book. In each, written scriptures play a very prominent role in the adherent's imagination. Also, the holy books share certain stories, such as those of creation and the call of Abraham, that appeared first in the Tanakh. Consequently, there is a family resemblance among the worldviews of these religions. This is evident in regard to their understanding of personal reconciliation, especially through the performance of good works.

BUDDHISM AND INNER PEACE

In places where the religions of the Book flourish, many people are less familiar with the worldviews of religions that originated in India or the Far East, religions such as Hinduism and Buddhism. Since their worldviews differ, so do their practices of reconciliation. Buddhists believe that reconciliation is the acknowledgment that unmoderated desire is the cause of all of our suffering. The four Noble Truths of Buddhism reflect this worldview: (1) all life is suffering, (2) suffering is caused by desire, (3) suffering can be ended by the termination of desire, and (4) the way to terminate desire is through the practice of the Eightfold Path.

The Eightfold Path is a path of moderation that involves right intention, right action, and right contemplation. This path emphasizes the

FRED GLENNON

Ho Tai, the Laughing Buddha, carved in stone, Buddhist monastery Hangzou, China. There are many depictions of the Buddha. This one shows the joy he experienced when he reached Enlightenment.

teaching of the Buddha that extremes give rise to excessive concern about oneself. It includes practices that enable the Buddhist to achieve interior peace and harmony. Thus, the Eightfold Path encourages Buddhists to adopt the viewpoint of the Buddha, to relate to others and earn their living in a nonviolent and peaceful manner, and to practice meditation that leads to enlightenment. In describing the Buddhist way of life, we have continued to use the term *reconciliation*. This is not entirely inappropriate, but Buddhists themselves would probably not use this term in describing themselves. It is probably more accurate to say that by living in accordance with the Buddha's teachings and by practicing the Eightfold Path, Buddhists believe they will achieve enlightenment or arrive at the state of nirvana, the *experience* that results in release from desire.

The account of the Buddha's enlightenment will help us understand the experience of nirvana and give us some idea of what reconciliation or living in harmony with their worldview means for Buddhists. The Indian poet Asvaghosa wrote this account at the end of the first or at the beginning of the second century, approximately six hundred years after Siddhartha Gautama, the historical person who became the Buddha, lived (563–483 BCE).

THE BUDDHA'S ENLIGHTENMENT

> He had conquered the host of Evil
> with his firmness: with his peace
> he wished to know the highest reality: & he meditated (the master of meditation)

he mastered all the ways of meditation and in the first
     watch of the night
he remembered all his former lives.

    (in such a place I had such a name I passed away
      from there
    & I came here): he remembered a thousand lives as if
    experiencing each one he remembered his birth:
his death in each destiny & the compassionate one
     felt compassion for all living creatures

& the conviction arose in him as he remembered (the
     controlled one):
    this world is insubstantial as a hollow reed. . .

(& thus he meditated his inner enlightenment in-
     creased) . . .

And surely awareness ceases when one yearns
no more for existence
(& the sage knew the causes one by one)
when ignorance vanishes

And he knew what was to be known: he became a
     Buddha
    awake from his meditation and saw a self
    nowhere in the world
    gained the highest peace by the eightfold noble path

I have attained this path: I have fulfilled this path
which the great seers followed
(who knew the true & the false)
for the benefit of others

And in the fourth watch, when dawn appeared
    And the whole world was tranquil
    he gained omniscience: the imperishable state

    & the earth trembled like a drunken maiden
    when he was enlightened
    the heavens shown with his success
    and the kettle drums sounded in the sky[3]

THE CONCEPT OF RECONCILIATION IN REVIEW

We have spoken of our human need to feel at home with ourselves and others. We have discussed the fact that our imaginations are shaped by religious and cultural stories and histories, and that these stories cause us to see the world in a particular way. For example, the religions of the Book teach us to desire the good things of this earth. Buddhism and some other Eastern religions, however, tell us that desire is the source of all of our misery. Should we cultivate desire or seek to eliminate it? From our own experiences we can gather data to support either view. The worldview we favor and accept as our own, however, often has to do with the circumstances of our birth and how we were socialized.

In any case, worldviews, to a large extent, reflect our values and contribute to our feelings of belonging or of dislocation, of being either at home or at odds with ourselves and the world. It is true that our stories shape us; it is also true that our stories are always in flux, subject to new interpretations as personal and historical conditions change. This phenomenon of change was the subject of Part IV. Although we can achieve a "comfort level" within our religious stories, many people, for several reasons, find it detrimental to identify themselves completely with the prevailing worldview of their religious institution. First, our personal stories are subject to continual interpretation and reinterpretation; since our personal stories change more easily and more quickly than institutional or cultural stories, there will most often be some degree of incompatibility between individuals and their religious institutions. Second, when we continue our dialogue with our stories, we discover which parts of the story help us to become who we want to be, and which do not. Third, if we become totally identified with a particular set of values, there is no longer a vantage point from which to judge either the values of the religious tradition or ourselves in relation to it. We could compare our relation to religious traditions to the relation of parent to infant. As children grow to maturity, they choose their place in the world. Even when their choice coincides with parental values, the choice is their own. They no longer depend on their parents to tell them what to do. We could also say that our worldviews provide us with the chapter headings for the stories of our lives, but that we ourselves fill in the content of the chapters to create our personal stories.

When we accept the values of our religious stories because they make sense to us, when living by them gives our lives a sense of meaning, we sometimes feel dislocated and ill at ease when we violate these values. All religions have rites, rituals, and practices—both personal and social—to reconcile us to the community, to holy mystery, to ourselves. Practices of reconciliation differ depending on the worldview with which we are attempting to live in harmony.

CONCLUSION

Our conversations about religion have revealed that religion is not only ambiguous, but it is complex. To understand it is in some ways like studying a gem stone or entering into an ongoing conversation. We can focus on one facet at a time, one topic at a time, as we did in this book. That gives us an in-depth appreciation of a particular part. We also need, however, to see and to appreciate how the various facets fit together to produce one phenomenon. We need to realize that our conversations never end; we merely pause. When we do that, it is difficult to know where one aspect of religion ends and another begins. We hope that you will continue your study of religion, turning it over again and again in your imagination, discovering new ways of looking at it and describing it. And we hope that you will continue your conversations about religion, conversations with yourself, with friends, and with all others whom you trust enough to discuss these important topics.

RESOURCES

ACTIVITIES

1. Select one of the practices that religions suggest are reconciling. Practice it for one week. Describe your reactions to this in a journal that you share with your classmates or discussion group.
2. Depth psychologist Carl Jung once stated that if his Catholic patients were still believers, he would suggest that they receive the sacrament of reconciliation. Often, Jung said, this relieved their neuroses and helped their recovery. Choose the work of one psychologist and research the place that self-revelation holds in his or her system.
3. Dietrich Bonhoeffer, the Lutheran theologian who was mentioned in the introduction to this chapter, said that Christianity was not an easy religion to follow; he thought that many people practiced it superficially, simply going through the motions. (This could describe various religious traditions.) Apply this idea to the concept of reconciliation.

How can an attempt at reconciliation be superficial? Write a short story or create a skit that depicts reconciliation that is only apparent or cosmetic.

4. Prepare a report for your class or for your discussion group on the similarities and dissimilarities between religious and nonreligious practices of reconciliation.

5. Interview three individuals who are the religious leaders of three different communities or congregations. Ask them to describe the place that the concept of reconciliation holds in their weekly services.

6. Select one of the spiritual disciplines described in this chapter and research both its history and its contemporary practice.

7. Discuss the ethics of Christian involvement in assassination plots againt tyrants such as Adolf Hitler and Osama bin Laden.

READINGS

Baum, Gregory. *Religion and Alienation*. Second edition. Maryknoll, NY: Orbis Books, 2006. A theology of religious alienation that employs sociological categories in its critique. It is a very good and reliable introduction to the topic.

Frankl, Viktor. *From Death-camp to Existentialism*. Boston: Beacon, 1959. Often found under the title *Man's Search for Meaning*. This is a moving, biographical account of one Jewish man's search for meaning amid the horrors of a Nazi concentration camp.

Griffin-Pierce, Trudy. *Earth Is My Mother, Sky Is My Father: Space, Time, and Astronomy in Navajo Sandpainting*. Albuquerque: University of New Mexico Press, 1992. This book portrays the worldview and symbolism of the Navajo sand-painting ritual.

Hammarskjöld, Dag. *Markings*. Translated by Leif Sjoberg and W. H. Auden. New York: Knopf, 1964. The diary of the former Swedish secretary-general of the United Nations. Its entries reveal this diplomat's experience of the sacred.

Hampl, Patricia. *Virgin Time*. New York: Farrar, Straus, and Giroux, 1992. An autobiographical account of the religious development of a contemporary woman whose questions led her to Assisi, Lourdes, and a Trappist monastery in the Pacific Northwest.

Merton, Thomas. *The Seven Storey Mountain*. New York: Harcourt and Brace, 1948. The autobiographical account of a man whose spiritual journey took him from Quakerism and Communism to Roman Catholicism and the Trappist monastery of Gethsemani, Kentucky. This is the first of his over eighty works on spirituality.

Niebuhr, H. Richard. *Christ and Culture*. New York: Harper and Row, 1956. A theological classic that cogently and incisively shows how cultures and religious traditions influence our understanding of who is Christ. The categories are easily applicable to the question of God images.

Potok, Chaim. *The Chosen.* New York: Simon and Schuster, 1967. A fictional account of a Jewish boy's interaction with his father. Within the dynamics of this interaction, the boy finds his place in the Jewish worldview.

Jalal Al-Din Rumi, Maulana. *The Sufi Path of Love.* Translated by William Chittuk. Albany: State University of New York Press, 1983. The poetry of a twelfth-century Islamic mystic who followed the Sufi path.

Paul Tillich. *Systematic Theology.* Volumes 1–3. Chicago: University of Chicago Press, 1951–63. A comprehensive theological analysis of Christianity. Throughout, Tillich, a theologian from the Lutheran tradition, refers to the modes of human alienation and reconciliation.

AUDIO-VISUALS

The Shawshank Redemption (1994). Castle Rock Entertainment. This film relates the alienation that occurs in prison and the power of friendship, which may be redemptive.

The Great Religions and the Poor (1995). Available from Films for the Humanities and Sciences, 132 West 31st Street, 17th Floor, New York, NY 10001. This video explores the religious and social aspects of poverty from the perspectives of Christianity, Islam, and Judaism. It also shows how these religions use modern means to alleviate poverty.

Principles and Practices of Zen (1992). Available from Films for the Humanities and Sciences, 132 West 31st Street, 17th Floor, New York, NY 10001. This video follows the path of a student priest of Zen Buddhism. It explores the physical and mental disciplines demanded by this way of life.

The Sufi Way (1980). Cos Cob, CT: The Hartley Foundation. Presents the ritual, dance, art, music, and philosophy of Sufism, the heart of Islam.

Taizé: The Little Springtime (1985). Mount Vernon, VA: Journey Communications. This film portrays the lifestyle and prayer style of the ecumenical monastic community of Taizé, France.

The Descendants (2011). Ad Hominem Enterprises. This film shows both the sources of alienation within a family and the path to reconciliation.

NOTES

1. William C. Chittuck, ed., *The Sufi Path of Love* (Albany: State University of New York Press, 1983), 234.

2. A. J. Arberry, ed. *The Koran Interpreted: A Translation* (New York: Macmillan, 1955).

3. Stephen Beyer, *The Buddhist Experience: Sources and Interpretation,* Religious Life of Man series (Encino, CA: Dickinson, 1974), 191–97.

Glossary

Acts of the Apostles: The second volume of Luke's gospel, Acts begins with Pentecost and the inauguration of the Christian community and ends with Paul the apostle on his way to house arrest in Rome. A turning point is the Council of Jerusalem, a gathering of such leaders as Peter, James, and Paul to determine whether non-Jewish converts to Christianity had to be circumcised and observe the Jewish law before they could be baptized.

Adam: In Hebrew the word means "red, ruddy," perhaps related to the Akkadian word for "creature." Akkadian was the language of Babylon. In Genesis 2:4b-27, the Hebrew word designates the human creature, the first step in the creation of woman and man. The tradition of understanding the word as a proper name traces back to the Septuagint translation (c. 250). In the Genesis account there is a play on the Hebrew words *adam* and *adamah,* "soil, arable land." The human who is a farmer in Genesis is created out of the land (Mother Earth?) it farms.

Allah: In Islam, the one undivided God proclaimed by Muhammad; this God is creator and sustainer of all that is and has revealed himself in the Qur'an.

Allegory: A method of reading narrative that assigns symbolic meanings to characters, events, and places. In Galatians 4:21-31, Paul interprets the story of Abraham, Sarah, and Hagar allegorically.

Amos: An early biblical prophet (eighth century BCE, during the reign of Jeroboam II, c. 786-46); unique because he was a Judahite preaching in the northern kingdom of Israel. He probably gained his knowledge of international affairs from travels associated with his position as manager of the king of Judah's flocks.

Arhant: Literally, a "worthy one" or saint in Theravada Buddhism; one who has overcome desire and attained enlightenment and will not be reborn.

Ayatollah: An honored jurist, legal scholar, and judge.

Bar/Bat Mitzvah: Literally, "son/daughter of the commandment"; the Jewish ritual through which one becomes an adult member of the Jewish community.

Bhakti: In Hinduism, religious devotion, loving adoration of a god.

Bible: Literally, "the book." In Christianity the volume that contains the Jewish scriptures (Tanakh), called the Old Testament or Hebrew scriptures by Christians, and the canonical Christian scriptures that are called the New Testament.

Bodhisattva: Literally, "a being intended for enlightenment"; the moral exemplar in Mahayana Buddhism who out of compassion delays his or her own experience of nirvana to help others.

Brahman: In Vedic religion and Hinduism, absolute and total reality.

Buddha: Literally the "awakened one" or the "enlightened one." This title was first given to Siddhartha Gautama, the founder of Buddhism. Subsequently, it was applied to a variety of buddha figures that are manifestations of the buddha nature that is understood to underlie the universe.

Chador: A large piece of cloth worn as a full-length outer garment covering head and body. It is worn by Muslim women, especially in Iran and Iraq.

Canon: From Greek *kanon* and Hebrew *qaneh*, "reed," perhaps used as a measuring stick. Today a canon is the standard by which religious traditions determine whether writings are authoritative for them. It is also the official list of books recognized as genuine and used in teaching and in determining doctrine.

Church: 1. The community of all Christians, presented in the New Testament as "the body of Christ." 2. A denomination within Christianity or a local group of Christians. 3. A building used for the assembly and worship of Christians.

Circumcision: The cutting off of the foreskin of males or the excision of the internal labia and/or foreskin of the clitoris in females. In a number of traditional African and Oceanic societies, circumcision is carried out as a religious rite either shortly after birth or at puberty. In Judaism and Islam, males are circumcised in commemoration of Abraham's covenant with God (Gn 17:10).

Code: In ethics, the tendency on the part of many cultures to summarize their moral obligations and duties into succinct summaries or laws, such as the Ten Commandments.

Codex: A book made up of pages bound together on one side; this Christian innovation replaced the scrolls on which scriptures had originally been written.

Communist Manifesto: Published in 1848 by Karl Marx and Friedrich Engels, it outlines the purposes and objectives of the Communist League.

Confucius (551–479 BCE): A Chinese teacher and public servant whose teachings on the principles of the good life form the basis of Confucianism, a Chinese tradition that is variously described as a religion or a philosophy.

Conscience: The internal capacity for moral discrimination that enables moral consistency by prodding us, through powerful emotions, to achieve coherence between our moral knowing and moral doing.

Cosmic law: The moral order that some religious traditions see as inherent in the universe. Indian religions, Hinduism and Buddhism, refer to this law as dharma. Chinese religions, Confucianism and Taoism, refer to this law as Tao.

Cosmology: An understanding of the structure of the universe.

Council of Chalcedon: A meeting of leaders of the Christian church that met in the city of Chaledon to define orthodox teachings about Jesus in the face of the teachings of the cleric Arius; this council also determined the four canonical gospels.

Council of Trent: Seventeenth-century meeting of leaders of the Roman Catholic Church in the city of Trent, Italy, to respond to the reforms that Martin Luther claimed were necessary. The council defined a Catholic canon more inclusive than the canon of the Reformers.

Culture: A shared way of life that includes material products, a pattern of social relationships, and values and beliefs.

Dharma: In Hinduism, Buddhism, and Jainism the moral order that sustains the cosmos.

Diaspora: Literally, "dispersion." The Jewish people who live outside Israel among the Gentiles.

Diatessaron: From the Greek, literally "according to four"; a harmony of the four New Testament gospels, edited and arranged into a single narrative.

Eightfold Path: In Buddhism, the eight steps to overcome suffering and reach enlightenment. They are broken into three instructions in the Theravadin tradition: concentration (right effort, right mindfulness, and right meditation), morality (right speech, right conduct, and right livelihood), and wisdom (right belief and right aspiration).

Encyclical: A Roman Catholic document issued by a pope as a foundation for church teaching on matters of faith and actions.

Enlightenment: 1. In Buddhism, the realization of insight into the nature of reality achieved by the Buddha; also the passing into nirvana of a person following the Buddha way who attains release from the cycles of birth and rebirth. 2. In philosophy, a European intellectual movement of the seventeenth and eighteenth centuries that celebrated reason and posited knowledge, freedom, and happiness as the goals of the rational person.

Eve: This name is derived from a Hebrew verb that means "to live"; thus she is "the mother of the living," a frequent title of ancient Near Eastern fertility goddesses. In Genesis 3, she acquires the knowledge necessary to create culture. In the New Testament, Paul holds her responsible for the fall of humanity (2 Cor 11:3).

Excommunication: The action of official religious bodies that excludes individuals or groups from participation in the rituals of that religion. Usually, persons are excommunicated due to perceived heresy.

Feminist hermeneutics: A way of reading texts whose aim is resistance and transformation. It uses historical and literary methodologies that focus on the text in its historical and rhetorical contexts, but also storytelling, bibliodrama, and ritual for creating a new feminist imagination.

Five Pillars of Islam: The basic obligations individual Muslims must observe, including the profession of faith, daily prayer, giving of alms to the needy, fasting during the month of Ramadan, and the pilgrimage to Mecca at least once in a lifetime, if possible.

Five Precepts: The rules for behavior that all Buddhists vow to keep. They include the precepts to abstain from taking life, to abstain from taking what is not given, to abstain from sensuous misconduct, to abstain from false speech, and to abstain from intoxicants.

Four Noble Truths: The basic teaching of Buddhism suggested by Siddhartha Gautama: life is painful, the cause of pain is desire, there is a way to overcome this suffering, and the way is the Eightfold Path.

Genre: Form or type of literature determined by style, form, or content. A first step in interpretation is to determine the literary form of the text. We read legal material differently than we do poetry.

Globalization: A process of international integration that comes about through the interdependence of markets and cultures.

Gnosticism/Gnostic: Early Christian movement whose members claimed they had gained salvation because Jesus had revealed to them special knowledge (Greek *gnosis*); only an elite few were initiated into these mysteries. Eventually condemned as a heresy, perhaps on political grounds. The Nag Hammadi Library contained Christian Gnostic writings.

Gospel: The literary form of the writings of the four evangelists; the "good news" of the Christian message.

Haggada: Literally, "narrative." The non-legal part of the Talmud consisting of history, folklore, poems, sermons, and the liturgical text used for the Passover Seder.

Hajj: The pilgrimage to Mecca (one of the Five Pillars of Islam) that every Muslim is expected to make during his or her lifetime, if possible.

Haudenosaunee: Literally, "people of the longhouse." The six nations of the Iroquois Confederacy.

Heresy: Religious teaching or opinion that is contrary to accepted religious doctrine. Literally, it means separation from the community. Those who withdraw their allegiance from a particular essential teaching of a religious worldview are named heretics. At times persons are declared outside the community by religious authorities. Often, those accused of heresy by one age are reincorporated into the community when their work is judged in a larger context by the thinkers of a more historically minded community. The case of Galileo is such an example.

Hierophany: Manifestation of the sacred.

Hogan: The traditional dwelling of the Navajo. It is a conical house of logs covered by earth with a smoke hole at the top. It is entered by a low, covered opening.

Holi: Hindu spring festival dedicated to the god Krishna.

Holocaust: The genocidal murder of six million Jews and others who did not fit the Nazi Aryan ideal by the Nazis during World War II.

Many Jews use the term *Shoah,* meaning "catastrophe," when speaking of this event.

Idealism: On the popular level, it refers to people who profess values that they refuse to compromise. Often, they are intolerant of others who do not hold the same values. Philosophically, it refers to the view that universals or innate ideas exist independently of the individual.

Initiation: The ritual process by which one attains a social and/or religious status.

Islam: Literally, "submission," that is, submission to Allah. Muhammad was the founder of Islam, a strictly monotheistic religion.

Jerusalem: 1. Capital of present-day Israel; 2. city-state David conquered and made his religious and political capital c. 1000 BCE; site of the temple, the central symbol of Israelite religion; 3. often personified in prophetic literature as Woman Zion, God's faithless wife, or Mother Zion, mourning her lost children.

Jñana: In Hinduism, saving knowledge or wisdom, insight into the unity of reality.

Ka'ba: Arabic for "cube"; the primary shrine of Islam, located in the Grand Mosque of Mecca. It symbolizes the center of the world, and Muslims on the hajj visit there.

Karma: In Indian thought, the chain of cause and effect that binds one to endless cycles of life, death, and rebirth.

Kerygma: A Greek word meaning "preaching" or "proclamation." Christianity's central kerygma includes the life and ministry of Jesus of Nazareth, especially his death and resurrection (1 Cor 15:3-5).

Kettuba: The marriage contract historically used in Jewish communities to provide a sense of equality between the partners and to protect them.

Koan: A mind puzzle given by a Zen Buddhist master to students to enable them to break free from the cognitive constraints of their culture and to achieve enlightenment.

Krishna: In Hinduism, an incarnation of the god Vishnu.

Kwanzaa: The ritual celebration developed within the African American community by Dr. Maulana Karenga in 1966. The celebration enables the participants to celebrate their African heritage while also leading them to reflect on ways to improve their lives and the lives of their communities. The celebration lasts from December 26 to January 1.

Liberation theologians: Originally, Christian theologians working in Latin American who reflected on the incompatibility between the practice of the gospel and the existence of mass suffering and poverty. Later, the practice of any religious community in any locale to give primacy to religious practice in order to change oppressive structures.

Mahabharata: Literally "great epic of the Bharata dynasty." A classic Hindu epic of over 100,000 couplets, the world's longest poem, which recounts wars between two related families, the Kauravas and the Pandavas. The hero of the epic is Krishna, an *avatar* (one who descends) of the Lord Vishnu. The Bhagavad Gita (the "Song of the Lord") is a section of the Mahabharata. The Mahabharata, which is thought to be based on events that took place between 1400 and 1000 BCE, reached its present form about 400 CE.

Mahayana Buddhism: Literally, "Large Raft" or "Vehicle" Buddhism; one of the two branches of Buddhism dominant in East Asia and Vietnam. This name refers to the belief that its teaching provides a "large raft" to carry people to enlightenment.

Mana: A Melanesian word that describes a mysterious power that inhabits individuals, objects, and events, enabling them to be particularly effective. It has been adopted as a general term in the study of religions.

Mass: The Roman Catholic form of the Christian Eucharist, the memorial meal of bread and wine that celebrates the sacrifice of Jesus.

Messiah: Hebrew term meaning "anointed"; designated kings and priests who were consecrated in their special roles by having oil poured over their heads. David and his descendants who ruled in Jerusalem were all messiahs. After the Davidic dynasty ended in 586 BCE, the prophets projected promises made to David onto a future figure who would restore the kingdom of David to its original glory (see Dn 9:25-26). New Testament writers identified Jesus of Nazareth as this figure (see Mt 16:13-20).

Metaphor: Application of a name or descriptive term to an object or state to which it does not literally apply; also a system of thought in which a term evokes a multifaceted experience.

Micah: A book contained in Hebrew scripture named for the prophet Micah. He promoted pure worship and spoke out against injustice.

Mitzvah: The Hebrew term for commandment. In Judaism, moral obligations and duties are often stated in the form of commandments.

Moksha: In Indian religions, release from the cycles of death and rebirth.

Moral perplexity: The internal moral conflict and confusion we experience when faced with an ethical choice or dilemma. We cannot make one choice over another without experiencing some moral blame or guilt.

Mullah: A Muslim man who is expert in Muslim law and theology.

Muslim: Literally, "one who submits," that is, a practitioner of Islam.

Myth: In Greek, *mythos* is "story." Today, a narrative expressing a religious truth that cannot be verified by scientific means. Myths are stories about divine beings and national heroes who represent the powers and energies that influence us but that we cannot control. Carl Jung viewed a myth as our inherited remembrance of primeval events that live on in our unconscious mind and that we repeatedly enact through ritual.

Natural law: According to Saint Thomas Aquinas, the moral order in the universe created by God and discernible through reason to guide humanity toward its true end.

Nirvana: Literally, "blowing out." In Indian religions the cessation of human desires and absorption into Brahman.

Om: *Om* or *Aum* is the most important sacred sound in the Vedic and Hindu tradition. It is used as a symbol of Brahman.

Parable: From the Greek *parabole* (comparison). A short narrative that has its hearers/readers pronounce judgment upon themselves through their reaction to its unexpected final twist. Jesus of Nazareth used parables extensively in his preaching (Mt 13:3–53, for example). At the same time, this use of parables kept many of his hearers from grasping his message (Mk 4:10–12 and parallel passages).

Passion narrative: A symbolic narrative interpreting the suffering, death, and resurrection of Jesus of Nazareth; each gospel interprets the event and the person of Jesus differently.

Passover: Seven-day Jewish spring festival that recalls the deliverance from Egypt. The festival begins with a service in the home.

Pharisee: A member of an ancient Jewish movement that emphasized the importance of observance of the Torah, the Jewish Law.

Polytheism: The belief in more than one supreme Reality.

Prayer: Communication with God or gods or spirits, often employing verbal formulas. Prayer may be public or private.

Priest: From Greek *presbyteros*, "elder." One authorized to perform rituals, such as sacrifices, for a community in order to mediate between God or gods and human beings, or to provide interpretation of tradition. The term is used in some Christian denominations to designate a minister.

Psalms: A series of 150 prayer-poems usually attributed to King David. They are widely used today in both Jewish and Christian worship.

Q/Quelle: A hypothetical collection of the sayings of Jesus of Nazareth; perhaps used by Luke and Matthew in the formulation of their gospels.

Qur'an: In Islam, the word of Allah, given as a revelation to the prophet Muhammad. The Holy Book of Islam, it is said to be a faithful copy of the eternal Qur'an inscribed in heaven.

Raja yoga: A mental, physical, and spiritual discipline in Hinduism designed to aid in the practice of meditation.

Reincarnation: In Indian thought, the endless cycles of birth, death, and rebirth through which all creatures are bound through karma.

Repression: A psychological term that names the defense mechanism that assigns to the unconscious events and memories so painful that they are neither allowed into consciousness nor can be recalled at will. Although they are unknown to the conscious subject, they still have effects on conscious life.

Rig Veda: Literally, "hymns of wisdom." A collection of hymns, dating from the second millennium BCE, dedicated to the gods of the Aryan peoples who settled in northwest India. The Rig Veda is part of the Hindu scriptures.

Rites of Passage: Significant actions and rituals communities use to mark the process of moving from one status to another throughout the life cycle.

Sabbath: The seventh day of the week, observed as a holy day of rest and worship in Judaism.

Sacrament: In Christianity, "an outward and visible sign of an inward and spiritual grace" *(Book of Common Prayer)*. Reformed Churches count only baptism and Eucharist as sacraments. Roman Catholic and Orthodox Churches add confirmation, matrimony, holy orders, penance, and the anointing of the sick.

Sacred: A modality of human experience that relates to that which is held to have ultimate worth and seen to be in a reciprocal relationship with the profane.

Sangha: In Buddhism, the community of monks who live together and participate in the practices and rituals that lead to enlightenment.

Sermon on the Mount: Found in the Gospel of Matthew 5—7, it contains the Beatitudes. It is depicted by Matthew as the inaugural sermon of Jesus, outlining his teachings.

Seven Principles: During the Kwanzaa celebration, the principles of unity, self-determination, collective work, cooperative economics, purpose, creativity, and faith provide the basis for reflection for participants.

Shahadah: The first of the five pillars of Islam, it is recited as part of *salat*, daily ritual prayer. It expresses the two fundamental beliefs of Islam—There is no god but Allah, and Muhammad is the prophet of Allah.

Shalako: Among the Zuni, an annual winter dance ceremony that renews the life of the cosmos and the community. Also, the mythological bird figures that come to visit and dance on this occasion.

Shaman: Among the Tungu people of Siberia, a religious practitioner who is able to contact and influence spirits. By extension, a similar figure in other religious traditions.

Shari'ah: The collection of interpretations and extrapolations from learned members of the Islamic community to make laws for people to abide by.

Shema: Jewish declaration of faith in the one God. Its first line, "Hear O Israel, the Lord is our God, the Lord is One" (Dt 6:4), is recited especially at morning and evening prayer and when Torah scrolls are removed from the ark of the covenant on Shabbat and holidays.

Sikhism: A religion founded c. 1500 CE by Guru Nanak in northern India. It combines the mysticism of Hinduism with the rigid monotheism of Islam, while it rejects their leadership structure and rituals. Noted for its veneration of its scriptures.

Simile: A figure of speech that compares two generally dissimilar realities on the basis of resemblance in one aspect. In making the comparison, the writer uses "like" or "as." Example: "My love is like a red, red rose."

Son of man: A Hebrew phrase meaning "mortal" or "human being" (see, for example, Ps 8; Is 56:2); the prophet Ezekiel uses it to refer to himself (Ez 2:1). In Daniel 7:12-14, "one like a son of man" refers to Israel itself or to a divinely appointed future rule. In the gospels it is the one title that Jesus of Nazareth consistently uses about himself (see, for example, Mt 8:20; Mk 2:28; Lk 12:8-10; Jn 3:14).

Sorcery: The art and practices of a person such as a magician, especially one supposedly aided by evil spirits.

Southern Baptist Convention: The representative body of the various Southern Baptist congregations.

Stupa: Bell-like or dome-shaped structures found in Asia that house objects of religious veneration and devotion.

Sufi: A Muslim who follows the more experiential and mystical teachings of the prophet Muhammed.

Sun Dance: Traditional renewal ceremony of the Plains Peoples of the United States and Canada.

Suppression: A psychological term that names the defense mechanism of refusing to think about unpleasant events or feelings.

Symbol: In a religious sense, a word, object, or action that evokes awareness of ultimate values or concerns. More generally, that which evokes or stands for something else by virtue of analogous qualities.

Synagogue: Literally, "assembly." The meeting of Jews for study and prayer, and the building in which the assembly takes place.

Synoptic gospels: The first three gospels (Matthew, Mark, and Luke); they share so much material in common that their texts may be viewed together as if "with one eye.

Synoptic problem: Term for the problematic relationship, that is, the nature of their literary dependence, of Matthew, Mark, and Luke. Although Mark was once viewed as a condensed version of Matthew, today most scholars agree that both Matthew and Luke depend upon Mark, which is then the first attested gospel that we know.

Tallit: The prayer shawl used by Jewish men and women during ritual prayer. They are received at one's bar/bat mitzvah and used in other rituals as well.

Talmud: A collection of Jewish writings made up of the Mishnah, written editions of ancient oral interpretations of the Torah collected by Judah haNasi in Palestine in the early third century, and the Gemara, further commentaries on the Mishnah. There are two Talmuds: an incomplete Palestinian Talmud compiled in approximately 450, and the longer Babylonian Talmud compiled approximately 500.

Tanakh: An acronym for the Hebrew words *Torah* (instruction), *Nebe'im* (prophets), *Ketubim* (writings), the Jewish Bible.

Tao: Literally, "the way" or cosmic order that underlies all reality in Chinese religions.

Taoism: Founded by Lao Tzu in sixth-century BCE China; its main scriptures are the Tao Te Ching and the writings of Chuang-tzu. Its ethical ideal is *wu-wei,* "active non-striving." By non-action, the wise seek to come into harmony with the Tao, the self-generating organic course of the universe, which accomplishes itself by non-action.

Tatian: A second-century defender of Christianity and an antagonist of Greek culture; produced a harmonized gospel, *Diatessaron,* used widely in northern Syria until the fifth century, when Theoderet ordered all extant copies destroyed; consequently, no copies exist today.

Ten Precepts: The rules a Buddhist monk vows to keep to become a member of the monastic community. In addition to the Five Precepts, they include the precepts not to take food from noon to the next morning; not to adorn their bodies with anything other than the three robes; not to participate in public entertainments; not to use comfortable beds; and not to use money.

Theology: Systematic inquiry into matters of ultimate concern and, in particular, study of the nature of God.

Theravada Buddhism: Literally, "Way of the Elders"; one of the two branches of Buddhism found in Southeast Asia. It claims to be the oldest form of Buddhist teaching.

Torah: 1. A Hebrew word meaning both "instruction" and "law," specifically the body of law associated with Moses and found in the first division of the Tanakh. 2. The books of Genesis, Exodus, Leviticus, Numbers, and Deuteronomy. In the Christian canon, these same books are called the Pentateuch (Greek *pente* = five).

Tradition: 1. Customs, beliefs, and practices transmitted orally from generation to generation and embodying the religious history and beliefs of a community. In the seventeenth century Martin Luther rejected the claims of tradition in favor of scripture alone. An example of a traditional Catholic tradition is mandatory celibacy for priests and permanent deacons. 2. In Judaism, oral explanations and interpretations of the Torah eventually collected in the Mishnah. 3. Recollections about Jesus of Nazareth preserved orally in various communities and later used as sources by the gospel writers.

Umma: Arabic for "community"; it refers to the entire world community of Muslims.

Vatican II: A worldwide meeting of the Catholic hierarchy called by Pope John XXIII (1962–65). Its sixteen official documents brought Catholic liturgy and theology more in line with the insights of contemporary culture and made major changes in the church's modes of engaging the world.

Veda: Literally, "knowledge." One of the four collections of hymns to the Aryan gods. The term also applies to the corpus of Indian sacred literature, which includes the four Vedas, plus the interpretations of them that are constituted by the Brahamanas, Aranyakas, and Upanishads.

Vedanta: In Hinduism, the main philosophical tradition that believes that there is only one reality and that the individual self is identified with the absolute and with every other individual self.

Vishnu: In Hinduism, the life giver and preserver of the cosmos. Vishnu appears on earth from time to time as an *avatar* (one who descends) to remind people of the ways to salvation.

Yoga: In Hinduism the way of salvation through inner discipline. It has eight stages: restraint, discipline, posture, breathing, detachment, concentration, meditation, and trance. There are four main styles of yoga that correspond to personality types: karma yoga, the path of action; jñana yoga, the path of knowledge; bhakti yoga, the path of devotion; and raja yoga, the path of insight. In postclassical Hinduism, yoga also refers to a philosophical system that teaches a dualistic worldview.

Zoroastrianism: According to legend, begun three thousand years ago in Iran by the prophet Zarathustra. Stresses living a moral life with concern for ritual purity in worship and in daily life and the worship of its God, Ahura Mazda, and the good spirits through sacrifice and praise. In addition to a deity who controls good, Zoroastrian theology also identifies a deity who controls evil.

Zuni: A multi-storied masonry *pueblo* (town) in New Mexico near the Arizona border and the more than five thousand Native Americans who inhabit it.

Index

Numbers in *italics* indicate images